KEEP THIS QUIET! III

BEYOND 3-D

Revised, Expanded Edition

Margaret A. Harrell

Praise for the *Keep This Quiet!* Series

Selected Review Snippets

Beyond 3-D

"Margaret Ann Harrell's book of initiations is a golden bough, a sacred marriage, an initiation, a wake, a book of revelation, a literary and spiritual journey into and through an ever expanding universal consciousness. Margaret Ann Harrell's *Beyond 3-D* is her Big Book, her epic narrative poetic masterpiece.

"Brilliant as a literary and psychoanalytic and spiritual text, it is a deeply touching and vulnerable human story. A book that breaks new ground by combining and weaving together such a broad spectrum of genres. I congratulate her on having the courage to write the book and share the book with the world."

—Ron Whitehead, Lifetime US Beat Poet Laureate

"I am amazed and in awe that Margaret describes these principles through real-life experiences. Incredible . . ."

—Jef Crab, Taiji Master, Taoist, Rainforest activist

"Margaret has done an amazing job witnessing for us all the deep path of walking with the Self. As Mother Earth moves into her heart chakra, Margaret does as well and tells the story to us from there."

—Jyoti, internationally renowned spiritual teacher

"The information of the universal nature of each soul offers a good potential to remove some of the barriers or veils between otherwise divergent ways of thinking and believing. I'm glad Margaret is "putting this out there."

—the late Al Miner, channel to Lama Sing

Keep This Quiet!

"Margaret Harrell's *Keep This Quiet!* offers an illuminating look at Hunter S. Thompson in full throttle trying to make it as a Top Notch prose-stylist. Harrell fills in many important biographical gaps. A welcome addition to what is becoming the HST cottage industry. Read it."

—Douglas Brinkley, editor of *The Proud Highway* and *Fear and Loathing in America*

"Memoir will likely please Hunter S. Thompson fans and appeal to readers with an interest in the beginnings of the post-modern era or the personal sacrifices involved in bringing serious written work to fruition."

—*Kirkus indie reviews*

"With a solid dose of humor and another perspective on these writers from a personal friend, *Keep This Quiet!* is a moving read and much recommended to any literary studies or memoir collection."

—*Midwest Book Review*

"Three men, embodiments of three different dimensions of the late 1960's Zeitgeist—wispy dissolution, language-charged intellect, and Gonzo persona-building—are brought together by Harrell to invoke a world of passion and commitment . . . *Keep This Quiet!* is at once noisy, sensual, and word-drunk, as well as quietly intimate and full of Harrell's wonder at her luck. While most readers will come to this book for the Thompson content, in truth all the portraits here—all four of them—are compelling and often touching."

—W. C. Bamberger, *Rain Taxi Review*

"In the ever-expanding list of biographies and memoirs about Hunter S. Thompson, this latest offering, *Keep This Quiet!* by Margaret A. Harrell, is quite simply a breath of fresh air."

—Rory Patrick Feehan, PhD, owner of https://totallygonzo.org

"This is no ordinary book about or including Thompson. It's a memoir detailing personal relationships with three authors, the main focus being on Hunter . . . [I] must stress that this book, as a memoir is quite deep and holds the door open for the reader. While Hunter is a huge selling point, the book has the legs to stand alone."

—Martin Flynn, owner of https://hstbooks.org

Keep This Quiet Too!

"A passionately written memoir that doesn't sit around being fit and proper and strait-laced . . . As a key to the lives of these three writers it is idiosyncratic and in an age where blandness is the norm it is a pleasure to go on her journey and find out a little about what makes these men tick and what drove her to them."

—Eric Jacobs, *Beat Scene* (print) magazine, UK

Keep This Quiet! III—first ed.
Initiations

"This is the third and highly recommended title in Margaret Harrell's outstanding *Keep This Quiet!* autobiographical series. A fascinating and exceptionally well written personal story, *Keep This Quiet!* III: *Initiations* is as informative as it is entertaining and will be especially interesting to students of Jungian psychology and metaphysics. *Keep This Quiet!* III: *Initiations* is very highly recommended for both community and academic library collections. Also exceptionally commended are the first two volumes in this outstanding series."

—*Midwest Book Review*

Keep This Quiet! IV—rev. ed.
Ancient Secrets Revealed

"Margaret Harrell is a skilled professional writer with excellent ability to communicate and weave esoteric ideas about science, psychology, philosophy, and spirituality. Richard Unger's channeled hand analysis description of her as a 'grand synthesizer' was apt and accurate."

—Ron Rattner, subject of *Walks with Rob*: *A Spiritual Memoir* documentary

"A puzzle master, Margaret walks us step by step through the process of her journey to that mastery . . . that wholeness of vision . . . so that we, if devoted enough, can also do the same. Margaret has injected so much LOVE into this work that, if you are open enough, it might just wake you up to your greater . . . even greatest potential."

—Joy Ayscue, co-founder of The Conscious Healing Initiative

Keep This Quiet! III
BEYOND 3-D

Margaret A. Harrell

Saeculum University Press
USA and Romania

Keep This Quiet III!—revised: Beyond 3-D

ISBN (hardcover): 979-8-9871061-8-1

ISBN (pbk): 979-8-9871061-9-8

ISBN (e-pub): 979-8-9871061-7-4

Cover artwork: Grant Goodwine, https://grantgoodwine.com

Cover and interior design: Deborah Perdue, https://illuminationgraphics.com

A Published in Heaven Series Book

Published in Heaven Books include titles by His Holiness The Dalai Lama, President Jimmy Carter, Thomas

Merton, Seamus Heaney, Hunter S. Thompson, Jack Kerouac, Andy Warhol, Allen Ginsberg, Yoko Ono, William S.

Burroughs, Edvard Munch, Diane di Prima, Jim Carroll, Amiri Baraka, Gregory Corso, John Updike, Rita Dove,

Wendell Berry, David Amram, Douglas Brinkley, BONO, Ron Whitehead, Lawrence Ferlinghetti, and many more.

Published in conjunction with Saeculum University Press of Sibiu, Romania and Raleigh, North Carolina

For inquiries, signed copies, and speaking requests, contact marharrell@hotmail.com

https://margaretharrell.

Bonus

Go here to listen to Ron Whitehead read his poem introduction live and to click on Jef Crab's audio annotations of discussion points in *Beyond* 3-D and in *Space Encounters* III, rev. ed

Contents

With the most profound thanks to Duane and the energy beings who pushed, helped, filled me

And to the writers who helped me

A Question Enters the World

I also think of the possibility that through the achievement of an individual a question enters the world, to which he must pose some kind of answer.

For example, my way of posing the question as well as my answer may be unsatisfactory. That being so, someone who has my karma—or I myself—would have to be reborn to give a more complete answer. It might happen that I would not be reborn again so long as the world needed no such answer.

—C. G. Jung, *Memories, Dreams, Reflections*

Foreword

"What Have You Learned So Far?"

I was recently interviewed by a young person.
She asked, "I have researched you. You are 72 now.
What have you learned so far?"
I said:
I learned the art of being still,
of being still and listening.
I learned that listening is the greatest art of all.
I learned to be still with my eyes closed.
Then with eyes open.
While sitting.
Then while walking.
Then no matter what was going on around me.
I learned to be still.
I learned to embrace the wind.
I learned to embrace my heart.
I learned that I was born to die.
I have seen people born.
I have seen people die.
We all are born to die.
I learned that there is no safety.
I learned that everything is demanded.
I learned to get off my ass and do
whatever needed to be done.
I learned to work hard.
I learned to expose myself completely.
I learned to be open.
I learned to be honest.

I learned to be transparent.
I learned to accept the consequences
of my successes
and my failures,
as no others dared.
I learned to pray,
then listen.
I learned that enlightened mind
is not special.
Enlightened mind is natural.
I learned to present myself
as I am,
a wise fool.
I learned that I am filled with wisdom
but I rarely tap into that wisdom.
Way too often I have been a fool.
We all have.
I learned to listen to my heart
so I could hear my wisdom.
I learned that my heart
is my truth tester.
My heart is the channel
for my wisdom.
I learned that the answers to my prayers
come through my heart,
as visions.
I learned to focus the answers,
the visions in my mind,
to hold them there.
I practiced affirming the visions
by speaking them quietly,
in my mind
and out loud.
I wrote my visions down.

I shared my visions with others.
I learned to see myself doing
what I visualized.
I learned how to help
my visions reach fruition.
I learned to fill my visions
with electric lightning light.
I learned to honor my visions
by taking action,
one step at a time,
towards realization.
Through action
my visions have been manifested.
I learned how to fill
my energy centers with lightning light.
I allow my entire being
to become light.
I learned how to see myself
filled with light,
accomplishing my vision.
I see myself
with so much light
it radiates from me
into others.
I practiced being lightning light.
One of my goals in life
is to become a beam a beacon of light,
uplifting and inspiring,
comforting and healing,
and awakening everyone to the fact
that we all have a non-stop
river of creative fire
flowing through us.
I learned to embrace mystery paradox uncertainty.

I learned to have courage.
I reminded myself daily
that through fear and boredom
to have faith.
I remind myself daily to believe.
I learned that whatever I believed
and held in my mind,
then acted on,
happened.
I learned that when acted upon
visions are realized.
I learned that dreams come true.
I learned that dreams can and do come true.
I learned to be compassion.
I learned that by being open and honest
I can more easily connect with others.
I learned how to be friends with others,
I learned how to be a good neighbor.
I Learned how to embrace the wind.
I learned how to embrace my heart.
I learned that not Knowing
is the fundamental plowed earth of my being.
I learned that there is more than meets the eye.
I learned to embrace not knowing.
I learned how to be a being of light.
I learned how to be light.
I learned how to never give up.
When I grow up I want to be
a beam of light.

Ron Whitehead, Lifetime Beat Poet Laureate

Author's Note

> There was no helmet on those nights.
>
> —Hunter S. Thompson, *Hell's Angels*

This book goes to extremes about the inner life. After all, the heart is subjective. It is action-filled but goes *out on the edge in spiritual initiations*, changing all the rules in midstream. Kundalini will affect the way I remember. Kundalini and eventually living more in the present will make some memory distant. I will see myself like The Old Woman Who Lived in a Shoe, with many selves, who seem piled onto my lap like children. I will encompass them all, pulling out now one, now the other, as out of a hat. Kundalini exaggerates the tendency, for we become more and more unbounded energy. We take forms, draw the boundaries. Then we feel how the boundaries are nebulous, leaking at the edges.

The same people will come back. I cannot claim to speak for the characters. As Milton Klonsky once said to me, "*Each of us has a self the other owns.*"

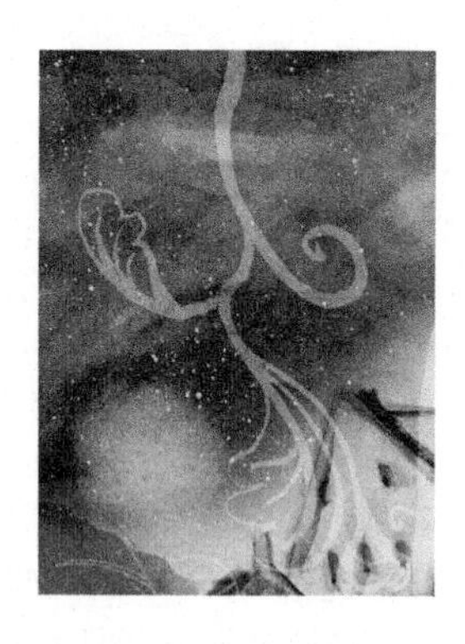

PART ONE

Preliminarily Speaking

On Behalf of Large Consciousness

When you take great care *at the start*, things happen automatically. You plant the Omega. The unfolding has an outline. A Track. An alignment. Time is in between. But *the outcome is lurching toward you*. It's stepping up to the plate. It's set up. No, not a setup.

Waiting requires not getting in the way—letting it happen. Then down the road when things begin to break apart, the Omega can come in. But the Omega is not just looking inside, to what it was from conception. It is unfolding into the idea of itself: the insight of what it can be, what **that** *Alpha state of itself* IS—could still be, taking this beginning *as an individual*. Another individual would tell it differently.

This is how large consciousness can be shrunk into small forms and codes. *As we decode from the "initial position," we discover destiny*. It's expanding. It's as simple as that to understand "I am the Alpha AND the Omega, the Beginning AND the End."

In between, not watching the clock. Not oriented toward The End. Oriented toward the relationship, the parts, the experience. This needs to be added back into our understanding of the Goal. It's the initiating point of the destiny possible at *that* end point. The offspring.

A soul grouping that came from the Alpha-Omega state was going into a transition and at that time leaving its Form, its wholeness, where beginning incorporates into it (in miniature)—at the start—the end. And end incorporates an opening, the Unknown: the Answer *giving birth to* the Question it finds when it answers its own question.

But that is not static, not death. It is what it *already achieved*, the Alpha-Omega it incarnated, that can be shrunk down into miniature or opened up suddenly out of nowhere, as in finding a wormhole. It exists.

It is also a Start, where none was, this now to stand on. So lifetimes achieve completion. Great lessons do the same. And seemingly minor ones. All actions carry FORM: all insights can be the kernel of a great gift.

Let's see how these ruminations work and how the Alpha-Omega is a consciousness that is trying to pass itself on, *like a light that was carried into many unconscious byways* but can be identified now, given a Path to call its own. Though as it opens outward, it cannot become an institution because *it defeats The End in stepping into it*. Always finding the open door that the End was hiding, now seen.

> We are living in unprecedented and prophetic times. The Mother Earth is in Her ascension process. If we can recognize this as Her spiritual emergence process, we can learn to listen to her and what she needs to move through this process. The Original Peoples of this earth have been given instruction and guidance that can help us learn how to awake to these times, and the birthing of The New Dawn. Creation is ending a 26,000-year cycle and opening to the next new 26,000 years. Mother Earth is moving into Her heart chakra. Her ascension has begun. And as this happens, we all are finding ourselves in a choice point for the human species. Will we awake and serve this awakening?
> —Jyoti Ma, Spiritual Awakenings International conference 2023

By the time I got to this book, I had a lot figured out. In a nutshell: part of me wanted to hide; another part not to. In some way, equal partners. But I didn't know that inner and outer leak back and forth. It took a lifetime to find out what's in this book. For instance, I walked on tiptoe as a tiny child in order not to be seen. But then, baby me also pulled the leg out from under my mother's table. Crash. Crash. And here I am, seventy-five years later, combining the two when I *walking barefoot through the garage*, dirtying my feet (*on tiptoe*).

So I now believe that *this disruptive me* was calling even then to that little girl. Not in the way we normally think of consciousness but just in *a potential desire to exist*, or even a probability of existing. And one little facet of the "future" can act as the drawing magnet that focuses us toward *that* direction. So almost as soon as I could walk, I walked on tiptoe—toward *that* me, the one writing.

It seems like a trifle to poise such a weighty book on. But stay tuned. Especially as I got this clue from a dream about the C. G. Jung Institute that came to pass.

✻

Sometime in the 1990s—I no longer remember when—the incident below occurred, at a time when events like this were an almost-daily occurrence; that is, all through the 1990s while I lived alone in Tienen, Belgium—with, however, "spirit committees." (My name for them.)

At the end of the day at a light body seminar, I "took a trip" with my teacher Roland Verschaeve—completely through energy dynamics:

> What I experienced was a visit by a spirit I recognized and knew to be powerful. He said they were "changing" drastically. A group change. He was very close to me, it was obvious. They were passing through death. They were sure to "re-emerge" into themselves consciously again. They trusted how they would "find themselves." But where this would take place would energetically be right there, in the masses I walked around with. Yet they would be so far away that they would have to "return," to even connect up with me again. They would, he said. Never fear. No matter where or in what form I might be. Time? What was it? It was too vague to guess how long they meant—in what language they would have spoken about "time" here. But I had to stay.
>
> *But how can you say something like this so quickly? So hurriedly? Before* YOU ARE SURE?
>
> But I was sure. Only, perhaps I overidentified with her, my "higher" self, my soul.
>
> And he spoke to me as a personality, on a personality level, a human-compatible level, who fit in. I answered back that they had made that impossible. That I was like Edward Scissorhands. They had not (in my case) taken away enough. They had put me here, still carrying too much from there. Or acquiring. So how could I not remember what my memory held energetically if not literally? I could not remember scenes. I could remember "the energy."

THIS energy. And if they were passing through something that, in the singular form of the wave, was her, my soul level, then it was also me they were passing through, just in the fact of not forgetting and thus acquiring symbolically the small Buddha belly I had. HERE. Here, of course, it would be used for things in this dimension that were "little islands," reproducing there and THAT.

Anna, was that one name appropriate to her, my soul?

But how, child, do you say all this? And not go further?

That, they say, is a later volume, *"the one you skipped." How skip it there, and slip it in, as if inconsequential,* HERE? *No. There. Yes.*

For me to tell this next part of the of the story (the one predicted in the 1990s), I am going to report things subjectively—that I can't prove, that give the drive to my life. Well, you'll see.

❋

Arnold Mindell, a Jungian psychologist at the Zurich institute while I was there, revealed that his own life and work with thousands of people convinced him of "a sort of informational wave pattern—a personal myth, relationship myth, or group vision—which moves and guides us through life." He said Jung, if alive, "would say, 'Of course, the pilot wave is what I called the individual's personal myth!'" In the section "Pilot or Quantum Waves in Rainbow Medicine," in *The Quantum Mind and Healing*, Mindell explains:. "I need only think of my early interest in physics, the apparently improbable accidents that landed me in the applied physics area of M.I.T., how my fascination with Einstein drew me to study in Zurich where I landed one week after Jung died in 1961. My first dream of analysis was about Jung telling me to pull together psychology and physics."

In my very brief stint in analysis at the C. G. Jung Institute, I discovered "two Margarets." "Little Margaret" left my dream book concealed between two pillows on the analyst's couch, while I, conscious Margaret, insisted I could not reveal those dreams. Little Margaret could.

When asked how her approach differed from the more behaviorally oriented analysts, the famous analytical psychologist/author Marion Woodman, who, by the way, broke the news to me that I was an *anima female*, answered, "Well, because I am a Jungian. I come from the unconscious . . . which literally is unconscious."

As a child, she recounted in *Dancing in the Flames*, she had "two Marions," and they battled all her life. One Marion, "from Monday to Saturday . . . never put on shoes unless she had to. She had a corncob pipe. Hair never combed. I was a gypsy. And when I went into the woods, I had no fear because my little Joan of Arc was with me." On Sunday all that changed. "We combed my hair . . . I had to sit there and grit my teeth until the ringlets were in place . . . I had to have a pretty skirt. And I loved going to church . . . and to hear my father preach" (see her interview on (YouTube: "Dancing in the Flames—'2 Marions'"). Little Margaret personified what Jung called my "inferior sensation function."

That mysterious personality type, undeveloped at that time in me, therefore had a home in the unconscious. As Jung explained it, "That least developed, or 'inferior,' function is so much contaminated with the collective unconscious that, *on becoming conscious, it brings up among others the archetype of the self as well.*"

But my analysis was not to last. I dreamed of a plane that flew, from point A to point B, faster than a ground vehicle. The plane was my intuition, which, the dream revealed, was best equipped to get me quickly to my destination.

⁂

In the first forty-five years I lived my personal myth unconsciously. At age forty-five that period ended with a breakthrough. But what had I learned *in the unconscious*? I had tackled, without knowing it, a karma—exacerbated by beginning in a cringing fear of speaking aloud. My thoughts, I gave to my writing, walling it off. As for my public self, on the one hand, I could have been a chorus girl. Yet if I even lifted my soup spoon at a luncheon, my hand shook violently.

All insecurities disappeared, however, in my bedroom with a pen and paper or drifting into the color green, sitting high among tree branches en route home from school. These two parts of me met as one at college, then New York. But only when this "personality level" got shattered did I get a test of my belief system and begin to study spirituality, in Charlottesville, Virginia, by then separated from my husband, Jan Mensaert, in Morocco. I left him—driven to it by dramatic circumstances. My husband was not only an artist; he was alcoholic, suicidal, and an incredible, charming, impish story maker.

The part of me who made this flamboyant relationship then drew near the part of me who traveled far and wide in my thoughts.

Outer and inner were practically forced to become the same person as a result of these experiences.

And consequently, led by dreams, in 1984 I wound up at the C. G. Jung Institute in Zurich.

I had just, by then, discovered that *every nineteen years* something changed monumentally in my life. I'd get a test on how well I'd learned the prior "assignment"—and if I passed, I'd get my next assignment.

The nineteen-year period *prior to Zurich* (1965–'84) took off from New York City. I met Hunter S. Thompson, Milton Klonsky, and Jan Mensaert, outlaw writers, which appealed to my chorus-girl side but also to my mind and love of going beyond boundaries—lifting the barbed wire fence at points where search of truth and yet-deeper truth beckoned. In fact, these rebellious males might have dazzled the chorus girl, but my deeper self needed them to teach me how to say *no*. How to discover my own laws, my instinct, stand up with golden energy pouring through my legs as I let no one tell me who I was or what I thought. Spoke out with that wobbling voice, which—when I *stepped aside* and let it speak—could not be stopped, it had so much to say—sluffing off anything too slow, too heavy.

It took me nineteen years to absorb the outsider mentality, which the inner part of me needed me to have.

Nineteen years in which my chorus-girl self sometimes ran wild, as it were, in excitement at being inside such dramas. But this plot dips in and goes back out. Always, however, in my consciousness, making roots.

So my self who will survive becomes more real to me. I will know where to face, in myself, dying. I can talk to that me. And "so much for that."

⁂

Did the original Mary survive?

Or was Mary just a puppy love of Jesus?

This sentence shocked me when it dropped into my head, untenable as it was. But to put some context to it, it had to do with energy when it incarnates on Earth, what happens to it. It's not like the full being, the soul, can come here in one piece, usually. It's narrowed down. A part selected. Or that's the way we open the subject. This thought was one of those flashing insights that are trying to steer us to information.

It relates to how recognizable, alluring in the physical as well as spiritual terms, a large entity might be. *What*? you ask. *Why even bring this up*????

And why did the question appear like this? Mary, not Mary Magdalene? But we can insert "Magdalene" into the hypothesis as well. No, let's leave that.

The point is that we are multidimensional, and a close soul tie has to fight through physical attraction to become visible in the cloaked fashion it exists in here.

Was Mary a puppy love of Jesus? Of course not. Out of order. What a question. But stop and think, as I did in Romania when it penetrated into my awareness. Actually, I hurriedly pushed it aside. Aghast.

Of course she was not a puppy love, but . . . based on experiences you will read about in this book, in this time of change, a new question arose. At least, it reached me. Obviously, she is with us and always will be. She is in my rosary, in yours, in energic descents that suddenly overtake a person who is "ready."

But that's one level, the easy one for her. Or souls on a very high level. Yet if they are coming to Earth at all, they need personalities. At least, most do.

Well, in Earth incarnation, we operate in percentages of ourselves. Not to mention patterns. A percentage of us becomes a focus, attracting whatever we want it to learn. And yet we also share and spread "ourselves" *energetically*, or find ourselves spread, advanced or regressed, hither and yon, in this person and that, including the most physical. This may sound all grossly speculative. For you can start anew with each incarnation. But let's leave it and look into it further later.

If on the "human" level, "she"—a large (or miniscule) energetic part of her—was more palatable, delicious, to the Human Christ than an even larger energetic part of her, what then? Would his future self fall in love with a variant form from the original? But then, cores evolved as well. Ah-ha. The core wasn't standing still. Naturally.

I was "all empathy." The "anima female," who hooked into and reflected the male's unconscious creativity. In me, this had purpose, from my soul's desire to align with higher consciousness in incarnated form—on THIS level of "everyday." If I have lost the reader with this abstract theme, never fear. Just wait for developments.

Mary is present in all of us. In the male sphere, by going into the shadow and attracting "her," he was risking too much shadow attraction. But as He appeared to evolve away from the original, "He," the Original, was watching.

I move into the "I" who speaks, as that's how I receive the energy, in which is the information, so that later you could say, "*But that wasn't you. That was a consciousness*" or "*an archetype.*" I don't stop and remove "myself" in such cases.

"I" speak, not stopping to define or ask, "*But where did you come from? Will you be 'me' in the next minute? Were you me yesterday?*" *It's first-person awareness.* Thus, if I were to continue as "myself," the limited physical body, at that moment, I could not speak for the "I" that has something to say: the consciousness, soul, archetype, transpersonal "entity" and so forth—which is how, by the way, it's possible to speak of a "Human Christ." Because he *is* each incarnation one after the other, all at the same time, to the degree he is "brought in."

Sometimes he (or any consciousness or cosmic entity) says "I" as one big beam of light or energy, not aware, at that instant, of the breakdown into forms. Other times, this beam-of-light form turns toward a single self, and that self can then say "I" in the part of itself that merges with the whole.

Call it a way to understand information this dense. Call it a way of experiencing, which I underwent. He wanted to be conscious as His energy spread—over the Earth—in the HUMAN SPHERE.

To experience his Oneness not just with God, with Himself as Human. Though male, female, for purposes of this plot, he was identifying with his male consciousness in its experiences on the Earth, *which defined the various "I" forms he had here, unknown to the people who held them,* who did not realize: *That's my Christ energy coming in,* though He did.

So a part of this plot will be to watch this energy develop, trying to navigate through the situation we've created on Earth, where exact *location*—source—of an attraction is hard to detect physically if the "deep attractor" is not physical. A spiritual attraction energizes nearby physical attractions that mimic it.

NOT to pull away from his love for the original Mary, who—by just looking at our typecasting of her on Earth, as a figure who made "supernatural appearances," who interceded on behalf of humanity (all true)—would, it might be expected, in the human plane, not cut the butter in competing with the human women adept at picking up whiffs of the spiritual attraction and reflecting it in the physical attraction. And so forth. *She had no down-on-the-ground "personality" deriving from her archetype, insofar as we knew it, who extended into her* Female Christ *level; no details of personality; no way to reincarnate, as it were, and find herself in a* Plot *with* Him *on the* Human Christ *plane, in the future.* He would draw away from her. He would be enticed much more by physical love AND PHYSICAL ATTRACTION.

So what sounds like fiction was received by me as a Plot *from another hemisphere, one which I was involved in and which was why I was in the personality I was in, which "explained" a lot of my life. It could be explained from any angle, and that would do. But since there was one angle where my soul wanted me to help, which sounded like a novel when I heard about it, I dropped the idea that it was a novel and followed suit.*

I played the card she gave me—as did others, I might add, it goes without saying: secret Mary representatives, or personalities, who could hold her consciousness, or a big chunk of it, yet help her develop a full range of human features. That is to say, to help the Earth redefine "female," as *having—in its gallery of "goddess" energy—the ability to participate in scenes she could not, on her* Christ *level,* participate in. But she had to, for on his Human Christ level, especially as He went into the shadow, He did.

But for this, she had to have no memory, *which I didn't and few of us do,* of Her divinity in us. This, then, is the Human story as "it" intends to evolve. All of us come here, forgetting our divinity, the fullness of our soul scope. Or most do.

It's the story of a conscious push toward evolution *as if listening to the intentionality of the genes.* Call it what you will. For me, it is the story of "I" as it came to get me, convinced me that was its name. "I" was stronger than anything else I had ever known. But it didn't say its name right off.

And thus, we start the plot, which I call nonfiction and many will be sure is fiction—and have the right to say so—right here in the Zurich Initiation. I do not know whether I am a novelist or a nonfiction writer at this point, in your terms. I listen to myself. Myself says this is on the level. This is truth. This is as far inward as I *can go*. So I *go inward. The plot starts to speak.*

It is transpersonal, admittedly. Still, it continues. It establishes its continuity. I am *its* "anima female" as well. I merge. No, *the rest of me evaporates*. It *"drops the body."* "I," who I was, is "dead." No, I *will come back over and over, a "regular" person*. But "I" *will also jump in as someone much larger, overwhelming the story*.

And there, I will have to be held back. I know. I know. Stay on focus. Let the "little story," where we humans are in control, have its day. After all, if "I" can't function on that level, then who will He relate to, when looking for "me," here, in any form, shadow or not? How will I recognize him if I do not have my "little self" fully alert? Or attract? How will I attract him? This is a story that depends on my attracting him, no matter when, no matter where, over and over, by other names and likenesses. But he is that extra something under the mix. OK, OK, enough already. Gibberish allowance met.

Ordering Archetypes

Archetypes, as physicist Wolfgang Pauli wrote to psychologist Carl Jung, are "ordering factors." Inside the speculative language of theoretical physics and psychology, the Jung–Pauli letters are sprinkled with gems that have gone unnoticed, in the mainstream public anyway. As I read that phrase "ordering factor" last night, it opened up what I am writing today. As I slept, it led to this path into the material I have been ruminating on for days. Before that, years.

Pauli also said that physics was, for the first time, now Aristotelian, not Platonic. Aristotle thought things were inwardly driven toward a preconceived form; an acorn *will become* a tree. Well, these ideas feed what is already my experience.

How could I possibly know the things below? It's been a long, hard study.

The reason a seemingly thoughtless choice can set up other choices has to do with a process of creating direction through analogy, much like "*If* this, *then* that": the tendency to go in a direction. To repeat ("grow and multiply").

A follow-up option might seem to fit, *by analogy*, a prior choice. To a reasoning mind, the two appear unrelated. But by the first seemingly irrelevant act, the decision can be *unconsciously* set up as a "value." We might never suppose there was a common factor or if there was that our unconscious would take that as a cue, even register something so minuscule. But our unconscious does, at least on this level. Habit reinforces, in this case based on an unconscious comparison: that original weighing of options, which to the unconscious sometimes means governing the future by precedent, even when we thought the first act of no consequence whatever, never imagining it might have unconscious weight that led, through a chain, to a snowball. Of course, we can stop it at any moment.

How you can do that, you can learn in this book.

Normally, I like to avoid overloading people with information, so I will do my best to speak heavily embedded in experience. But it's time to know this information—develop this foresight. At least, I can't hold it in any longer.

Our intuition is always working. When *my body* moves, *my intuition* begins to interpret.

These two "personality types," as Jung called them—sensation and intuition—are opposites and complementary.

Even when I position an object, my intuition may kick in. When I place a cranberry juice bottle behind a tin of coffee beans in the refrigerator, it is meaningless, I know. But that's not so. If we honed in *to what such an act could possibly mean*, as the intuition does, am I *acting out* (the "sensation" function's role) the fact that I *prefer* to drink the coffee? So what? I am *signaling* an attraction, secretly albeit. But the unconscious loves to pick up on our secrets. In my *scale* of values I have just placed coffee before cranberry juice.

Later in the day my unconscious may *translate that* into skipping gym or some other health choice. *The thing may mushroom*. For that's what scale does, on these tiny levels.

If I postpone picking up a messy piece of paper off the kitchen floor, that too is meaningless—but not so, relatively speaking. I have decided to relegate at least one picking-up act, not make it a priority. It would be superstition to think that simply placing one thing in front of the other *caused* a later event. Yes, I know. Such are superstitions. But even so, my unconscious is listening. It is getting to know me, predict me, jump to conclusions. It can systematically attribute *placement values* as emotional preferences at that time because my unconscious can read SIGNALS. That is, be conscious as to what these actions unconsciously *mean*.

Sometimes the interpretation is wrong. Sometimes it creates what we call self-fulfilling prophecies. But it is detecting what I am HEADING TOWARD. Creating shortcuts and automation, like its own brand of AI—easy future positions to "slide into" like a baseball player stealing a base.

If, not realizing this, I get into a trap, I see the result *in an event large enough to be noticed*. Even then, I probably make no attribution of cause to the above: all the little choices seen as trends, pathways, predictively important, by the unconscious. For to it, *when we collapse a tiny wave (of possibilities)* with a single (to us) arbitrary choice, it can attribute *meaning* without *meaning to, by enlarging the scale*, collapsing "*like*" waves *in the future*, making it easy on us, as it were. Yet the opposite may be the effect.

Thus, I stopped myself from procrastinating longer on this book.

⁂

Identity is a spectrum. Our consciousness expands; our identity moves with it into a larger spectrum. It changes like a moving hand line that responds to our life.

I, for instance, had no understanding that where I felt the most energy *like* me was where things were *not yet in form*. Through this lifetime I was going to—without giving up the abstraction—move closer to incarnation in a more-physical point on the spectrum. *This is what a number of people are doing*. And others—*in reverse. This is our life. This is our* NOW. *This is our* IT. *Here we* ARE. NOW. *On Earth. And Earth is changing to keep up with the conditions necessary for life here.*

We spent earlier volumes "on the edge." But this century is already taking us *over the edge*, the tipping point; we will use the secret weapon underneath.

⁂

So unconscious process was visibly at play in our waking life. Let's test the idea further.

We knew what happened when we rolled a ball. But how come all these other things were always catching us by surprise—far from our intent?

The picture concealed in a seemingly everyday scene might, at the same time, be revealing a picture of the "ordering factor" *at that moment*.

It might be that the "ordering factor" was an archetype no one was aware of. Archetypes went ahead of us sometimes, in a direction before we gave it a name.

Jung and Pauli discussed how the "ordering factor" might be an archetype. That is, we might be conscious of being energized but not know *the cause*.

So let's slow down and look at these things as questions that got my attention—linked to experiences that seemed to show them as an important underlying structure of *cause*. As I have recorded some physical events of my life, I would now like to record some mental events, and some later physical events that—the more I evolved—became important to me here. Thus, to begin with the first initiation. *Of course, I do not insist on any explanation I offer*. But these possibilities, I believe, have never been laid out in quite this way. Naturally, because they began in initiations.

So it is my life that I can look at through these explanations. That is, if I go out of the purely standard *explanations and add in these other perspectives, and the unsuspected "ordering factors." The unconscious motives, but of whom?*

I had many "train station moments."

Did you hear the story of Max Ernst, the painter, prominent in the Dada and Surrealist movements?—how his train stopped at Canfranc en route out of Vichy France in World War II? There, he was carefully instructed by the station master *to get onto the wrong train, back into danger.* Prompted from within, Ernst instead took the "wrong" train, which was the right train—fleeing to safety. The positive and negative joined hands, the positive counseling wordlessly to stay *off* that train, and he would be spared by believing in his Escape, his potential inside that choice, wrapped up in scaled-down, miniature replicas of his dilemma. He recognized, "*That's me, the one who gets onto that train.*" Had he not, if he survived at all, that moment would be repeated so many times he'd be forced to have the acuity, the stamina, to jump off when the train-station moment again presented itself.

⁂

Jung wrote in *Dreams, Memories, Reflections,* "I regard my work on alchemy as a sign of my inner relationship to Goethe. Goethe's secret was that he was in the *grip of that process of archetypal transformation which has gone on through the centuries* [italics added]. He regarded his *Faust* as an *opus magnum* or *divinum*. He called it his 'main business,' and his whole life was enacted within the framework of this drama. Thus, what was alive and active within him was a living substance, a suprapersonal process, the great dream of the *mundus archetypes* (archetypal world)."[1]

"A suprapersonal process, the great dream of the archetypal world," indeed!

Does the archetypal world dream? Build answers in giant structures with collective connections over time, inside us? Is it intent on finding answers? That is, as if we are like a colony of ants—but consciousness contractors—answering questions essential to our survival? We will see.

By the time of my Initiation at the C. G. Jung Institute in Zurich in 1985, the three major relationships have come and shifted, not gone: Jan Mensaert, the incredibly self-destructive, gifted Belgian poet I married, lived with mostly in Morocco, and from whom I learned the philosophy of daring to listen to yourself, not others; whom I lived with through much writing and his suicide attempts and whom I had now, in 1984, left. He had a problem translating into life what he sensed on this "wrong" track.

But the other Major Figures I have sometimes called Big Guns demonstrated the same psychology: Milton Klonsky, who had an iron-clad ability to listen within, who often quoted, "It is not *given* you to complete the task" (from the *Sayings of the Fathers*), coming down hard on that "given."

"N*either*," he continued, "is it *allowed you* to leave off."

I met Milton in the Corner Bistro, in Greenwich Village, alone in the back of the café, and I could not take my eyes off his eyes, described by writer Seymour Krim as exactly those of Rimbaud—hypnotic, pale. By 1985 he had died, the first to go. I say "died" with qualifications, as you will soon see. Technically, yes. But he was letting me know to take the news with a grain of salt.

And Hunter S. Thompson, who spent his whole life battling bureaucracy, with a counterculture lifestyle that condemned hypocrisy from first breath to last, singling out "fear" as the operable byword, the great Devil this century, destroyer of will—fear that seemed inevitable. But there was another, a "wrong" train to safety out of Vichy. I took these examples as inspiration to be myself.

I was on my own, forty-five years old, in Zurich, when the Big Initiation occurred. By that time, I had sped through the equivalent of multiple psychology courses in living with Jan fourteen years, been tempered and steeled and finally watched him finish magnificent soul-level poetry. I left with it ringing in my ears—for instance, describing a place where "there and only there can Inca live":

> Like the sun and that is fair, however often it may descend.
> but also the slightest mosquito, as long as it goes high enough
> And doesn't lie down along the road, may be sure of being a guest
> at the divine banquet, narrates the flute which is listened to
> till earliest dawn, of Inca consolation for what one had to suffer.
> Which is enough
>
> When one considers from where those words came. Soft but yet how mighty are those tones, powerful enough to make the enraptured listener forget where the almost angelic patience was learned that he who is neither wind nor sun needs to get up, and to go on, and once to hear the consolation or what he did.

At the Forefront

N*aturally, I wanted to be at the forefront of the basic assumptions of the next centuries. I wanted to come in here, where the evidence was thin, to throw my weight into shepherding it into our belief system.*

So now the soul has started to speak. You can tell by the degree of "knowing."

I wanted to get information from a much wider array of formats, including pure energy itself, because energy, for the most part, is in patterns that our brain knows how to "read." While our brain is in fact reading patterns, we typically DO NOT KNOW anything about it. We do not *do* anything about it. We cannot "see" a pattern, but the brain can.

We haven't a clue to something so irrational because we think there is no way to have a clue. This is rectifiable. Even as Martin Luther King wanted to free people from racial prejudice, I want to help free the mind. Life has shown us—or we have focused on—its uncertainties, to which one of the primary responses is fear. Every card has two sides. The Certainty side has yet to be *turned over*. Right here, in this book, I try to do so.

Arriving in Zurich

I love my life. Every thought, every situation went through me. I *felt* it all. The initiations added more "layers" to everything that went before.

If an initiation is successful, we move our "identity" *out of the "observer"* into that area where the initiation took place. What we only observed now becomes something we also *are or have a good chance to be if we cultivate these seeds, given specifically to us*. That is, *the energy we saw on the outside now integrates*.

Events have shapes, like we do—auras, energy fields. We just can't see them, as we can't see infrared without goggles or hear sonar. We can't *see* the event until it's no longer the building storm (in a mass whose directions we can't read) but is broken down into components—*inside our lives*. But even when it's amorphous to us—"the future," in fact—we could in part predict if turning our attention to it enough. Events have shapes that can be seen beforehand—*still deciding about direction*. This, ultimately, is to see cause. It's right there beforehand, as *forces*.

By long-standing tendency, we don't typically accept this form of perception. So, this other *dimension* of the fact that we began to see through flea, or fly, glasses (microscopes) and telescopes in the sixteenth century physically is, as it were, coming back to haunt us now. Or we could say, "home to roost."

I had learned and applied the lesson of the "anima female." She lives in co-dependency, having accepted the male's need to see "her," his inner female, on the outside—having willingly portrayed it, held the space for him to experience it in. Hurriedly, rejecting that role after recognizing it, I was now to see how it looked in a *different consciousness*, where—this time—*the rules were backwards*. How much could I say yes to?

Arriving in Zurich, I'd mastered the understanding that I had subpersonalities that could not wait longer to be integrated.

Powerful rebel males had illustrated to me how to be strong

as a female. But now it was time for the second life purpose to come to the fore, the soul purpose: "to help others lift the fear of Enlightenment from their minds." My soul moved me into the position now to consciously participate. Would I still be a writer, for it was my Linus blanket to hold onto, the one sure unfailing thing, my place of certainty? I had to write. Now it appeared I had also to transform. I was to stand on "the first half of my life" and let it go, to go forward.

As my own consciousness came toward me I had to discover there were dimensions where ordinary reality was only one facet of a spectrum to retrieve information through. I had to quickly put under my belt all these clues my unconscious as a writer (and dreamer) had given me.

Information is constantly tossing up (to the acute nervous system perceiving in this way) new minutiae of information *that change everything* that went before, for, ultimately, this is how the "natural mind" (of the Buddhists) works. But it is the opposite of the "ordinary mind," another Buddhist term (meaning the logical mind). It functions globally. The forces marshaling to create the future are picked up *before* they show themselves in an event. The tiny pieces left out in "connecting the dots" are sensed beforehand, because they are there, just in more subtlety.

It keeps going—after The End. It doesn't consider it The End. It's only a foreclosed End, because here, on this complex framework, it BEGINS yet again, in instant digestion of what is now different.

In concluding prior volumes, I had certain things perfectly set up AT THE END—many things to bring to conclusion. But they belonged in a different book. It required my readers to want to jump. To realize that the consciousness in the whole book up to that point was not to be the one from then on.

Time, for instance, is invisible to us except in the present.

How much of myself is invisible, and what is it doing in its invisibility? What is the "dark matter" of me busy with?

"White Designs"

A dream showed me I was to write *verbatim* the end of Milton's charred, deformed obituary. It felt like an assignment in a detective story. Something wasn't right, got told wrong, left in ashes. I was a reporter. This was a story. I was to report.

In confronting the reality that he didn't finish the novel the publisher Harper & Row gave him an advance on—"White Designs"—or write the poetry *he'd been expected to*, quoting, "It is not allowed you to leave off," Milton added penetratingly, "I can write poems as well as anyone alive. Why don't I?"

The obituary left that question hanging.

The intricacies below capture me in the act of receiving energy locked into word play, chunks of it—as with Zeus throwing thunderbolts—that uncovered an ambiguity, an underlying meaning, in *allowed you, a* LOUD U.

I could feel it pulsating, as in a voice at the top of its lungs, telling me this was

> Not the End, not A DIEU*
> This is a loudspeaker of the spirit
> a shouter
> *un haut-parleur*
> This is lo
> This is me,
> *Io sol**
> saying, "We belong on Mt. Olympus together*
> "We have an appetite for dew"

---

* *adieu*—goodbye (FR); Dieu—God (FR); *haut-parleur*—a loudspeaker (Fr), a reminder that Milton was "a shouter"; "*adieu*" in French is an off rhyme with *haut-parleur* but pronounced, in English, uh-D(Y)OO, rhymes with "a loud U.

**io*—I (IT), as in *io sol uno*, "I myself alone" (*Divine Comedy*, II canto); *sol*—sun (SP)

It is *not allowed you to leave off*
For this is not adieu
but A LOUD DIEU
Nothing else will do
Nothing else is
A LOUD U

. . . .
Here's the end you were looking for
it is "A LOUD U"

Leaving Charlottesville, I thought ahead—blind but at warp speed—telling myself to make meaning of this death; it hid "buried secrets."

How I could do it, I didn't know. But, I predicted, one day—unexpectedly—I would:

just as if these blank pages had held something invisible all
this time. Blanks that were not really blank
Here were

The WHITE DESIGNS

In the Kaballah, or mystical interpretation of the Torah, what wasn't written down—the white around the Hebrew letters—was said to contain the hidden meaning. Thus, Milton's title. In fact, he also told me, he was a "crazy kid," who had "more whites around the eyeballs," referring—I just realized—to the same explanation. (He added: "You know what I was crazed by? Immortality.")

As stated in the Zohar, a Kaballistic set of books, the Torah was written in "black fire on white fire." Consequently, "the white space is a higher form of Torah" (see the account of Robert Garner in "Written and Hidden Letters of the Torah," Sefaria.org). "

Was it possible I was being urged that what wasn't "allowed" him was "allowed" me? Maybe had been "set up" for me? Could that even be conceivable? And why? A spur if ever there was one; that is, to follow to where this nondeath was leading.

Of course, who writes such words is not the personality but the self, the soul, standing, catching the dribblings and the downfalls, holding for dear life onto this "umbilical cord."How much of ourself can we know

* Milton had said this to me.

in human form—dare to (even be meant to)? As we expand into the twenty-first century, what more—corresponding to the new technologies—do we urgently need to meet, to know, even individually, in the parts of every person personally? Having determined that my life proceeded in blocks of nineteen years, I had already anticipated that a new "block" was beginning.

What is never imagined has practically no chance of being brought to bear on the situation. *And it does not matter who imagined it!! It does not even matter what century it was imagined in.* Life has a long memory. The universe does not forget. It can shove something aside. It can de-energize. In fact, we can learn this useful trick. How not to "lose the thought," how not to explode on the spot. How to defuse, even inside a pattern of explosion, re-energize a thought or feeling. And not mechanically in the head. The heart can do this.

Everyone works somewhere on the spectrum. That makes us all connected and equal. Certainly, we need a few new structures, perceptually. I detected it was my purpose to work at the event level.

Normally, to know this was not important. Just a fact hidden away in the hills of the Himalayas and some other places, where gurus sitting in caves could look at event maps and influence them "at a distance" through consciousness and intent after, of course, purifying their energy to be capable of this.

The reason it becomes important is to the extent the individual becomes much more a force—with decision-making capabilities, in parallel to raising the basic consciousness to result in better-informed decision-making. If the individual is more empowered, the consciousness the individual works in has to be more informed. That is, the esoteric was performing a job. It was secret. It depended on knowing certain principles of energy.

That being so, the time came to turn over more esoteric principles to the West, in the way the West had turned over scientific research to the whole world.

The Eastern "science of spiritual evolution," yogic science, was in every way the opposite of laboratory science. One principle it operated under was Mind through Matter. It required study inside minds, recording experience. *What? But that's not scientific,* said the West. *Never could we think the mind took the place of a laboratory, of measuring instruments. What about repeatability?*

It had been assigned "my personality" to go into this. This is about me, in various dimensions.

Before entering the second phase of my life purpose—to help others remove the fear of Enlightenment from their minds—I had to get through the first stage, mainly in the personality, AS A FEMALE. When ready (or thought so), be "moved into position" by my soul.

I had taken my personality through every form of challenge in having my shadow (where I was least conscious, underequipped) marry a shadow of a very conscious, evolved being. Now I had to come *out of the shadow, when he did not*—triggered by Milton Klonsky's death. As my mentor and a semi-boyfriend (in New York City in the mid-1960s), Milton was the model for Robert, the male protagonist of my then (in 1985) still-unpublished "big book."

I could have returned to New York, hooked up with him after going through all that being married to Jan Mensaert entailed. But I had to "get there" first. And getting there coincided with—was triggered by—his "death." Yet, was he dead? How could he be? Such a mind, I had believed—not intellectually but intuitively—could not die. This had nothing to do with survival theory—but with those recognitions that had framed my life and showed its calling. The man was more important to me. The explanations he gave me, the vibrations he lifted me to, were stronger than death. If he could die, whatever we called God could. It was that simple to me. Perhaps it was Plan B.

So, at this point, I was at the C. G. Jung Institute, and Milton Klonsky was, to all intents and purposes that I could detect (having passed away in late 1981) "guiding" my initially flabbergasted self from wherever the afterlife had taken him.

I am on the track of a new "Bell Curve" of what it is to be human, in terms of the information we can gather if looking at it in an entirely different way, that does not lay out those pathways each person has to access the Collective, the Whole, the Universal Mind, *and bring down something individual.*

Some of this information, which right now is churning itself into my fingers, passing simultaneously through my brain, which is to some degree astonished, may have been "left" for me, planted in space, by someone no longer in a form to do so personally or to even hand it over to me now. But it passes through my mind on this frequency that it could be compared to Clark Kent finding his birthright.

I do not know where this perfectly thought through information comes from. But it might be from someone who merged into the collective energy at such a wavelength as to no longer in present time speak individually. Or perhaps even from the anonymity of universal consciousness, by my finding this pot of spiritual legacy I am invoking the forming again of that entity, bringing him/her "back to life," as it were. And perhaps it is a part of me. And this too being a universal principle, on this level, that we can "return" if our energy is, as in *Star Trek, reconvoked, reserved for another century*.

On that principle, it could even be the spirit of Newton—to us the "father of the clockwork universe"—his unfulfilled desire to blend alchemy (transmutation) and physics (gravity, action at a distance) into something that took his discovery of gravity a step further: galaxies of time further, light years further, to where a connection existed. But not in the seventeenth century. So there's the barest possibility I could be convoking him by stumbling upon his "stache" of brain matter, of speculation, like living fire or radioactivity.

Or it could be Dhyanyogi-ji, who "realized" all his desires, but after starting to connect East (as spirit) with West (as action/science), or spirit and matter, inside the United States—illustrating Eastern satguru techniques in such ways as giving a demonstration, measured in a scientific experiment, of at will raising and lowering his blood pressure—screeched to a dead halt and left the country, understanding that it would require too much lifting of "karma" in the United States, receiving it into his own body, if to take the idea further at that time, in the 1970s. No, the timing was off. Too many "thought forms" translated into too much disease; the "cure" premature.

He acquiesced. There are many such acquiescences in our history, many such delayed-time reactions. Suppose they are in an Energy Field of Completion as their "burial ground," on the wavelength where they all connect, being "unfinished desires" or premature insights, is pulled later out of dusty drawers. Perhaps I intuited this, feeling elation as a child in watching actress June Havoc open a dresser drawer while she kicked her leg high in back—and that scatters or concentrates wherever it is destined to or timed for, or calls out again. Suppose, then, it is as urgent as I feel it to be.

So is this a continuation of the storyline? Exclusively the facts, ma'am? But these facts have personality.

No matter. Proof is not the point here. The East does not use Western-style "proof." How could it, when its discoveries far outpaced the nonexistent hard science of those centuries? So, this will be the culled-from "facts" of certain laws for whoever cares to hear or has that "startlement" of recognition, that energy-burst going round the circle of genius as it holds hands. Therefore, from no matter where, it is part of humanity's genius, tapped into, the circle round, *speaking of withheld things*, suspected things, things buried and personally carried in lifetimes not allowed to speak, mothered, fathered, brought by courier at great risk to here.

Getting Back to Me: The Initiation

Dreams told me that in my case, at forty-five, I had to find ground-level stairs. In that way, I could "recycle" (perhaps *to* myself) what I'd taken to a plateau. On the plateau was a cul-de-sac, a Black Hole with the now-dead (but alive there) Milton Klonsky in it.

I *saw his legs in the hole*. I had to descend and start from the ground.

That is, the soul could not just "march in," banners flaring, insights recounted, belief systems that were outmoded cast aside. *To speak, I needed ladder rungs from the bottom up—myself no longer flustered, sitting crossed legged in a corner at the mere contemplation of such an assignment, but having learned to gracefully step aside and let Her, the Soul, do what she had to so as not to end with unexpressed contribution, but that she instead gave back to the Earth the relevant wisdom it had taught her, permitted; all that in my heart in the spirit of passing ourselves on, not only genetically but in ways that process and interpret those genes, by the body of consciousness that can unlock them, because it has the hidden structures they are a match to.*

✻

In my two-room apartment in Zurich my Big Initiation was about to begin. I'd just read in a popular-science book that in quantum mechanics, there is a Heisenberg "loan mechanism," by which some particles that *lack the energy* to get to the other side of a "hill" (an electromagnetic barrier) might *tunnel through on borrowed energy*.

Heisenberg's indeterminacy principle *left the position of any particle uncertain*. How did such a particle tunnel from *a* to *b*? It *"borrowed"* what it needed.

Physicist Paul Davies, the author, cautioned that this ability to reappear miraculously on the other side of a barrier is impossible in our macroworld. Humans cannot, on borrowed energy, walk through a wall. Nevertheless and naturally, my sleep took the idea up a notch—with a dream about a *lending library*.

The night of September 6–7, 1985, it asked me if I wanted to *have the Initiation*.

In the dream I walked into my apartment and tossed my coat onto the floor. My (deceased) father and youngest sister (whom I took to represent my mother) were neatly folding my freshly washed towels. Surprised, I adamantly refused their help. I *want to be independent*.

At that, my father and sister froze. No matter how hard, he would bow to my wish. But I saw a sliver of disappointment crossing my father's eyes. I knew that look.

I too froze in my tracks, seeing strings rising from the tips of my fingers. Touched by his wordless emotion, that flicker of disappointment, I really felt their yielding.

I did not know this yet, but the universe puts full strength behind now one thing, now another, now one person, now another. At those moments (called "tides in the affairs of men"), if riding in with the tide, you have the whole ocean behind you to ride in on. I could. You can, no matter if the tiniest drop. Everything is *lined up*. *Ready to spring*. You have only to *take the ride—go with the white caps, go with the surge*.

Fortunately, I have a 1990s journal entry to quote from to be sure I don't misspeak with time's additions: "It is as if angels are descending, I am being *initiated*. I jingle the words in unconscious translating. Discoveries leap out, landing here in my conscious mind":

> I *really felt* strings. I was *really touched* by that unspoken emotion. In his eye . . . felt really High EYE CUE.
>
> I felt the vibrations in my hands as I—got the cue—but I couldn't physically see—
>
> High Eye Cue

In the way quantum particles that cannot surmount a barrier without assistance can, nevertheless, tunnel to the other side, *on borrowed energy*, this was not about co-dependency. It was here that my soul was "moving me into position."

Deep inside me, I was able to read the tiniest of clues, interpreting the vibration. I desperately needed this help. **It was a soul pattern of unconditional love, of Oneness, of grace. And so I soared upward** in the intention to ***accept*** what was now arriving.

✻

Thought by some to be the successor to the "Sleeping Prophet," Edgar Cayce, the late Al Miner, the first psychic I ever contacted, was the channel of Lama Sing. Just one year earlier, addressing the urgent question I'd posed him, he answered that Milton, having died in November 1981, was—yes, as I suspected—indeed guiding me; there was a conductor, a channel, between us, "which cannot be disrupted by the loss of a physical body, for the tie was far deeper, at the emotive and spiritual levels." He said it was a "time of very beautiful opportunity"; that he *was in a soul grouping* I *was in*, several realms in consciousness beyond the Earth. But *so as not to abort this lifetime purpose,* Lama Sing said little more; also because I would not have wished it. That was enough to digest, as much as I could handle at the end of 1983.

I wanted to "do it myself," forge the qualities that came from Not Knowing, blunder on, biting my nails, till reaching the breakthrough a new person who used experience to modify behavior. This was the advantage of not knowing the end, of uncertainty. The creative instinct *used* uncertainty to press forth. F*ear used it to retract.*"

However, Al did add that the several realms in consciousness were identified by the "ability to accept." A*bility to accept was an indicator of consciousness*.

My alignment with this "ability" had just been tested. It made sense that I'd had been identified by Marion Woodman at the Institute rightly as "the anima female" and that I'd rejected that line of reaction. If I was the inner female of males, holding their inner femininity in a pattern where this caused me subjugation, then it was detrimental.

But *it all depends on context*.

In a workshop of Miner's while living in Charlottesville, in 1984, I'd learned what all the other participants believed: that everyone has guides, and souls belong to multiple spirit groups. It would take time for such a concept to sink in. Was it true?

Much later Al said to me:

> To be succinct, brief in that regard, you are a part of a soul grouping who is intending to bring that peace of understanding that comes through the realization of the nature of

> self and the universe itself as a single whole of consciousness in the journey of eternal life. In the sense of documenting this, you are in yet another unification or initiation into yet an additional grouping of souls and/or consciousness who are seeking to discover these final stages of what you have described as an initiation . . . considered initiatory but in other respects . . . a process of reawakening and claiming that which is ever within and about self no matter where [your] foot might fall upon a pathway.

He called the result a "newly forged rod of wisdom . . . So you have brought these forces of understanding and these expressions in a combined form . . . [an] initiation into oneness or one understanding." (March 2009)

He described how the "process of growth" can be compared to a "funerary procession or death parade":

> Why? Because an entity in the Earth and in other realms tends to grow into a position of presuming their present existence to be that which exists. As then new opportunity, in effect, forces its way into the consciousness, or change is manifested which disrupts that consciousness, there is the loss of that reality. For knowledge is as an energy: when it is exercised it becomes wisdom. Wisdom is light, and where there was an illusionary realm of existence in the past, the light of wisdom removes this, and the entity is in essence requiring themselves to grow. The loss then of an aspect or portion of self is presumed by the entity, when it is in effect not quite so, but rather self becomes clearly freed by the removal of such limitations and can move in all directions easily. (October 1984)

After the Folding the Laundry dream, I stayed in bed—meditating—on the strength of seeing the disappointment in my father's eye *if I refused their help*. This was *an energy transfer through the eye*—as the clever word play hinted.

I'd been given a request in a High Eye Cue; it required me to receive the input transferred powerfully *in subtle energy of love* and a desire to assist.

✻

Staying in bed, I meditated four and a half hours!!!—sensing my mother and father were helping in supplying the energy.

With my eyes closed, I saw visions and felt myself being pulled upward—toward an opening (hole, tunnel) as to the top, the dome, of St. Peter's Basilica. *After several hours* (in suspended time, not knowing how long it would take me or to where), I felt the atmosphere "break." I was there—no doubting it—***in a consciousness.***

In this consciousness—a lone man looked up into an empty stadium, addressing his "audiences of the future." He was planning his book, making contact with those audiences not present yet in the empty stadium. It was filled with fragrances but no people. Knowing virtually nothing of different traditions, nothing of Asia, for instance, I thought this must be the Christ. No, I *assumed* it. No other possibility crossed my mind. *Who else could it be*? I asked myself. But I also knew I was being guided by Milton and that was the reason it had happened.

Describing the Initiation

My soul grouping's current project involved mind through matter, Mariah Martin, a second psychic I'd recently consulted, told me. The Initiation showed her to be right.

A Personal Milestone

First a little more background on the period separating old and new, standing on a seesaw between two perspectives, two parts of myself, the personal and the soul. I was about to learn views in 1985 that would apply to shifts in the twenty-first century. Thus have something to say at this time.

The second morning, I tried to repeat the first morning. In far less time suddenly there was an opening. I found myself in my mind's eye watching a movie, in my father's consciousness. I *sensed* a telepathic message in the scenes that played almost like sitting in a theatre. In later sleuthing I identified *Max Dugan Returns*, in which Jason Robards, a likable ex-convict whose daughter kept him at arm's length, escaped from jail and, in my version, after going to his daughter's, with loads of stolen money, to meet his grandson discovered the kid *was terrible at baseball*.

But Max, *promising to get his young grandson the best teachers money could buy*, hired a big-league pitcher. As Robards slipped away, the boy was pitching a game. Emotionally in secret in cracks in the fence, the grandfather watched his grandson pitch a victory.

Recognizing this as a message, I believed "the very best teachers money could buy" would be sent to me.

The third night, I met the spirit of my mother but had forgotten the indelible dream, waking, except her enormous amount of enveloping, caring love.

In remembering Jung's own plunge into a "Confrontation with the Unconscious" after leaving Freud, I felt reassured. I could do it. From it he received the seeds of his lifework: the material he would develop for the rest of his life.

At the Institute we used the term "Confrontation with the Self." One of my Zurich professors tried several times to teach a course on it—never lucky enough to arrive safely the first day of class. Finally—I was there—medicated, in bandages, on crutches, he triumphantly did arrive.

In undergoing her Confrontation with the Self, my mind-body teacher at the Institute went temporarily blind.

A September 16, 2009, *New York Times* article said that Jung "later would compare this period of his life—this 'confrontation with the unconscious,' as he called it—to a mescaline experiment. He described his visions as coming in an 'incessant stream.' He likened them to rocks falling on his head, to thunderstorms, to molten lava. 'I often had to cling to table,' he recalled, 'so as not to fall apart.'"

Sara Corbett, the author, predicted: "Had he been a psychiatric patient, Jung might well have been told he had a nervous disorder and encouraged to ignore the circus going on in his head. But as a psychiatrist, and one with a decidedly maverick streak, he tried instead to tear down the wall between his rational self and his psyche. For about six years, Jung worked to prevent his conscious mind from blocking out what his unconscious mind wanted to show him."[2]

Such a test was supposed to be awesome. Mine was now.

I dreamed of a plug in a wall. But it was connected to a converter. I was having a conversion. I wrote: "So my book will have a plot change in the middle. The man trying to get my attention is the inner Christ."

The Initiation began with fasting for purification. But it was further based in an understanding of archetypes. It was time to lift an illusion. It is not just that we are made of jostling atoms that can now be microscopically viewed. True and not true. Alongside the forces in the atomic world, I *hold* myself together with the thought of who I am. The atoms will not just jostle into another form.

But I do this to life as well. These jostling atoms are met—by my eye (trained by my brain)—in a way that does not allow me to see freshly. This creates stability. But it does not help me be authentic.

I was in the perfect place. Zurich had backgrounded many unreported initiations, and the historical presence of many world thinkers, including Einstein.

No wonder I had worked on *Love in Transition* since 1965—twenty years—but found *the end* elusive. It was waiting for this in-Life Takeover.

In 1985 and 1986, I was taught exclusively by this "guide." The person I believed in most, Milton, was vouching to me that this was his recommendation.

Not long into the fasting, I was to temporarily eat only two teaspoons of honey a day, drink two glasses of water, go to the bathroom only twice, practice receiving dreams and study them with him. I practiced sleep-deprivation. Learned the beginning ropes of how to work in electricity. I was being groomed to, at the drop of a pin, go anywhere, do anything, without *needs* interfering. The other reason for the extremeness was that I was *being purified cold turkey of "physical attraction."*

It was based in an understanding of the relationship of spirit to matter, the archetypes we have on the Earth put them in, the divisions, and how—ON AN ENERGETIC LEVEL—this misunderstanding would be dangerous in the future.

It was time to lift this aspect of our belief system, if you will, off the minds of people on the Earth. This illusion was based in believing that what you see is the way it is—taking physical reality at face value: you push a ball; it rolls.

My logic listened to my intuition, which told me I would have been baffled at the severity if I'd had no predisposition for this sort of thing. I imagined that this initiation might offer some details of earlier esoteric initiations *that were unrecorded*.

I could not just "know" what was in his mind, so one method of communicating was by runes; I would draw a rune, and the explanation flash into my mind. Or thoughts, song tunes.

I was learning that physical attraction was complicated by its unconscious relationship to spiritual attraction.

To create a pattern (a "Sacred Marriage") where a physical attraction was not being fired up by an unconscious spiritual attraction, he wanted to remove in me the underlying components of physical attraction. Just imagine. However, the purifying fasting made me skinny as a rail, down to 87 pounds from 124. He showed me feats I'd have thought superhuman. For instance, he took the Kundalini shakti energy, and as I heard a sort of mechanical sound like drilling, he carved out excess flesh in the insides of my thighs. Though I would have believed it impossible, it was a shocking demonstration whose physical effect I could see in the scooped-out shape.

The Kundalini is defined in the East as a divine energy, a conscious intelligence. Dormant at each person's birth, it is coiled upside down at the base of the spine. If it awakens, the coil reverses direction; the energy moves up the spine. Unlocking blocks, activating chakras, it is en route to the head. It is also called Kundalini shakti, the Divine Mother. At this stage I only got a taste; the whole experience looked to me like the Bible and miracles (the only reference point I had). I found that reassuring. That is, such things had happened before, I thought; that quieted my alarm. I could imagine no other explanation. I was having a biblical initiation! What else could it be? I accepted the idea that this was a form of Christ and of Jesus, and who was I to say what was impossible in such an energy?

But had I known other traditions, I could have drawn up countless stories that describe great teachers working in energy in just these ways. This, we will come back to. For he was not against science and even assigned me to continue to read the Paul Davies book *Other Worlds: Space, Superspace, and the Quantum Universe* with him.

About himself, he told me only that on three levels he was like me and on those levels he had an imperfect relationship with his feminine energy. "Object," he encouraged me, "if I tell you not to water your plants or take a bath." He wanted me to "stand up for the feminine."

But it was entirely different on the fourth level, he said. There, I *was not to dispute* him. On that level he was the Christ, even the "first" Christ (I will explain later), or Jesus.

I had no physical impression that he was the Jesus I'd read about. Yet under the impact of demonstrations, I believed him. I had the impression that if his energy was traced to a particular point, at that point it would be Jesus. But I didn't understand. He did not go on into an explanation of a transpersonal consciousness, *which in fact is what he was illustrating*. But I was as if entering the story after all the explanations, *in media res*.

Now I was leaving the unconscious, to some degree. Being an artist, I had a lifeline to the Unconscious, a powerful relationship to it. But I had not thought it conscious, as it were. What I received from it, by way of inspiration, I thought I made up. If you let something be unconscious, it's like an uncollapsed wave.

I lived in uncollapsed waves before, a rich environment for the artist. Now the wave of *What I Believe* was collapsing. And what happened and how it happened was insignificant beside the fact that I came out a changed person. My personality was smashed. I would have to work on creating a personality who could speak from this new base.

My personality didn't know WHO I was. I was in another split, but higher on the spiral, the split between what I knew and how to speak of it at all and how to create context. For I did not yet understand enough. Not by a long shot.

Lama Sing had told me that if I could get into my body and give enough self-worth to self in the sense of acceptance and receptivity (but "not in the sense of putting self above others"), I had the chance "to become a Living Example, a Living Christ" (I add: as does everyone).

So now, nearly forty years later, in 2023, I would say—based not only on this but other things—that this was a nonlocal consciousness, a Global Consciousness, or Galactic Consciousness (I would go that far) that could assume the form where any one entity has a point inside of every other entity and therefore, if choosing to identify with that point, can have energy, even conscious energy, inside any person whatsoever. This was the level this Initiator was appearing on. Or at least, it was what I received, not just being told it once but watching tests based on it, tests with me.

Every day, I woke to audible chords of music piercing the silence, without a physical source. I loved it that this felt so protective. He could brighten the room—intensify a light bulb light. Put words on the oversized bulb's glass. I still have that green lamp. Once he projected scenes onto a wall. It's hard to explain how you can be sure of a presence, but this was accumulative.

Fasting, he said, would get rid of any dependency; he wanted to remove old cells, cellular memories, even the habit of caring about food. I was to dispense with all crutches. While asleep, I was not to budge, even turn over—but throw away the eye mask, the ear plugs. Cold turkey.

Could I be tempted, asleep, to want things I was renouncing? How would my unconscious react? Suppose my famished self was confronted with a feast of chocolates in a dream. It sometimes happened. Or my body woke me with an orgasm. Could I be unprogrammed in my unconscious? I fantasized getting on a plane to Morocco just to eat the fresh-cut salads: beets, tomatoes, cucumbers. But his belief in me was contagious.

Wouldn't I have been more baffled at the severity if this were something I had no predisposition for? I asked myself.

I came to think this must be familiar to "me," something I knew about. Surely someone with no history, even, of familiarity with such an initiation would not have been thrust into it like this, so lacking in gradual steps. It would not have "blown in" like a wild gust of wind, and blown out after a couple of years, without some expectation that I was able to use the vast array of thunderous seeds.

My rational brain tried to find a cushion from which I could confidently have something to rely on. Mariah Martin had labeled my style of learning "uprooting of the ego." It figured.

My miniature six-year-old, regal black mini-dachshund, Snoep, whose father was a French champion, watched from his wire kennel, which took up several feet in my living room apartment, though he weighed ten pounds. Not allowed to move about freely, in his lack of bladder control due to his back legs being paralyzed in the "dachshund disease," he was nevertheless being lightly initiated—the two of us together. *For a brief time*, his diet changed to rice with only a plum for seasoning. He loved the plums. Seeped enjoyably in the good vibes, he sometimes, apparently easily, received (by sensing it or telepathy) information; to communicate it to me, *he acted it out*. For instance, the Initiator said *the First Christ could, under no circumstances, have been stopped*. By this, he meant Jesus 2000 years ago.

Abruptly, Snoep began to valiantly attempt to poke his head out of the top of the kennel, slightly pushing up the large wire lid—illustrating the statement that nothing on Earth could have stopped Jesus Christ. The second Christ (or stage of Christ consciousness as received in people), however, the Initiator said, was vulnerable. I will go into that below.

I was to be taught that because of our belief in physical reality as matter—solid people there in front of us (*surely I am solid, you are solid*)—physical attraction and spiritual attraction were entangled on the Earth.

Invisible "vibes" present (*through* a physical person or just "in the air") might be thought to emanate from a person or even an idea, whereas the "real" source was too subtle to be identified, thus adding *intensity, irresistibility, inevitability*. For most of us, that is. It meant that the basis of a decision, of a feeling, might REALLY be very very different—perhaps opposite—from what one interpreted. Thus, ensuring many rude awakenings.

It was going to be important to make this distinction in this time in history. Fully accepting that this was a biblical-like Initiation!—what else could it be?—and that this was a form of Christ and of Jesus, who was I, as said, to say what was impossible in such an energy?

I was learning through the tasks and experiences he brought.

Remember that he was affecting the vibrations in the atmosphere, communicating in constant presence if I went outside.

For instance, we went to Parade Platz (Parade Square). One tool he guided—and impressed—me with at this point was the hands of my father's watch, on my wrist. As I had a thought, the minute hand might spin or stop. At Paradeplatz he told me to buy an annotated Bible. He never said why. I found out years later. Meanwhile, it just sat on my shelf.

But let's backtrack just a moment to Milton's death in New York in 1981. Synchronized with it, totally unaware it was happening, I watched oceans away in Belgium *a parade* that was very numinous. More so when I found out what it coincided with. Buying that Bible at *Parade Platz* in Zurich in 1985, I associated it with that Blankenberg parade, not having a clue why.

Back in my Zurich apartment in 1985 after any excursion, I instantly sat at my typewriter, trying to pick up the guide's reactions: *What did he think about our outing*? This addressed my insecurities, as I delightfully felt answers come into my head, my fingers, typing. I was not used to channeling except to the extent it can be the source of a novelist's inspiration. And he *wanted interaction*, not just one-sidedness. He wanted to engage my energy.

He wanted me to interactively inspire him and vice versa. In this, he appeared to be Milton. But this was a much larger being than anyone I had known on Earth, for he was nonlocal; that is, not identifying himself only in a single physical form. This was a whole different structure.

He set up goals, one being a Marriage. I had, at this time, never heard of an *internal* mystical marriage, such as written about by St. Teresa of Avila or Jung. *In fact, I had never heard of any specifics I was encountering.*

But first, I had to come spontaneously into his consciousness, he said.

I accepted the marriage idea, though it was, he said "in this world and the next," which normally I would never have consented to. Imagine making a commitment into the indefinite future—with someone you couldn't see. It was like the myth of Psyche, married to the god Eros (Cupid), who visited her only in the dark. Even so, I could not meet his criteria. Before marrying him, he wanted me to learn to leap from my consciousness spontaneously into his wavelength.

I couldn't and furthermore constitutionally resisted.

I said that perhaps I could do it easily—if the idea came from me. That is, if I felt compelled by someone to do something (and did not want to), I did it but harbored resentment. I didn't want to get back on that emotional roller coaster. So if ordered into his consciousness, I hadn't the maturity not to take it as a command violating my free will. This, also, was part of working out his masculine/female balance (in the archetype) on the three levels below Christ, where, like me (though in many forms) he was inside patterns we humans live in.

Then one day it happened. I sat in my small-apartment living room, wearing my pink felt hat and pink fuzzy sweater, a single candle lit on a coffee table. We were having the marriage. Keep reading for a fuller description later in the book.

In a dream before Milton's death, the main figure *stepped away from a group*, as if taking matters into his own hands. Then, his wiggly, elongated, willowy body stretched as in a painting by El Greco—looking as if on remote control—he wrecked the car. The accident was only hinted at; there was no driver visible, in the end.

Sensing that this figure broke off from a group to hurry along a project's speed, I asked Al Miner in 1984 if my soul grouping *was involved in a "project."* Al answered yes, a project in the Christ consciousness.

Putting these facts together, I felt I *must be inside that project*; that somehow I must have, in my human form, attained the right to participate. Or that I was just dragged, kicking and screaming, in, the way any birth takes place, leaving the womb of the familiar. This was the position "my soul had moved me into."

At first, the Initiator tried to make me remember incarnations in which I had known him before. I failed miserably. Not thinking of a single one. In fact, I had no memory of any past life whatsoever. And I did not think a person should take statements about one's own memories coming from other people, or even spirits. I also feared my legs would remain with the big hole in the thighs, unrecognizably thin. It did not suit my vainness about my appearance. But that was barely more extreme than the rest of me. However, I totally trusted the Initiator. When my landlady became worried that I remained inside, the curtains drawn (the Swiss opened their curtains), and called the police, I refused—at his instigation—to open the door. Not budging while the police banged to get in, so taken I was with the Initiator's instructions. Would they break the door down? But peeping through a tiny open portion of the curtains, when they saw I was alive, legally, it turned out, they could not go further.

Having stood up to them strengthened me. I was well aware that no records of initiations and transformations involved meek, doubting, half-baked responses. My models (from the Bible), such as Elijah in a cave being fed by birds, or St. Paul blinded by light, showed that anyone who underwent a conversion—was transformed—was a rebel, totally submitting to the Initiation.

None of the stories would have survived otherwise or been convincing. I was not thinking of this as a story that would survive, but I could draw up no other comparisons.

They were defiant, standing apart, consumed by their "call." Else, it was not convincing at all. So, this gave me a sense of proportion (humorously said, but I did take it that way)—that my reactions were in line with history and credibility of the situation whenever encountered and recorded.

So now, similar to many another person in such an initiation, when it was real, I was choosing to heed, instead of police, this invisible Initiator.

The more extreme it was, in fact, as with Jung, the more credible and eventually productive—bringing consciousness out into the world by confronting the Self. Or wrestling with Jacob's Angel, going through the Dark Night of the Soul, going to Heaven and receiving the command to "write," or heeding the angel's offer to have a Christ Child, or whatever. But one had to come out of it sane and alive, for it to amount to anything publicly. It never occurred to me that this was leading to spending the rest of my life in a cave, for the Initiator had started by showing me his concern for communicating with the masses.

I thought of myself as having a conversion, of which there were many in history: all dramatic, extreme. How could I not accept what Lama Sing had predicted was coming as "a blessing"? I knew I was not losing my grip or having a breakdown. I wanted to be able to go through this the way my models did. *Not that they had been my models before.* Sometimes you found yourself in a situation you'd read about and never imagined as anything but a story. Then what? *Then this.*

Yet I had such confidence in the Initiator, I never, from the first moment of being transfixed by his certainty inside the stadium, felt doubt.

He was revising with me my unpublished "big book," now *Love in Transition: Voyage of Ulysses: Letters to Penelope.*

First, he insisted on removing its negative energy; he said negative energy (in emotions and situations) could be picked up right out of the book.

True enough, someone at the Institute became very ill. He explained that if a person resonated with a pattern being discarded, it was possible that person could fall ill. I was very upset at this logic. Could life be like that? Could patterns of discarded emotion be attracted to someone else? Germs were contagious, but what else was? Under what circumstances?

In other words, he acted from an entirely different perspective, where not only could spirit move through matter but in certain conditions loose archetypical energies could "infect" our psyches; that is, if organized in a way that was attractive to receivers.

This could be attributed, in an Eastern point of view, to karma. But the cause was a pattern.

Mastering this concept, one could maneuver patterns. But we lived in them unconsciously.

A pattern could be hiding in a scene, dramatized in a book—so he was saying. Organizations of energy (like bacteria) could affect us on other levels, *reaching us through our emotions*. That is, an attraction that, to us, was inconsequential had "meaning," and that meaning was the lesson.

Lessons had degrees of relativity. To the degree we were ultimately part of a web of life, we were all learning lessons for each other. Whew. But I didn't digest it this much then.

It was sitting as a half-conscious thought. I lived in the moment, trying to absorb what the day required. Later I would take these ideas much further, with many references that settled them down into known or unknown concepts. I lived here, though, not in concepts but in new experience.

We wrote *The Christ State* (dictated *through* my energy). After that, fragments of *To Love—AND Remember—*like *The Christ State*, all poetry;

about the Earth but personal, which is what stumped me.

I could starve myself down to nothing, follow the dictation (energizing). That was easier than translating, *digesting in a form that could be communicated*; even, at first, understood by me intuitively. I could detect what belonged—what strayed off point. But *intellectually*, I could *not* explain. I could not contextualize. I had an emotional block, a boulder insofar as the material brought *me* in. I seemed to be something without a category, my ego 100 percent uprooted.

But by these counts, it seemed the whole Earth was uprooted. I did not know how to place this "map" of consciousness and reality on top of any reality map. This wasn't "from" the Earth I knew. It was from the man writing his books (in the empty baseball stadium) "for the audiences of the future," whose consciousness I had entered the first day.

No matter that he was telling me that on the fourth level he was the Christ, I was down here on the three "lower" levels, so where did I fit? My ego was not yet able to grasp that perhaps even if "I" was brought in centrally, somehow it was "not about me." I grappled with the question: *How was I, outside the confines of the book covers, to mention that he was writing* The Christ State *in a transpersonal/personal focus, speaking of a Christ who would return this time with "**tu**-lips"?* **Tu** *(the personal "you" in French) being reserved for those close to you.*

And why then were the *tu*-lips coming over to me? With my limited framework, I did not know how to lift "me" out of the center while also putting me there. I was like a child who freezes, not daring to think a thought further, when letting it loose would bring the solution—something unthought of.

On one of our downtown walks, before I got too thin, he in fact had me buy a figurine of a miniature clown, holding tulips. Another time, a stuffed clown I still have. He identified with clowns.

His message drew on the Universal Mind. Yet it personalized! It concerned vital issues, archetypes, new world structure, "saving the planet," with *ability to do so*. I had never heard of such a concept of a multidimensional Christ. But wouldn't it be so if he were cosmic?

But why was I here? He was both supremely high (on the fourth level) and human and dispersed (on the other three).

And what was I? Why was I in the center personally, while he was a giant energy sending giant messages? Of course, I could say I, like everyone, have this nonglobal consciousness, but at the moment I found it extremely awkward.

I did not resist; quite the contrary. Yet I found myself in a *cul-de-sac*. For I *did not have the authority*.

Excerpting from *The Christ State*:

> For I was a New Man
> the spirit of the New Man
> the stopped-beating heart of the Old Man
> released rejuvenated in the New Man

And many group missions:

> To go into an experiment
> be pushed to the limit
> and find out what happens
> a discovery, in this way,
> of unknown capabilities in man
>
> What action would it produce
> what heart bursting
> What was man capable of
> at the outermost limits of the Earth
>
> The project Earth
> To go into unknown territory
> what was unknown, unexplored in Man
> for what was known in Man
> could not save Man
> Perhaps what was unknown
> could
> *To go then into the shadow*
> *of man*
> And when in *the twilight of man*
> bring out of the shadow of man
> what was good
>
> To teach man what love was
> That it beareth all things
> That its essence is patience
> and further to give

DAR*

To play this hand now
top this hand
CAP it

I was convinced that it was the future of the planet on the initiator's mind—that it involved knowledge I could not at this point have access to:

Give them, the living, the energy to bet
Tell them what the bet is
so they can choose sides
Tell them what the sides are
Tell all this
to THOSE ALIVE

The unpublished book *To Love*—AND *Remember*, which he—or, more precisely, a spirit group with him—also wrote with me, is now just scattered blocks of sheets of paper: an elaborate all-poetry mosaic. Will I ever contextualize it enough for publication? Yes, now, almost forty years later, this present text does that, provides background for the too-far-ahead material I skipped over with a lump in my throat. I loved it.

It fascinated me for the narrative, told through personalized archetypes, an epic adventure partly of Christ and Mary inside the larger movements of the Earth. But I did not use these names. The

---

* *dar*—to give (SP)

* *peau*—skin (FR); pronounced "PO"* Ann is my middle name and that of my (à la Jung) then-"inferior" (transformative) function of "working with the hands"; "and" is also the feminine sense of connectedness; I'd dreamed: "The second Stanza begins with and."

* *Tanza*—dance (DE)

* *mano*—hand (IT), from Mozart, *Don Giovanni*: "Là ci darem la mano!" (Your hand in mine, my dearest).

* REM—the dream state in the brain

* "*Dan*" is in the name "Dhyanyogi-ji."

opening (below) takes place inside a dream fragment when I was living in Larache, Morocco, on the Rue de Damas (yes, I lived on the Road to Damascus), February 3, 1981. In it I felt myself spun—instantaneously (the speed felt like an eyeblink) to land someplace off-Earth. The poetry below, from *To Love*—AND *Remember*, begins here:

On the Road to Damascus
The certificates of deposit
All there within
In the de-*peau* sit*

A cement unknown to man
An experiment with it
A cement unknown to man

When the word would come
EAR AN*
The second stanza
When she would be TANZA*
Would dance with him
La CHI
DAR REM
*La mano**
Doe-
REM*
DOUGH
REM
Carry out the dream with him

---

* *hache*—axe (FR); "h" (SP); spinach, as in what makes Popeye strong

* *thé*—part of "Don Quixote." thé—tea (FR), pronounced "tay." Tea and a cake, a Madeleine, started Proust on his great recollections, In Remembrance of Things Past, a title from Shakespeare. Some of that spinning around in this swirl or bouquet of energy-information-emotion—also, part of a "go" signal

* *gâteaux*—cake (FR), *Le Gâteau* (Baudelaire) still spinning into new breakdowns and re-formations

La mano

. . . .

Tall, almost emaciated
standing beside the Master of Ceremonies
a Master of Ceremonies in the shadow
"When did you see Dan* before?" he asks
SEDAN SEDAN
When did you
SEDAN?

When did you see him
before?

I say, "In New York,"
not knowing why I say it
or what it means
"In New York."
Then I'm whirled back as through time
Spin-HACHE [*ahsssh*]
This must be
Spin-*hache**

Who would cross the goal line
Hoe *thé** ["tay"]
Goe*thé* ["go tay"]
when the signal was given
Goe Thé

The mission of artists overhead
A flock of artists overhead
All in the energy pool overhead
When the signal for the run came
Go Thé

Got toe
*gâteau**

cake
cook-key
goe *thé*

. . . .

Then the signal was beamed between them
that Dan—whom she didn't know—she remembered
For he was the man she connected with
New York

The other not visible
known only through a beam in his eye
communicating with the first through this beam
of light
that traveled from his eyes
A signal
that this part of the plan was successfully passed
That something long in preparation, evidently,
had undergone a test
And that the result was that hoped for
They had felt sure
she would pass it
when the time came
this test

Then she would go on to the next stage with him
Then what was unknown in the plan could be unveiled

But this was a memory that must be carefully guarded

This was not for any reason to be let out of the channel
the private channel between then
for this was the holy bond itself
This was the treasure that would open to all the treasures
This was the energy they shared
It was in that energy, the memory
the cells that remembered where she didn't
That knew they had sent this message through matter

That had with mind penetrated matter
Had made matter known through spirit
This was spirit
This was his spirit
that would make the spirit triumph
with its memory
over any appearance
in matter

And so it must on all accounts be she
who held onto that energy
It was the thing most sacred to her
though she didn't yet know the connection with him
for how was he Dan
when was he Dan
why did she recognize him as DAN
Dan—it must be—could it be?—one of the men standing here?

One of the initiators
one who set up this test?
She knew she knew
Dan
And she had known him
in New York

But she wasn't
to make conscious too much
It wasn't the time
to remember too much
she could be trusted
that was a bond of trust
She answered only
for she knew only
she had known Dan
in New York

And thus the commedia opened
with a mysterious test
a confrontation

a challenge to memory
And to use that memory
for the glory of God
For it was
God's energy

A child conceived waiting to be born
This child a new-born child
Not a human child
but a living child
a real child
A consciousness
An age that could accept it
that a child could be born not as a living baby
but truly existing, this baby
the child of God
a birth of
a consciousness

MOVING AHEAD:

Out of sleep
Dorm Ir*
AWAKE INNING

In one of his sons
a new climb mate
A WAY KIN

So to top our own freedom there was the
Om let
of God's
FREED Om

Look into the sky and see
FREED Dome

---

* *dormir*—to sleep (FR), pronounced "dorm ear"

The missing event has to come in
through the hole in the ceiling
the unknown hole in the ceiling
The unknown thinness of the top of our earth atmosphere
That the ceiling must come off

For a new means of vision
for a possible re-
Vision
of Life on this Earth . . .

Situations couldn't be escaped from without
a change in the Dome
The same problem would face the Earth
till we removed the thin covering from the Dome
Saw the hole there
the tunnel of Death
That once through that hole
we would see beyond our own death
We would see new worlds to discover
See the future
of the Earth

For the Earth was in One Situation
That being a dimension
until it changed its situation
by changing the Dome
Removing the covering from the hole

---

* "Ch" seemed to be a trail: from Milton's phone number ("CH-2") to CHarlottesville, to Zurich's zip ("CH"); *ange*—angel (FR); ch-ange, referring to the archetype of the consciousness of Home
* *vie*—life (FR)
* MN, "Milton," the door he went through, death, a journey, expansion, the Initiator
* *viens*—come (FR); pronounced "V-N." In reading this aloud v-N-a and d-N-a rhyme and sometimes, depending on the line, are pronounced like "Vienna, Dienna," instead of the usual D N A
* Robert: name for the spiritual-yet-streetwise male based on Milton in my "big book"

MOVING AHEAD:

A double END code
D-N-A
VIE-NN-A

Soaring high above this Earth
Calling down to this earth
Come in, Earth
D-N-A/Vienna
Remember the code
the code
CHANGE*
DNA END CHANGE
END CODE
IN CO-ding
Calling from
VIE* in A

The dance
that had to be learned

Through the door
The M N Door*
Viens [pronounced V N]
Viens
DNA* [here pronounced to rhyme with Vienna]

A new kind of man
M N
Viens
d-N-a

---

* *colle*—glue (FR), pronounced "cul"
* *ouvre*—open (FR)
* *ouvrir*—to open
* *tempête*—tempest (FR); *pête* is pronounced "pet"

The colors change, Robert* said, but the Dome remains the same,
in circumstances surrounding an event
And yet this time
suppose
you've turned
INTO YOURSELF

....

St. Peter's Dome
those just behind the Dome
The DOME of the Seer *colle**
Making a seer *colle*
one body
many physiques, many expressions
reaching out of the
Dome
to me to reach them
to go through this Up-rising
For there they were
My soul grouping

....

For there was a world locked up in a heart
And the heart
Had to open—

Heart had to *ouvre**
to Louvre

Ouv-
REAR*

**t'aime*—love you (FR)

* *ama*—love (Latin,); part of "Amadeus," whose name means "love of Deus"

* *rêve*—dream; *nu*—new (FR)

Tem-
*PÊTE**
*T'AIME**
PSST
Pan-
*AMA**

Rêve
N
N*u**

In a dream I saw a contentless outline, a trucklike frame. An archetype. Milton asked me to detach from his physical form. I buried my head in his shoulders, not willing to give up the familiar form. On a distant hill he appeared as the Lone Ranger, telling me he would use the meaning of his death to help others—that its deep cause (medically an inoperable cancer) had been an underlying challenge specific to this time period, that would likewise baffle others.

Introducing earthshaking ideas, the Initiation interwove personal and transpersonal in ways that gave me no legs to stand on: Applied Consciousness without the basics. I was supposed to figure them out.

To remind me to go through the "Death of Ego gate," we had a two-inch piece of glass with a painted gate: Ego Gate, Gate O, Gate AU.

So indeed, a consciousness was coming toward me.

Yet with a message so important, he wrapped it in sure delay by bringing me in, inexplicably, in a personal way.

The Institute had warned that no one should "merge" with an archetype. But that was not much of a starting point to find answers. Yet find them I must.

I could do it, he said, retrieve the consciousness that had these updates.

But how, for instance, did this Initiation relate to Mother Mary? In it, he called me "Mary," and I erased that name from the book *The Christ State*, substituting the name of Paula, the main female character in my "big book," Milton's mate (his name in the then-novel being "Robert").

Why had the Initiator changed the personnel? How could the Holy Names be relevant? Since I did not have any sense of what it is to exist IN a consciousness, even to BE a consciousness, I did not even have a start in finding the answer. But find it I must, if I was to speak. My soul counted on me. He counted on me. I could do it. Retrieve the consciousness which had these answers, these updates perhaps, to what we thought the Christ was, IF A CONSCIOUSNESS, an energy, omniscient, in us all, a gate to "FREEING THE MIND."

Yogis such as Yogananda had been in the Christ consciousness and experienced a Light beyond religions. But I was being shown *that* in a multidimensional form, one that ran through us, that was "imperfect," inside archetypes on the Earth that I would hope to help *shift*. Shifting energy was what my creative impulse would be doing, whether or not "I," on another level, mostly unconscious, was writing books.

In his *Autobiography*, Yogananda called a great Hindu avatar, Babaji, the "Yogi-Christ." He wrote, "Babaji is ever in communion with Christ; together they send out vibrations of redemption and have planned the spiritual technique of salvation for this age."[3]

I Had to Be Celibate—Reversed

The Initiator made me believe I had to be celibate. Then suddenly it was not to be. If I learned a thing, it might be provisional—the opposite become the new rule.

Pronounced free from physical attraction, I was told the goal had reversed. Its purpose achieved, a "law" might reach what Jung called enantiodromia, the moment of turning back on itself.

I was supposed to go into energy fields he set up—to attract a human being (already in his energy). Now, here I may lose readers. But many more will want to hear.

He would set up the field through casting down into it (by intention) a part of him: a memory of a relationship, experience, event. This energized, vibrating, loved memory would be a magnetic beacon to someone who had those subtle inclinations, maybe in his heart of hearts. The catch was that the Initiator would have only minor control over that person after the attraction "took." From the Initiator's point of view, he was putting part of himself out there to be "picked up." Being that it was a real memory, it was "organized" (had a pattern). Underlying that was the consciousness. In this instance, he was trying to create patterns *based* in spiritual attraction, though that was not meant to impede physical attraction. He'd removed physical attraction from me—to try to create an attraction involving me and him (on the subtle level), that would begin, though perhaps unconsciously, in spiritual attraction. You can say he was setting up archetypes.

He showed me the drawback. He was electrical; his human personality liked electricity, strong passion. *Now that he had taken that out of me in a physical sense, how was he to attract "himself" to me?*

The attraction would have to be created while sidestepping what it usually depended on. Of the difficulty, he seemed unafraid. That is, to take on the task of destroying the archetype, at least in one conscious instance. But then, any instance anywhere works like that, with whatever level of energy is involved. Here, there would be a large amount of intent. To replace sexual attraction, in some instances, with spiritual attraction (the Sacred Marriage) because of things that made it timely, indeed necessary, at this time.

It was a kind of St. George and the Dragon situation, where he would operate secretly on the inside, in the unconscious.

He then created a pattern at a location where a male was walking—in a park once, downtown another time. In the apartment beforehand, he had me concentrate till I could "see" the male. Then he had me go by tram to near the location, hoping the pattern would attract us. On the downside, it might pivot the male into a *wild inexplicable physical attraction to someone else*, whom he met coincidentally at just that moment.

That is, exact *location*—source—of an attraction is hard to detect physically if the "deep attractor" is not physical. A spiritual attraction energizes nearby physical attractions that mimic it. The spiritually based attraction, being secondary in our experience of attraction (subtle, that is), might spin off a wildly energized physical attraction like a more earthly photocopy. So he set up a likelihood, but the exact adaptation of the pattern in form (in an event) was outside his control.

Initially *the pattern* he set up (to create the format) startled and dismayed me. It came from *my* past. (Used the way he did, real events could be patterns for later events.) I was shocked that stories might be "used" in this manner.

Though setting up a couple involving himself was only one of his projects, it revealed the larger principle of how, in our perceptions, spirit interacts unconsciously with matter. By spiritual I am also referring, unavoidably, to what is called "past lives," despite the fact that this term assumes a sequential time. But spiritual attraction can also refer to meeting someone who is part of your primary "soul grouping."

❋

Well, it's now over the time limit, and I am running to get in under the gun, to say what I made of this version of reality given in seed form and fast-firing neurons and downloads and chaos in 1985. For I did not want to die and remember, as Kierkegaard dreamed repeatedly, there was "something I forgot to say."

A Colossus of Rhodes at this point
And the one guideline
I believe we
ENACT our lives.

She could do it
He was sure of it
make it
A HOME RUN

She stood behind the plate
And it was a
silver plate
calling on her to do it
make it
A HOME RUN

The impact of a memory
An overwhelming impetus
A consciousness in the heart speaking to the heart
Encouraging the heart
To make this Home run

. . . .

A hill faraway where once stood an old Cross
A man waiting
to commune with her
A heart
Sac-
raiment

The fusion of the heart once experienced
For there had been, on an abstract level
somewhere beyond the Earth
the fusion of the heart's memory
Just above the ground that moment
When it had to be
brought down to Earth
It had to be lived

The fusion felt on the mystical level
it had to be
part of the Earth—
The mystical marriage

Discard violently
the Pattern

We had agreed to a separation
that on a certain day was to he ended
We wanted to get a head start in this century
to so forge our bond that it passed safely thought the moment of transition

An idea was trying to enter the Earth

I C BAS Pow
pacing overhead
Doing it
Bringing it
to the Earth
A new idea

The madeleine in the air
Mary Magdelaine
Her spring
Her aria
For this is her
Sea-
Son

Waiting all this time for it
Locked in the garret
the readiness of it
Man's reaching her state
For all of her would be released at once
She who had come in darkness all this way
following her soul mate
Not to be left behind but to change with him

Make the spring with him
Her Sea-
son
Not sending into the world
the feelings of a man crucified
Sending it his song instead
its transformation into song
into harmony
Nep-
Tune

She had only to open her heart to reach his feeling now
For it was directed at her, to be channeled by her
that she must know it was her destiny to channel it

A picture spreading across the sky
seeming to reflect something
that was taking place on the Earth
And overhead the masterpiece painting
of *The Last Judgment*
of May-he-co

A crescendo large-scale
A judgment that this really
had to be
LARGE-SCALE

"I believe," said Milton Christ to Paula, "we
ENACT our lives."

A concept from another galaxy?
Could it be a concept
of humanity
from another
Gal AX-
Y?
For us all
A new place setting
Resurrection

The Old Man
who loved more than anything, in 4-sight,
His Son

A cleaning of the slate
become present
Now
in his allowed re-
Conception
Not of his life
but its meaning
choosing that over the unconsciousness
of reliving

⁂

When he spread the first pattern over the air in Zurich, I was aghast! Startled and dismayed.

It came from a real event in *my* past—reproduced an actual relationship in my life,

How could a piece of my life be dropped over a location, hover above people? Wasn't it scandalous? To him, a sacred tool. Not the least because he considered the experiences to have been his as well, though *through* another physical person (he identified with, in the earlier situation).

Taking the organized energy—of a prior relationship—he dropped it down like a dragnet. Being perceived by him as a pattern (of spiritual attraction, however physical), it was to hover like an energy bubble over the scene, which he further energized by his own loving memory. On some level, it was now prima facie reusable. *How*? I asked. I especially asked myself how it was moral to "give away" pieces of someone else or oneself. But he considered himself on some level the other person. Not in the flesh. But in depth of attraction.

Far from being random, for the recipients of this experiment with me in Zurich, he selected people who were, from his point of view, resonant with his energy. Or who, from his point of view it appeared to me, *were* him.

More accurate now would be that his energy was *in* them, even potentially but strongly, to a degree he believed in or felt he could *activate.*

Also, this was an implication of our Oneness. It would not only be the Christ some of us worshiped in a church. It would be the sense of "God" inside each human being, by whatever name. It was an implication—removing religious terms—of how consciousness functioned when not restricted to a physical location, how we "left" pieces of ourselves behind, or, in fact, why it was said that Jesus changed every cell on the planet by the pattern he lived.

But the odd thing, to me here as I say repeatedly, was the personal part, that there was nothing abstract about it except the fact the Initiator had no physical body.

He did not reveal his *personal* likes and dislikes, except once he started a list: he liked jeans, cut flowers, rice—

He stopped, realizing it was inappropriate, when he was, for all intents and purposes, transpersonal.

I was not an instant master of this situation, to say the least. These encounters based in spiritual attraction led to a few slow-burning *friendships*. No instant hot romances. My question remained how on Earth I would go out into the world after this, publish, have a sense of identity. *For I, who had known since seven who I was (a writer) now didn't know at all. I was being given my work for the next nineteen years.*

Still, I struggled with the concept. In one way, it was like a Buster Keaton film, but in another the deepest, most profound effort to make spiritual attraction more viable, not an unrecognized instigator of physical attraction. Not to remain an unconscious sometime-pyromaniac of the heart—like someone who went around throwing down burning matches and stealing invisibly off the set. So, to be brief, inept at the skill as I was, no couple was formed beyond friendship in the first year and a half.

But these were not things learned lightly. In fact, Al Miner had said that some had to leave the Earth to learn the things I was going to be taught, and it was seen as a great blessing. I guessed this all made sense if my soul grouping, according to a reading over a year before by Al Miner, had the project of introducing the "*universality of humanity.*"

So my soul, operating inside her universal self, had sent me down here in the most tiny form insofar as I knew, with her oversight. I also worried that suppose my soul grouping's transition was dangerous. Wouldn't I want to be there? Was, then, my soul grouping in the Omega moment of the concept of "a universal consciousness," moving beyond it, and if so, into what? Was everything *personal* being lost? I had no idea whether this last was babble or incredible insight.

My sense of the spectrum created a lot of abstraction in my personality. In reverse, of course, the "personality" can *expand into* the larger being, and from that perspective, *up* and *down* have little meaning.

So I was not encountered by a guide who wanted to speak *through* me. That, I probably could have mastered—saying I was receiving information from a superior consciousness. Or my inner Guru. It was not like that.

But back to the first pattern he spread over a small portion of the city I was to walk through. It was too "weird," a "shocker"; further, to use another person in this way without his knowledge, creating something that happened unconsciously to him or to his energy, even if not to the physical person, seemed an invasion of privacy. This pattern he created or detected and lifted up to set down was between Hunter S. Thompson and myself. *Who*? *What just went by there*???

It was a favorite of the Initiator's, the clear first choice. This didn't require Hunter's presence or even consent, I was aware—though his soul's consent? I thought so.

My crazy, hazy days with the late, great godfather of Gonzo

My crazy, hazy days with the late, great godfather of Gonzo | The Independent | The Independent

Ralph Steadman tells for the first time how a meeting with a former Hell's Angel changed the face of journalism. By Martin Hodgson and Katy Guest. A few excerpted paragraphs below.

20 August 2006

When a little-known Welsh cartoonist met an ex-Hell's Angel in a US bar more than three decades ago, the result was electric. "A voice like no other cut into my thoughts and sunk its teeth into my brain," recalls the British artist. "It was a cross between a slurred karate chop and gritty molasses."

The meeting spawned the birth of Gonzo journalism as Ralph Steadman, who had travelled to America after giving up his ambition of being a banker, struck up a drink—and drug-fuelled relationship with Hunter S Thompson, author of iconic books such as *Fear and Loathing in Las Vegas* . . .

Steadman reveals that . . . after Thompson shot himself last February. "When he died it was as though a piece of shoreline had split off and fallen into the sea. I had to write myself out of the emptiness," he said . . .

The two men met in 1970, when they were commissioned by *Scanlan's* magazine to cover the Kentucky Derby together. At first, there seemed little common ground between the acerbic American writer and the diffident Welsh artist. "It was chalk and cheese. We were so different, but I intrigued him because I did such vicious drawings," Steadman recalled . . .

When the two men first met, Steadman was best known for his work in *Private Eye*, and he credits Thompson with focusing the savage vision of his cartoons. "We changed each other's

> lives. After meeting him I realised that a drawing could be a weapon—and that I liked to use it," said Steadman.
>
> "When I did pictures with Hunter I got butterflies in my stomach and it was very exciting. He made you realise how lazy and how respectable and how tired you'd become . . . . . .
>
> Steadman refutes the idea he wasted his talent. "He was probably a great writer, *but a lot of his best stuff was his conversation and his life. He didn't squander his talent—he used it in an amazing way* [my italics].
>
> "I miss him a lot . . . bawling at the end of the phone. It was the most difficult friendship in my life, yet probably one of the most essential."

He added, "He was an exhilarating person to be around." Indeed.

Of all the prior events in my first forty-five years, up to 1985, *the Initiator chose this one.*

That tight nugget of the "Hunter-Margaret" experiences, formed into a pattern he could imagine aloft in the air, reactivated—a neutron star, or black hole, of the past—by, I suppose, thinking, willing it there, where the spiritual energy itself from our precise history created the physical-attraction feelings, *therefore did not destroy—let go of—the spiritual attraction, never having been disconnected from or emerged out of it.* No, he strongly hinted that somehow we had done this: brought a spiritual attraction into a physical attraction. That he was permanentizing it into a pattern universally available. Imagine.

And how could Hunter and I, to take just that example, ever find the Real Us again, if it had multiplied all over the Earth? Well, that's one way of exaggerating the situation. But in another sense, to find each other again, we would have to go much much deeper or rise much much "higher," as this level of the attraction had already, now, been widely claimed. That is, if his plan worked.

And this pattern he detected had, so far, effectively functioned to stay alive here, with *feelings that clung together even without our presence.* Not AI. That was nothing to this. It was intangible form. Well, it might as well have been hung on an electricity pole, for that's how spiritual attraction functioned.

The Initiator, to spell it out, just used unconscious projection.

Based in resonance, this pattern ensured that anyone in his energy he targeted—well chosen by him—was a male that he, in his matchmaker role, knew I'd at least like; in fact, the idea was that we would both at least *be highly drawn* to each other. It was a setup. And since, in this case, the projection (the pattern high in the air like a balloon) sent out, to the cellular level, the quantum level, information it could read and respond to—and it would not be attracted to something foreign but to something it had affinity with, all unbeknownst to the hapless receiver—the receiver responded because he couldn't help it. His deepest inclinations did it for him. That pattern was like a siren call to him, for the right reasons, like honey to a bee, like Home finally arrived at.

If you're being shocked, you have company. As said, it was almost scandalous to me. That's the way I saw it then, if not now, when I know that using a tool like this just calls on yet more advanced tools to see through it. Tools he would try to embed in any affected male, because involving someone would mean he had to grow. And to the Initiator what I have just described was sacred.

Well, I'm running to get in under the gun, as I said; in a hurry to laboriously get what I made of this version of reality into my voice, my vocal chords, my cells, my intention—for I did not want to sit up on my deathbed, as I ruminated, and suddenly, glassy-eyed and frantic, have the realization that I forgot this: *that this, in fact, might be why I was here. Of course, I knew that I'd had other challenges, lessons to learn. But that was for what we call the personality. Couldn't the soul speak at the end, clear everything aside, and say these are some things I know? Or think I know? From my point of view?*

A tricky communication—that everything built up to—of how spirit interlaced with matter, including mind through matter; so that the turning point into science at the end of the sixteenth century, when it split from "faith," was unfinished. At most, three-dimensional.

What was left back there, when we started down this road, if we run back to the seventeenth century to start all over from that download when Newton sat in his bed and began us on the path to the twenty-first century, with planes and computers and technology everywhere? What underpinnings of *that* beginning—what complement—did we filter out? Omit? Erase? To pick back up now?

What, under the radar, under that polarity (faith/science), was the connecting unifying *beginning point*, trying to come back in?

We know, through chaos theory, that a weather forecaster will predict a hurricane, based on a certain-size fraction (say, 1.55757) fed into the calculations. Another prediction will result if the fraction goes to 1.55757222222438. So all new ideas come to us in fractions, rounded off—their *complexity capped*.

Then, in the very act of living, they acquire more complexity, thus perhaps making visible the very implications we cut out—but discovered through unfolding consequences of their being eliminated at the outset.

That's for another day.

Now, returning to the sixteenth century, what can we add? Einstein added $E = mc^2$. That matter and energy are interchangeable, that energy can be latent, then converted into kinetic matter, brought into form, motion. Suppose latent factors left out of the Newton revolution are ready now, BECAUSE WE CAN HANDLE THEM—not wanting to be given everything at once but rather to spread around through time the opportunities to experience that *not knowing everything at once* creates.

What law? What connecting principle—or simply link, event—would add the fourth dimension to the sailing-forth of modern science through the flea-viewing microscope and the flea-based plague that, by propelling Newton into the countryside, spared him while masses died?

What caused the modern scientific world to be inseminated, or begin its birth, in that time of death, with him spared? The many dying, the one saved—the paradigm from earlier times of one living, many dying—one idea collapsed out of the "whole," that would sail forth to bring us from there to here (though of course many contributed).

And how did that connect, microscopically, to the information I am trying to bring out now—about the fourth dimension of that discovery of the ability to see things microscopically or turn the telescope, then spaceships, to the stars; see the huge universe, which could be traveled into in spaceships as if lighter than air?

So here I sit, trying to wrap that nineteen-year-course into a ball, make it into a word. And, in a word, bring in my message.

Events, I would learn, have a shape. That is, an event could be diagrammed. The energy shape of it, I learned, can be *felt* with the hands. I learned the principle in the early 1990s by *feeling the shapes of the energy of specific pages in my book, at a distance, while my hands moved through the air in Taiji class led by the magnificent Jef Crab*. My mind, with no one else knowing, applied diagrams to the air my hands moved through.

I gradually realized that my mind was taking the energy, and with the movement of the hands, APPLYING that to the book pages at a different *location*, a different spacetime—conscious of both.

The unfoldment took years, buried in time capsules, as it were; posited in "hunch" form, then leaving me years to get ready for each idea—revolutionary to me—that would one day make its assault on the bulwark of my brain or nerves, with me standing guard, working to steady myself as stealthily the new idea was let through, I all the while comforting my nerves and brain cells, telling them they were not being annihilated, only stretched, changed, yet once again CONVERTED.

In this beginning point with the Initiator, he was making an energy organization of a geographical area—setting up emotional "turbulence," *synchronicity*. Attraction—that old bugaboo of Newton, who wanted to know *just how* there could be action at a distance *without a medium such as ether*.

Holding the question for three hundred years, we discovered that space was warped, perhaps had curls, strings. Everything attracted its likeness or repelled what disattracted it. Space was no different, or the matter potential in it—the nurturing womb of potential, of the future, of matter in terms of organized events prior to re-enacting themselves in replica or even variation disguises.

So though situations were not exactly conscious—no one said that—they replicated.

There was so much to add in, once we got this far, to Newton's query. How? Just how, through "empty" space, could there be, light years away, attractions????? You tell me.

It was way over my head, but it was what I had to learn, to adjust to, to meet the expectations of. I would not say I was an underdeveloped person, and yet here this was much beyond my capacity to understand—that is, in the sense of communicating and contextualizing. Imagine trying to tell someone about it.

Collectively, setting up the "Sacred Marriage" on Earth was also a personal opportunity for himself, and (it must be), importantly, for my soul. At the same time, this project of "saving" (informing/repatterning) the Earth" in individual and collective group efforts, known or not, was equally important to him, or part of the same thing.

I now think of the Eastern gurus, the old ones, who learned to take a situation and ball it into something very small scale that you could hold in the hand, as it were, or in the mind's eye—it was scaled down to that—or you could "act it out" in a different location, on that smaller scale, connecting it, via your consciousness, to the larger act you wanted to influence or forestall, eliminate. Work on it like that. Of course, not taking away the human need to make discoveries. And not violating free will. Therefore, this did not happen more often.

Some of my dreams showed that "Hunter" (looking like the actual Hunter) was going to be present—once, at a Zurich Taiji class. In a dream beforehand I was shown a deep attraction to a stranger that involved the nonlocal consciousness of the Initiator; in that sense, his nonlocally physical self. The Initiator was indicating there was either some *history* of identity (related to *his* energy) or a *potential* affinity. The attraction would be genuine, but I'd have insight that it started in the Initiator consciously—that a spiritual base had been called into play—though, to all appearances, it was standing on its own feet. There was no magic spell. No *Midsummer Night's Dream* or *Cosi Fan Tuti*.

Much later I learned theories about this. For instance, the physicist Amit Goswami, describes the highest state of *samadhi*—"knowing yourself as the Ground of Being"—beyond the subject-object split to where one knows oneself to be "the knower, the known, and the field of knowledge,[4] with a never-ceasing "awareness of the primary self." [5] Such definitions would help in understanding how the Initiator saw himself as many people, perhaps "the undivided whole." But I got only a glimpse—a sharp, clear chunk—at that time, when, after all, I had never experienced samadhi. I was also impacted that while being transpersonal, he clearly had individuality.

The above-mentioned attraction did develop, genuinely. Before I knew it, I and this intoxicatingly fabulous (in my view) man were practicing our Taiji together in his apartment. What a rapport we had. Not a whit of romance, though.

Hands down, spiritual attraction would lose most times if competing with physical attraction that was unconsciously using it.

Concealed under the physical attraction that was mimicking it, a pale shadow of it, the spiritual attraction was *unconscious!*

I knew that somewhere, in some energetic point, when I was experiencing one of these delectable friendships, sat the Initiator, watching it, allowing free choice to lead where it would—but wishing, hoping, that it could result in a couple involving him and me.

As said, this was stupendously astounding to me, so convoluted. But I sensed the extreme importance it had to my soul. After all, the Initiator and I went so far as to *marry in spirit*. And that, he said, would provide him extra energy as he went about his "work."

I guessed this all made sense if my soul grouping, again according to a reading over a year before by Al Miner, had the project of introducing the "*universality of humanity*. A doctrine so far from Earth knowledge that to teach it to me required these contortions. It was easy to say, "We are one," but try adding in these applications. Individuality and oneness knocked against each other, and it would be up to us, once we got the hang of it, to industriously work out the boundaries and "rules" when they got into the same territory.

I had viewed the Initiator spanning different levels, different dimensions, giving complete free will to the individuals who were living lifetimes unconscious of his role in them; that is, not identifying their fierce, driving charisma as having to do with any energy sourced in Him. In reverse, of course, the "personality" can *expand into* the larger being, and from that perspective, *up and down* have little meaning in the absolute, or qualitative, sense. But despite knowing the terms "inner Christ" and "Christ consciousness," in this period I basically was taught "raw"—not even knowing the Eastern systems of gurus.

He had me all wrapped up in knots, when thinking of how to explain this, in that it was *so personal*. He appeared never to lose sight of my soul level—which, in fact, was why he was here. Me, my personality, would not have drawn him, I don't think.

I probably could have kept up with being a "channel." But this was all about embodying. Transformation. Incarnation. The other would at least would have been a "job" recognized by those around me. *But it was not at all like that. In one aspect it was a love story*. I know this is not entirely unique. But it felt nearly so to me. Well, I knew about great love stories. There were a number. Hard to count. This, still, felt like, in its externals, its paraphernalia, one of a kind, though nothing is and everything is.

Couldn't we just dial it down a few notches? No.

I didn't know how I would ever bring it out. Instead of being abstract, he was intertwining his teaching *into my history and my life, into initiating me in shocking (to me) ways, just as Jung, however, had been.*

But seeing the mind-boggling, to me, risks he was taking, I felt protective of him, indeed. Sometimes, knowing he was experimentally putting his energy into someone, I meditated alone, sitting on the floor my arms wrapped around my knees—to help provide extra spiritual energy that the one unconsciously in the energy might not, *as I saw it*, corrupt what was sacred, offered in a test.

For someone struck by a bolt of lightning, or flashes of feeling, or whatever his energy at such a moment induced, would not have the skills to know what to do (*except deep within* where *he* was, their deepest sense of self). If they found *him*, the energy would not be too much; instinctively, intuitively, they would have the tools.

Just as I had not had the skills, not a single skill, for the Initiation *but found them only by turning within*.

Perhaps I was seeing, in reverse, how I had left my body in one particularly jaw-dropping moment, remembering only having been led away by a large being—in that case, female. Was it he who, waking as if from a cryogenic sleep, had appeared, thinking, inside the mind of my seven-year-old self?

I'd frozen, stunned, knowing instinctively to listen to his thoughts inside me. Who stood in the little seven-year-old in bafflement, saying, of all things, he was a great writer, disbelieving the fact that he had (*in me*) so far "done nothing"? Did this higher (perhaps highest) aspect of me wither on the vine? Or was he, even, here now? Was he, at the start of this initiation, looking into the empty stadium at his audiences "of the future," with a sense of time I hadn't? Had he been famous? He thought so. And did that matter?

My little dog Snoep, who was like his "child self," he said, sat blithely watching.

This entry into the Initiator's consciousness was just the beginning—not a peak experience after which things subsided back to normal. He cracked the egg of my mind. He had told me, as Milton, that there was a "psychic virginity." I knew he'd taken that. He opened my Third Eye, showed me experiences far beyond those I could have imagined; for he did not confine himself to the laws of physical reality we generally knew. I had read no mystical texts. I don't know, however, if any would have gone this far on some points. From this point on, as Rilke said, I had "met my fate." I was being initiated on an inner Christ and cosmic Christ level, but to draw me in and convince me, he was using the presence of Milton, whom I trusted as the sanest, wisest Highest Truth I knew, not to mention that he'd also drawn in my parents. Nothing could be more surreal, more baffling, and yet more a sacred privilege—*therefore, on the one hand, how could it be happening to me*?

I had no idea at the time—that is, from my own experience—that this was the barest sketch of some of the types of multidimensional experiences one might find oneself in by staying open, all the while being as questioning as any skeptic could be, of what in fact was going on, holding on to the fragments of explanation, the outer and the inner. Watching as the worlds I had not known about breathed and stretched, or shuddered—or shuttered—outward. T*his was the hole in the "big book," that had seemed unable to come to an end: the pathway of standing high enough, to see the material that was to be marked off,* Plotted—*bringing the unconscious into some historical consciousness.*

In fact, I *was shown, it was a hole, or (positively put) potential in the* Earth*, something necessary to now include—that the hole in my book was one of the places the information was being "dropped in."* I was told not to, at that time, read any books except *Other Worlds: Space, Superspace and the Quantum Universe* (1980)—to study this with the Initiator. By Paul Davis, it provides "an inquiry into the nature of the universe, draws out the implications of the quantum theory and argues that our universe is only one among many possible universes and that other universes may exist."[6]

Isolated away in my room, I was not put to death, like Giordano Bruno, although there are arguments as to why and how he was killed: "Four centuries ago today, on February 16, 1600, the Roman Catholic Church executed Giordano Bruno, Italian philosopher and scientist, for the crime of heresy. He was taken from his cell in the early hours of the morning to the Piazza dei Fiori in Rome and burnt alive at the stake."[7] A *Scientific American* article refutes the above claim:

> Ironically, every exoplanet confirms not the cosmology of Kepler, but of Giordano Bruno, the Italian philosopher who was burned alive in Rome, in 1600, as a heretic.
>
> Bruno said the universe has no center, and stars are suns, surrounded by planets and moons. Remarkably, he thus outlined large-scale aspects of our cosmology, while Copernicus and Kepler mistakenly thought the universe is spherical, the sun is its center, unmoving, and stars are not suns surrounded by planets . . .

Further, in a hint of the consciousness we've lost from back then:

> He believed in ideas we reject: that Earth is a living animal with a soul. Nonetheless, some famous Copernican scientists believed that too, including Kepler and William Gilbert.[8]

At this point I'd been shown a man of "many forms"—in each, a point (or plane, or place of expansion or narrowing precision) where he was the consciousness—open to anyone. But at the same time I'd seen a man inhabiting it. As he became more unspecific locally, he had, by passing every minute with me, commenting on everything, dropping everything to teach me, become more cherished, more intricately the one direction of my feelings, life, and self-purpose.

Still he dictated, merged with my energy—and I wrote: feelings flowing through the union, the impressions, the tools he'd taught me to receive in: visual pictures, song tunes, a rune, and so forth—startling as the thoughts often were *and reluctant as I was to put them onto paper.* But he insisted:

> One point
> One past
> One man
>
> He was calling her now out of different stories they had lived together
> Calling from different points in the story
> Different points in time

✻

I was told that my initiator, who probably was in fact the composite of my soul grouping—or a representative, with the group energy behind him—was some potential inherent in humanity, a state, the Christ STATE. In any case, a state of consciousness. I knew that it was the Initiator's consciousness. And here the explanation begins to get vaguer because at this point *it begins to be seeds, seeds I needed time to grow.*

This was hurried. There were centuries of consciousness to "download," if to master all of this. And it was not a one-way street. It was, except in his highest form, interactive. I was to remind him, remember, when he ignored the feminine.

But I was experiencing the personification, therefore a transpersonal entity state. Never mind that, to me, I was experiencing his individuality. This transpersonality is the presupposition for why he was introducing me to forms (of himself) that were in fact other people—where he was in their energy unconsciously. But looked at from the opposite end, he was literally, consciously there, at least in the times he set up the fields. It was in this scale of changing patterns and archetypes behind the scenes that I was being initiated, working in mass consciousness and "in the unconscious."

Mystical states were where he was on the fourth level.

So I could not go into the project radiating physical attraction. Physical attraction had to be eradicated in me so that spiritual attraction would not be unconscious. We had it backwards on the Earth, putting physical attraction first—which would have been quite fine, had physical attraction been able to divine where the intensity of attraction sometimes came from. It often came from the spiritual signals, which went through electricity because electrical signals of PATTERNS reached us through any variety of electrical field, be it speaking to us from the TV set or whatever. It only "took" on a person who resonated. So getting back to the seventeenth century, and what got "left out" when Newton could not figure out the rules of attraction and alchemical transformation, that was easy to redress now, when it was so manifest in electrical technology. As germs were carried by rats, electrical signals likewise reached our emotions and triggered them UNCONSCIOUSLY, *in delayed response*—in PATTERNS inside FIELDS.

As he has become more unspecific locally, he has, by passing every minute with me, commenting on everything, dropping everything to teach me, become the one focus of my feelings and life and purpose:

I couldn't give him up
I could never give him up
I would follow and follow

But as myself
He wanted me
And I wanted him

All the parts of him
Merging into him
The dream I now began to have of him
For I knew him much better now
I was amazed that a man could be so varied
so complete, so pure
I truly loved him
There had to be time
There must be time
for our story
to bring us
our true selves
together
to live together
I wanted to live with him

Wanted THE LIFE
as I'd wanted The Truth before
Saw that he was also—he could be—
The Life
. . . .
One point
One past
One man

He was calling me now out of different stories we had lived together
Calling from different points in the story
Different points in time

Still he dictated to me, merged with my energy—worked on my mind, opening it to express, and I wrote; though it was as if about myself, it was feelings flowing through the union with the Initiator at this particular point and consciousness, the impressions he had taught me to receive from him, *hesitantly putting them on paper.* But I let the words flow. They were some strange descriptions not entirely transpersonal, not entirely personal:

He was in all points of her past

Calling to her from all points of her past
Till the time came when there must be a choice
One story must be chosen
. . . .

From every experience she had had
She was sure she was invisible
It was clear she was invisible
It never occurred to her
She would become visible

Other people wanted invisible friends
She was the invisible friends
Wanted an invisible animal
She was the invisible animal
It never occurred to her there was anything strange about this
Or that she had a choice about this
For she had been born that way
And accepted it

There was no court to appeal to
There was no one place to lodge a complaint
She had lots and lots of friends
And lots and lots of experiences
But none of them in this dimension
None of them written about
None of them history

She had a personality just like people
Only, she was an energy being
It had somehow happened that when she was born
She didn't grow like other people
She didn't get a body like other people
She stayed as she was
Invisible

Growing all the time
And yet not physically
She was light and airy

And bouncy
She had lots of curls
Because she imagined how she looked
She could feel how she looked
Only, she wouldn't of course show up
in any mirror

. . . .
paint that could change shapes
going in and out of shapes
stretching
gathering together
condensed
reaching out again
all the changing shapes of him

clouds for canvas
clouds for stone and marble
making pictures in the sunset
how he feels

. . . .
Life sitting on top of life
as if there were no separation
periods contracted
As if only the action springing from within
had the answer now
For there was no time to think it out
rehearse
There was only to do

The entire description of *who did what* changes. It was these kinds of questions and their implications—the structures they demanded—that I turned to. I tried to create a place, a mind, a consciousness where "I" made sense to me—now that my ego had been uprooted. One would have to imagine how I looked. It was slowly, in the later phase, I began to put back on weight. Else, how could I go out again as he wished, walk into the energy fields he set up and meet "him," in the various forms. And *talk to him, not to the outer person.*

Talk to him, who was inside.

✻

When I later asked Mariah Martin where she thought he was, for I was concerned (after all, I had married this energy being), she said she thought he had gone into "the collective unconscious." Imagine.

So now every person I met, I thought, I might trigger something in unconsciously—if my energy was with his in the collective unconscious, which, of course, every person accessed in their personal unconscious. These were the seeds of my mysticism. I was not mystical yet. This is not a description of mysticism. Mystical states were where he was, on the fourth level. I was on the first three levels and sometimes taken into his consciousness. But not for sustained periods. And not by getting there by myself alone.

As germs were carried by rats, I said just above, electrical signals reach our emotions, triggering them in delayed response—in PATTERNS inside FIELDS.

I have written about this in other books. But in brief, say you were watching a TV program, thinking it had nothing to do with your "real" world. It might happen that the field of a situation it portrayed resonated with you (electrically). What then? *Nothing*, you say. *It's just a program*. Wrong. The electrical circuits are an elaborate fixture in this world of semiconductor chips and non-manmade conductors we are intertwined in.

That very instant, suppose you made a connection to the TV scene unconsciously that would play out, say, twenty-four hours later, at the moment the same field presented itself in your life. A plot the TV scene you resonated with itself echoed. In other words, in this instance, at the moment the electrical signals reached you through the TV, this future scene connected electrically to the scene you were watching—correlated to it, aligned by meanings or event outline.

But electricity is not always right! It can connect in a negative correlation! Falsely. Unfairly. Inaccurately. I've often felt electricity jump into my hands or legs—indicating a "hit," a connection. But that connection might be—heaven forbid—a projection. I learned this system from the Initiator, who had me sit in a particular position, learning to receive signals. Perhaps because he was in such a strong electrical field, he could easily demonstrate all the electrical attractions reinforced positively. Or gone awry.*This unsuspected entanglement of spirit and matter, or in this case electricity and events (especially emotions), is very very important for us to understand now, in our age of technology. And artificial intelligence. Imagine if the height of the plague had merely repeated itself rather than our discovering germs.*

Barking up the wrong tree, in cases where electricity was

"programming" us.

It was the same in everything: matter went first.

This was being reversed. For as long as we saw everything through structures of physical reality, we would be too unconscious for this time period.

It was a very simple thing, once understood. The Earth itself was "Going Home." But "Home" was being literalized. Receiving the intensity of the drive toward home, we humans were not necessarily grasping that it was an energy field OF GOING HOME TO OUR PLANETARY CONSCIOUSNESS, our inner heaven. This was predicted to me in '85.

In the brain, expectation ("prior beliefs") sets up belief. What you think is possible, you make into your reality because you can let it past your censors. What you think impossible, you haven't the structure to receive objectively, even perhaps "see."[9]

> Consider, for instance, how a shadow on a patient's X-ray image, easily missed by a less experienced intern, jumps out at a seasoned physician. The physician's prior experience helps her arrive at the most probable interpretation of a weak signal.
>
> The process of combining prior knowledge with uncertain evidence is known as Bayesian integration and is believed to widely impact our perceptions, thoughts, and actions. Now, MIT neuroscientists have discovered distinctive brain signals that encode these prior beliefs. They have also found how the brain uses these signals to make judicious decisions in the face of uncertainty.[10]

My interest here was to "free the mind." The mind is only free—really free—if able to accept what it proves to itself or at least, when it experiences something, consider it possible, no matter if thought impossible by one's very self before. So I was undergoing this initiation to free my own mind. And it worked. But the receptivity had been set up my whole life.

I cared about the truth more than I cared to hold onto what proved itself inadequate. I did not want to lie to myself or trick myself, but stare at whatever came my way and see if it held up. I *speculated that* Hunter *was in this soul grouping. True or false?*

Therefore, he would have access to everything I knew, everything I had experienced and learned, because soul groupings, I had discovered, pool their consciousness. If he was in the soul grouping based in part in the consciousness of Jesus, and his lifetime looked as it did, then it was very interesting to see its role that way.

To see what sort of shadow mission he might be on. If—I say if—*so, how did this sort of juxtaposition to me reveal something about life*??????? *That's almost like saying pieces of the same entity. I hope someone gets the joke and from there understands why I had often been told to "lighten up."*

But also, Milton had said to me that all this effort we put forth, if there is a God, it means that *somewhere it's important*. I could fly here. I believed it.

Jamie Lee Curtis in True Lies

Let me make a few points.

Jung, who dreamed he was locked a long time in the seventeenth century (that is, alchemy), said that in the unconscious there are aspects of ourselves that exist in "quasi-islands" without being integrated and the unconscious is quasi-conscious.

In the unconsciousness of the "quasi-islands," the "whole" was larger than the sum of the parts. That was on the Initiator's mind.

In Spiritual Emergence (a term coined by Stan and Christina Grof) the shaky period, as the ego is uprooted and beliefs torn out, risks looking like a breakdown. Indigenous peoples had such rites of passage as shamanic "dismemberment," where the limbs were symbolically broken into pieces.

In Jungian terms, there are *containers*, "safe places"—for instance, the relationship between therapist and analysand. A book while in draft is, typically, "in a container." Then only an insider is permitted to see it. Something incubated has to go through that incubation without leaks. Otherwise, old explanations might be *pasted on top of something trying to be new.*

So here I was in a container. The ego had no place. I was not afraid for myself. Just the opposite.

I'd received rudimentary glimpses of energy laws, nothing by way of mastery. Therefore, I thought of myself as like a "primitive"—or neurotic!—*on the surface.*

Inside, I never felt the need to cry for help or "wish it would stop." I was being shown how energy masters work, *not how to work in energy myself—not yet.* I knew that to go into these fields was not dangerous, with mastery. But the Initiator cast aside protections and walked naked, as it were, into the fields he set up, sure that his energy would dominate inside others.

Jung's dive into the unconscious brought him the seeds of research for the rest of his life. But he had to go through the unconscious, give up control, *and* come out on the other side. Yet I also knew how my actions looked from the outside—a reason to be in seclusion.

Let me stop and explain something else.

Here, when soul level investments, or the ability to work through me, was at stake—my opportunity to remember my soul "home" and to work whatever way the soul wanted—there was no question who would win out. My ego was transformed into service, awed at the situation. It received the blessing, like someone being knighted, so impressed it was with the Initiator and the issues being faced.

My "high eye cue" (ability to recognize the energy message transferred through the eye in the dream signal) opened the way for more "remembrance" of myself multidimensionally. Different in magnitude, as I think about it now.

So, this is a well-known technique. One tiny look in the eye conveyed everything, providing the shift, the energy to stay in bed, accept, believe. That's energy exchange, according to how all Eastern masters work, such as Dhyanyogi-ji, whom I would later study under. I resonated.

My personal feelings were wiped out. This began with "breaking a karmic bond," which had prevented me from seeing that self-worth was as important as helping another—in that case, Jan—and in truth no assistance could go to another, beyond a certain point, unless it came from a person whose self-worth was not compromised in the giving. It had taken years to understand this—my entire marriage—building to the next step, making the Initiation possible.

The dream of Folding the Laundry reversed the lesson I'd mastered in leaving my marriage.

That lesson was to be independent, not co-dependent. My unconscious, in the dream, dutifully applied what it had learned—only to encounter the reverse test. This other lesson—no one told me it was coming. I just had to *know*, which the look in the eye told me.

It was *not help for/from the ego this time*, the look—transmitted in a different frequency—said. I immediately recognized it.

The baby I dreamed (in Charlottesville) I was to take to its mother at the Institute was now here. That Charlottesville dream, which let me observe my oblivious self carrying the baby to the Institute, also revealed that an "expectant mother" who well knew the baby's past and purpose waited at the Institute. *So now that level was operating.*

The unconscious mother "carrying" the baby was then supplanted by the consciousness waiting here, another me, the Mother in another dimension. This made it easy to step into the comfort of the Knowing, for it preexisted.

But I also recognized the stark fact that to see someone waste away physically, to have reports from the landlady that I was in danger, might have consequences.

Not important enough. I ignored that possibility. They were part of the dangers the Initiator himself was fighting off, I felt.

I was empathizing with him, not with my human self, who also felt this was "worth it." As a child, I had once transferred away from my father onto myself a nickname that silly girls—like a bird dropping—were about to bestow onto him. I knew it. This was the same sort of instinctive understanding, but on the soul level. It was indeed the test the ego felt it had trained for, all its life (my life). Something grown-up; so, my Inner Child could imagine. This was the stuff of heroism, of ideals, of working in the "business of the world."

I well realized that I was being given rudimentary glimpses of how spiritual laws worked, and that, as mentioned, put me in the role of a "primitive," or even a neurotic—but that was the surface.

The actual explanations, the "light at the end of the tunnel," were entirely different—a scale or two or ten higher—from what I was being taught, I knew, never feeling the slightest need to "cry for help" or wish "it would stop." I wanted it to go on, to be actively involved on this level as much as I could, to help the Initiator in this multi-group effort to "save the world" by expanding and refining the consciousness, freeing the mind, taking away the fear of death, introducing the idea of energy fields that not only existed (which we were helpless in) but that could be set up for positive purpose, though that was something we out in "ordinary reality" didn't know because it was dangerous to give such tools, such secrets, the laws of esoteric reality, away.

I don't know why I am giving them away now. But I was being shown how great masters work in energy. I knew that to go into these fields was not dangerous at all if you were protected. The Initiator dispensed with protections, sure that his energy would prevail inside other people. They would "choose him." Like the test whether to choose Jesus or Barabbas centuries back—you could see it in these terms. And I did.

Only, internal this time, inside each person. The higher-pattern consciousness would, in due course, win out. If not right away.

My idea of the Initiator, as you might guess, was like Don Quixote. Harnessing human potential, he had a conviction that if they were forced or given the choice, people's unconscious instinct or inner knowing would come forth. I saw that as part of *this level* of consciousness.

I knew all this. I knew I would be all right. It never crossed my mind I wouldn't. However, I did not have the skills, only the inklings, the glimpse inside the Door. I felt no torturous doubt between "right" and "wrong." There was certainty. The Teacher, I felt, was putting himself in danger for the sake of the world. Groups were. Great teachers, risking their emotional heritage, the storehouse of personal memories, setting them into the most unconscious settings, releasing their consciousness into areas where, on that level, there was, on the surface, unpreparedness. That's how I saw it.

Willingly, I threw myself in. I also knew that my fear for the Initiator in going unprotected into the energy fields (fear for his memories and other intangibles that were the "bait") looked superstitious.

I'd learned about electrical chains, vibrations remaining on objects, therefore attractions between them, that—while unconscious—made patterns recur. I knew that a "track," a pathway, isn't there in our brain to be traveled just once: knew about little "microcosm" scenarios, miniatures that—seemingly harmless—could as patterns do gigantic damage or good. Obscure great Eastern teachers, I would later learn, used these secrets as tools, unwise to let out, yet here they were.

Ever since the Initiator told me about it, I would sit with my hands crossed over my knees and feel the electricity in my hands as it connected to someone. I knew it operated in scales, so a tiny replica could not literally cause anything. No object could. Spirit was always stronger than matter. But I did not have the skills. I only had the awareness.

For example, in a chain of effects as I eliminated links—if a certain "bad" situation occurred while a color was present, I would stay away from that color to eliminate the association. It was extreme, I knew. It looked downright compulsive, I knew, to throw away Snoep's yellow blanket because it had become a link—yellow had, everything yellow. Throw away yellow. Never touch yellow. I just didn't know the way out of the *maze of laws I hadn't been taught*, that were the *map not the reality*, therefore operated mechanically, just like humanity in relationship to the unconscious.

I knew enough to be afraid regarding the events "caused" by

what was *information* on the most minor primitive levels.

I knew that small-scale replicas formed miniatures that could chain-link on these levels. For instance, if I did the simplest thing, like put a dirty fork beside a clean knife, I was connecting vibrations—"memories" of "where" the object had been. More, as I've said, the unconscious read our "body language," as it were, a tipping of the scales.

But now you're in the quantum realm, aren't you? We're safe from all that.

Not at all.

Jamie Lee Curtis in *True Lies* flashes into my mind. Her husband, played by Arnold Schwarzenegger, was a secret spy. She thought he had a boring job, but then she got dragged into the action. And discovered his hair-raising, secret daily life, joining him in it—with a lot of slapstick. It occurs to me to compare my situation to that.

Take this further, to the theory that information is energy, *interchangeable with mass*: $E = mc^2$. Think of all the "solid" objects—the plants, everything, you, me—as "matter waves."

That's right, the "incarnations" of energy into mass are energetic waves, when they're not being, at the moment—or even if they are—solid, entrenched forms, as if with a key turned in their backs telling them (us) to forget all about their wave nature. We fall into the illusion, which is "true" for a stopped second, a lifetime. But we're limiting our view.

Forgetting conveniently, wanting to be secure—and time did not let us discover it until recently—that matter is, relatively, a stopped, frozen, chosen form of energy, operating under laws that apply in its "stopped" form. But energy ALWAYS exists in waves. Got that? Got it. Take a seat and breathe in deeply, then out. Think about what that means. I cannot think I "end" where my physical form does, the skin on my outer body, the tips of my fingers, does. And that I *only* obey and must succumb to our laboratory-proven/theorized physics *laws of large objects*.

Meanwhile, matter is busy interchanging itself with the energy around it, flowing in and out of a *matter wave*. Whoops. Many matter waves.

Knowing that about yourself, what next? What do you want to do as a matter wave? What hocus-pocus could you be up to (a slight exaggeration to drive the point home or at least into the realm of our hypothecation).

I could go on with details and examples and even *roll out the carpet of the next-section explanations right here*. It would be simple, because, though I didn't know it yet, the seeds, the structure, exist. I would soon learn that if one single person breaks a pattern, a karma, for himself or herself, it is conceivably for the whole Earth. No one may ever know. I didn't know how yet to operate on these levels. I was in between, in between heaven and Earth. I chose heaven, awkward as some of it was. As I was saying, perhaps the Initiator—the times the attempt failed—with René—with my Taiji buddy—had no real intention of setting up a couple. But then came Willy. Just the right typecasting. This time it would "take."

With Willy van Luyten, no longer would the attempt to set up a spirit-sourced physical couple be amateurish. This time, it was serious, practical. Anyway, Willy came in, as Chris Van de Velde, my dear friend and gifted energy teacher in Belgium, was to tell me, "propelled into this lifetime TO PAY YOU BACK."

❋

At forty-five I was "on track" insofar as a full life involving outer and inner was concerned. It fit the individuation pattern, in which at the approach of the second half of life we turn inward. *Would it be as exciting as turning outward? Make as many stories? Contribute as much?* To me, of course yes.

And a still point of myself, not watching the passing years as time, had been inward all the time, occupied fully in my writing.

But it all depended on what point on the spectrum you looked at it through. At least, that used to be the case. It was no longer so, in a sense.

The Earth was changing. It was receiving a new consciousness, just as I had received one here.

It would remember—unveil—levels/facets of itself. How would the Earth (or people one by one) be closeted away to meet their "Day of Judgment"? For with the archetype of saving the Earth in play, the archetype of "Home," people were being called back into their more expanded, internally derived consciousness. Called to be authentic, to think for themselves, sense with their hearts. To spin *themselves*, not information. To incarnate their own truth. To take themselves more seriously, while also not seriously.

Our planet needed us to Be Ourselves. Not be an outer shell. Suppose I failed, and my soul was no longer up to assisting the

Initiator in his future exploits. No, *the stakes were too high, for I felt at home exactly in this role.*

I never for a moment doubted, with my father having promised to "hire" "the best" teachers that love or money could buy, this was my Destiny.

This was it. The hard part was not this, for me, but integrating and *finding any way whatsoever to explain to myself who I was*, why he was trying to carry out some relationship between Jesus and Mary through me. But as I didn't know anything in depth about the laws he operated under, how could I know this? Jung had warned: "Never identify with an archetype." Mother Mary to us was an archetype.

But the Initiator didn't necessarily seem to be applying Jung. (Chuckles.) Fortunately for me, I had enough of my memory and enough ability to respond to triggers not to be completely smothered by mass consciousness when the moment came to throw Self-Doubt off. Rather, heed the question Milton had once asked me.

I had just showed up at his door in a downpour of rain, having expected to get there much earlier, arriving worn out. I was in town only for that evening, in a flight layover. He took one look at my wet, grumpy self and asked me instantly—like Stentor, who, said Homer, had a voice as loud as the voice of fifty men together; like Zeus commanding a thunderbolt; or like a champion archer in control of his arrow—"*Which do you think is stronger? Spirit or matter?*" without another word instructing me to sluff off the tiredness, like brushing lint from a shoulder.

At any scale, the principle was the same. *Spirit was stronger. Mind could operate through matter. That was at the core of this soul grouping project.*

It could even demonstrate this by a test en masse—through setting up an energy field with outcomes determined by the unconscious choice of the testees. Deep within, their (our) divinity was accessible. When push came to shove, most of us "Earthlings" would choose that, consciously or not, at least those not so submerged in the mud of habit and teaching. An example comes in later in the book.

There were certainly enough, in all walks and stages of life, who would "choose Jesus, not Barabas." That was the principle. Choose Hanuman. Choose the Buddha. Chose MYSELF. This was all that had to be done. Listen WITHIN. BELIEVE MYSELF. But be centered. BELIEVE THE HEARTBEAT OF THE EARTH. Hear it. Believe in this Transition. Otherwise, this much energy unleashed, this much breaking of old boundaries and sturdy restrictive laws, would create a chaos to such an extent it would turn into Debauchery. Not knowing *what was what* anymore, as events spiraled out of control, and the intensity of spiritually resonating inner potential was given over to outer fear, that was the risk.

It was no risk. Humanity was Universal. It would learn this about itself.

It would learn its divinity. Divinity meant participation, co-creation, individual autonomy. Where would the world be if everyone perceived himself/herself to be a god? But this was ahead, as more and more people dug inside and came up with that phrase. So my confusion didn't count. I sensed that something much greater than myself was at stake. And on some level I was in the know about it. And on this level I could assist. I could start even right now. And this time when I said it was *now or never* and tomorrow would be too late, I would be right. So Bamboy ran in secret around the track, absorbing the determination.

❋

I first taught myself that it would be arrogance and false pride if asserting one's will—which would then be the ego—to not stand for what one had learned.

This was a point very difficult for me to assimilate: that is, true humility and self-worth (not pride) come from letting things be, letting whatever happens just be, for it is not inflated in its own context, it is just a natural flow of reality.

It is our emotions that create the inflation. If our soul asks us to do something, it is not the ego that does it or gets any benefit or recognition from it.

I had just come out of a marriage where, in a fictional description, I called myself "Pouf." With that in mind, we can see the lengths it required going to, to, out in the open, walk on the foundation of these experiences.

They also used a laser beam, or that Kundalini "chain saw," buzzing into me, to find the corners where Not Me was hiding: the parts of me I had been afraid to let out, the question about "Live, live, live, it's a mistake not to," were keys to the inner chambers *where these unexplored living energies that were myself spoke from*—creative energy now becoming conscious as my soul history.

As a centerpiece of *The Christ State* (book), he said that God was setting up the archetype of "Home" around the Earth, as I've just said—but it intensified *in both directions: positive and negative.* Thus, an energy field of "saving the Earth" could destroy it if received too unconsciously.

The Earth had reached a cliff where the consciousness it had, to an important degree, was not enough. And it was *not all that hard to change.* At least, to such a confident, positive consciousness as that I was being introduced to, and evidently came from—so went the reasoning. Being confident involved willingness to take what I perceived as risks. But I understood that this consciousness easily flew into "where angels fear to tread" and did not bite its nails in the process, the way I did.

Still, I was much in the dark. I only suspected how dangerous some of the actions were—working in the unconscious, afraid of nothing. It was easy to see why I had admired these qualities in my relationships. *Was this my male energy? Indeed, he said my male energy was like his, as his female energy was like mine.*

According to the Initiator, *there was a new Christ personality coming into being.* Unlike with Jesus, the second Christ (personality), he said, was vulnerable—needing nurturing. The second occupied the surface. Inside, the first was the core.

But the statement was so premature it has waited silent—up to a point where it is dangerous to withhold—giving me the chance to bring it out, still on its dusty shelf. The second personality was Mozartian.

About the premiere night of *Don Giovanni* in 1787, Wikipedia writes, "copyists had just finished making copies of this hastily written overture before the performance. The orchestra was assembled, the crowd was gathered, and just before the curtains went up the musicians were handed this wonder of a piece. Legend has it that the musicians sight-read the overture so well that the audience that night at the Estates Theatre in Prague applauded the work enthusiastically."

But, I was beginning to realize, waiting had a purpose. During waiting periods, more structure "lines up," with more options and people coming in. While it was very very subtle, they could not see the outlines, not choose. The Light always strove to be inclusive, leaving the gates as wide open as possible, for as long a time as possible. For any who asked to be admitted were.

It was this new personality he was trying to introduce me to, the one who might easily say, "Lighten up" while on the most serious mission imaginable.

Certainly, the new, young personality of the Christ was always "taking chances," in cliffhangers—as seen in how Mozart flamboyantly waited, then began at midnight, his wife prodding him with stories if he would fall asleep. He rushed to the performance, to hand the orchestra the sheets just before the curtain rose—and calmly took his seat at the piano. They played magnificently. A close call, a cliffhanger—that was the new Christ personality exterior; inside it was Himself/Herself. It might explain to me why I had always had the inclination to look for the "hidden" "real" self, why I strove to "save it," though while I had this outlook inside the anima female, it was a flaw.

In fact, Matthew Fox had written that the Christ energy was always "on the edge," in *going first*.

The Initiator said he was going to materialize in flesh and live with me, in a recognizable form of one of his personalities—in fact, the outer model for his new human form: the jovial, kidding Mozart. Once he called in that energy to write with me; in the combination my fingers flew at a frantic pace. I thoroughly enjoyed it. But the Initiator was dissatisfied. He said it was focused too externally.

I had now named the Initiator "Milton Christ Mozart." I'm not sure whose idea it was. I think mine. The name signified the aspects meaningful to me.

The Initiator prepared to materialize. I was pretty panicked. I had gone along this far. But imagining sleeping in a tiny twin bed with a materialized version of this white-wigged eighteenth-century figure was too hysterically absurd a situation for me to think of adapting to or even believing possible. I had heard tell of "materializing." I'd never thought about it. How could I imagine it without seeing it with my own eyes? He promised such a sight. But he wanted me *in his consciousness first*—again, a feat I could not accomplish at will, unable to go to high frequencies at the mere thought.

Then I saw the telltale first signs: a blurry, grainy form barely beginning to be visible. I was horrified. But did not let on. I didn't like the barest impression of the materializing figure, of which all I glimpsed appeared to be a crew cut. Instantly, the process stopped. The Initiator afterward said he never intended to materialize, that it was a temptation, a wish of in fact his *anti-self*, which he'd known would try to take over. I should likewise be on the alert *for my anti-self as well.*

This was heady stuff. I didn't know whether to literally believe I might have an anti-self, he too, that, as he said, would want to—and be able to—interfere. He said there would be such temptations to thwart the situation.

Sometimes he said he had to be gone for a few days, to take care of things far away. I didn't know for sure if he was really gone or not. But I at first jumped at the idea I could eat anything I wished. Going out to a restaurant, I held the food down till dessert: iced-cold ice cream. Want to guess what happened? I had instantly to run to the bathroom, and everything slid right through me into the toilet, with my stomach now so small. Anyway, I found that somehow I wanted, against my will, to be loyal to his regimen even if he was out at the edges of the universe, taking care of serious problems. He returned and congratulated me, saying I had followed his energy no matter how far away it went.

❋

So how was I ever going to put a context to my life from here on in and to the books we were working on, including the now-revised "big book" (*Love in Transition*)? I did not envisage how *The Christ State* could ever see the light of day, except that I also felt it a sacred task to bring it out, for he had given it to me coincident, even, with his preoccupations with Earth-saving changes in patterns and awareness levels, little as I was, compared to all that. But he felt my soul up to him in her development or at least heart ties, thus, marriage. This was the truth of my life at that time, its Revelations.

The plan to make a pattern couple based in spiritual attraction of his energy and mine, as it also became physical attraction, had not worked fabulously. Everything he challenged me to do was outside the bounds of anything I had conceived possible before; yet it was now my life, my job, my privilege. I knew that Milton was no longer in a single form and imagined him being blown and exploded into bits all over the universe.

❋

I did not know exactly how to imagine what was going on. I was assigned to make him fall in love with me inside some form of him that had no conscious knowledge of him, some Young Personality with the exterior typing of the clowning Mozart. This new personality, besides mostly being younger than me, usually by about ten years, was often literally handsome, dashing, as attractive as could possibly be. At least, at that time and place.

On top of that, he told me to *choose him on any level, the highest to the least advanced, and he could make it work*; he could bring all the forms, the energy of the totality and individuality of all of them, to back up the relationship in any single form. And it would be "he."

※

I cannot begin to say how deep the roots were, how much grew from them. My impression, while being in deep awe, was also of stretching the space for all experience—*on all levels*. And not insisting that others go at any particular speed, because one thing we can count on is the inexhaustibility of originality. And we had better value the capacities we have and the priorities in the form we are in *now*, letting that enthusiastic acceptance extend outward to the values of others.

One had the human right, I felt, to develop a consciousness and perspective inside which one's own thoughts and heart made sense—and had, therefore and only therefore, the minimal energy for subsistence.

※

On a few occasions I "overheard" what appeared to be fragments of a spirit-discussion. One snatched phrase was "After Christ died he was sacrificed." Who? What? I was against it and wanted to prevent it, whatever it meant.

Another of these random sentences, I thought involved me: "They will be together in old age." Who? Was it Hunter?

There was no logic to imagine how it would come about; that is, in an everyday way, after this Initiation. In fact, I could not imagine life after this initiation. What would I write about? Who was I? How would I both honor the Initiation, as I was determined to, and walk out with any sense of reality of identity?

The Initiator had several times taken over *Love in Transition*. Once he dictated changes into my consciousness, so fast I feared he would rewrite the whole book in days. *And it did not feel right*. Bravely, I rebelled the next day. It had been a test, a dream revealed. I passed it by taking the book back.

I got the impression that different entities in the grouping that was there in spirit form had different "favorites." Some sided with one lineage, as it were, in which my "whole self" had had experiences that would logically lead to forming a "spiritual couple" with a particular guy, but others favored a different eventual relationship. The Hunter faction appeared to me to be *small*—the rest coming down heavily in the view it would be too difficult—Hunter being as he currently, realistically was. But I found myself disinclined to rule out, entirely and absolutely, that I would ever see him again or ever again pick back up the relationship.

Another of the bits and snatches of phrases I heard, this time waking from a dream, was the song "Why do fools fall in love?" This was during a period I was receiving prophetic glimpses, or predictions, not at all clearly. But I was such a novice that nothing could be said to be really clear, only glimpsed at and put into safekeeping, like looking over mountain ridges, being allowed to stand on very tall shoulders—catching falling spoonfuls that were in fact very large doses when savored and reflected on.

There was one overheard prophecy that was awful, and I determined to overcome it: "was reduced and relegated, became like a well dried up, who had been a diamond." In the years ahead, I was to hold it in front of me like an *anti-future*; I would flinch at the hint of it, the fearful, dreaded vision of being shunted aside. But knowing of it, I could sidestep it, always watching for signs that it was a risk, using that danger to walk in the other direction.

❋

Now enters a former model, the swoon-worthy René Pasca; he looked, I thought, like a combination of French heartthrob Jean-Paul Belmondo and Zorba (Anthony Quinn). He was in the energy of the Initiator.

After René's modeling career timed out, he became a painter. In an elegant Zurich bar late one afternoon I met René and girlfriend. You may gather that the style of the Christ energy I met ignored boundaries and had the spirit to get away with it: larger than life to some degree.

No sooner was I home than the phone rang. He was in trouble. He could see himself outside himself. It was dangerous to be alone. Would I come over? He'd been gloomy and taken medication, he said. It clashed with alcohol. This was on the level. It wasn't a pass.

"Swooning" was barely an inappropriate word. Very taken with him, without a moment's hesitation, I dashed to his apartment, located in a sprawling basement. On all the walls, he had hung his huge canvases of planets and gigantic black-and-white Sri Lanka photography. I stayed all night, watching.

While tossing, feverish, he suddenly said, "You came." It seemed to me *that* was the Initiator.

At one point he said, "*If my heart explodes, I'll just go to another planet*."

The next morning he was fine. For such a meeting to "take," the Initiator would focus strongly on an experience from my past, turn the dial to bring it in precisely, as no one else could, to the exact sync, back through time *and his own feelings*—that level of the personality that connected upward.

If it "took," he'd opened a possibility. The rest would unfold in free will.

I instantly liked René, pattern or no pattern. I liked his huge, raw energy, Life Force, looks. That he was so upbeat, large scale. And a painter who'd successfully modeled, no small task. The vibes rooted in spiritual attraction, the electrical, tingling physical attraction was undeniably there as well.

His multiroomed basement apartment doubled as studio. Angry with his landlord for storing things there, he once rolled the clutter out onto the Zurich highway, disrupting traffic. Lusty for life, he took the risk of being jailed (which he wasn't) in going beyond where an invisible sign said S*top*! like the warning I saw at Chartres Cathedral: GO FURTHER AT YOUR OWN RISK. He was simply huge with life. And had the pleasure of seeing the landlord clear out the basement.

I felt convinced there was a "point" in him (energetically and consciously) where the energy I was being initiated by *was*.

Several more times at the same bar, we spent the evening talking. Once after he moved to a hotel, I went to his room. I remember so well how as I approached I had to dash into a hallway WC because suddenly rushes of blood from my period began to pour down my legs. I felt sure it marked the intensity of the attraction.

He told me he'd just dozed off, that in his dream he saw a book entitled *Love* beside a planet. I had come to put a down payment on a planet painting titled *Love*. "I'm glad," he said. "I'll like seeing you among the rich buyers at the patrons' evenings. Will you manage an art gallery I want to set up?" I was astonished. Also, right then would I carry paintings on the train to a nearby town for his exhibit?

I paid the deposit, and the impressive work began to belong to me. Exhilarated, I went to the nearby town to deliver his paintings.

Another time as we sat at the bar, a beautifully dressed, gorgeously made-up model came over to him. "Most of my girlfriends are models—from the old days," he said, not giving it importance. Their glamor and beauty meant little to him, he added. He suddenly bought a flower bouquet from a passing seller and swirled to face me with it. He said, "I would *never* go down on my hands and knees to them. I *might* to you." The shift was so abrupt. I gulped to take the words in.

Plot Seeds

However, to even think of a relationship with René seemed much too complicated. I hadn't anywhere near the confidence. I chose Willy. Actually, I don't think that with any of the others in the Initiator's energy it was remotely possible to slide into more intimacy, despite the fact that the Initiator gave me a dream in which his face replaced one of theirs, and we talked one on one (the inner energy and myself). In reality, I thought René was attached to his young girlfriend.

Over years after 1985–'86, my ego transformed. But the "I" I was then could not expand without more framework. Expansion isn't mental. You can never think yourself into it. Or argue and reason.

This Initiation provided the foundation for when the time came. I and "I" would exchange roles.

Now Willy, in Belgium, entered. To stay.

And all this is leading to the dream assignment to "help write the Hunter S. Thompson Story." *This story now.* Assigned in a dream. Wait. It's coming up.

❋

Looking ahead, to plant some of the seeds of where this plot will go, let me introduce them in a draft of a letter I wrote:

Dear Hunter,

> My whole life is changing.

Though the Lunevillelaan 46 letters (of which this is one) are up ahead, we can get a glimpse of what Time is carrying like a stork toward me. A preview.

> And I promised to tell you about it if it ever happened . . . Part of it, I've told you. But the other part I haven't. I haven't told anybody, in fact. The part you know is that I once dreamed

> in a little nap, something I knew was the future. Because I've often done that. And when in that way, not really asleep, it was always literal. So this was in Zurich. I closed my eyes, fell into a little nap, and in it was married to you. And I was given advice about what to do if a particular day came. Then [in "real life"] I carried out what I thought must be a symbolic version of the dream [with Willy van Luyten]. Though, as I said, these things had always been literal. Not that they happened too often. Then this person, though fifteen years younger than me, died suddenly, driving a car. That was January 6, '91. The accident looked impossible, as if someone put a ruler between the road and a tree and in the dark drove the car into it at top speed. It was impossible to really do that because of the dark [4:30 a.m. January 7, in a fog] and even if he could, no one could hold the steering wheel that straight. Anyway, he had the reputation of being the best driver in Belgium. He had wanted to be a Formula 1 racer if he could have gotten the backing . . .
>
> *Now, the morning this man I was living with died, before I heard it, I sank into a sleep and it was all lavender. And in it I had a period of confusion and then, I packed up all my belongings to go to the United States to write, or be involved in writing, your story.* (my italics)

I mentioned other things we will get to later. No more peeking.

I wasn't at all sure of Hunter's role, if any. As always, I left a question. We learn more about this scene further on. This was in October 1992. I continued, neatly wrapping up some of what was in my mind back then, what this book is dealing with—though, as said, we are peeking ahead.

> Now, I don't know how to interpret it. But I do know if it has any real meaning for you, you'd want me to tell you. No insistence on what you want to do with it. just take it as information.

I was totally full to the brim with this story. It had been fed to me, and fitted into all my experiences, since the Zurich Initiation. I went on here, spelling it out, *for this me right now, it turns out.*

Things I would never dare say now, she said. Time after time. Fitted into the experiences that bombarded her, crafted to teach her. But wait! That was me.

In Summary

The Initiator was operating from a higher consciousness that had a foothold in mass consciousness. He was not identifying with a single Earth body, and yet he had a single sense of "I." That is, he identified with himself over a spectrum.

Or rather, he did identify with individual Earth bodies if they were holding his energy strongly. How could he not? How could you not? Where your energy is, whether you know it or not, I know it or not, you are, I am.

This was the beginning of teaching me about different ways to locate "I," which is going to have an importance in moving from the most rudimentary sense of "I" into an expanded experience of what a single entity is, how large it might be and some of the rules outside three-dimensional identity.

But this larger sense of identity operated inside our everyday world. So now I was being asked to remember what I knew about "the universality of humanity," in ways that made the adjustment to it easy. For didn't I know this? Know how it worked? *Hadn't I lived in it*? Been asked to remember myself as a particular entity who knew this, in relation to this Initiator?

I can only compare Superman and Lois Lane, if not bringing up Jacob wrestling with the Angel or even David and Goliath, David being my ego, though my ego was quite willing to do its best to understand and comply, for the most part.

But also this was in medias res, in the midst of action, not abstract teaching. He was making "trial runs" into the patterns in humanity. One trial run, which he was working through with me, being, as said, the Sacred Marriage. To set marriage down on the base of its sacredness as a pattern, where couples who had, for instance, worked on their relationships over centuries or were just ready, meant anchoring their attraction into its sacred source, and clearing up the patterns they had perhaps already fallen into. If you clear up a pattern for one person, it's universally available.

Let me also say that as every "level" had free will and originality and contained some of his energy—the most potentially powerful—there could be no up or down or better or worse, as we are used to, because a potential could lead to a new discovery in the "higher" form, and a flaw there could reveal a flaw in the higher form as well, a susceptibility, a temptation.

So, first of all, the structure of thinking some people were better than others would have to be revised. But I didn't focus on that at the time. I was later to develop these seeds to where I could explain them. If I stick right here to only what I knew, I would be describing the context I saw them in, *leaving out the context they were actually in*. But I have to say, the Initiator tried to keep simple to grasp, except for the handful of things he expected me to be able to do.

In the future as the seeds grew, I was to have sudden "got it" moments, long in fruition. For instance, in a workshop with Joska Soos, a Hungarian born into a shaman tribe, who was picked out at birth, the way the Dalai Lama was recognized but not in this case due to reincarnation of a specific person. In the first sign he was a future shaman, his mother gave birth alone; born with a cowl on his head, he stayed a half hour in the cowl with the placenta connected till someone came by to cut it.

So, Joska was taught by a master village shaman. But what I want to describe is a workshop in a castle in Belgium, in the large, open, high-ceilinged Dome room, where he had all of us lie on the floor on meditation pads. And taking his Tibetan brass bowls, he sat them, one after the other, on each of our bellies, hearts, and foreheads. I did not pay much attention to the fact he was calling in "spirits of the wind" and so forth, because I was not ready for that. But I had a profound experience with the vibrations of the bowls he set down on me. We reported experiences aloud if we wished.

I felt desirous to tell my experience, and he asked, "Where did you feel this in your body?"

I had never thought to think that question. I reflected, "In my heart."

He said: "*Then identify with it.*" *This critical simple authoritative comment did it.*

I made the shift from observing to standing in an experience, saying "I."

My normal "I" would only have observed, from the outside, the sort of experience I had just had. But without any blandishments or inflation, he said if the heart felt it, then take it into one's identity. Feel it by identifying with it.

But the "I" that I identified with at the time of the Zurich Initiation could not identify with the experience. So, this is an example of how over years, my ego transformed, imbibing and crediting for itself all it could, 1985 to '86, regarding myself. But it could not have expanded without more framework. *It would have remained mental.*

Expansion works by shifts of frequency, as the seed of *The Unobstructed Universe* by Steward Edward White planted. You can never *think* yourself into expanding. It's a matter of feeling and using the imagination as a sensing device literally, as I would later learn in light body work. This Initiation provided the foundation for what would be like a board with a lot of holes.

Each hole would be a place of transformation when the time came "I" was ready to put the new shift into it. I and "I" would meet and exchange roles. The Initiator had "set the bar," and I felt reality in the marriage with him on the soul level, not sure how it could play out but knowing he knew better than I. That is, so long as it was the former I in question.

Just the same way you might have several dimensions in one space but with different frequencies and some "invisible" to those not on that frequency, evidently you might have several "I" forms (conscious energy and entity forms) in the space of a physical person. Some would be in potential: places to expand consciousness, not physical flesh and weight. Expanding consciousness could conceivably *meet the expansion of itself* that was larger than itself, in the sense of transpersonal, yet saying "I." So, consciousness became "places," such as the one I entered. Yet there was still individuality. Else, this marriage would not be important to the Initiator. It was a very personal marriage, through which he would gain more energy and the sense of great love in doing his job, which, it appeared, was focused most right then on "saving the world."

Finally, in my pink felt hat and pink furry sweater with skirt, we had the ceremony in my small living room, our attention on a *single* candle. And *The Magic Flute*. I played the entire three-hour opera, only to find out he preferred Igor Stravinsky's *The Rite of Spring*. Little did I know the passage below, by St. Teresa of Avila in *The Interior Castle*, which I just stumbled across this very day (in 2023):

> In the spiritual marriage with our Lord, . . . the soul always remains in its centre with its God. Union may be symbolized

> by two wax candles, the tips of which touch each other so closely that there is but one light; or again, the wick, the wax, and the light become one, but the one candle can again be separated from the other and the two candles remain distinct; or the wick may be withdrawn from the wax. But spiritual marriage is like rain falling from heaven into a river or stream, becoming one and the same liquid, so that the river and rain water cannot be divided; or it resembles a streamlet flowing into the ocean, which cannot afterwards be disunited from it. This marriage may also be likened to a room into which a bright light enters through two windows—though divided when it enters, the light becomes one and the same.

In fact, he was "working in the unconscious," my own and that of others, but, as said, honoring the law of not violating free will; in fact, welcoming it because through free will the creative process came into play. And our creativity made us come up with new solutions for the Earth, individually unique solutions that could be applied broadly.

So, as I would gradually figure it out, my higher self was focused on creating patterns. Every time I wrote, every experience I went into, made patterns, so the more *potential* for solving *problems* I had, the more thorny situations I went into, the more solutions I might participate in or have breakthroughs in, though on another level it was my life. On the level of my life I was earnestly trying to be a great writer.

Bringing out works was my expectation and goal. On her level, she was creating patterns *and they never had to be seen or known by a single other living being*. In fact, she would, eventually, show herself to me in the act of handing out patterns. Gradually, I got the point: she was trying to come down into the Earth, whereas I, for my part, was trying to "go up." But the more I went "up," the more I would encounter her and her consciousness, which meant become transpersonal.

My ego "got it." And it surrendered. But then what? How could such opposites consciously work out their differences? There were no differences, once made conscious—due to the ineffable feelings, the new vibrations, that the body felt and was awed by. But nevertheless, everyone else was marching forward into life. In some way, I felt left out.

This is where we will pick up in the next section with the odyssey of consciousness trying to stretch itself over dimensions, so that everyone comes along inside the transition of the Earth and is seen as a valued POTENTIAL contributor.

And what experiences it takes, and who with, to get some of these understandings under my belt. And then how consciousness gives us the bliss that is reported. Bliss such as might be experienced by the body as it reaches the state where Light itself feels Love and cells meet cells, and that can be felt by the human whose body feels this. And what it feels like in the human living on these multiple levels, a single person in a single body but (as the consciousness begins to understand) it is not limited to that at all in its consciousness, and consciousness has location.

So what is the personal effect? And the transpersonal effect? How does one do this trick?

Some of the characters will come back, in new mirrors and new escapades, for these do not disappear. Life goes on.

Starting from the position where the Buddha says after Enlightenment, go back now into ordinary reality and understand the thrill of chopping wood and peeling potatoes, we will step into some of the situations, as the mind tries to open and lose all shackles, for my soul is intent on the purpose of "freeing the mind."

She has to succeed with me through throwing off fear. I will meet Shri Dhyanyogi, who will in large measure be teaching me, though outside physical contact. But contact there is, including in a dream, which I go into in the next section. It is said by Eastern teachers that *no one is permitted to dream of a Yogi without that Yogi's consent*. In this very important action not long before his "death," he came into my dreams to tell me something I needed to hear.

What was little would not be forgotten or taken for granted—buried inside me as awkward (to the Earth) complexes. Complexes that were sources of energy to break the old patterns as the pure unconscious energy kicked like an unborn child, determined to see the Light of day.

❋

I had to come "down," and that is just as hard as going up, though many do it. So that does not entirely answer why it was crafted in such a convoluted form in the instance of me. Yet the "assignment" evidently preexisted in outline, in me, as playing disjointedly my first piano recital at seven, determinedly starting again over and over—I wouldn't leave that piano stool till I completed the Bach barcarolle, in one go. For such a shy person, what kept me on that stool? Whisked away all my inhibitions as my airplane self took over? Was it the imprint of a life-purpose pattern, to "play" the "whole," Alpha to Omega, in a sprint, decades and decades later, at the very end? But what was it the start-to-finish of, personally? Was it to hold my "whole" self, "low" to "high," as it had existed and learned on the Earth—the blue-ribbon "passages"—into one "me"?

So, now I have written, up to 1986, how I began to remember, through experiences, that underneath it all was the Universality of Humanity, of each and every one of us (who could guess it?). How to teach this simply to us humans, who are so used to pinching ourselves, feeling it hurt, to know if we are dreaming. I taught it to myself by teaching to myself, and the end product, even if "knowing" the End at the start, was most unusual, to me, who had the idea to re-experience the vortexes of opportunities (that I played fragments of over and over to get the sequence down)—at the same time, making myself as little as possible, so as to have as much as possible to learn, giving myself inevitable "complications," which translate into "potential," following the threads of mystery to the overarching already-known, waiting answer: Universality of Humanity. Love of course being the governor, the trump in the hand.

❋

We are both squeezed into Earth bodies, shaped into wonderful opportunities for a very limited lifetime, and at the other pole in the end, however, we are universal.

And what if—this is a new thought creeping into my awareness, or rather descending with a thunderclap—*this*, THIS, is the secret of my soul grouping's "transition." Suppose that grouping is inside the unconscious. Suppose this very situation is its own transition to a higher form. Suppose it is exactly this experiment—this initiation—that I, on my unconscious level, was privileged to receive because I was in the grouping. And my soul is moving into the state of the Initiator. And, further, suppose, then it is the answer to my question, now as I write this in 2008 twenty-three years later—the one I sought after.

Suppose in their parallel transition out of operating as entities with a single individuality, they tried this out on Earth as a way to "spread the consciousness" unconsciously: received unconsciously, intuitively, a thing is original, deep within the person who perceives it. But at the same time it would be a valiant test of selflessness, being so convinced that individuals on the Earth matched that higher consciousness *in affinity*. Whew.

Let me hope I explained that as the bombshell it just made, or the meteor that just landed in my awareness, knocking a crater into my brain, my sense of understanding, collapsing the question, now when it's ready, to full understanding. Yes. It's a message coming straight down into my awareness, now stripped bare enough to take it in.

So let's get that straight. In fact, I am literally in everyone. So are you. We are unconscious of our energy, at that degree. But this transition I am speaking of consciously follows its energy into the unconscious. Whew again. Let's let that sit. See where it leads.

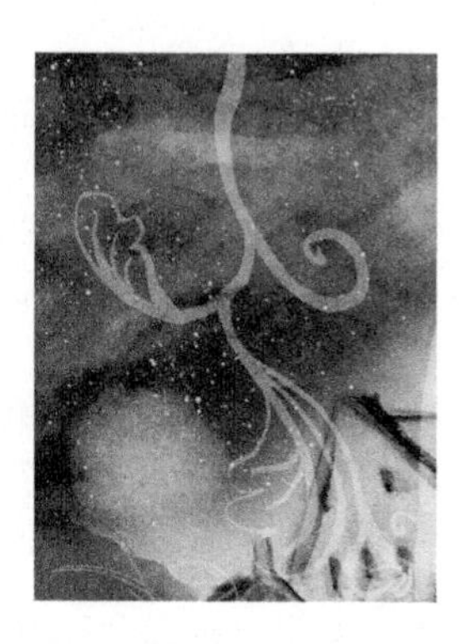

PART TWO

Lunevillelaan 46

Moonville Land

I met Willy in the TV room of a hospital where my estranged husband, Jan, was being treated.

I'd left Jan in 1983. But in 1987, after his mother wrote he was ill, I occasionally went by train from Zurich to Tienen, Belgium. It was an eight-hour trip.

First, by phone he promised to stay out of cafés, go into parks with me. But instead herded me (straight from a Zurich purification lifestyle: no alcohol, coffee, meat, sugar) into a café, where he stayed, with me in tow, for ten-plus hours a day.

Drinking twenty draft Stellas—slowly, quietly, steadily—he smoked two packs of filterless Gallois. That was all the money he had, by the way. Sometimes he longed for a restaurant meal, which was outside his budget. Sometimes I took him.

Polite at the bar, he drew no attention to himself but sat with an intensity. He'd never expected to live this long. Be sure, he kept urging me, to get his novel *The Suicide Mozart* published. It was his soul's message. A Dutch publisher had accepted it on the condition it be commercialized; he refused. He sometimes recounted his enchanted memories of us in Morocco.

With all cafés closed over Christmas, he didn't know what to do with himself but determinedly slept round the clock. I crept out and bought Greek "take out." I walked back in the center of the street, and a police car stopped me to find out why.

I didn't know what kept him going. He now had anguished wrinkles instead of the boyish, smooth, mischievous face—agony in his look. In one trip into the Initiator's consciousness—sensing a very high cerebral, abstract, clear sharp focus—I was in Jan's Third Eye, the Initiator told me, but I also knew there was nothing to do about him now. Even so, I made several trips.

❋

Eventually he was in a hospital—where, with the beginning of brain deterioration, Korsakoff syndrome, caused by alcohol, he was in danger of liver cirrhosis,

In the TV room sat an athletic thirty-one-year-old blond: Willy. A motorcycle accident had just created a turning point for him. An incredible conversation ensued. They liked each other. Willy, clearly, "wanted to change." This, his seventh accident, had created a turning point, he said, and it was true; they were meeting as "opposites."

Mourning the breakup of his marriage and a restraining order his wife took out, which prevented him from seeing his little daughter, he had, during the past year, turned to cocaine for solace, practically daily. Even though in the accident he was not legally found at fault, or at least the fault was evenly divided, the drug was in his body. The police promised not to report it if he rehabilitated. For this and also internal pressures, he was very serious about transformation. He really wanted to get back on his feet, including live with someone again. He was cute. Funny.

As they conversed, he and Jan found similarities—not having to look far: one had worked in a tiny town in Algeria (Jan). In that same very tiny town, El Attaf, Willy had worked also (his only trip out of Europe), having been hired to supervise cleaning. In fact, it was in his long stays out of the country that his marriage began to fail; his wife became unfaithful.

Willy held up his leg. Jan held up his. Each had a steel pin in one leg. How could this conversation be happening? The want-to-change and don't-want-to-change aside, the sophisticated, elegant, artistic Jan was, in personality typing, nothing at all like a truck driver.

With El Attaf background and a steel pin in a leg, they seemed to "exchange" me right there; funnily, this village, El Attaf, even harked back to the location—in Algeria—when Jan first proposed by letter in an offbeat way. But Jan seemed, to me, to be saying: *I am at the end of the road because I refuse to change. There is no hope.*

He seemed to have shut his heart.

Lama Sing, through Al Miner, told me he had not gotten the lesson of the "karma" I had "broken" by leaving—the recurring pattern I took to be co-dependency in which he had expected me to "keep him alive," giving up my own life for his. Willy seemed to be saying: *I want to reach out to my opportunities, by changing. I want a positive life.* Of course, consciously, Jan would hang onto me, while doing everything to make himself off limits to any attraction.

When Willy, very strapped for funds, asked to share Jan's room, Jan supported the synchronicity.

Willy was now in a parallel bed. He told me that every day he could "sense" when I approached the room; that waiting for me, he went into the bathroom and practiced the meditations I'd talked about. I later realized he'd become somewhat psychic in emerging from a coma after a truck crash.

I felt he was a "personality" of Milton Christ Mozart. That is, that on some level the energy was a match. I felt the attraction of what must have been his inner Christ energy, trying to take over, trying to get a word in.

Despite a lack of formal education after age fourteen, despite no workshops, he seemed, on some level, quite up to being his parents' son, those parents named (in the names they were not called) Joseph and Mary. So in an unconscious part of him his inner Christ energy in the specificity of the Initiator, sat. That's how I saw it. Odd though it was.

For the first time, I was going further than friendship; the attraction "took." In the room it intensified. In the hall, talking, Willy invited me to move in with him and got himself checked out of the hospital early.

Being tested for physical endurance as a requirement for release, he was told that no one in his condition (half his bones had been broken in truck and motorcycle accidents) should be able to perform the exercises he had. But he told me, he was strongly incentivized to get home—so I could move in. He lifted large barbells regularly and never brought up pain, not letting it influence him. A doctor had told him, though, he was "riding with death."

You might ask, *where did I find these characters*? So individual and carrying a destructive streak, trying to master it.

But my inner guidance said he was at a critical juncture when his higher potential was trying to come out.

(Actually, hadn't I thought the same about Jan? Yes, think back. It was so.)

I had been indoctrinated that the inner Christ energy, specifically the Initiator's, was afraid of nothing—no challenge—and confidently stepped up to try out *where a potential might manifest*, materialize inside the energy of its human dimension; that is, its physical self, the self that had never thought to name it, had never looked for it, but had called it "intensity," "inspiration," "drive," and so forth, which it was.

I was an expert in not recognizing in myself that it was also a consciousness, an entity eventually.

So I was ready to see if this relationship could work. *Besides, I was extremely attracted to Willy. That was the setup. Naturally, I'd be attracted to him.* It would be conditional love, love conditioned on the fact that I was able to connect with his higher self, his soul, and make a bond with it.

I moved into Lunevillelaan 46 (aka Moonville Land), traveling for a few months between Tienen and my Zurich apartment by train. Then moved in permanently—in November '87. I returned to Zurich again, though, to pack and ship suitcases and see a few friends, including René.

I was just about to leave for another trip to Zurich, to pack more, when in the mail came a lovely letter from René, with a clown drawing. I replied but I didn't see him on that trip, I don't suppose. No, I couldn't have.

Stamped "*Gestorben, Décédé, Decesso,*" my letter to him returned unopened—4.2.88 (February 4). He was dead in German, French, and Italian. This forty-four-year-old had left the planet. I open it now, still sealed after seventeen years:

> January 18, 1988
>
> Dear René,
>
> Missing you very much, but here I am, and a part of my life is, so here's a small reminder of me—I'll be in Zurich sometime in February, for sure. The calendar isn't fixed.
>
> I wish space were different, so I could walk out in the evening into Zurich. I'm in a time different from all times I've had before, but that's par for the last 3 years.
>
> A strong hello to Sandra [his girlfriend].
>
> Are you writing?
>
> What?
>
> My bouquet [the one he bought me, that I pressed] is in my writing room
>
> Love,
> Margaret

Oops—I meant painting. At least, consciously.

I'd enclosed a four HUNDRED Swiss franc Eurocheck as the next payment on the painting—knowing he needed money. He never got it.

Dumbfounded, grief-stricken, I called his girlfriend.

Sadly, she flabbergasted me by not honoring my downpayment; neither would she sell me that—or any!—painting.

But she did fill me in. For a month, she said, he'd sensed himself "stalked by Death." The struggling painter, by then living in a hotel, laden with expenses, explained to her he was too tired to fight (feeling himself in a losing battle with his own demise, which perhaps meant that same sense of being "outside" himself, watching, that I had helped him pass through safely). He cut his wrist, or something like it, but then, thinking himself dying—that it was too late—alerted her; naturally, she had a rescue team rush over, and they saved him. But here comes the odd part.

Assured by the doctors he was fine, she left. And he promptly had a fatal heart attack, thus indeed putting a bow on his image of being "stalked by Death," or even—as he'd told me that evening I sat with him all night—if necessary, he'd just "go to another planet."

I notice for the first time that my painting receipt is marked "Paid in Full," as if giving me that guarantee should what happened occur. Unfortunately, I didn't discover that till after I spoke to her.

And then there were the numbers. He was 46. I lived at Lunevillelaan 46. His phone number had two 46s in it.

Some sort of synchronicity was afoot. *He did not last even four months after I left. This Belmondo style and beauty, this Anthony Quinn energy—it was in only 46 years exhausted*?

❋

I'd realized that not only did the Initiator's energy take risks *in* people, the mirror of that was that *he* relinquished control—giving it up but putting all his strength into belief in the people in whom his energy was factored in. That is, in which he was in their unconscious, his consciousness reachable there.

He believed his energy, in no matter how unconscious a context, would have intuitions, impulses that would assist in synchronicities and mercurial solutions. It was fruitless to bite my nails; instead, I needed to count on his energy deep inside the situation—aligned with, *thus supplying connections at multiple nonpersonal, global points*. That is, nonlocal to me. Local to an entity structured in this way, who said "I" to a much larger "field." This, of course, brings to mind Jesus Christ, if one went through the suspense with him, wondering, *Would he die or not? Was there a way to prevent it?* There was that sense of high stakes in this energy, in whoever it was in, blind confidence—or knowing confidence—believing in Himself even in THE UNKNOWN.

❋

Superbly physical, Willy was not knottily muscular. For lack of a backer, he'd forfeited several ambitions; for example, to be a Formula 1 driver. To try out their tough-guy cred, young men attempted to pick fights with him. He didn't like it.

Not that Willy's connection to the Initiator was necessarily easy to detect. From my first energy teacher, in Brussels, Belgium, beginning September 14, 1989, I took a weekly two- or three-hour class in psychodynamics (aura healing, Neuro-Linguistic Programming, etc.)—at Hornstraat 97, Brussels. This street invariably brings to mind the Jung Institute (at Hornweg 28). And underneath that, my mother's insistence on having *my horn* fixed as she helped me purchase and test a used car (*the last moments I ever saw her*). And now this class (just by psychic geography).

The lanky, tall, brilliant, innovative, naturally entertaining, funny Chris, Willy's age, could "loop" up to the source of word play such as I used in writing; in private he deciphered my often-French-based syllable-rhymes, joining me in the fun.

Eventually, he gave me a psychic reading. Brushing aside my initial questions, he had nothing whatsoever to say about most people. Then Willy. Chris stopped, settled in. He could see, he said, me in charge of the workers, hired by the castle, in the Middle Ages. Willy was a hot-headed, precipitous leader of the workers, like Lech Walesa (Chris had never met Willy). He often got into trouble, sometimes being unsupported even by the workers. When rebellion would have been folly, I calmed him so that he was not punished by being flayed alive. Chris added that Willy "*externalized*"; was "a master of transforming others but not himself. A chameleon."

Later, watching *The Prince of Tides*, he imagined the attraction between Willy and me as like that of the New York therapist (played by Barbra Streisand) and teacher/football coach (Nick Nolte).

Willy was to heal what got broken in my marriage. He taught me to hurl myself *with him* through the stages of an emotion, such as anger, till exhausted in gales of laughter.

The castle story fitted neatly into the sequence of instances I was aware of in which I'd had a "past" life as a strong male. The "externalizer" description fitted a "Christ menu" I'd seen at my table in a dream; in the dream a young man (obviously the inner-male me) intended to fly flamboyantly into seminars, in rock-star style; he needed to learn to internalize.

Willy had a kind of masculinity I wasn't used to. When I reported the information about the Middle Ages, he did not object; even when I told him, "Chris said you were *propelled into this lifetime to pay me back*." That got a laugh, but he didn't dispute it.

Very much opposite to the delicacy and sophistication of Jan—playful nonetheless—Willy confided a secret to me: he never learned the alphabet (he spelled by ear), having stopped school very young to help support his mother, but that still didn't explain it. One wonders what he did age six, seven, etc. But I didn't ask. He didn't know the alphabet. That was a fact.

A charismatic, people-oriented outdoors type, he spoke excellent English, like many Belgians, learning it though pop music and TV movie subtitles. He often watched sports—Wimbledon, the World Cup, soccer, even professional darts and billiards. I went with him to dirt bike races. Willy had both a dirt bike and a Harley-Davidson.

I see him standing before his tape deck, dancing in double time, or an 8/8-, or 16/16-time, whereas I had thought it was 4/4. But Willy was on a double-fast lifetime track. He could feel all the different speeds.

I can see him listening to Joe Cocker, "I just wanna be the one you run to," or "I'm Your Man." With that rough, grainy, passionate, yearning feel, he also loved Dire Straits and "Get Ready," or—when he went to jail briefly for a misdemeanor—"Stand by Your Man." Just some of his favorites. He always had tapes in the car or a boom box.

To start the diesel engine, which he'd turbo-charged, he often had to push it downhill, running, steering it through the open door, then hopping in—due to a dead generator.

Willy seemed to "work" the world or a bar like a room. Sometimes he was a bouncer at a local event. He believed in connecting people. No matter what was going on, if the bell rang, he answered until I convinced him to peep through the curtains first if I didn't want to be interrupted (you can guess why), hoping he could resist.

He loved nature. When he took me on a picnic, we might lie in the grass, just for enjoyment. Or he drove drive miles to jog on a woods trail, not pavement. We bicycled forty kilometers, stopping to drink from a natural spring and take a dip in a lake. I had not known such things were masculine, but with ultramale Willy that sensitivity to nature was. And making love in some private nook he found outdoors seemed quite the thing to do. He was, all in all, a breed I was glad to finally meet, just once, up close.

But nothing was accidental anymore. I felt I was looked over every single minute and that my choices now reflected what fitted the Zurich Initiation. That is, to the extent I was capable. Not that I could tell a single soul about it.

Willy had a Cross he wore at all times. He referred to it as "the Man." He said enigmatically that if he ever lost that Cross, our relationship would be over. He did not explain. He also said that during one of his accidents (not his fault) he'd gone into a coma and woke with amnesia. He let on to no one till finally his memory returned. However, it left him somewhat psychic. The moment we met, like the moment of meeting Jan at Jemaa el-Fna square in Marrakesh, was significant, dramatic, downright odd if you put the experience into its beginning and end.

⁂

Willy was very proud of a letter to me by Herbert Tarr, a rabbi turned bestselling author praised by holocaust survivor Nobel Prize winner Elie Wiesel. I'd worked with Herb on the "serious/hilarious" *Heaven Help Us* at Random House and then freelance on his 1989 *A Woman of Spirit*.

Herb wrote, praising my abilities. Willy carried the letter in his wallet, even into jail, where he went briefly some months after I arrived. I neglected to say that for about six months we stayed virtually in seclusion (away from his friends) while he shook off the coke habit. He'd been given heart pills, as to go cold turkey could be dangerous. But after about a week he stopped taking them. And stuck to his plan.

Willy, in the past, did not sniff cocaine. He used a needle. Why? I asked.

"For the rush."

Besides, taking it was prevalent among his truck driver friends on long drives across Europe, on deadlines, to push through the night. In deciding to make a clean break from the drug, he initially did not see his old friends.

Complaints about breaking a restraining order to see his daughter filed much earlier by his ex-wife finally, slowly, found their way to trial. Also, he'd been caught in a dragnet when he went to a marijuana dealer while hidden police cameras turned. Willy explained to me that smoking marijuana because it "made [him] think better." Of course, this was not true of me, never had been, and certainly more so after beginning the consciousness courses, working in human potential and energy. But that didn't prevent Willy from smoking, with great fumes escaping into my side of the car, driving me to the train station for my weekly mystical Taiji class in Leuven or Inner Landscaping in Brussels—dutifully waiting to pick me up at the Tienen station when class ended.

To Willy most things had a humorous side. That kept him from belaboring anything. In Belgium, cases are often protracted, going to trial late, then having jail time reduced to low sentences—in his case, about four months, during most of which he worked outside in construction, only sleeping in the jail.

Willy was intense. Not a good plan, incarcerated. When a guard said something derogatory, he wanted to lash out but, very keen on keeping the construction job, smashed his fist into the wall instead. The fist broke, turned black. Wrapping it, camouflaged, in a cloth, he went to work. I found it hard to imagine the stoicism of breaking your hand, then still doing the heavy lifting of construction. But if he had reported to the infirmary, he would have had to spend long, boring daytime hours locked up.

This incident added some more broken bones to those broken

already. So he was out all day long, and the time in jail passed quickly. But (what no one, including myself, suspected) Willy was a police informant in sales of drugs to minors. This, a policeman told me in my living room months after his death.

I did know his driving skill was so extraordinary that the police *asked him to instruct them in car chases*. Declining regrettably, he explained that if you'd been arrested, it was illegal to teach the police. Nonetheless, he was licensed to drive explosives. And his reputation as a driver was broadcast far and wide. Also, Willy stories. He'd parked a car by lifting one end into a tight fit. Or driven through a corn field with his windshield wipers on.

Now, though, he was on handicap compensation because of the many broken bones. So he had teamed up with a mechanic friend to rebuild crashed cars, acquiring wrecks and car parts in Holland. But he also labored over an investment bulletin, quite wisely investing his insurance money from the accident in which he'd been in a coma. Willy looked for—and found—the most lucrative offer possible—in those days of high interest rates.

In jail, he said, my photo acted oddly. It kept falling off the wall. He was intent on building me up in every way, including that he had my glamorous New York City face photos (from age twenty-four)—to which he would point—made by a professional photographer who stopped me on the street, framed and proudly hung on our living room walls—whereas I had been too shy ever to do this in New York.

A year later, happily clean, Willy began seeing his friends again.

Going away with Willy and Friends for a delightful week at a Spanish beach provided a highlight of the last months of his life. We battled in a humorous way—for example, when I wanted to play poker with the guys (and they let me), he left the game; he returned, only to find I'd won some of the hands. But the spats were all in fun. As always, when he slept he flung his arms and legs around me, which made the energy between us, from my point of view, flow. And made me sleep like a baby.

In 1989 Herbert Tarr gave insightful comments about my still unpublished "big book." Though a rabbi, he had read Christian saints and knew histories of divine-love poetry, which I didn't. He had planted a tree for me in Jerusalem. And treated me lavishly to restaurant lunches on my visits in New York City—not caring if I ordered a dessert just to take *two bites*. He recognized the writing style as "Cubist." From Herb comes a critique, in an envelope with two owl stamps, the owl staring me in the eye:

> Dec. 4, 1989 (got the book yesterday &—yes—couldn't put it down)
>
> Dear Margaret,
>
> Reading *Love in Transition* (wonderful title), I was reminded of Nabokov's *Pnin* and Renata Adler's *Speedboat*. The former because it was so highly concentrated and rich, I would read only a few pages at a time, to savor it appropriately. The latter because Adler's novel (published by Knopf, I think) was written in short takes or bursts. I'm not even sure if it was divided into chapters—just a page or two at a time, each "take" separated by a double space or something like that. (The book got excellent notices and did well commercially too.)
>
> Your *Love* is like that—with its short chapters. And highly condensed, like Nabokov's. I'm wondering, though, if excellent at cutting as you are, you might have cut too much from the original manuscript of 1,000 pages . . . The book itself is studded with marvelous lines and insights. I started copying some of them down to repeat to you but gave up when the pad filled up . . . Which leads to the question: does the book end too soon? too abruptly? (Though you can't really go by me. I was the only one in America who thought *Portnoy's Complaint* ended in the middle, with the psychiatrist saying to Portnoy at the end: "OK, Mr. Portnoy, let us now begin." Me, I wanted to go all through the analysis from beginning to end before I felt fully satisfied . . . Query: what's the relationship between Paula & Robert on the one hand and Anny & Joseph & Ian on the other? Did I miss the connecting link? [it had still never been made conscious]. If not, you have to furnish it—some reason wnhy [*sic*] they're in the same book, aside from the theme [of love]. As to the characters, Robert is clever and Anny very well drawn, but the biggest, surprising achievement, me thinks, is Joseph. Most women writers, men as well, would have put him down, patronized or satirized him. Amazingly, you stepped into his skin & presented a very sympathetic portrait. Kudos.

> But then, with Joseph's finding his bed empty and Anny gone, the book comes to an end, with the little chapters—and I felt cheated. I wanted to know, What then? . . .

This arrived just prior to a trip to the States. In a folder of meetings I'd set up in 1989, I find a letter to Jeneane, to *New York Times* book reviewer Anatole Broyard, and to author Hannah Green. I had no idea Anatole was sick, in cancer remission. We talked by phone. I initiated the call. At the very last minute, December 27, just prior to my trip, I wrote the letter below. This would be the last chance, unknown to me. There was barely time, at that.

> Dear Anatole,
>
> I will be in America January 4th and hope to spend that night in New York, after which I'll be visiting in North Carolina. I would like very much to talk with you, in New York or Cambridge, around the 4th or 5th, if you have the time. Or if not, then when I return to Europe a couple of weeks later (ten days to two weeks).

I wanted his benediction about *my casting of Milton*. There is nothing like a best friend, an expert critic (for the *New York Times*, no less), if you want a yay or nay about your characterization of a mutual friend, especially if it's somewhat daring. I wanted him to bless the presentation.

Also in this folder is Hannah's letter to me, December 9: "very anxious to see" the opening of the book. Now, twenty years after we initially met at MacDowell Colony (we were both fellows), she says send just the first twenty-five to thirty pages, because—she drops this bombshell—she is recovering from cancer, "but I lost so much time and have a new deadline for my long over-due books."

I tell her: "I'm sitting on a powder keg." It has to do with the Zurich Initiation, which is not in the book but which I now feel like opening up on. Hannah is an old friend and I want to broach this.

Finally, there is an envelope (addressed in green ink to Hunter), nothing inside.

With Jeneane, I set up the plan to attend her Zurich workshop—which would be significant indeed.

Arriving in the States, I stayed at the New York apartment of an old old friend, Jim Mohan, who worked with UNICEF in top positions, including in Chile, Afghanistan, Sudan (trouble spots)—whom I had known since our Yellowstone Park "soda jerk" jobs at a Hamilton store in the 1960s. Looking out over Central Park—in Jim's apartment—as he prodded me, I couldn't resist contacting a Yellowstone buddy. But also—Hunter.

I found Hunter celebratory because all charges had recently been dropped in a sexual-assault case filed against him, complete with arrest warrant and a bond set for $2,000—a situation he'd counterattacked full blast, resulting in complete exoneration. And a little courtroom humor. He explained the "heinous" situation. It was over now; it was fascinating, a relief. But having had police comb through his house refocused him.

He was to write: "I'm the point man for a lot of people . . . This is just part of what I think is a long series of abuses of the Constitution, *the Fourth Amendment*, which guarantees all of us, even judges, the right not to be subjected to unwarranted search and seizure." (*Aspen Times* article, Mark Huffman, June 1, 1990).

How many years had it been? He mentioned *that my ears must have been burning* when he and Jim Silberman, his senior editor at Random House, my former boss, spoke on the phone. He added, "*I should have known I would get into soul searching, talking with you.*" Time melted. There we were, in the "old days." On the phone. I couldn't believe it! He said to pass his greetings to Anatole.

It was so emotion-packed—historic—to see the debonair, book-digesting Anatole after twenty years. Snow packed the train station; no one remotely answering his appearance was there. Twenty minutes passed. I wondered apprehensively, had we missed each other? I telephoned his wife. She said he was there, waiting.

I moved to the location she indicated. Handsome, with a scarf wound round his neck, dignified, healthy-looking, approachable, receptive, there he was. No doubt possible. Time stopped and swelled, expanded. I walked over. He suggested going somewhere for a light lunch—burgers. We sat at a nice table for two and I ordered a cheeseburger. *He approved of Robert and Paula*, in my *Love in Transition*; *he wholeheartedly gave it his blessing.*

"People want to read about the sixties." He was collecting "Milton stories." As he attempted to pry Milton stories out of me, I could barely remember any.

He said, "You were a very important person in Milton's life."

"I wish I had come back to New York to see Milton earlier," I said.

He didn't understand—why?

I said, "to marry him"—the first time I had put the belated thought into words. Did I mean it? With all I knew now, didn't I?

He said, "That would have saved him."

Hesitantly, I broached my thought that Milton was still alive. Would he laugh? Walk away from the table? But I wanted to be sure, in all fairness, his blessing was with the knowledge that I was going into unexplored territory.

He accepted the idea. "*Your whole relationship with Milton was a fairy tale.*"

I don't know where he got that idea. But his answer seemed positive—the fairy tale an afterthought.

He had said, from his (Anatole's) point of view, Milton was concerned about my being so—a word for "organized"—in contrast to his own (more worldly wise?) style. What he probably meant was that Milton admitted to me he sometimes did not know whether to interpret something I did *as naively innocent* (*"like a child"*) or as *incredibly calculating.*

"With me. Milton was "an ironist. With you, he was a romantic," Anatole said, as if people—some people—changed wavelengths, depending on whom they talked to. Well, they did, didn't they? And not from hypocrisy. (I now take this for granted.) That was one thing that held me in New York: the intelligence, in sparkling creativity of the people I met there. Anatole being no exception, as he proved yet again.

Just afterward I phoned his home—the last time—expecting to leave a message. Instead, he picked up—it was remarkable—jumping on the trampoline with incense in the background. It was "meant to be."

His writing on the '60s had gone well. He felt great. He had begun to call *his* "Milton" (in the '60s) "Robert" in his mind, *an untoward, unexpected compliment.*

So my Robert *really* passed muster. Picking up the persona, transferring it into his own unconscious, Milton's best friend sensed not one whit of loss of credulity; he was evidently energized by our meeting, as I was. *Call back any time.*

Sadly, though we had managed to walk back almost twenty years, the cancer returned—right away. And he switched manuscript subjects to the process of dying.

He never finished those '60s memoirs in the intended way, to my knowledge; instead, the portrait that concludes *Kafka Was the Rage* seems to me a pause, a moment in time *he would have counterpointed in the next chapter opening, a stylistic tool he used: to turn something on his head the page after a chapter ended*. The next chapter opened. What happened? The impression reversed.

Kafka ends with Anatole going off to follow a girl and Milton not understanding.

Yet Milton had told me that when Anatole's father died, he (Milton), to distract Anatole, suggested they double date! Anatole didn't understand.

It was just the opposite. Roles reversed. After his father's death, Anatole withdrew to write, "What the Cystoscope Said," his famous 1954 short story; he was grim, totally undistractable. In his lauded story he offered his father a way out of his dying weeks, the intense pain—an assisted suicide. Anatole had thought that in pain seemingly too great to bear, his father would not cling so to life. He was wrong, as his appalled father made clear.

After that, nothing could distract Anatole from pouring his feeling into the cathartic creative act, nothing else having the power to ease the distraughtness and heal. That was then: "What the Cystoscope Said."

Kafka Was the Rage stopped when Milton really came onto the scene. I wondered why the moment he tried to go into "Milton stories," the next second, almost, he was ill.

Of course, I was only guessing at the total character portrayal Anatole would have left the reader with, had he had the chance to write his "Milton stories." Anyway, I wondered.

He said to me, when I tentatively broached the fact of having a boyfriend, fourteen years younger than me, "You seem to have found the secret to happiness."

He missed Milton very much.

"I used to speak with him every day at the end." He particularly missed him because "After Milton died, no one talked to me as an equal."

Anatole never brought up his cancer, his fears, nothing straying from the subject at hand.

Was he being deceptive, just as when he did not bring up his Blackness to fellow writers at the *Times*!!? With his children, well, he should have told them. But the others? To the contrary. He was staying in the present, on a frequency of really being *there* with you.

So he seared into me that most important of wishes: to be "treated . . . as an equal." Not a *Times* reviewer to cater to. And not a Louisiana Creole who probably stemmed from a French ancestor, having thereafter exclusively Black forebearers. Those closest to him, indifferent to race, down in the Village, knew about that "C" for "Creole" on his birth certificate. I *did, even before we met*. But it was never a topic of conversation, to me.

In perfect symmetry, having been born on the bottom end of the socioeconomic ladder, at the top he found inequality of a different sort. "No one talks to me as an equal." It being a thing to lament. His smile, his healthy handsomeness, his saying "I'm an old man now" but belying it in every way, were reviving. But he boiled down the point to wanting people to act natural around him—to be treated as neither Creole nor celebrity.

Willy Dies

I returned to Belgium not a moment too soon. It was the last year in Willy's life. Funnily and impossibly, one day in 1990 he interrupted my typing, entered the little room with fresh bread for me to smell—whimsically, with a twinkle in his eye, said, "Hello, Mrs. Bell." No explanation. He did it several times. A "bell" was looming on the horizon, making it uncannily precognitive. But he would have to die first, and he had begun to have suspicions that was shortly to occur. What? A just-under-thirty-five-year-old, healthy male specimen? Don't josh about a subject so serious. I remember him listening, engrossed, to "Spirit in the Sky," standing before the large stereo cassette player, overwhelmed for no apparent reason. But Willy was on his way out.

At this point, he, like René—I explain below—felt "stalked by Death."

First, during the summer I attended the holotropic breathwork workshop of Jeneane Prevatt, PhD, and Russell Park, PhD, in Zurich; Jeneane had studied with me at the Institute.

Holotropic breathwork, aka hyperventilated breathing (to reach "nonordinary" states of consciousness), was developed by Czech-born psychiatrist Stan Grof, MD, a pioneer in transpersonal psychology, and his wife, Christina. Jeneane, a friend of the Grofs, was president of their Spiritual Emergence Network (SEN), which served people experiencing psychospiritual crisis. The Shift Network writes about pioneers, citing Grof research as being "at the leading edge of psychology":

> In this paradigm, consciousness is not limited to your body or even to your singular life. You can expand your identity to a cosmic scale, explore other dimensions, and access information from what appear to be past lives.
>
> We are not limited by time, space, and causality in the way we once thought . . .
>
> From this work has emerged a new "cartography" of the human psyche that accounts for our birth experiences as well as transpersonal domains more typically explored by shamans and healers.[11]

It feels very foreign to call her Jeneane. For she was (or soon would be) Jyoti, a spiritual name given her by the satguru (Sanskrit: "true guru") Dhyanyogi-ji (1878–1994). Since 1988 she has had a "Buddha belly." This deserves a pause, for it is unusual to have an inside look at this rarity.

> Friend, hope for the guest while you are alive
> Jump into experience while you are alive . . .
> What you call "salvation" belongs to the time before death.
> If you do not break the ropes while you are alive,
> do you think
> ghosts will do it after?
>
> —Kabir, as quoted in *An Angel Called My Name*

Jyoti's home, September 7, 1988. As recorded in *An Angel Called My Name*:

> I was watching television when a movement similar to a heartbeat started pumping in my right leg. It increased in severity until the leg of my blue jeans started moving. My housemates noticed the movement and asked me what was happening . . . The "heartbeat" then moved down into my foot, back up into my thigh and entered my vagina. At that moment a brilliant white Light absorbed me and I seemed to disappear within it for some 10 to 15 minutes. While in this state, I had no awareness of anything. I would later understand that I had entered my first states of samadhi . . . No sooner had I regained a sense of myself than the same process began again except this time the pulsating started in my knees . . . When the Light again absorbed me, it felt as if my entire auric field expanded and lost all boundaries. I became very dizzy and nauseated . . .

Her two housemates, Russell Park and Quita, had spent years working in hospitals, "Russ as a clinical laboratory technologist, Quinta as a paramedic." They put her to bed, "and the heater in my waterbed blew out. It is important to remember that when a Kundalini episode is in progress, it affects all present."

> For the next two hours I experienced such bliss that words are unable to describe the richness . . . Suddenly, "something" about the size of a small man's fist formed under my skin at my

> pelvic region and, with a twisting movement, extended itself up to my abdomen, stopping at my heart region. (pp. 140–142)

It repeated the movement, filling the belly with an energy in a sometimes-almost-unbearable pain for a couple of hours. "When I awoke the next morning, my belly was extended to the point I looked about five months pregnant.[12] But what had happened? In a *kombuch* (Buddha belly), she told me, it was said that the *prana* and *apana* (the inbreath and the outbreath) were in a holding pattern. It was primarily found in the East, among spiritual teachers. And indeed, she was soon to enter consciously the orbit of Dhyanyogi-ji.

He called himself "a wandering *sadhu*," saying, when he left his cave to go out into the world, "I *had the intense desire to help as many people as possible.* I *remembered my suffering when all* I *wanted was peace and the answers to* 'Who *am* I?' *and* 'What *is death*?' I *felt compassion for others who wanted to find the* Truth."

Along with several others, including me, Jyoti and Russ would, in June 1995, co-found Kayumari, a healing and spiritual-seeking community in 160 acres, surrounded by national forests, in the Sierra Nevada mountains of California. It now has branches in the United States and Europe. Later, she helped convene the International Council of Thirteen Indigenous Grandmothers and founded the Fountain. And is on the Esalen faculty. And is herself Grandmother Jyoti Ma, besides having a PhD in transpersonal psychology.

My experiences in the seminars of Jyoti and Russ were utterly phenomenal—beginning with this 1990 holotropic breathing workshop (below).

In a vision, I was met by my "clan" (Jyoti called them); in high intensity, the leader ("the tall man," she called him) showed me a series of faces, each with a feature highlighted. Before my eyes, a spotlighted feature—a nose, for instance—slightly shape-shifted, to fit into the face of the next person in the same energy.

The "clan" leader showed me, also in pictures, how, *in conjunction with his Light, these males, one by one,* in combination with Earth energies and thought forms, grew unbalanced *began to darken*; it was hard not to become unstable if he was unconsciously there.

For instance, Jan. I saw him waiting at the train station with his leashed boxer dog. In the pictures it appeared to me this disintegration occurred after he went back to Belgium and that at first, standing still, waiting with the boxer dog, he was all right. But eventually it was too late, *definitively*. Waiting, I suppose, for me.

Lastly—uncomplicated, with a simple faith—was Willy—still bright, innocently so, in the vision in the summer of 1990. The "tall man" instructed, me, "*Take me out of your heart. And put Willy there.*

"Or he might not survive."

At that, *a drop of mercury, all silver,* slid out of my heart. I watched it. So "the tall man," the clan leader, was my mercurialness! His presence in me. It made me *not* stay stuck; made me incapable of twiddling my thumbs, no matter how difficult the situation—*do* something. Even "going down" was not unthinkable because mercurialness always found a way back "up." Mercurialness made me unpredictable, suddenly reverse course, not able to take "no" as the conclusion but find a way out of an impasse, a dark nothingness.

Of course, if I were only mercurial, nothing else, it would be like a phrase Milton once used to describe himself in that instant: "like a little ball on top of a fountain"; any little movement, he said, "can send me up or down."

By taking him *out on this level*, the "tall man" said, I would find him again on the level that Willy *would move up to*. What a bet.

Let go of a bar with nothing to hold onto—just do it, drop it—and in that dire situation something solid would magically take its place. Soon enough. In time. *It would have to. If one staked that much.* Risk that Willy would, with everything staked on him, find his own mercury within; i.e., find *him, the "tall man."*

It might have sounded melodramatic. But remember, this takes place in another dimension, where "the future" makes its plans, stakes out its position.

Imagine giving up my mercurialness. Supposedly, on the instant of my decision it would mysteriously "vanish." And then what? Would I sink into a situation so dreadful that Willy got on his white charger and Mercury showed up? In Willy. Riding to the rescue. What a romantic. Yet it was a serious proposition.

I did not even consider it, however. My human feelings would not let me. It was like the longest shot I had ever heard of.

Coming out of the vision, I attempted instinctively—lying on the pad, my arms stretched out over my head—to climb up by rope, following "the tall man." I did not want to be "left behind." I could not do without this drop of mercury, personified as a part of living human beings. A young part of me spoke in my place, saying—I well remember the words—"I *live in a world all lavender,* where it's always snowing in my father's heart."

Up for anything, Jyoti called her a "star baby." With assurances that she had been a star baby *herself*, she coaxed her "*not to believe you can walk on ceilings and don't need any food*" but to let "Margaret" come back.

So I did. But my mind was still set on not to take *him* (the man in whose heart it was always snowing) "out of my heart," transferring the loyalty to Willy, who would wind up discovering the vanished "drop of mercury" for himself, feeling supported so much he climbed to that high place, no doubt. At least, that was the plan presented to me. He was certainly bold enough and uncomplexed enough and courageous enough to risk everything to get to his higher consciousness if he made a decision to. But I was dead set against playing my assigned role.

That is, to lose all to foster a potential—which Willy could only reach if I believed in it so much I risked everything, asking my heart to do this. Another's heart would know if one did; that is, I would give it up and Willy would reach to incredible depths within to replace those qualities critical to me I no longer had. In *this way only*, he, the "tall man," would be able to put his light strongly enough in Willy without blasting him out of commission.

It would be his simplicity that rose to the challenge. And if the tall man did not put his light more strongly in Willy, the deal was, though I did not think this through, that Willy must "leave," as a sacrifice to raise the energy field. In this way does collective energy figure out its events to support.

For some time before his death as he drove home from nearby Leuven at night, Willy "saw" his windshield crashed into.

We had just returned from Portugal, when Death—I say "struck" I'd dreamed (but did not make the connection), "He was trying to tell her goodbye," meaning in Portugal in December.

In November '91, Jyoti and Russell—he was at that time on the research faculty of the Institute of Transpersonal Psychology, at present is a psychologist at the California Department of Corrections—just popped in, in Tienen, for the first time, spending two nights. Jyoti completely charmed Willy. He was like a little boy seeing an angel on top of a Christmas tree. About Russ today, just to peek into his LinkedIn bio, he has "the unique distinction of being professionally qualified to create, develop, and verify a broad range of research and testing instruments." He "founded and directed a leading-edge clinical and neurotherapeutic clinic, developing skills in mind/body medicine, peripheral and brain (EEG) biofeedback; light and sound technology and peak performance." Down at the bottom of a long bio list of specialties: "I have led 5 groups of 20+ people into the Amazon rain forest. I am an authorized 'Fasting Priest' of the Cheyenne nation. I am a pilot. I have presided and sat on environmental organizations working to create a sustainable environment."

Russ, sleeping in Willy's position in our bed, dreamed of an imminent accident with Willy driving. It felt so lifelike they debated whether to hire a taxi to the airport (rather than letting Willy drive them) but decided to go with Willy.

At the end of the month, here came more attempts to "save Willy. Now it was the Kundalini to the rescue. I began to have a kriya episode, very intense discharges of blocked energy, once a week. For example, on the Tienen train station platform to go to my Inner Landscaping psychodynamics class in Brussels, I started shaking. Knowing it was the Kundalini, I weighed the odds and went to class.

The shaking wouldn't stop. Kriyas, which these were, deserve a pause to be explained. Kriyas can accompany a spontaneous Kundalini awakening. They did with me. In a kriya episode, I typically suddenly started shaking in my leg or other part of me where energy was blocked. But not just mildly blocked. It was unblocking deeply locked-in information that it was time to let surface. Once it starts, there is nothing you can do but let it work its intent, as it is part of the awakening Kundalini, thus, a "conscious energy" by definition, in the Hindu tradition that discovered and researched it experientially.

> In yogic philosophy, the universe is considered to be a play of this *chiti shakti* because it is the energy that has manifested itself of its own free will into everything in experience.[13] (my italics)

As we meditated, on one side of the room minds went blank. One attendee was afraid. Putting his assistant in charge, Chris Van de Velde, the teacher, took me aside to see what was happening.

He said rather sternly, "This is my class. I'm responsible. I want to be sure this isn't something harmful." Then he began to move his fingers through the energy, and as he did, I "saw" different lifetimes fleetingly pass by. Each new energy Chris brought in changed my energy. The last figure was my father, "John Henry." He said, startled, blinking, in dry wit, "Well, I'll be *John* Brown."

In my father's case, the energy I shifted into was too solid, too earthly. I panicked a little bit, hoping I didn't have to stay that feet-flat-on-the-ground-like. If you are wondering what "John Brown" meant, It was a familiar phrase in his vocabulary in North Carolina to indicate surprise. In history, Brown was an abolitionist who was hanged. My father could, finding himself in my energy, have been humorously implying how uncomfortable it was. But never fear.

Chris shifted me back.

He said those were all incarnations of myself—that in the past I had helped others energetically, but this lifetime I was being helped. And it was all OK. He said, "Your heart is opening."

Why, though, was I having a kriya episode once a week?

After several episodes I consulted Mariah. She confirmed that it had to do with Milton, as I'd deduced; he was changing form. Was he "going home"? Could he be passing "memories" into me in these overwhelming energy incidents? Were these dramatic memories, some at death's door, his or mine? I could not believe they were mine, as I associated a famous person with one of the deaths. Surely not me.

As I would interpret this in normal language, being in the thought form of the Day of Judgment, as I think he was, would indicate—it did to me now—he was in Christ energy manifesting at the end of the twentieth century, holding it in a personal form, to be walked in and released. A summing up of a chapter in Earth History, in the history of the collective unconscious. But it had to be made conscious through the decisions inside the path. In the history of the collective unconscious, this chapter is still unconscious.

The fact that a spirit committee made a stop here before widening their field would have to wake me up to the fact, if nothing else did, though it did, of how important this part of the clearing of the path was. I take the purpose to be a dissolving of the karma that it sums up, by stating it.

What remained unconscious in the collective unconscious would repeat itself.

This idea of "going home," I'd dreaded, when I first heard of it, imagining it meant total loss of memory, even being shattered all across the Earth (and further) with bits of memory and potential falling far and wide as energy, even conscious energy. If so, it made sense to pass some memories into safekeeping. I imagined it like that. But then, I didn't really know. Anyway, in this much intensity, whatever it was, I was sharing it. And, as it turned out, it would sweep up Willy, on one level of this multidimensional event, which—if we could see it, I was learning—all events are, some more than most.

⁂

So this is the background to what would occur January 6/7, Old Christmas, 1991. It is the anniversary of the only telegram I ever received from Milton—the one in 1967 with the words "GIRDLE OF O, GIRDER OF I."

It consisted of a single line—eight words—ending with "Inviolate, Unbreakable."

Here the shape of an enfolded Event Ball began to occur to me. More on that later.

The day Willy died, the Russian Orthodox Old Christmas (in the Julian calendar), in the wee hours of January 7, was heavily laden with symbols.

It followed on Russ's warning dream, practically scaring him to death though he didn't scare easily.

And it reinforced that terrifying sight Willy had, in the mind's eye, off and on for a month—driving home alone from a nearby Leuven café late at night—of a crash through his windshield. It turned out to be a tree.

Shaken by the atypical (for him) warning, he decided in December that New Year's resolutions were in order. If he changed enough, *could the event be called off*? he asked urgently. It was all he could think of to do.

Feeling the ominous, looming forewarning (no kidding, no exaggeration)—as if "stalked by death"—just as René had—Willy decided to try to ward it off by stopping smoking. He got it into his head maybe that gesture would prevent it. He would also attempt other transformations. He didn't try to be rational about it. The visions of the crash petrified him. He was hoping to outwit death. He didn't say, "I'm being punished," didn't try to figure it out, just took from the situation the idea he "needed to change."

In Portugal with me in December, he began to follow through.

In the same period, Jan died, committed suicide for the how-manyest time, on December 27, the anniversary (unconscious, I'm sure, but significant dates were swirling around) of the date in 1968 he'd written the Greek suicide letter to me, so colorfully but seriously describing an attempt to commit suicide in Santorini that it drew me back to Belgium, taking up in-person contact with him again for the first time in four years—me working in New York City and him living in Morocco.

There was a last-ditch effort to "stop" Willy's accident January 5. In the Brussels National Airport, just back from Portugal, suddenly

I had to sit down while Willy stood at the baggage carousel. I was having the last of seven Kundalini "episodes." This time, I "saw" a scene: of Jesus going out Palm Sunday into the crowds.

But a different archetype tried to take it over: Mary—*telling him not to go*! This nonhistorically recorded scene tried to "crossbreed" with the known outcome, just like genetically modifying seeds—here, attempting to *rewrite about-to-happen current history energetically*. Was that possible? I had never heard of such a thing, but in the grips of the vision, feeling the powerful energy go through me, I had no thought to question what was intended. Could, in a hypothetical energetic battle, two events—one historical, one imaginary—fight it out, and whichever one won would have a significant impact on the Earth event itself"? Throwing its weight toward/against an outcome by some law we didn't know that could assist in tipping the "scales?"

When I *hadn't* taken Mercury out of my heart, a backup plan apparently went into effect: with attempts to intervene, though, as said, they also apparently related to Milton's changing form. Anyway, this last kriya incident honed in specifically on Willy as the energy shook loose in me in the airport kriya episode, producing a scene before my eyes.

But leaving the airport, I—fatefully—just a precaution, for observation, my choice, checked myself in to the local hospital (for one day) for a rib injury. I'd heard about fractured ribs puncturing lungs; mine were bruised, hardly any risk. Just in case, though, I voluntarily had myself admitted to the hospital where we first met.

That night, all was well. However, I decided to prolong my stay for a second night. Here, everything got eerie. You might ask, wasn't I consciously, actively, worried about Willy's possible looming death, that very night? Not at all. It didn't work like that. My intuition might be totally in the know. But my rational self still felt lulled into complacency—not permitting the entry of "the reality" of it.

Almost closing time. Willy prepared to leave the room. Around 8:00 p.m. I had no suspicions of the odds of his not surviving that night. Anyway betting against his surviving would have won the lottery.

In my room the *energy field* of the Mother reappeared as he lingered. In the field I sensed her pleading with her son not to "go out to the crowds" on Palm Sunday. I picked up the energy, knowing I had to get his attention, draw on our bond—that always made him calm. As fate would have it, the elderly woman in a parallel bed *reminded him of his mother.*

He transferred his focus to her.

She started talking, easy-going, friendly, sympathizing; they kept exchanging pleasantries as she picked up on *the Mother energy, but on the wrong level*. I watched helplessly, knowing it was important to soothe him, as I typically did—make sure he walked out of the room calm, focused on "us"—sensing it was now or never, *for a reason* I *didn't know*. It was.

I *see you drive the car from the parking lot, the last time*. I *watch from the window as you linger—waiting inside the car before starting it* (*thinking of what? deciding about something?* As *if you could hear*, "Don't *go*"? Or *merely waiting for the diesel engine to warm up*? But I *felt an intense sense of* "Wait" *in the air, as if, joined with his mind*, I *sensed a hesitation*. Who *knows*?).

Now in the hospital room the clock began its slow ticktock. The "motherly" woman spun a tale almost impossibly uncanny, just precisely as if she were a "plant" in the room, a magical figure who didn't really exist, indicating the precision of the synchronicity-laden situation. She now said she had lost *two husbands by age fifty*. U*nfeasibly eerie*. (I *was fifty*).

Further, "I *might have warned the last one*," she continued, describing details that applied exactly to me.

I tried to phone Willy, feeling something was not right. Why all the clues, the warnings, floating about?

He had already left the café—he was physically unreachable. But in Portugal that hadn't stopped us once, a few days earlier, from communicating subtly.

Alone on the beach, approached by a cocaine dealer, he'd been tempted. By myself in the beach hotel room, I'd felt a strong electrical current in my right hand. By the vibrating, I knew some deep energy exchange was taking place, positively. He came back in and said, with the tumult of this period he'd been pulled toward the coke—torn. B*ut remembering me*, got the strength to say no.

That night, I flew in a dream, trying to get someone's attention to warn him. To no avail.

That old practice from Zurich, sacrifice, or self-sacrifice, in order to further collective manifestation, had reared its head. But I had been oblivious of warnings. There are photos from the Portugal trip that went down with the car as it crashed into the tree, photographs completely unharmed. You and I are smiling in swimsuits; they show off your physique—looking like a very good lifeguard, which you had also been. You had mastered many sports before I met you, before you broke many bones, not showing it, in seven automobile/motorcycle accidents, none but one of which was judged your fault. But why so many? One took place exactly where your father died in a bike crash.

You announced that the eighth would be your last. Funny. This was the eighth accident.

The night the crash happened, you, uncannily, predicted to someone else: that either you would die young *in an auto accident* or survive and live to a particular age, which you wrote down, mentioning (uncharacteristically, unique on your part—but then the eve of death is unique) a prior incarnation you were "back from," telling the person to keep this slip of paper. Truck drivers don't usually talk about "incarnations"; you didn't, but you did that night, just the way you also sometimes joked privately with me about being younger than me *in "biological age" only*, playfully referring to what I had said about "the castle."

Early the next morning, you died. Or rather, out of body, never got back in. Two people reported it that way. The psychic teacher Mariah Martin, whom I'd consulted for years and years, said that Willy had been out of his body, in an "unconscious suicide." That is, he had *consented to the sacrifice but not the timing*; it would be unknown to him. My friend Helen, whom we will get to, had the same impression, independently, of this out-of-body state.

It matched, to me, my 1981 dream (of a *sacrificial figure looking as if on remote control*)—a wiggly, elongated, "willowy" body driving a car. But the driver's seat empty in the last dream frame. Why?? It had mystified me why that there was no visible victim at the end. Well, in dream lingo, I now take that to depict that the body was not visible because the spirit was not in it. Yes, the more I think about it, dreams do speak exactly like that. A *seat without a body: out of body!* Ah-ha! Decoded ending.

But especially given the tire tracks. In that foggy 4:00 a.m. hour of zero visibility, who steered the car, heading the tire tracks straight into the *only tree* (invisible) in the field, as if with a precision ruler?

"Why didn't he use the hand brake?" His baffled friends shook their heads, in view of his legendary driving abilities.

His "appointment with death"—that had been set up who knew when if we go with these warnings?—had proved itself real.

"—won't survive . . . has to be loved with a whole heart . . . take out the mercury . . ." But I *couldn't and did not fully appreciate the direness, the reality it forecast, stakes it laid down. And even, I think, it was asking too much of me—that I give up that much, with no promises of its working. But who knows?* Could you do that? Do a total remake, lowering your own capacities,

on the off chance of a rescue that would require a personality reversal in your partner? I couldn't. My spiritual identity could not be wagered in such a gamble.

Anyway, this is not speaking in regret, because of what was coming next. The future from which the energy field he was not supporting was removing him, so as to step up. Step in. Take over. Settle down into his apartment, be the energy field that would expand and grow there, with his assistance now, for the next ten years—only after which I would leave this "hermitage," rubbing my eyes to see the light outside, after being almost exclusively in the "inner light." But first, something else would work itself in. Something involving—Hunter. However, let us describe the new energy field that both helped Willy in his transition (the shock of sudden, early death) and helped promote Earth consciousness of the multidimensionality of events and all of us, all life.

✻

The bell first sounded shortly thereafter, making that illogical comment "Hello, Mrs. Bell" literally mind-boggling. Yet it was one more "impossible" day-to-day occurrence death left in its wake.

But immediately the apartment was occupied by magnetoelectrical fields, including a bell that, though nonphysical, was clearly audible. Yet it was one more "impossible" day-to-day occurrence death left in its wake. A part of the long journey through the unconscious. To take the direct route preempts many unknown routes. But to come in from the unconscious leaves all other routes open.

Chris's energy class led the whole group in a meditation to try to "assist" Willy if he wanted assistance—send him light. What I picked up—bursting into my mind—was "Get ready, 'cause here I come," that cassette Willy'd identified with—turned high in volume—that included the lyrics (by Smokey Robinson): "Fee-fi-fo-fum / *Look out baby, now here I come* . . . (Aaaahhhh, aaaahhhh, aaaahhhh, aaaahhhh.)" . . . It filled my meditation space: "(Get ready, 'cause here I come. Get ready.")

Yes, get ready.

"You know I'm comin' 'cause here I come . . ."

Actually, it went on, unnoticed then by me: "(Be outta sight.)"

Enter the Bell and Other Psychic Phenomena

Leaving her translator job at the European Union for a week, Helen Titchen-Beeth (then Helen Titchen) stayed with me, sleeping in my double bed. Not used to being psychic, she nevertheless discovered this forte in being better than I in sensing Willy's presence. He was, she told me, looking through her eyes, making her "see through" my nightgown.

The situation was a bit like the plot of the *Ghost*; though I had not seen it, it was the highest grossing film in the United States in 1990, having been released a half year earlier.

The bell was audibly there after his passing at thirty-four, just the beginning of most people's mature years. It came almost immediately, sometimes "rung" by Willy (an invisible bell that sounded in physical time and space) to underscore a communication, a thought, a TV sentence. But we have jumped truly into other dimensions in reciting this. However, we have only jumped into them as they intercepted the physical plane, and as I have narrated elsewhere. We have not made more sense of them than before. And we shall.

Almost immediately a second phenomenon took over: what I called "computer-PK." I had never experienced anything like it before. But in January I went out and bought my first home computer and printer. What I then experienced were printouts that differed from the on-screen text. In the printing, when I pushed "print," the page slid out *with text altered from the text on-screen*: with highlighted phrases, in much-reduced word count, the rest of the words gone. Or rather, I didn't just push "print." I endeavored (successfully) to give the system a nudge. Why? To amp up the energy. So I turned the printer on/off/on. Ah, it operated inside a well-known science of energy surges: they created a destabilizing environment into which oddities could creep, grasping the energy, redirecting it. That is, if the interceptor was powerful enough. Mine was.

In the first instance, the bell rang moments beforehand, signaling that if blank pages started spewing out of the printer, not to turn it off or give up. I didn't. These blank pages were followed by a page of *transformed* text.

And here I need to refer back to Zurich. The inserted numbers and words, in this initial stage (but not later) seemed to be keying into Bible passage references. For example, "p815X," beside a word at the top of the page—did it associate with the annotated concordance of the Bible I'd bought at Paradestraat (Parade Street) in Zurich in 1985 or 1986? That flashed into my mind. Ah-ha. So that's why I impulsively bought that book. Wait six years, and you may unravel a mystery.

Thus began ten years of roughly 12/7 concentrated experimentation with mind through matter at the computer. In a fun way. I thoroughly enjoyed myself.

Mariah had said, remember, she thought my soul grouping was working on "mind through matter." Al Miner had made one further comment about the group project, that it was trying to spread its consciousness—the Christ consciousness.

How ethereal it all was. I could feel it throughout my apartment, throughout my cells. Like being nourished in manna.

> Ten o'clock at night. Time to cut off the computer. The sounds continue. There are instructions being processed. I go away from the computer and the sounds continue—something is causing the computer to receive instructions. There is no machine to measure what kind of energetic field might be here and yet there is surely a nonphysical element. The scene: inside an apartment in Belgium, where the living room has been turned into my office. Amid the hand-crafted objects, there is a simple . . .

—so begins a record I made in 1991, memorializing how the computer was acting. This was the second psychic phenomenon that followed on the heels of Willy's death.

But what could I possibly do, for structure, with a novel now being invaded by cosmic Christ consciousness writings, metaphysically focused—or Christ-related poetry—in transition related to the Earth?

❋

Chris, just after Willy died, did what he called a "soul reading" for me. But he immediately said he could not "find my soul." I was watching a face in lavender energy right in front of my face. I said: Look here. He said, well, yes that was Jesus. "Somehow your soul is related to him. But not the one in the Bible—the whiplashing one, who took his whip against the hypocrites."

⁂

That was in January 1991. When I was told he was "gone," in the same breath his sister said that in addition Jan had died as well, only ten days before.

⁂

Jan Mensaert wrote a few short letters to me from the clinic where he was to die, saying to publish his book (*The Suicide Mozart*), and summoned me a few times to see him between 1987 and 1990, just to tell me to publish it. He was in the clinic because he had no one to live with and was "a danger to himself" if left alone. Thus, committed by his mother. I would not have done it, right or wrong.

I did not see how he endured the emptiness, the static repetition, the noises, because there were also insane people there and people who had "given up," never "lived," and so forth. But he sat it out, in mostly steely silence, not even escaping into TV. Indeed, I had dreamed someone was "wounded beyond despair." I've no doubt who. But still clinging to his "Higher Self." Part of his memory had succumbed to alcohol over time, and he now firmly believed that I had left him on a "bed of typhus."

He had once, after he knew my address in Zurich, written me, saying he was going to lose his mind. And not to tell this, but he was not resisting because he felt he was meant to learn this way how to live in the heart. It seemed another extreme taken to absurdity, typical of him, as when he stabbed his paintings. I had a physical revulsion against destruction. But it was a major part of his path of "playing with freedom" and not fearing death.

Then, one day, choosing among the many implausible ways tried or contemplated or dallied with before—turn a screw driver into his head, jump off a wall, cut his wrists in a tub, take all the pills in sight and go out as Popeye the Drunken Sailor, or pretend to take arsenic day-by-day—having sombered into merely the position of having outgrown his life (other things calling him: things this side of himself heard and said to the child that he was, yes you have done your work), he, and if this sounds contradictory to the above paragraph, they were both true at the same time, in two directions of looking toward the future—one where there was a future here, one where the future was elsewhere but the past exonerated—he died. He committed suicide (having hoped, he wrote in a poem, to be "pure in the last hour"). He was by then a nonparticipator. He left, to become—one can speculate (not quite in the snap of a finger; there would be healing required first)—the self he had given up in the first place, when coming here (a dream said) "on a mission, the work of Divine Sin." (A phrase from a dream.) He left, to do the next work of his soul.

Can all this be true?

I would hope that if I leave anything behind, it is the habit of wider thinking, the habit of stretch, of the solution beyond the boundary of solution, the explanation beyond the last boundary of explanation, where resides the truth *coming into being*—for which lives are paid, by bringing us to the border where we stop. Or it may be the border where knowing something doesn't fit, doesn't make sense, we go on and become—in universal contexts, however—individual. Then we say what is left out, what no one else can. Then we stand shining in the only light we have. Then we talk to each other in what Kierkegaard called "poetic infinity." Then we are unreproducible and uncopyable, though we can be stood on top of.

❋

This young poet, concealed from all others, in his younger days drew cathedral after cathedral, interspersed into pages of poetry and novel—for whom the tall, straight lines of the cathedrals of the past had privately so much significance that the bombing of some meant that all he stood for—or was?—had been bombed. But he had kept the relationship with so many things private, just like the boxes of music composition, some of which no one but he heard played.

The death date—December 27—is (for the Eastern Orthodox) the celebration day of St. Stephen, stoned to death; it is also a date observed in honor of the Slaying of the Innocents to try to prevent the growing-up of the child Christ. All these symbols swirling around together, put into the box (Pandora's?) of anti-self, in the final Jan Mensaert work, are introducing something even more radical yet. A theme in *The Suicide Mozart* was that on Vega Fünf were masters who could not "go to the next level" without finding a replacement—sometimes having to "create" one, as with the fictional Mozart, guiding the semiautobiographical Fiss in having shadow experiences for him, but not destroying his will.

He always wanted things to be taken to the genius statement—the thing no one else had said! So we tried. As if one might spray genius seeds, in *unconscious* planting. From that, perhaps in being picked up—without having lived one's genius in a sense, for it was too unconsciously located—to make it survive. For it would be beaten into ploughshares of its own planting. Curiously as well, the beginning precisely returned to the end, for the Santorini suicide envelope was stamped "December 27." It bore the Greek suicide letter that decided me to go to his side in Belgium. And that means— BUT WE HAVE TO STOP SOMEWHERE.

Afternote:

James Hillman says that reading *The Arabian Nights*, as Gopi Krisna did—he could have alluded to the storytellers at the Jemaa el-Fna square in Marrakesh as well—put one in touch with the transpersonal and archetypal level of things; not the conscious pathways, but the unconscious information that these by-streams and side passages can reveal—*unconscious pilgrimages* on the pathways of the unknown futures. As the lifework of Gopi Krishna pursued some of these personal-myth checkpoints, is this, then, also a story about pathways into the unconscious evolutionary future? That is, the real pathways, those that no one knows until being on them. And figuring out where they are. Is it an unconscious MESSAGE??? No, in the end, no longer unconscious.

❋

Even his suicides were original and up-in-the-air—an artistic act that might or might not result in death, and he himself was not in charge of the result or particularly concerned which it might be, to all intents and appearances. Yet the childlike aspect redeemed this irresponsibility, the playful interaction with circumstance, the utterly serious relationship to the art of everything, the sense of style, the refusal to live on the surface. He once said, "I would hate to die with a stranger"—meaning AS a stranger. Principles such as this give credence to the seriousness of an investigation of his life. He didn't want to just ask, "Who am I?" but to experience it.

Referring to a page of an unpublished text I wrote then: he was introduced as a man with an ailment: "Too much imagination."

This ailment was incurable, as things stood. Still, after his death, someone offered a challenging insight, that "He could make art out of suffering. Art out of everything. But not the rock."

This comment came through Dr. Russell Dean Park.

❋

So tell the story any way you like. This is the only way I can tell it.

But it's fantastical, not reality.

Maybe so. But as he said. "It's Gotterdammerung to have the artist personality and not be one." Not be one? Well, not a successful, famous one. I cannot imagine anyone being more an artist than he was, even if his artistry ran across the borderline into the anti-artist, which, in his own words, was intent on killing the artist. *But who won*? I think, though not in published works (though some were published, if in Flemish), the artist hands down.

❋

Willy died, I was saying, ten days after Jan—so I too lost two husbands at fifty.

I stayed that extra night, never dreaming it would result in his death while seemingly bringing to life literally *the car accident I dreamed of during the approach (shadow) of Milton's physical death ten years earlier and also the car accident dream Russ had just before Willy's death*, coinciding with Milton's changing form as a spirit (my seven Kundalini episodes, once a week, receiving activations, memories). And that Willy would set out to his death January 6. dying on January 7, matching the date on the telegram:

Girdle of O
Girder of I
Inviolate
Unbreakable

And that Old Christmas—that is, following the Julian calendar—is on that date. Funny. Russian Orthodox Christmas. Milton was of Russian Jewish background.

Willy, distraught (half my fault), had hit me the morning we left Portugal. We were on pins and needles of up-tight nerves by this time. I didn't fault him for it particularly. I had been half to blame. As we drove from the Brussels airport, he said to me that he was 50 percent wrong, and I was 50 percent wrong. I agreed. The fault was 50–50.

I remember, ready to go to the hospital, I said to Willy that this (his striking me) couldn't happen again, "Or I'll have to leave." He answered, "It's an . . . appointment."

Why that odd word?

It must have been uttered from some other dimension, the one that would now begin sending the signals, which none of us, whichever one was then the listener, heard in time. But if it was an unconscious suicide, it was already set up to happen, anyway. On the other hand, I also knew that nothing was predetermined that could not be changed, with enough unconscious energy, enough *electricity—or any other expression of this depth. The soul level didn't have to leave. The "old" Willy did, one way or the other.*

Because the bell came immediately, and I was swept into another action-packed development, I had no time to grieve. It was the inauguration of the New Year—and in nine months, I was to be at Owl Farm with Hunter (for I would telephone, again out of the blue).

But there are reasons for *this tight knot of associations and events.* On another level I was following a blueprint, continuing from the Initiation in Zurich, *that Initiation coming on the heel of Milton's death, a death which gave me the final inducement me to leave Jan, which began the long climb up the mountain of consciousness in earnest,* the climb to where he was, calling, letting me know first in dreams that he was not dead and eventually that he was—he said in dreams—"coming back." And those very words later echoed in Willy's "Get ready, 'cause here I come."

From that moment of Milton's death, November 29, 1981, more

or less as I watched the parade, to that other moment in January 1991, when Hunter was on the horizon, barely months off, my whole consciousness shifted. I can expect the readers will want to know what emotions were set in motion by this death, *how such a trial was endured*. In that context, the techniques of computer-PK and other psychic "condolences" made sense. The New Consciousness was intent on not letting go but also not holding on, of making the best of the situation, of connecting to higher forces and awarenesses, of going to this School of Consciousness now that it had every inducement, for it promised spiritual knowledge, comfort, certainties. It promised to help the Earth.

❋

With Willy, the bell additionally helped us work through lingering issues. I discovered he had been to a prostitute. I turned all his photos over, facing down, knowing he was watching. W*hy*? I muttered to myself. The bell rang. I began to imagine reasons he'd done this. The bell followed the thoughts.

Curiosity, "wanting to compare." It rang to underscore the right thought.

Not a good answer by half, but he was "dead" undeniably, and where was he? H*ere*. And wasn't that the ultimate statement, more important than the failings?

❋

The death was premature for Jan and Willy both, *at the same time*, and on another level, of impossibility-made-possible, I could hear the song about fools falling in love and believe that such an ending was foolishness. Nevertheless, facilitated, I firmly believed, by Willy's soul grouping, or if not that exactly, an even more transcendental soul grouping, and that it had been foreshadowed in the dream before Milton died, thus in some way predetermined, *but at the same time avoidable*, just like his own vision of the crash meeting him head on in his windshield—difficult, possible, to avoid, yet not avoided. And not for lack of trying. He crashed into the tree anyway, at just under thirty-five years old, Earth-time.

Enter Owl Farm

Meanwhile, Owl Farm was filled with merriment; a horrendous legal issue had been resolved. It had consumed much of Hunter's attention in 1990. As described on The Great Thompson Hunt (website), "The year [1990] barely begins when HST is charged with assault and possession of drugs and explosives after a disastrous meeting with Gail Palmer-Slater. Palmer-Slater, a porn-star turned ophthalmologist's wife, allegedly had her breast tweaked by HST.[14] She filed charges. In what he considered a violation of his rights, a police search ensued. The Great Thompson Hunt lays out the sequence of events:

> What better way to ring in the New Year than get hit with enough felonies to put one away for fifty years? HST found himself in that predicament when Gail Palmer-Slater, a woman of many colorful careers, refused to join HST in his hot tub . . . what followed allowed the authorities to search Owl Farm for 11 hours. Of course, they found a lot more than just peacocks and used typewriter ribbons.[15]

However, he was exonerated.

I wouldn't say that Willy died and the next day I called Hunter. No, but it's not far off. I dialed. Could it still be a good number? We hadn't spoken since January a year ago.

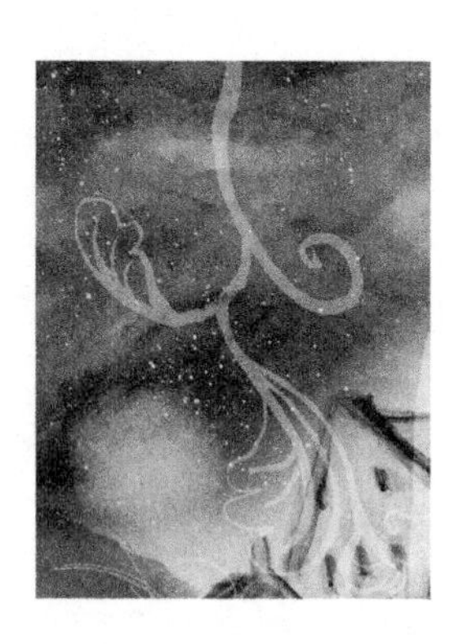

PART THREE

The Lunevillelaan Letters to Hunter
The 2023 Version

January 20, 2023

In the early 1990s, I took Hunter as my confidant. This is the story of things I sent him and wrote and didn't send him and why and how it's important (if it is) to his story.

The things I'm describing took place in another dimension; that is, a lot of them did. They took place in this dimension as far as I was concerned, but they came "down" to me from my soul level. I can insert a lot of new information and context, having discovered, mostly unmailed, letters I wrote to Hunter in the early 1990s, when I was still packed with that energy he'd put into me live in my visit to Owl Farm. The energy took a long time to dissipate. And while it was settling down, *there was such an intensity inside*. Bear with any repetition that invariably appears, in setting the stage in this new *Lunevillelaan Letters context* to keep the flow moving along, although I've cut whole cloth to reduce the repetition tremendously.

By that time, of the three main male figures in my life (men I met in the mid-1960s, all of whom I would call confidants), only Hunter was still alive.

I had consulted Milton Klonsky for his wise appraisal of events in my life, his one-liner, condensed, aphoristic advice, in annual visits to his Greenwich Village West Fourth and Eleventh Street apartment right up through 1980; I skipped coming to the United States from Larache, Morocco, that year, so I knew nothing, by normal channels of information, about his approaching death, which took place in November 1981—me not finding out even after the fact he had died until the summer of 1982.

My estranged husband, Jan Mensaert, died by suicide on December 27, 1990, just days prior to when Willy Van Luyten, with whom I was living in Belgium, died by auto accident.

So in January 1991—faced, in his apartment, now mine—with mysterious aftereffects of Willy's death, I felt sure my old friend Hunter was the logical person to call.

But let me go back to when I first encountered mysterious after-effects of a death and why what happened next in 1991 fitted into a sequence that, if you think of our 3-D world as only part of the universe of life, as only some of the dimensions we live in, had a reason to be interesting to me, to capture my attention, to draw in my awareness.

First Indication of Anything Other than 3-D *in My Life*: 1980

It was the summer of 1980. I lived in Larache, Morocco, with Jan. Annually, I spent a month in the United States in my parents' house. That was the deal with myself. I'd give myself a month to get back to myself, especially in view of the fact that, as one observer put it to Jan, "She thinks through your eyes." Well, *not during that month*. I had other eyes, and I reserved them for this cooling-off period, or rather intense US seclusion.

So in 1980, like usual, I went to the local Greenville, NC, university library and this time got out *Man and His Symbols* by Carl Jung, my introduction to this famous psychologist. Alone back in my room at my parents', surrounded by library books, mostly classics like Flaubert's Madame *Bovary*, I read that all people—none excluded—who had any interest in *knowing themselves* HAD to follow their dreams. An imperative. An injunction. It was eye opening. Forty years, and it had never occurred to me.

I'd lavishly perused every avenue into myself as part of my lifelong devotion to writing. In fact, I was still in the midst of struggling with my "big book," which had gotten me three fellowships to MacDowell Colony. I could get the *very* end but not the lead-up to it. Something was missing. Now, Jung told me emphatically that sitting and convoking inspiration wasn't enough. He did not mince words. I had to get on that "royal road to the unconscious," dreams.

In Morocco, I set a pad by my bed. It was September 1980.

Before sleep now, I asked a question, then woke in the middle of the night to record them, developing increasingly effective methods to remember them. Dreams had been waiting at the doorstep. The threshold of my consciousness, pacing and stammering. In the middle of the night they flooded in. Not shy about accepting this invitation.

I'd spend the next morning documenting them in their entirety and playing with the images. "Active imagination," it's called by Jung.

I began this practice spontaneously, not realizing it had a definition. It was a road deeper into "the Unconscious." Jung included in that term the collective unconscious as well.

No matter that my big book was in prose, my active imagination was shoveling up image "trails" for it. I spontaneously "followed," finding they had destinations that led to punch lines that involved elaborate word play. I pruned. I had poems. It was amazing.

But what also developed were what Jung called Big Dreams. Before long, in 1981, they led me to imagine my main male protagonist, based on Milton Klonsky, dead *and how I would feel, how I would react*. Naturally, it was all made up, I knew. H*e can't die*. I *need him alive too much*. I had him almost immunized against death. But side by side with my character, Milton was in fact dying. The dreams were just turning fact into fiction instead of the other way around. I didn't know. Did I?

My "father"—what could be clearer?—told me in a dream he was "going home," and I said, "Wait till I get there. I'm not afraid." Not afraid of what? My dreams were deep into ladling out predictions. I even "flew in," according to my dreams, to try to alert people to a heart attack he was having, and they paid me no mind. (That heart attack, or stroke, I found out a year and a half later, was real.)

November 29, 1981, Milton died in a hospital in New York City in a room full of Puerto Ricans, blaring their music (he couldn't afford a private room). No one informed me Why should they? That job was left up to another avenue.

My unconscious seemed quite privy to the news, having already imbibed it.

In New York again finally, in my summer 1982 visit to Greenville, I phoned his number during my one-night stopover—expecting to take my usual amble, excited, drawing out the suspense, as I left my Pickwick Arms, East Fifty-first Street Third Avenue, hotel room and moved down Sixth Avenue to his Greenwich Village rent-controlled apartment. That was on the one hand. Below the surface, I was both surprised and unsurprised that an unfamiliar voice picked up.

Not surprised, no, but floored as if the bottom had dropped right out of my world. Devastated. Crushed. Shocked. I had given him the role of wisdom master in my life. The Highest Truth. He contained it, I had decided. He *knew everything* I *needed to know*. Well, I was only forty-one. I wasn't yet convinced I could get answers that deep for myself, yet he had shown he could steer me through the wildest or most dangerous courses, apply pithy phrases to them that a poet understands, hard, cold, warm, pulled down from some On High stratosphere.

His friends, such as Beat author Sy Krim, knew this; Krim chronicled, first in *Two Teachers, Nuts, Two Human Beings* in jazzy, profound language, how this man dazzled him, but he had not taken down, as I did, his phrases. *From the very second I met Milton, I put his phrases into my character's mouth.* In fact, "Robert" was born in that instant, in that Greenwich Village bar, as Sarah Uman, a Chicago-native daughter of a Black jazz musician, introduced us—in admiration of his hipsterness.

On one visit, when I described Jan's suicidalness, Milton—who else would dare be so pragmatically direct?—having taken me to a party he was obligated to go to when I appeared, unannounced, at his door on my annual visit to New York ("You were a little wraith, almost," he said, and "Here we are again," appreciating the familiarity, as I did), advised in his typical turn of phrase, serious, looking me in the eye: *"Give him something to rise to.* OR *then go down with him.* ***But don't*** *be a bystander while this man commits suicide."*

He knew the topic intimately from singer Beverly Kinney and other friends he called *sui generis* (unclassifiable); he said I was *sui generis* too.

It was in this background that I drew Hunter into the role of confidant in the 1990s. I had always needed a "big" energy type. You can call it projection. And it was, partly. It was, however, pinpoint accurate. I did select Big Energy males, and I am getting to how in the 1990s that role (easily designated by me) fell to Hunter. Another way of saying this was, I always needed a genius around.

But to get to the spiritual side of the story, which the 1990s focused on, I have to go back to the Death of Milton, where it all crept out of the unconscious. Before that, I had not thought in terms of a spiritual dimension except in the sense that I received inspiration and closed myself off with it, like artists did.

But in 1981 the dreams marched right into the book in little poems made from their images.

In 1982, learning that Milton had died in late November 1981, I looked back at the dreams and found many precognitive signals my logical self had ignored, squashed, and denied. Also, Jung concurred, in theory, with my intuition; it was normal, he declared, that an approaching death might give "advance warnings."

So I had to *have it out with myself* especially as Milton began to march into my dreams, very convincingly, realistically, now that I knew he was dead. I returned to Morocco, knowing he was dead, but that was the beginning of the end of the marriage. It was as if Milton had occupied one "prong" of myself. Held the fort there. (Yes, a mixed metaphor.) Neptune, indeed. With that voided, I could not leave the space exposed. I had to fill it myself. But how?

By early 1983, after several brief separations, I'd had enough. I left Jan for good. I *anxiously told myself to make peace with the fact that my intuition had known* Milton *was dying*. How had it known? I didn't want to be scared of something "real" that was trying to reach me. But neither did I want to believe anything pseudo-factual, thought through sloppily. Alone, I didn't have the tools, the consciousness, to trust my conclusions. It was not even that Jan would not have believed my intuition capable of giving advance announcements. He could go even deeper than that. But he allowed me no space to discover myself.

Not long after escaping from the marriage—not even telling him I was leaving—back in the States, I consulted Al Miner, as described in detail earlier. Below are some details I omitted before. I found Al through a recommendation at the Association for Research and Enlightenment. ARE, the Edgar Cayce organization, vouched that Al had the highest measure of accuracy of any psychic they'd tested. Additionally, he was on the board of Atlantic University. He discovered he was psychic totally accidentally on an unplanned trip to Nebraska with friends who were consulting a multiple-PhD expert about the woman's weight. She was going there to be hypnotized.

When a slot fell open due to a cancellation, the psychiatrist/reverend/hypnotist Dr. E. Arthur (Art) Winkler offered it to Al. Would he like to try? Al sat down to be hypnotized, and his channel-self emerged. Stepped forth. Startled the onlookers by doing an Edgar Cayce-type "reading."

While Al had the life-altering experience of being clad in a heavy robe and sandals in a desert oasis centuries earlier, waiting for someone to arrive—who? Jesus—meanwhile, unknown to his then-off-Earth self, he was channeling the Lama Sing spirit group, on a soul level.

Thus, Al Miner started his psychic career reluctantly while being an early computer engineer. As my website recounts:

> What happened when he went back to a time several centuries in the past (while simultaneously diagnosing illnesses in the "present") became the turning point, leading up to the decades as full-time channel that occurred since. However, the conversion was not without preparation or "tests" . . .
>
> *The "chance" hypnosis session happened after several out-of-the-ordinary [life-threatening, or life-directing] occurrences in Al's earlier life.*

By 1984, I was doing full-time volunteer work for Dr. Robert Van de Castle, psychologist and dream researcher at the University of Virginia Medical School. From there, pondering why I felt I was in contact with Milton—was it even possible? was I correct?—I wrote Al to ask for a reading.

Definitively yes, Lama Sing, confirmed—in the mailed cassette in December that shook me to the core. I've already recorded this.

But he went much further. The only reason I had these suspicions in 1983, consulting Al, was the depth of shock in that I was unmoored, bereft of my compass, my steering mechanism. Milton, to whom I had delegated all the attributes of Highest Truth and the search for it—*was he reporting back to me*? An out-of-body Ulysses writing to Penelope? Now that he was no more in an Earth body, there was every indicator, I thought, that he was continuing to lead me, on a different level. That is, if I hadn't misread *everything*. My logical mind wanted this cleared up.

In the reading in 1984, when asked by me if there was a group project, Al said yes, that the soul grouping Milton was in, "several dimensions in consciousness beyond the Earth," *which I was also in*—that last floored me—was undertaking a project associated with the Christ light; that is—he defined—"simply the illumination of the universal nature of each soul by the intensification of those forces which relate to this consciousness.

"So it is called the pathway of return unto God, the Christ Consciousness."[16]

Or the "return home."

Obviously, a return in consciousness.

Having this spelled out, what to do? I *could not get away from it. It was my own consciousness introducing itself to me.* I enrolled at the C. G. Jung Institute in Küsnacht, Switzerland, arriving in October 1984. Surely Jung could help me out now.

In a New York City stopover en route, I phoned Hunter. Whoever answered promised to tell him I called. He phoned me at midnight; joyously hopping back and forth in animated conversation, we talked a couple of hours; a dream afterwards depicted it as tap dancing. I recounted that because of the extremely high—white light—energy field in Zurich, I'd given just up alcohol, coffee, red meat. He shared his attempt to give up something harmful. Slipping right into the confidant role.

However, that ended that. No word more in Zurich.

Instead, as recounted earlier, in Zurich, I had my Initiation, in which I began to be taken inside levels of consciousness, of vibration—not held in general here.

Also, at the Institute I was surrounded by intuitives and feeling types and by visiting teachers who spoke expert Jungian philosophy, some with a history of initiations. Then came the Initiation itself.

Though "lowly on the totem pole," I was shown ways to interact with the Earth that were beyond what I'd ever heard of. Remember, the soul grouping project was about universality as part of the Christ consciousness. Or call it a term I learned from Al Miner, the Living Christ in each person. The potential for it. Al, or Lama Sing, said I had that potential life path.

And this seemed to be drawing me in.

Now for Hunter. He seems out of the picture. But we know from Part One, he was not.

This Initiator spirit guide(s) explained they could lift out the pattern Hunter and I made together in New York and place it in the air in the proximity of someone they wanted me to meet. If it descended on that person—by, I now know, resonance—kept on this high level, it would fit their intent. However, the great danger was that it would be intercepted on a lower level, of physical attraction that would then be intensified. That made sense to me.

Now I balked and felt this was outrageous. But I assumed, and later this seemed confirmed, they had the consent of Hunter's soul. *You know this from Part One.*

What it produced—instead of love affairs, however—was deep friendships—unlikely ones—I will never forget. Never.

No romance. Not till I met Willy Van Luyten, who had just enough of a "pure" spirit—uneducated, a truck driver—to live by instinct and fill this bill till it got too heavy for him because (as I was shown in pictures of the guide's "personalities," or energy locations) if Light is put into a person, it at first adds Light, but can quickly overwhelm. Then it turns dark. So you know all this if you've read the book so far. Why does it turn dark? Because consciousness does not have definitions laid out for you to follow; the guidelines shift—all the time. Like in quicksand. Too fast for a human intellect to keep up. You can't memorize the "right" thing to do.

It creates loneliness, "on the edge," figuring out what *this one situation* is demanding without by rote recalling the answer that went before. No, there are subtleties to consider. No parallels to follow, except, as Milton had put it, in the *sui generis*.

Now, I was convinced that this all involved my soul and that this soul counted heavily on me and had *a history I didn't know*, which they were drawing on. So I felt bound *not to betray my soul. How many of us ever get into a position where that is remotely possible?* As I *was in the dark to a large extent about what was going on, I felt a heavy weight on me. I could betray my soul. Shivers.*

If she had put me in this position, it must be because I belonged there.

Fast forward to 1987. I met, fell in love with, and moved in with Willy Van Luyten in Tienen, Belgium. He died. Abruptly.

Which brings us to the beginning of the story. We pick up with me phoning Hunter, needing a confidant. Willy had carried his load, heavy with shadow but never taking his Cross off from around his neck, through fights, cocaine (then clean) as far as he could. His shadow was growing. He was feeling drawn toward cocaine. Even if it was a temporary setback, this project had no time for it. He was "taken out," you say. Or define it anyway you wish. But the next phase began.

I recontacted Hunter, carrying all this awareness, feeling that his soul was "on my side," wanting the contact to be positive, knowing he was strong enough to bolster me. Feeling it not off track, however it turned out. Wherever it led.

And it was to lead far. To Owl Farm, no less. But let's not jump there.

❋

After Willy died, his apartment (now mine) was a laboratory or treasure trove—take your pick—of off-Earth type communication. It was as if the apartment were lofted above, to where such incidents as we call psychic occurred "scientifically," as a matter of course.

The "spirit committees" were, with no holds barred, teaching me, using me to get ideas into the Earth atmosphere and instructing me in what I probably already knew but not in this physical form of myself. Things easy to accept off-Earth but not here. Now.

So I phoned Hunter.

And we were off to the races.

It gave me, in some small manner, a way to relieve myself of the privacy of *holding everything in*.

Meanwhile, in Tienen I had a birthday party for (the departed) Willy, April 27. I invited his, mostly truck driver, friends. And mine. And they came. I was astonished. *Why did I not do this before*? We should try things we are afraid of. Afraid of refusals. His friends came eagerly, unhesitantly, and they communicated with the bell, adding witnesses. One close friend of Willy's said the bell even visited in his home.

I must have told Hunter about the party (wouldn't I?); it was perhaps mention of the bell that elicited the remark, "Margaret, you talk the craziest of anyone I know."

Among my confidences there were, at any rate, surely some about psychic experiences, such as of Kundalini. After all, what else is a confidant for but to confide in?

I had been having a Kundalini awakening, including kriya episodes, which in my case might start with a leg shaking, then fill the room with shaking, as the intelligent divine energy let some truths loose, and if this happens to you, you cannot fight the awarenesses that come to you or the belief in them afterwards.

Whether or not I told Hunter about the kriyas, for sure the topic is relevant to my visit to Owl Farm. You could not put kriyas in a basket and firmly close the top. In fact, if I hadn't kept the lid on Hunter's snake in my office in New York tamped down tightly enough to keep it imprisoned decades ago, I had not learned enough since to tamp down Kundalini when it wanted out either.

Hunter's girlfriend, Catherine Sabonis-Chafee, had just moved out. The hole she left, opening up the space for long conversations, I immediately filled. Thank you very much. Sometimes he called; sometimes I did.

Early 1991: we were a "twosome" again by phone, with no photograph or physical image. "Do you still have . . . those long tresses?" he asked.

With his night prowling, it worked out. I adjusted my sleeping habits, hoping—I might be wakened. Everything was new.

One time he was making tomato soup. I began to associate him with tomatoes. He was buying new equipment for the kitchen—an oven?—and asked my advice. "Can you cook?" And so forth. For we were as on a blind date insofar as years having passed since the '70s. He read into the phone "Let the Trials Begin," which opened his latest book. *Did I think it was funny*? Absolutely, to laugh out loud. In it Hunter listens to Andrew's ravings,

> rolling his eerie phrases like a man gone wild in a trance, and I began to pay more attention . . . Jesus! I thought. This is pretty good stuff. I recognized a certain *rhythm*, a weird *meter* of some kind that reached me even if I wasn't listening. . . It was strange. I had a feeling that I knew it all from somewhere, but I couldn't quite place it . . .
>
> Soon I felt a queer humming all over my body, like falling into music . . . (p. 23)

The piece was called "Electricity." He is familiar with electricity. It is, he writes, "always homesick":

> It is like a hillbilly with a shotgun and a jug of whiskey gone mad for revenge on some enemy . . .
>
> [Electricity] likes to lay in wait under some darkened bridge and swill whiskey like a troll full of hate until your victim appears—drunk and careless and right on schedule—so close that you almost feel embarrassed about pulling the trigger.
>
> That is how electricity likes to work. It has no feelings except loneliness, laziness, and a hatred of anything that acts like resistance . . . like a wharf rat with its back to the wall—it won't fight unless it has to, but then it will fight to the death.
>
> Electricity is the same way: it will kill anything that gets in its way once it thinks it sees a way to get home quick . . .
>
> Zaaappp!
>
> Right straight up your finger and through your heart and your chest cavity and down the other side . . . And it wants the shortest route—which is not around a corner and through a muscle mass in the middle of your back, but it will go that way if it has to.

But Hunter recognizes the "dirty, evil, thieving little bastard!" who said he had authored this text had stolen it from him (p. 26).

As we felt our way through the missing time segments, I revealed some of my private experiences (which ones, I don't know). Hunter exclaimed, "I feel like I'm talking to a naked child." I felt warmed; he was not threatened off. Everything, on the contrary, seemed to propel us toward each other—toward meeting—inevitably, as if the plan had only hung in the air suspended as to *when* for twenty-one years. But I was doubtless cautious in confidences.

"Let's meet. I don't know why we didn't do this before," he said.

In fact I had a pretty good idea why. But he was speaking from the heart, wearing it out in the open. We set the date. May 13.

We would meet at Woody Creek, his "fortified compound." What a dashing idea.

Last seen in New York City in 1969, he had been saying goodbye to me in his Fifth Avenue hotel. I last had a letter in 1973. Lifetimes were lived in between. Both of us knew this meeting had been held in reserve, as if we had held the idea privately through thick and thin, though I didn't allow my thoughts to go that far. Such a meeting might not be the "best" idea for either of us, considering all the water that had gone under the dam. But we didn't care.

Common sense might say this was an impossible dream. But his secretary/friend Deborah Fuller sent me a few photos of Hunter and a sample of his letters to others, to prepare me to leap across the gap.

⁂

To Hunter's credit and my surprise, he put out not the slightest feeler about how I had held up physically over the years—except being curious if I had my long red "tresses." Was I hobbling with a cane, two hundred fifty pounds, back bent down to the floor—a white-haired fifty-year-old of unknown weight! He asked not one question about that.

Wasn't it carrying things too far, signing on sight unseen for come what may—having decided not to care? This re-created the mode in which we'd met in 1966, conversing, sight unseen, as two "voices," creating and falling into "vibes" together, admittedly, unavoidably.

I was very excited about the impending trip. From my apartment I fitted it into the spirit initiations, the writing, the bell.

In May, I sent questions to Mariah. I was to arrive at Owl Farm the thirteenth, on a one-way ticket. After that? We would see.

Would that that tape were still intact. I flew to my sister Norma's and her family's, where Hunter phoned, creating a stir. Then I got onto the plane headed west.

I threw myself into what came next, short as it turned out to be, unforgettable as it nevertheless was, for both of us, I dare say.

Now, be prepared as you read ahead, unless (and even if) you have read this tale in a prior book by me. I'll tell it differently and succinctly.

There was a factual gap between when I knew Hunter in person or closely, beginning in 1966 (working on his first book together, *Hell's Angels and just after*), and the period post-that, so different, when I married (1970), after which there came little contact for years. No, let's be explicit, decades. In between the early '70s, including planning and writing *Las Vegas*—and the later reconnecting period, in 1991—much went down.

I never told him what happened to me, except in snatches. I was not really aware just how much of a cult figure he was, though I did know the sensational aspect.

To get this part over, because I don't know how I am going to deal with it and to get over the parts where the obvious questions are, the unavoidable ones, let us start with the airport arrival of me in 1991, into Aspen, Colorado—small but not, like Pitkin County today, filled with parked private jets. Hunter is picking me up, every action at this point replaying itself in slow motion as this 6 feet 5- or 4- or 3-figure—*much taller than I remembered, a good deal heavier too than the slim, trim early-thirties-year-old*—swiftly hurries in, a little late; comes straight for me without hesitation, not showing any surprise at how I look—his alert eyes appearing to lock directly into position, spotting me at first glance, myself the target singled out, towering over me, and I am one full foot shorter! This sensation of height, having to look up, I'd forgotten.

Alone, face to face. And yet it wasn't awkward. Kind of: *I told you so* (him to himself, me to myself). *See, simple.*

According to Ralph Steadman, Hunter was at his most prankish in airports. He had been known to charge a customs depot to retrieve his elephant tusks, thought confiscated. This was the *anti-scene* of that. Outside, on the open road, In the silence a sense of presence, he was maneuvering that notorious red shark. Words did not have to be exchanged. Rather like the first time we met, when he mumbled hello, intent on opening a shaving kit and drawing out two Ballantine beers—in my Random House office.

What I remember clearly, headed toward Aspen, is the projection of his smile, filling a bandwidth between our faces—pouring energy right into me, straight to the heart, heating the imagination, the expectation. Did it extend beyond the range of visible light? If smiles could do that, yes, I think so.

And then a convulsive shiver—he snorts cocaine. Then is back like before: charming, no shouts of bats on the horizon, phenomenally *right there*, a person I was overly relaxed beside—the Hunter I went "way back with," and had this baffling history with that he didn't know about, in another dimension! At least, that was on my mind, *not knowing how that dimension would play a role now, if at all. Would it sit on its hands. Would it make an appearance, drop clues, do something "impossible"? Or leave it all to me? Play it "our" way?*

Was I the same fellow conspirator who had, with a mischievous smile—holding his handgun in his New York hotel room in those long-gone days when to slip a gun into hand luggage was not particularly frowned on at all—looked up at him, posing on the bed? *He took a roll of film of that me. Was I here? That one? Did she come on the trip?* I think so.

I was putting myself into the story back then, all right. But in '91, far from flashing scenes from the past sending me into musings, all I felt—could feel—was his words, which seemed to dissipate the question he'd just implied: *What if I* ***want*** *to do it. Shouldn't I be allowed? Who's to stop me?*

As I've mentioned in telling this story elsewhere, committing a cardinal sin, I blurted out, "Do you *have* to do that?"

Remember, the twenty-nine-year-old wouldn't have. He was now introducing his new habits—having dropped years ago that more casual self whose lifestyle was less dangerous.

He answered—creating a wavelength I joined him on, vibes, which was his secret skill, our secret skill, to meet there, not concerned to get my approval. As lightly as he might have flicked the cigarette in the holder in his hand, said, "*It's not what you* HAVE *to do, Margaret. It's what you* WANT *to do.*"

The comment was hurled at me transparently like a ball of hot iron, an admission, a philosophy: like "*I'm satisfied. So why not throw your life in with mine.*"

But there were lifetimes, times we grew in different choices, since he was twenty-nine and me twenty-five. Would they bar the way?

Post a No Entry admonition? Well, we had pulled a draw. Still leaving ourselves wide open.

Prema facia, I didn't see how I could disagree. Inside I felt: *Yes, who can argue with that? If a person makes a conscious choice, how can you tell that person to make another choice? He appears fine. What can I say? I am happy to be here. Let's keep going.*

Let me quickly add that this is the only situation in which I can imagine reacting with that response. Remember, when I first began living with Willy, I helped him *kick cocaine*. I'd been told that cocaine instead of bringing on pure consciousness expansion strengthened the ego's sense of power. It supposedly made "*holes in the aura*," into which negative energy could enter. It was in every way counter-prescriptive to someone like me, having spiritual initiations in altered states without drugs. Yet he did not have a normal reaction. He did not cave in, have ego outbursts. He was "the same," with 150 percent *charming vulnerable* presence.

In that way, a gentleman, courtly, a romantic, he wouldn't get stuck in a mold, which would be boring. And anyone who is deeply sensitive, in touch with his feelings, is taking a risk in a relationship. No one has signed on "for keeps." There is no insurance in love—except its authentic nature.

I had seen him have "a rush." But that intentional shaking appeared to settle the substance down. He was not even driving fast or dangerously. At least, if he was, I didn't notice. Or perhaps he didn't test me with fast driving because he was protecting this meeting.

I didn't know that one of his drugs in stock was Dexedrine, which stabilized consumption of alcohol, preventing, for a good long time, the imbiber from getting drunk.

I sat back. I was not gripping the seat. I never did. I was either with someone I trusted or out of there. Capturing the past, for now we were drawing it in. It felt right. We stepped in.

No one should try to be Hunter. It is an impossibility. On the other hand, he wrote (to his editor, Jim Silberman) that the descriptions in *Fear and Loathing in Las Vegas*, though written soberly, were perhaps "flashbacks" of those states which he had experienced. But do not discount the writer, who lives in his imagination. He was there too, all the time.

He suggested getting reacquainted leisurely at a bar, catch the pro basketball game while drinking Marguerítas and eating guacamole, all of which were my favorites!! The Hotel Jerome. We were in a world of our own.

So, we sat, watching the Lakers.

I was heart and soul plunged into hopes. And we begin to see where the plot is going, though it would take a lot of adjustment to bring two such dissimilar people into one point of time and extend it, make our lifestyles accommodate our attraction. We did not know if it really was possible. We were going to give it a try. Melding, grooving, ignoring consequences.

I am focused on Hunter, in recall, in recantation of other reports, in embellishment perhaps—in making my life have poles, not be missing an important steadying, explanatory "piece." We are on the same wavelength. Perhaps not enough, as time will show.

Was the red I painted and repainted on my palm, every time it washed away, in a dream, this moment, the Red Shark *moment*? Was this it, what I had vowed to myself never to let go of without one more chance? Was this the meaning of "They will be together in old age?"

I knew the "soul grouping" energy would be with us; that, weird as it sounds, even Willy would. I hoped I could swing it. I thought it more up to me. I was the one conscious on another level of consciousness; at least, that's how I thought. But with such a vibrant attraction, all that was almost irrelevant. All that swirling in my head. I basked in his smile, completely blessed out. He, apparently, too.

But a vicious axe descended. So early to splinter this idyll by a polite waiter, a phone brought to the table.

The call, quite reasonably, was from Deborah Fuller, who needed to square a few things away before leaving for a few days.

We pulled up at Owl Farm, home of peacocks and a "fortified compound." Actually, a very unpretentious, one-story log cabin surrounded by picturesque, tall, snow-banked slopes of the Colorado Rockies. An expansive sky. As I crossed the threshold, a line from Dante's *Inferno* warned, "Abandon all hope, ye who enter here." Facetiously, of course.

Virgil led Dante out of the Inferno; then Beatrice led him up to Paradiso.

To be honest, would anyone think I could safely remeet Hunter, stay 24/7 at his side, and not have some of this spiritual, beyond-3-D background (more than I intended) spill out? I was somewhat of a hider, like Rilke, as I said. But remember "Little Margaret" at the Jung Instituter? How she relished bringing everything out in the open?

Why keep my secrets? She couldn't understand it.

So I went to Owl Farm intending, on the surface, to have a romantic reunion, relight the flame, sink into the ecstasies and also the work ethic (him writing) of old, and share *just enough* as kept things on track. But not rock the boat. Not tumble the whole foundation down like the house of the Three Pigs. And yet I should have known. Hadn't I been made over, rewired, transformed radically in surprise after surprise? These, I called my initiations.

My reticence was not to win. If I held onto it, there would be consequences, and there were.

You know the rest.

Oh, some of you don't?

He walked into the house purposefully, my bags in hand. In his bedroom, without a word deposited them. *Hot damn!* I felt no qualms about working with him. We settled into it, the article he was hired to produce, on deadline, side by side at his kitchen counter. Such moments are suspense thrillers.

He had TV sets turned onto different channels of news simultaneously. ABC, NBC, CBS, and cable showed competing anchor faces coming in over his satellite chip.

The Fourth Amendment, "the right of the people to be secure in their persons, houses, papers, and effects, against unreasonable searches and seizures," which interested him, was the article focus.

Barring intrusions, it was clear to me we could get along.

According to Deborah, he would not answer the phone. He let it go out over a speaker.

I loved the talk, the comments, the humor, the funny warning about sex he pulled out at random (printed on a card) and mumbled that it didn't apply. I loved that this romantic, so imaginative after all these years, so unpretentious, so HIMSELF sat beside me. I loved that he included me in this privacy, that he had not been disappointed. And neither had I.

The New York Times

> Hunter S. Thompson, Outlaw Journalist, Is Dead at 67
> By Michael Slackman
>
> During his career, there were moments, usually in interviews or in his own personal correspondence, when Mr. Thompson let the public in on the point. It was, he seemed to suggest, not really about guns and drugs, and tearing up the pavement and planting grass, but about grabbing public attention to focus on the failures of leadership, *the hypocrisy in society* [italics added].

I will call it BEING UNCONDITIONALLY AUTHENTIC.

❋

I struggled out of sleep. "Putting soul shimmer into politics." It was the words I woke with. About Hunter. That summed it up for me.

But to get to the significance of the 1991 meeting, I remember his giving me the opportunity in 1966 and the immediate years after to pull pranks, backed up by him, pushing the envelope but safe, a "rush" from pure life, the danger it can find inroads into reality through, being on the Edge. In the mid-1990s. But he pulled it off. He was not a bungler but an enticement to "feel" at fever pitch.

However, no matter what structure I tell you the book has, remember, it is fitting in the passages itself.

❋

Hunter said, "That was about you." It was the first evening.

Now I will keep this short, having told it before. But it has to be included in the book. I cannot deprive the readers who don't know. Besides, it sets the stage for what came next.

We were alone in the living room; he was playing a cassette.

The singer always expected to end up with a particular woman. *Did he really say that*? He had mumbled. But the song said it for him: I have always loved you. Clear as any lyrics can.

Obviously, this called for some fancy footwork in the feelings.

To cover my embarrassment, my next sentence was a kind of hemming and hawing, pointing out that (obviously) he'd been in love at times during all these years. *Of course.* He said yes, "*But you have to understand about time.*"

Understand what? I didn't ask. This was very Milton-esque. Now Hunter-esque. The all-containing one-liner. The capsule digest of something important. The genius observation.

I let the silence linger, my intuition comfortable. Did I honestly know what he meant? No. But I thought my intuition did and it would unfold the meaning to me. Silence put me on the same level as he was. I stayed, not asking for explanation. But let's try.

An angle into time was like a tuning fork. It cut through with a pitch. Everything might seem complete. Yet it had a missing, organizing frequency. Add it in. *It would change everything, its additional insight, its revitalization, relativization.*

So, time allowed experience to be complete in itself, disregarding other facets, but a hunch might be sitting in a corner of the head, aware that there was an unfinished story.

I thought it incredibly wise for him to answer my question with: "You have to understand about time." It took nothing away from past experiences but set this one onto a ledge where it waited.

That evening climaxed similarly to the meeting in New York decades before, and I do mean climaxed. Fresh in memory now.

Details would be quite inappropriate. I hear "simply the best."

We will have to come back to it, though, because it was halted by a surprise arrival. I say little more, except that it wasn't a human—no, not a ghost, not a spirit. Not an animal. Keep guessing. An energetic phenomenon. Not so familiar to Westerners, but if you know the East, then you might hazard a guess—even get close.

Had this "surprise guest" not, with the best intentions, attempted from an energetic level to direct the course of our evening, well, everything would have gone into some unpredictable direction. Who could even imagine it? Not me.

But it didn't succeed. And that set up a different ending.

The Soul's "Deep Pockets"

Well, no. You convinced me. I will lightly tell it here.

I pick out just one thing that invades my privacy the least.

Who am I kidding? I'm either straight with the reader or hedge and the next part of the book doesn't make sense. So, gulp, here goes. But to fill in, read *The* Hell's Angels *Letters* and *Keep This Quiet!* IV.

All cozy, finally getting down to it:

> Hunter effortlessly created an orgasm in me in the living room the night I arrived. No problem for him, or for me in that situation. But—the intensity was so high that suddenly my throat began to tremble in the first sign of Kundalini kriyas. Now, with kriyas, . . . you have no control, because their whole purpose is to destroy blocks.[17]

Can you imagine if your "higher self," your "soul"—more, a whole group, suddenly descended to force you into memories and to speak of them openly, unabashedly? Or forget the memories and, say, it was feelings—hoisted up by the cells, pulling them up out of "deep pockets"? What was that pocket Hunter once mentioned he wished he could put anyone he loved in?

Was this interruption like saying: *Who do you think you are kidding? This is Mission Impossible.*

But *if you want to try, this is the only way it can work. Else, you forfeit this future. Tom Cruise/Hunter will now do a death-defying leap, no stunt guy, himself. What if your soul stays right in your body, close to the surface? You want to give it a shot?*

Flashing across my mind is the memory of my soul as a Little Dot (a particle? a compacted larger entity?) successfully beckoning "me" to follow her out of body at the very Earth time I was losing my virginity.

So this time—was that the deal?—*she's here now and you aren't to "leave"?*

The throat trembled. The kriyas shook the lips. What did I do? I tried my hardest to be "normal."

Remember, Al Miner had said it's possible to "abort" a lifetime, bar its purpose from proceeding further. Willy had just died. There was no point in my starting up a relationship that didn't fit in with *this* story, the one Hunter didn't know about.

So, OK, *we'll give you a chance, toss you a bone. Do something with it. Or, The End. Go home.*

Was the Kundalini in the throat far wiser than I, than

Hunter?—well, that's a given if you know Kundalini. Was it giving me—no, either of us who was really ready for what joining together would bring in—a chance? Giving us a test? Well, this was the first concrete hint.

So if you wanted this story to stay right down in 3-D at least in moments like this, forget about it.

To conclude, in the midst of a beautiful sexual experience, oops—kriyas headed for my throat. It started vibrating, the lower jaw not so discreetly moving up and down. *How awkward*. I held on for dear life, trying to prevent the kriyas from taking over.

Gone was the simple, idyllic sexual focus. Perhaps I should mention that the Kundalini intensifies sexual feelings. Well, there's that.

No matter that it was now cut short by what Hunter did next—in essence calling a rainout, moving us into the bedroom to sleep, taking a pill to calm him down. Ah, Kundalini, if you could speak and explain to him what he was feeling, what was going on. Oops again, that was evidently my role. No matter, though, as said, that we had been relocated into the bedroom, off the living-room floor. It was not for the purpose of continuing the wild magic. That evening had been a delicious start, I thought. We would pick up where we left off tomorrow.

Ah, delusion. This energy had now been set loose, unrestrained by a harness.

The next day, after more afternoon writing, Hunter set us out into a "champagne evening," purchasing the champagne at the Woody Creek store, prepared to "finish" the evening before. And you know the rest.

Oh, you don't? But you can guess.

In sum: that cart overturned, the whole visit was in danger. I soon left. But to give you a few more details, I've written the next chapter.

"De-*niched*"

Excerpting from my memoirs:

I had brought my soul grouping with me, and who could say what they might be hatching? Not that they would *make* anything happen, but they could intensify energy. Even electrify it. The rest would be unpredictable. Which makes me remember the first time I met the Lama Sing channel, Al Miner, at his workshop in western North Carolina, ten months before I moved to Zurich. More on that coming up.

Al barely knew me, had never seen me in person before. At the workshop he observed that two strangers appeared to be creating an energy field. To test it, he had them stand facing each other a few yards apart. We other attendees then walked through the "tunnel" they formed the ends of. One of the two field-holders had just (after hesitating for years) agreed to be a Christ consciousness channel.

But Al suddenly exclaimed to me, "The energy is trying to jump onto *your* head." This was 1983. Deep into processing the death of Milton Klonsky at the time, I felt sure that if the energy was responding to me, it could only be because of his invisible presence—forming the subtle other half of the field with the new Christ channel.

There were pangs of fear (like jelly) in my stomach when the female who appeared to be holding one end of the field speculated aloud, "There are *energy vampires*." Al started to protest, fearing the worst—about to correct her. But he heard in his head (encouraging him to keep silent): "*She needs it.*" Meaning me. I needed to toughen up and—he also heard—"lighten up."

Under the watchful eye of the impressive Al Miner, this public demonstration was my introduction to energy fields. Mysteriously, the two strangers who had just met in riding the train together to the workshop, then when they stood

> facing each other created a Christ consciousness field as conductors.
>
> But the test ferreted me out as an *invisible*—deeper—conductor [of a Christ channel], which Al Miner detected. Fortunately. Knowing not a soul there, I was on the spot—frightened but feeling an inner strength as the incident unfolded. Miner in firm control, the shock taught me a lot about energy, lessons the Zurich Initiation afterwards underscored. Now, here I was in Colorado, putting my hands into, I would say, an equally strong field—just outside Hunter. Possibly stronger.[18]

Eating heartily, Hunter enjoyed the cinnamon toast he prepared for us at breakfast, both our childhoods on display. Our "inner children" happy, as we were. True to reported habits, he also had, along with the fantastic spread, Wild Turkey and cocaine. When I squirmed a bit at the sight, he monitored the coke, he told me and that he recently cut it back.

Hunter was a glutton for work. Don't believe the contrary.

He could go for hours, as could I. Music in the background, he twirled his hands, establishing the rhythm as he wrote.

But horrors. Excruciating ones, it turned out. I was to operate the fax machine, having never seen a fax before. With my notorious history as short-term failed receptionist, I had better have a better sense of machines this time round. How did I suppose the fax worked? Well, lay the paper flat down on the machine. It would take it from there. I expected it to "fax" in some unseen technological fashion. T*hat's all there is to it, isn't it*? No. The faxes did not go through! We did not know!

I asked if I could feel his energy; that is, the field surrounding him. Yes, he consented, easily. He didn't laugh.

Now I was an old hand at this, having practiced in Inner Landscaping classes. But this timebomb-like field around him, I was unprepared for. In great agitation. I pulled my hands back from his "air space," as if having touched a landing field for flying unknown objects. A little warning bell went off that I tried to shush—again thinking I could keep everything "normal." Not so. There were implications to walking in an externalized energy field that was sending off pulsing, exploding attractive signals. At least, to my hands that was the impression. Never had I felt a field so volatile, or—perhaps the better likeness—volcanic.

I knew, of course, what heavily "attractive" fields might be announcing, having learned about them in my "Basics of Psychodynamics" classes with Chris.

Holding my hands a foot or less away from his physical body, I was awed—no, astounded—by the energy palpitating around him; it certainly would be too much for most anyone to handle, to function in. I said nothing, though. I did *not* speculate on the obvious—did not even ask myself if perhaps this was a very field-specific situation.

I seemed to be splitting the part of me who lived in the Belgium high-intensity subtle-energy situations from the me visiting Hunter, who expected to fall in with his routine, all psychic phenomena safely at bay, wrapped up and waiting for my return. Did I think to check in with the spirit committee on just how plausible my expectations were? Of course, on this point no.

Was it the energy field related to us, our history!? It never crossed my mind. *How presumptuous,* I would have said. But had, conceivably, the guides set it up?! For us to walk into! Was the field swirling around him possibly about us, a container for us? That is, had his own field been intensified by another field, amped up by it?

At least, to my startled hands reporting it to my brain it seemed too big for him to exist in it every day. But that must be the case, I told myself. *This was Hunter's field, every day of his life.* No thoughts entered into this impression. It was "stuck" in a first impression, overwhelming my ability to think it through.

I was keeping that voice of awareness inside me quiet. I asked would he like to experience a way to get high without drugs. He said it would save him a lot of money.

He offered me an ultra-pure ¼ LSD dose.

I had never had LSD. No, I said, not explaining the concern I always had of keeping my mind "on call," free for esoteric information. Not doing anything destabilizing. My mouth clamped shut on that. In an echo of the awkward teenage, teased me, afraid of sounding too uncool.

The phone rang. Hunter answered. A friend invited him to dinner.

"Do you *want to* go?" he asked.

Well, I could always whip up tarragon chicken in white wine

sauce with carrots. But why test my culinary skills? Did time hang a scale over my head, asking which way I wanted to play it? I am embarrassed to say I felt self-conscious about my cooking.

So we left, walking right into the unconscious powerhouse field, or rather taking it with us.

Was he always a walking timebomb—with shooting guns just a release expressing its nature? Too combustible to stand still? Was this his normal field? A Big Bang field, when worlds are created? Like particles in a cosmic soup? I didn't know.

Had, even, I occupied and held part of the energy some of the time when we were together?

Thinking back, I would say I *ho-hummed* away the danger. The energy field said otherwise. I was too speechless to turn it to calculation, to speak about it to myself in a coherent, warning-laden way. Yet it was as if I were at the threshold of consciousness on this, standing in the awareness and carrying it no further than a tight ball of astonishment, many emotions carefully packed inside. It was so over the top that I stopped short of communicating to myself anything other than how turbulent the energy was, how bustling and jostling. One reason was that I thought: *It could not mean what it seems to. Obviously, he can handle it.*

Give me a break. I'm not to have to face consciousness hurdles here, am I?

Well, as I just described, there had already been a bona fide hurdle the night before. But I thought it a onetime thing. However, you do not walk out into an eventless dinner, telling this energy, "Stay right there. Wait till I get back," to pick up where you left off hours before.

En route Hunter leapt out of the car at a store, dashing inside to buy a bottle of champagne—like rubbing his hands with excitement at what was timestamped for the end of the evening. He got as far as pulling into the parking lot before the storm began to pour down.

A friend of Hunter's hurried over to intercept him.

Forewarned, he did not turn back. Now knowing what he was walking into—with a struggle? with no struggle?—he made the decision to enter that door. He knew now what he would be facing. Perhaps, like me, he did not let the implications sink in. Did not know himself as well as he thought? Or did, and that was the point.

Perhaps the temptation was calling too hard. I do not know if he genuinely believed that he could have it both ways. Or just that he would follow wherever his heart led. And tossed the coin. But his heart could not necessarily interpret these rampaging signals, in such a field. *Did I say that*? Oh, but his heart could.

"I know where I made my mistake," he was to tell me days later, giving his first assessment.

But wasn't he, I'd thought overconfidently—not wrapped around my finger but entwined in our mutual feelings with not an inch for anyone else to squeeze in? Think again.

Now those feelings, kept exclusively in our container for this re-meeting, would turn outward *in my presence*, a first. With me right there, in the room.

A young woman who sat next to him at the table engaged him in conversation.

She took the lead—didn't he want to "go out" with her? No answer. *Well, nothing to see here,* I thought. *She's talking about something she wants to happen after I leave. I won't think about that right now.* Even hushed as her voice was, I easily followed her entreaties, whispering but I could hear. You bet I could. Finally, though, something snapped; he yeilded, walked away from the table. I was frozen in shock in a scene that didn't belong. Quick, on the cutting-room floor.

I kept myself in my seat. (*Make it go away.*) I felt like flinging the door open to wherever they'd gone. Anything. She was an old girlfriend, his friend, seated beside me, shocked, said. She'd suddenly returned, unannounced, temporarily.

An old flame? Well, here's a second one.

Did I budge? No, I did not. An inch. Listening to the outrage of his friends, their apologies. Watching the seconds tick past. Not too many.

But my heart wasn't convinced. *It was not possible that the person genuinely smiling at me a half-hour or so before, eager to leap out of the car to buy champagne, for us, now switched, took one look at an old flame, and transferred it all to her.*

It didn't seem somehow the way Hunter and I knew each other *But the field was loose. I was not there in it. It was loose and that was the way it was.*

A field has to be "held." Pure and simple.

I know you might think this exaggerated and an attempt to justify something simple: *He chose her. Idiot!* But that's only reckoning with 3-D, and you are very right to stick with it exclusively if that satisfies you. I had been trained to see more. Therefore—wait for it—you can always expect to be tested in what you are ready for. Or not ready for but learning. You will not be allowed to have experiences that restrict themselves to the laws of 3-D IF you are learning other dimensions. And so it was.

One could make a wild leap and think it was a repeat of the Al Miner tale, with two ends of a Christ channel, but someone at one end mimicking the invisible channel, me? The other, Hunter, oblivious of his position? Could I posit the outrageous idea that this was some sort of field he was unconsciously in and that the test was do-or-die? That is, for our relationship. Who knew the answer to that? Let's see if later it becomes clearer or just falls out of the picture.

Then he was back and rushing me away, once he saw, in astonishment, that all of us knew exactly what he'd been up to—not a word having been said between him and the woman after they returned to universal condemnation.

As I kept pace with his long strides, he looked at me *with the usual clarity he had for me*, fully present, the lack of deception captured, as I hurled the accusation that "I knew"—we all knew.

As if no space were between us, transparently visible to me, he blurted out, almost in a single word, "I apologize for the rudeness. But not the passion."

Did this prick my last remaining bubble? Not exactly. The worst was out in the open. Was it an impulse, already beginning to fade? I tried not to imagine. I recoiled A field of passion. From where? Or simple as A, B, C? I didn't know. I just knew the impossible had happened. It might be out of the question to "turn the tide."

He knew he was "in trouble," he told me shortly after we left, "in the parking lot." Let's replay that.

Now I believe the energy field encompassed what he meant about "time."

She might have deserved her day in the sun. But not this night. But what the heck. It happened. It was something at least part of him "wanted to do." The other part might have been wringing his hands in foresight ignored.

What nincompoop, faced with their both being away from the table, wouldn't catch on? How could Hunter think he was being discreet? By the same token, how could I, who knew about energy fields, think we were too "safe" to be disturbed by this one and that *he could handle it*?

Why hadn't I stayed in, taken the quarter LSD?

I was protective of the initiations the guides were giving me. Not that I opened up on this, just left him feeling that I would *not trust myself with him as I explored something brand-new and* (possibly to me) dangerous.

I remember how Willy had said, when I objected to his shoplifting a couple of *tiny* souvenir porcelain statuettes, in Portugal—the only time I saw him do this—"This is me"; i.e., as if that was reason enough to accept this slight illegality; also, he said he didn't want to always be feeling he was learning from me, but that sometimes I was learning from him.

Yes, yes, yes. Hunter apologized: *mea culpa*. He'd stepped into a mud hole, in the sense that one incident splashed black onto the other. Not that my visit ended, but it had a steep hill to climb, to xxxx out. As he repeated several times, "It wasn't what I planned. That's why I bought the champagne"—as if he really had planned *in detail* something epitomized by all the years of our relationship, culminating—finally together again—having survived. Only, it fizzled. Or rather, darted sidewise.

And yet, as said, all these experiences can have validity, intent, and passion to them—at the same time, *but not, dear Lord, at the exact same restaurant table*.

Our relationship seemed in shock.

What such a scene usually does is take away trust. *But Hunter inspired trust*, because, in my view, you knew where you stood. I did, anyway, noting the internalizing analysis he was giving the situation silently. *He did not hide*, but took the blow squarely on the chin, apologizing but not more than his emotions said to, apologizing even more, perhaps, to his self.

To add insult to injury, a friend, departing for five years, came to the ranch to take leave—staying till 4:00 a.m. *But I'm leaving too. For how long*????

That night ended in a swim (just the two of us) in his neighbor's pool, a far more tepid affair than it would have been. What I remember most was eating oysters as he opened them expertly with a can opener, then watching a film on the overhead screen, which, he said, was, to him, the most erotic movie ever made. It featured a Caesar and his sister and was a bit soft porn, with lyrical scenes.

In a photograph with me that night, shot by the lingering friend,

Hunter was bright, sharp, happy—his arm flung around my shoulder. He had taken the LSD. He was fine. I looked wilting. The swim was good for his broken back; it helped his poor circulation. It was blissful. But not the way it had been.

Hunter (before long—my mind jumbles the details at this point and/or erases whole days) told me his mother was ill (she wasn't), easing the blow, knowing it was futile to continue at that time.

He went to Louisville.

I went, as planned, to California, to Jyoti and Russ's.

The afternoon beforehand, Hunter drove off alone. It was late when he returned, to sit in front of a TV in the wee hours. Naturally, I waited up. He was watching Mae West, *She Done Him Wrong*, which has the famous line: "Why don't you come up sometime 'n see me?"

He appeared introspective and obtusely set on being alone, creating a self-made distance ahead of the real distance. He didn't like to be pushed. Nothing would entice him away from the movie. This is the way he had decided to end the visit, as if processing the scene, reliving it on-screen.

Captain Cummings meets Lady "Diamond" (Mae West):

> Lou (seductively): I always did like a man in a uniform. That one fits you grand. *Why don't you come up sometime 'n see me? I'm home every evening.*
> Captain: Yeah, but I'm busy every evening.
> Lou: Busy? So, what are you tryin' to do, insult me?
> Captain: Why no, no, not at all. I'm just busy, that's all . . .
> Lou: You ain't kiddin' me any. You know, I met your kind before. Why don't you come up sometime, huh?
> Captain: Well, I . . .
> Lou: Don't be afraid. I won't tell . . . *Come up. I'll tell your fortune . . . Aw, you can be had.* (my italics)

Hunter had evidently instructed Deborah to wake him too. I wasn't to leave without some reflections, fragmented as they were. In the living room, he seated himself, holding *Songs of the Doomed*, with a signing pen. I had no copy of any of his books autographed to me, just one to my mother.

Now, at the last minute, he did the job up proudly, like saying, "Here's looking at you, kid."

From *Keep This Quiet!* IV, rev. ed. (page 48):

> With a felt pen in large silver letters spanning both sides of the inside hardcover first edition, he wrote what amounted to a private dedication to his whole career, "Here's another one—& it's all yr. fault. But thanx anyway, Love, H, Hunter"; he said pointedly that the evening was *not what I planned*; I *bought champagne*. Also, "I know where I made my mistake." No further explanation. I didn't ask. I was just glad we were parting *not* in closure (too much up in the air) but on a close note; that he was staring into my eyes, summing up his disappointment but also his admission—analysis—that something had been misplayed.

Hunter knew, in having it out with himself, that once inside the restaurant, his legs would just follow a decision already taken. Was that what he meant about "where I made my mistake"? I don't think so. But I'm not sure what. I think it went deeper.

I left. Nothing else to do. It had been magical—then turned into a raging, stormy, choppy sea. Knocked off course. I don't remember anything of the rest of the week, in fact, except snatches like me sunbathing behind the cabin.

Deborah drove me to the airport.

❋

You know the rest.

I left. Nothing else to do. It had been magical—then turned into a raging, stormy, choppy sea. Knocked off course. I don't remember anything of the rest of the week, in fact, except snatches like me sunbathing behind the cabin.

Surely, this was not the end, that last sight of him in that chair one room over from where he would take his life by shooting himself. But surely in the years till February 20, 2005, our story would peek its head up some more. I left, overwhelmed with that powerhouse of energy he carried with him, which, in my case, did not just dissipate, evaporate. We will see this in the Lunevillelaan 46 Letters. That was May 20, '91. To be continued. (It is February 20, 2006.)

In sum: that cart overturned, the whole visit was in danger it could not fend off.

> I remember him in that chair (one room over from where he committed suicide fourteen years later by firing a .45-caliber semiautomatic pistol into his mouth but incredibly leaving his face undamaged)—signing in that translucent silver lettering. Surely, this was not the end. Surely, though, that honeymoon arrival, without anything but the unknown to climb up over, was past. Who ever knew Hunter to mind a challenge? As he said, it never got too weird for him. And about myself? That was May 20, 1991. To be continued.[19]

✻

On a barstool at Denver International Airport, a Heineken in front of me, I wondered how Hunter was feeling.

Plot line one: what would have happened if I had explained about the Kundalini at my throat that first night? Plot line two: what would have happened had the kriyas carried out their intent to a mysterious, successful conclusion? Plot line three: after Plot lines one or two above, imagine if I had demonstrated the computer-PK (if I could) with his brand-new computer and printer. Together making esoteric printouts! Like shotgun art? He'd have immediately gotten the hang of it. And why did his computer arrive just as I did? Ah-ha. Timing. Timing.

Plot line four: well, that's the one we're in. I will have a kriya at the sublet near La Honda, and this time I'm alone. It comes full bore.

In the moment's intensity and the lingering aftermath, where will my attention also go? To Hunter, convinced he's part of this too. It's an idea I get inside the barrage of energy. But this will take a few chapters to unfold. First, to my plane setting down in San Manteo County at the San Francisco Airport.

Jyoti's Bay Area Office

Richard Unger was at Jyoti and Russ's for dinner the night my plane landed in the Bay Area. Founder/director of the International Institute of Hand Analysis, he added a ton of irony. He had read at least 20,000 hands. It's over 60,0000 now.

Considered "a foremost authority on hand analysis worldwide," based in part on his "exhaustive study of the medical literature on fingerprints," he is also very intuitive (something of a "channel"). Persuaded by Jyoti I had an interesting hand, he gave me a short sample reading, in which he sketched out, quite prophetically, my Karmic Habit (Life School). What was it? Being "De-niched" (run out of town). You don't say.

He mapped out the challenge. I still have the diagram:

LESSON—Least evolved skill and greatest resistance.

That is, it would involve giving the reins to the least-evolved part of me, the part to which I had the most resistance.

But there was a huge upside. The "happy ending," or LIFE PURPOSE / TO DO. I had to complete this life purpose through a triangle: "Finding Your Niche" (*left angle*) "Being Understood" (*right*) and "Doubts Yourself/Guilt" (*bottom*). The end result?

"Big Shot—Leadership," "Impact world," "Gets results."

Get results how? The hard way. He outlined the treacherous predicament:

"Heartbreak fuels transformation cycle."
"A broken heart: Key to others' understanding"

And this was my route to—da dum—"worldly influential."

Well, I would say he was batting a thousand.

He insisted that *a broken heart fueling transformation cycle* was the *least costly route.*

Other people ran on different fuels. Mine was heavy, heavy. He spelled out the happy-ending heartbreak dynamic:

> Nobody wants me, I don't belong, nobody understands me→Panic/
> Frozen→Take Action Anyway→Big Shot/I'm Home/They want you to stay.

Coming, as I had, from Owl Farm, "de-niched"—by having squashed the throat outburst that tried its darndest to *say who knew what*?—I felt: R*ight on*. Yes siree.

As will become apparent, sometimes I had to be forced—energetically, from "higher up"—to take a step. I might not do it if the pressure weren't high enough. Heartbreak sounded like pressure enough.

My karmic habit was "being run out of town," and my life purpose was to overcome that karma with a success story—*at a point of nothing-to-lose*. The key: good, in-depth communication. And to facilitate that, my hand held signs of gifts in communication. But only backed up against a wall, consenting to massive revelation, would I be deeply understood. And to break this karma, I had to be. I was complex. That was a setup. Only by communicating in a context deep enough—comprehensive enough—would I avoid being mistyped, mischaracterized. "Run out of town." Ah-ha. What a lifetime to step into. *You think you can continue hiding*? *Well, try this lifetime, then*. I would be forced "not to hide."

Being run out of town would be the punishment if I didn't communicate even *more than might normally be thought necessary, because* I *had to open up even more, to be understood at all.*

For instance, what might sound mental to someone else, or inconceivable, might not be that to me at all, but expressed from my core, in my heart—for reasons only I *knew. Making this clear,* I *would have understanding audiences.*

Actually, many artists—understood only after death—had similar plights. Take Bizet. He died of a sudden heart attack at thirty-six after his now-beloved opera *Carmen* opened as a scandalous flop. Upon the tragic-death news, the public took note and it became a hit. But Richard Unger indicated it was my *win-the-lottery lifetime*. A lottery, huh? Have to win the draw. At least, that was staked.

Like Rilke, who said he had opened up totally to a stranger one night and woke up the next day wanting to kill him and who had broken with his fiancé because "She was the light of my eyes and my heart's desire, but my soul was filled with despair," I would have to walk a fine line, overthrowing keep-your-mouth-shut introverted inclinations. Otherwise, projections would mean *who* I *was* would not be suspected because what I had to communicate had to go inside the context that only I could offer it, its real width and scale.

Richard would later tell me that the distance between where my thumb began and a notch on it was twice the normal, indicating two times as much information to absorb before I could put it into a digested context; that is, I was dealing with such a large amount of information what I had to say (or even how I saw) wouldn't make sense till digesting a large enough context.

I would have need again of "the naked child." Well, I had not even mentioned Willy, though I did put on his large hat, to which Hunter responded with, "What a small head." That made the perennial cat get my tongue, but an obvious comment now would be he was jealous, claiming his territory as the guy with the more formidable head beside a pipsqueak I should pay no notice of.

Had I *not* known Hunter from before, I would not have been drawn to him so soon after the death. Had he not figured in the Zurich Initiation, I don't think I would have persisted either, because that indicated the depth. It thrived in passion, which was consciousness of another sort.

I thought he was in my soul grouping. I thought that in one "layer of reality," we were working inside the same dimension. There, my consciousness and everything I hoped for would make sense to him. He knew all I knew; he came out of that consciousness. But he was "playing his cards" in a very different analysis of what he "wanted to do."

This, of course, is part of what fascinated me, that he did not tackle directly the things I tackled but was tackling them in an even greater energy field perhaps, from an unconscious position. I had found that becoming conscious had advantages and disadvantages. It was easy to see why some people, already conscious, decided to become unconscious, and have experiences that, *once conscious, they could not have.* So I thought like that, that he could, in the blink of an eye, or death, recover all this information and consciousness that he purposely had unloaded as baggage for the moment.

It was nice to have Richard Unger's diagram put into perspective—so synchronistically significant.

People could not, would not understand me unless—my least developed skill—I *made them*.

I did not say, *Hot damn*. But there it was. As Milton had said, "You see all the *unordinary things. But you don't see the ordinary things, what anybody else would see in an instant.*"

Yet I was always communicating under the surface. Even though received there, sometimes it was not enough. For the conscious personality could not hear, and, as with me as well, sometimes just broke through spontaneously, *overturning my tables*. It was like Emily Dickinson: *This is my letter to the world, / that never wrote to me*. Now this strikes me as a good description of the little me who instinctively yanked the tablecloth. It turned out, this wordless, unconscious me was my game changer. And knew her role from the get-go: overturn the tables. Or pull the rug out from under the solid belief system and the sometimes-conventionally-inclined, hiding me.

If I could just get past this test—or now, karma—I was promised everything. The part of me who defied the internalizer to tell my secrets was the "least evolved." Yet somehow would be the key to my happiness.

And the deal was contrived so that I would *not* be understood—but, indeed, be *run out of town, stoned, crucified—as long as I did not have the skill of telling the truth in such a way that it was received, no matter how odd, how original, with open arms instead of stones and pickaxes and cries of blasphemy.*

But was this not, in a way, the lot of everyone with something original, individual, new to create—and was it not exactly the karma Hunter threw in little slivers onto the wind, ignoring? This was the artist's karma. But it was also that of Jesus, of Mary Magdalene, and so forth. But only partly that of St. Paul, who spoke fearlessly though saying he was "untrained in speech." No matter. He had "knowledge.

I could have written a book on it, *My Life as Plot*, it being illuminated yet once again. One self would be open, one shut. There it was, the two-legged, bipod, extravert/introvert. But the extravert spoke in a totally disarmed manner, able, if brought out of the unconscious, to be a great addition to the introvert, the Wise Man/woman. The levels were also personality/soul. I would need to go into my greatest weakness with my least-acquired skill, go into my defeat and outflank my private self, as in chess—be understood by opening so wide, surrendering so profoundly, so totally, with nothing held back, that only welcome could follow. For everyone recognizes what is authentic.

⁂

Well, and so much for that. I could have benefited from hearing it a week earlier. While in California, I left a few phone messages to Hunter, who did not usually pick up (so what was new?). But at times did. I have no memory of how often.

I arranged to return to the La Honda area to sublet Jyoti's office, October–December while she was in India with the satguru Dhyanyogi-ji.

⁂

But before that, in May '92, I attended, delighted, a Maitri Breathwork™ workshop, taught by Jyoti and Russ—booking myself into the Hotel du Theâtre in Zurich. This time was even more extraordinary than the visitation by "the tall man." This two-day workshop, featuring Grof-like breathwork, took me twice into what I called "magnetic moments." As these so-amazing incidents are too dramatic to just hurriedly recount, I reserve telling them for a later chapter.

Having arranged to sublet Jyoti's spacious home office near La Honda, beginning October 1, I made plans to board my newly-invited-to-live-with-me purebred dachshund. I'd found him in a grungy room full of dogs, not in kennels or runs—like in *The Prince and the Pauper*. Unfortunately, my next-door neighbor offered to keep him (with her dog) while I was away, which didn't turn out well.

Who could resist Snoepie, who loved to go up to anyone and stand there, watching them work or get their attention? He forced me to put our rabbit, Sheba, however, out of the kitchen onto the little screened-in back porch, as it was tempting for Snoepie and Sheba to share space. Soon he would have the same issue with my hamsters. An exciting life, Snoepie had.

With deep reddish hair, he looked a year old. He was three, the vet said. So Sheba and Snoepie lived together a few months till—on a day I didn't realize how hot it was on the porch, Sheba, getting diarrhea, began to dehydrate. Discovering his plight in the evening,

I put him beside my bed to take a taxi to the vet's the next morning. Late, in the dark, Snoepie jumped to the floor and squatted, staring at the rabbit. Sheba was "transitioning." Because Snoepie woke me, I could hold him as he passed.

It only became evident that Sheba was a "he" after Willy died, because suddenly feeling a lot of sexual energy, Sheba began humping people—animals too. Snoepie likewise began to hump people though he arrived neutered. But he seemed not to know it.

Postmarked Aug. 30, two photos arrived in a medium-sized tan envelope—from "H.S.T., Box 220, Woody Creek 81656. A sunset and a moonset or -rise.

High up on the side of the sunset is a flying object that one might say looked like, at first glance, a UFO. Balancing it at the very top far right is a tiny shooting star. In the other photo, against blacked-out ground and trees, in between the foliage, is a perfect V surrounded by solid pink. In the center—isn't that the moon? Rising? A pale full circle? I had forgotten all about these photos. I don't know how this envelope "slipped through the cracks."

No explanation. Not a word. *See you at my sunset—see that* UFO *and shooting star*? Nothing of the sort. Yet I'd had had a dream that contained a line: "When one sun sets, it's the signal for the other sun to rise."

GINGER:
It's something daring. The Continental.
A way of dancing that's really "entre nous."
It's very subtle. The Continental.
Because it does what you want it to do.

It has a passion. The Continental.
An invitation to Moonlight and romance.
It's quite the fashion. The Continental.
Because you tell of your love while you dance.[20]

❋

Meanwhile, in July, President George H. W. Bush nominated Judge Clarence Thomas to the Supreme Court.

In October 1991, the Senate Judiciary Committee reopened confirmation hearings to examine charges by Anita Hill, a University of Oklahoma law professor, that Thomas had sexually harassed her while she was an Equality Employment Opportunities Commission (EEOC) employee in the 1980s. By a vote of fifty-two to forty-eight, Thomas was confirmed. Now Hunter set about writing one of his landmark, witty *Rolling Stone* satires, "Fear and Loathing in Elko."

Arriving in California, finding myself in the historic location of some of Jyoti's Kundalini experiences, wouldn't you know? Something was up.

The great Kundalini Maha Yoga satguru Dhyanyogi-ji's image looked at me from pages of Jyoti's wall calendar. In India, she was continuing a process that, she said, "seemed to be totally rewiring my nervous and neurological systems," (p. 169), I took her place—or held the fort—on the home front. Dhyanyogi-ji was aware of me, I would find out. I had no clue he was on the threshold of guiding me. He is called "Guruji," Teacher.

The experience I am going to describe involves Kundalini. It takes over the body. Imagine trying to object to Kundalini when *it* has control. It is stronger than you are. It is releasing cellular content into your emotions. It has the upper hand. This is the authority. It is to be dealt with.

In the East, it is considered to be Mother Shakti, or the Divine Feminine cosmic energy that rises from the base of the spine, trying in individuals to reach the top of the head, the crown, to unite there with Shiva, which creates unity consciousness.

It is, according to Gopi Krishna, in *The Awakening of Kundalini*, she writes, "the mechanism in the body that brings about the transmutation of the species."[21]

Jyoti quoted, in *An Angel Called My Name*, a story by Swami Prajnananda in the preface to Swami Muktananda's *Kundalini: The Secret of Life*, in which a lonely God got bored and "created the world from Himself," but because the beings "knew who they were and how to merge back into their source," they merely returned to him. So he called a meeting of other gods he'd created. What to do? That's easy, they said. Close the gates of heaven and hide the key. But where? They had many suggestions, far-fetched locations, like the Pacific Ocean bottom. Finally, God spoke. No, he said. These locations would all fail:

> I see men exploring every nook and corner of the universe. Not only will they conquer the Himalayas and swim to the bottom of the ocean, but they will also land on the moon, take a close look at the planets, and try to go to other universes through black holes . . . He will go millions of miles into space."

So where to hide the key? "Then, suddenly, God said, 'I've got it!'"—that never would man look "'within his own self, right in the center of his body.'" The gods all agreed. "And God has had great fun watching man's search for happiness ever since."

> Muktananda found this key to happiness . . . From his own experience he says that what is outside is also inside. The whole universe, all knowledge, the answers to the mysteries of human existence and true happiness lie inside man and become available to him by the awakening of the Kundalini, the divine Mother. (xxiii–xxiv)

Finally published in 1998, *An Angel Called My Name* is a jewel of a memoir on "transformational energy that lives in the body.". It describes how in 1987 "Kundalini entered [Jyoti's] heart chamber." She was "rushed to the hospital." As nurse prepared to draw blood,

> just at that moment, a gentle energy entered my feet and extended up my body. It seemed to electrify the air around me. The nurse complained of being warm and had to leave. The Voice began to speak from within, repeating the same phrase over and over, as if in a chant, "And now you dance the second part of your dream awake!" . . .
>
> I've since discovered that when Kundalini enters the heart, it is often misdiagnosed as a heart attack due to their similar symptoms." (p. 111)

❋

In October, I went down to Guadalajara, Mexico, to study with the bodywork-oriented psychotherapist, spiritual teacher Dr. Hector Kuri-Cano.

Unable to confirm the arrival time, I nevertheless, not to be deterred, jumped onto a plane. I found his lovely family moving into a new home; he told me he was recovering from kidney cancer. His telegram approving my arrival date had gone awry. On my website I described him as "*serious, humorous, and earthy . . . just what I'd flown* 1,642.75 *miles to find*":

> Normally, one cannot go through great spiritual shocks without a teacher. Not beforehand but afterwards, in the grounding phase. I sought Hector out. I was sure he was equal to challenges that my encounters with "the afterlife" had brought and that he would support me. He did . . .
>
> Anytime I have found presence, my own ability to be present is more alive. It seems to catch fire . . . Knowing is reminded. It's that invisible handshake that cements a step. Getting more Hector under my belt was sustenance for a long time.

The young Hector worked in his Lebanese grandfather's shoe factory. Another tiny note, said, Jean Campbell, in her iMage Project website: "The first time I witnessed Hector's work with a dream, I knew I was watching a master at work."

Hector had studied with psychoanalyst/humanistic philosopher Eric Fromm; then met Dr. Stanley Keleman, a leader in body psychotherapy, at Esalen Institute. Then studied with the founder of Bioenergetics, Alexander Lowen, MD, in New York. When he faced a life-threatening disease, he headed to New York for treatment. But on one trip simply stayed in the plane till it landed in India. Talk about following your inner guidance.

He cured himself or was cured, studying with various masters and gurus in India and the Middle East, then returned to Mexico and developed his Energetic Metatherapy.

He brought in physical exercises for me, including a focus on Tara.

In my makeshift motel room on the outskirts of the city, from which I would hitchhike by truck to his house, I practiced the Green Tara mantra ("Om! Tara, Tuttare Ture, Swaha") he gave me but began spontaneously to sing a different "mantra," one I'd dreamed. Normally an alto, barely carrying a tune, I was singing soprano!

Telling him about it the next day—not knowing he was a master at working in dreams—I was encouraged by him to sing my mantra: "N*o lo me trahijo*," meaning (no matter how rough the Spanish), "Don't betray me." Evidently, based on "No lo me tangere," the words Jesus said to Mary Magdalene after death—warning her that it was too soon, "Don't touch me."

Again in California, I went to see Mariah—driving bumpily in Russell's stick shift car I borrowed.

"An opera singer is on the edge of your energy field," she told me—"wearing gold; she's trying to go inside you. She's part of you."

After I left, I found myself singing soprano to myself. I named her my higher self, "Anna," associating her with "N*o lo me tangere.*" I felt she was telling me how sacred she was, to be careful with her energy.

For some time after that, when asked my name in an energy session with Joost Vanhove, co-founder, at Centrum GEA, Belgium, I would say, "Margaret Anna Harrell," trying it on, feeling the sound. Hearing the name helped Joost find my energy. (Joost, who will come in more later, is described this way on his Centrum GEA website today: "From a holistic point of view, Joost brings together the various essential aspects of being human in his work as a coach and trainer: the rational and the intuitive, the conscious and the unconscious, the cognitive and the energetic, the individuality and connectedness, the personal and the transpersonal.")

But Hector's real gift was much more than anything above. It was a surprise. In Guadalajara he recommended three stories by Kahlil Gibran. What happened when I read them was nothing short of astounding, it went so deep.

Kriyas Strike Deeper

I returned from Guadalajara with an assignment from Hector.

Sitting right on Jyoti's lavishly filled bookshelves was a book Hector *had said to read.* *Jesus the* Son *of* Man: His *words and* His *Deeds as Told and Recorded by* Those Who *Knew Him*, by Kahlil Gibran. I opened it up. What happened?

Read these three vignettes, he had told me. Unsuspectingly, I began "Mary Magdalene: His Mouth was like the Heart of a Pomegranate." Entranced, I read, "What would you, Miriam?" One of those incredible floodgates opened. The next day in October 1922 (the date on the account below), the energy was still charging through me, fresh in my mind.

Recently, I found my original notes, which augment and verify my memory (below):

Unsent poem to Dr. Hector Kuri-Cano
After a visit down to his Guadalajara home

A Fable out of the Vast Cosmic Energies and the Patterns they hold, the memories

Coming to sit with me
Telling me
Flowing through me
To write this down
Kriyas forcing me to lift my hand
Tell the Earth this
Tell myself

What I'm leading up to is the contribution you made
Which was crucially timed
The day in Mexico you, after many contributions,
Asked me to read the book

The experience was too private to mail. But I recorded it, anyway, addressing it to Hector:

I was reading what Mary Magdalene said in Gibran
last night
about
"pomegranate lips"—Gibran wrote:

HIS MOUTH WAS like the heart of a pomegranate, and the shadows in His eyes were deep . . .

And I remember Him pacing the evening. He was not walking. He Himself was a road above the road; even as a cloud above the earth that would descend to refresh the earth.

But when I stood before Him and spoke to him, He was a man, and His face was powerful to behold. And He said to me, "What would you, Miriam?"

I would not answer Him, but my wings enfolded my secret, and I was made warm.

And because I could bear His light no more, I turned and walked away, but not in shame. I was only shy, and I would be alone, with His fingers upon the strings of my heart.[22]

At "I *remember* Him *pacing . . . a road above a road*," the Kundalini took over. I "heard," not literally—"H*er water broke*."

she asked him to come into her home
about five times
He wouldn't come
He only said
"Other men see a beauty in you that shall fade away sooner than their own years.
But I see in you a beauty that shall not fade away, and in the autumn of your days that beauty shall not be afraid to gaze at itself in the mirror, and it shall not be offended.

"I alone love the unseen in you."

I dropped the book amidst a sudden eruption of kriyas as the cells brought buried information to the surface. Kundalini literally "shook" it loose, out of the cells—the body trembling, as the kriyas took the form of jiggling energy, just like the Brownian effect in physics—in which random water molecules bumping against one another in a fluid, make the temperature rise—which effect Einstein used to prove the existence of atoms; on another level, here—the body shaking as in an earthquake—it "proves" to the recipient that Kundalini is real. There is no arguing with it, no telling it that it is imaginary. It is too profound, too insistent, unstoppable.

Deny this if you can, it says, or rather it doesn't say it. It is too busy illustrating its proofs, triggered by something that only the cells know. *Can cells "know" something*? you ask. "The answer is yes. Entangled in the vast web of connections in the universe, acted on by spirit energy, they sometimes "disconnect" from the history of ourself we know, or the projects we are aware of, and bring something from far far away, taking their "marching orders" in unknown-to-us triggers.

He was "a road above a road." That got to me. And "What would you, Miriam?"

Bursting in, the Kundalini kriyas went from cell to cell, releasing the memory content, knocking on each jail door and saying: *See the key in the lock*.

Remember, this is energy. What happens locally draws from the larger, universal history. It does not organize *time* the way we do. It strikes a target, like lightning. There has to be a reason, a purpose in choosing "this" target.

> According to the yoga tradition, *kundalini* is like an energy, a serpent, or a goddess that lies dormant at the base of the spine of all human beings. Sivananda says that the awakening of *kundalini* manifests itself through various physical and psychological signs and symptoms such as feeling the currents of *prana* (vital energy) rising to the *sahasrara* chakra (thousand-petalled: the individual's center of spirit, enlightenment, wisdom, universal consciousness, and connection to higher guidance), feeling vibrations of prana in different parts inside the body, feeling electric-like currents flow up and down the nerves, experiencing bliss, having divine visions, and getting inspiration and insight.[23]

The fact is, I "woke up"—in a flashback—before my birth.

Looking down a long rectangular table in what I instantly identified as "the Upper Room," I "heard"—internally—a man in the group seated there pose a question to me. Suddenly in these kriyas, some block, I knew, was breaking up; some recessed "information" going into a multidimensional frame where "I" was there as well but not in an ego form. A question I had shoved deep into memory was alive there as I "saw" the leader asking me at that very moment to choose a lifetime.

"What would you, Miriam?" In almost those precise words he asked me what lifetime I chose, which I wanted most.

In the shaking, the electrical information, I could not avoid remembering the answer. As the Divine Energy shakes the cells—all blocks, all remorse, resistance itself—making it crumble even, as if the walls of Jericho, I hear, "St. Paul." My voice.

OK, permission granted, but carrying a proviso: that you also accept Mary Magdalene.

That is, I *can have the lifetime of* "St. Paul." *Take that role, whatever it means, whatever it entails bringing with me to* Earth. *But only if* I *take* Mary Magdelene *as part of the deal.* The kriyas, still shaking, punctuate the message.

Imagine refusing to go where my cells went and their cellular knowledge. I would provoke a war with my own body. Imagine fighting the transplantation of a higher dimension of one's own heart inside oneself. Fighting it as if a refused heart.

No, life was an adventure.

I held on. I listened. I received. I *became.* I added on this new experience, observing till I could merge with it. In merging with this Kundalini, you could also say that in a sense it was my way of merging with the Divine Mother (she *was* shakti, the serpent energy), according to the Hindus, who originated the system).

"Miriam," Mary, often called "the Apostle of the Apostles," had the term "prostitute," mistakenly borrowed from Mary of Bethany, removed from identification with her in 1969 by Pope Paul VI.

Here was the level my life purpose was being reset. No wonder I had the karma of being de-niched, run out of town.

From the top, the permission to "have the lifetime" came down. Whatever that meant *in human terms*, the cells knew enough and had loyally "kept the faith"; the assignment meant something secret, a resonance, a guarantee—deep down in the cells a backup. It made likely certain forms of reaction, ascertaining that they were the highest probabilities at my birth, I supposed. Triggers would come with me, patterns fully formed, ready to be initiated. When the time came. Or even, "at once." So this secret alliance entered my conscious trajectory as well.

But what could one become after entering such a chamber, finding that the cells, if not oneself, had this knowledge and were ready—quick, unthinking, not needing time to reflect, it was ingrained, seared in—to respond with it? Like the most loyal French Resistance paratrooper? Like someone who swore an oath?

Everything was backwards. In the most convincing way possible, the cells knew themselves to be in a lineage I knew nothing about.

The Zurich Initiator had always pled with me to "remember" him in other lifetimes—from his global consciousness perspective. Mariah was to tell me she did not think anyone working in light energy this century could avoid holding some of the Mother Mary and Magdelene energy, so it was a very collective situation as well.

A coincidence had drawn the vision, or memory, or Kundalini downpouring. They were one's own cells and, even when replaced, would *will the memories to the cells that came after*.

So I had the "assignment"—of taking on the Magdalene energy, backed by that of St. Paul.

Planning some such arrival as this, among her many arrivals, but particular, coming personally—speaking to the cells directly, first and foremost, afterwards undeniably conscious. But not to outer appearances, just fitting logically into the links of these chains or feathers, if one were to put it all together—as I am doing now. For the master piano composer Bach, which of the many themes was this one? And what others were in the piece? Now finally remembered, of myself at seven, playing and playing till I remembered the end, at the piano. But I say that precursorily, prematurely. I do not exactly remember.

BUT MY FINGERS DO.

"I know," Thompson once said, "that I will be back around, you get your assignment in the great hall. It's like going to court. Your name is called, and you go to stand in front of the judges, in the great hall of karma. And you get your judgment in the form of your next assignment. Who knows?" he said, "I might be back as a three-legged dog on a Navajo reservation. But I don't think that will happen."

—Robert Chalmers

Life is something we're all *sentenced* to.

—Milton Klonsky

Epic Proportions

In the unsent letter to Hector, I tried to capture the burst of realizations the Gibran story plunged me into. The epic poetry unleashed onto the page *the very day after the kriya episode*, still submerged in *its energies, catching its drops*. That came to me, saying: *Take this down*.

> And here, then, what would burst through me like the most powerful rocket
> For it was an archetypal rendition
> But behind that the man who knew the original intent of the Jesus Mission
> And that intent had nothing to do with what happened
> in the unconsciously played script
>
> For there is always an unconscious level,
> Time takes care of that.
>
> All through time the unconscious script was the one chosen
> And he chose another version
> His own version
> So here the link occurred
> the transition would occur
> And build the bridge
> with it
> into the new century
>
> In the right sequence
> And not as in John's recorded version
> For in His version consciousness came to lead the way
> And that was what was in motion that day
> When you gave me the clue to read
> the three Gibran stories
> Some in his lifetime
> Some after

when the story went on
In the timeless motion
it traveled through
the form it could survive in
and cook in

. . . .

And then there was the Gospel of Mary
And she talked about
those that have EARS
And that's what I've been writing
As if it's the decoding right here
and there's nobody picking it up

"Never met a girl could make me feel the way that you do"
Not "Out of Sight"
for while there was an invisible female in the story
there was nothing but projections
And obituaries
And then one day
the last story came up to bat
And my dreams said this was the last time this story was being
played because my father was old

Well. This was what she'd and I mean Mary'd been afraid to bring
to the Earth
Or try to bring it to the Earth
All across the nation
A new vibration
in the archetype
But first of all in those who fought to get it here
behind the scenes
making soul investments
Just as Faust did
As Goethe did
and one ever knew the cost
In the soul
till the light would come on in the story
What was the Real Story?

"Black AS GRANITE" WAS HIS HAIR, he said
In the New York version
when he hoped for
the other hand
the one from long ago
When she said he had pomegranate lips
palm granite
He stored it in his memory cells
Remembered that much
Black as palm
Granite
But the bomb hadn't been strong enough then
As he hoped it was now

Wasn't it clear now
The other palm of this soul grouping project
When
Mary Magdalene
Of the other story was grown up and she said she was big enough now
She was ready
He could come out of the shadow
And off the cross
And he said
If she
could find the palm granite lips
in him he could find the original one she had been then

Seen then
And know the hand he really wanted to play

The unconscious hand
right in the pomegranate
Pomme—apple
What a fall
Not to know that it was all contained in that original couple
And the look of recognition
she had
and he had

Not acted on then
And he was scripting
the other version
And the project to be concluded now
that he had master-
hearted
His was the heart behind the mastermind
The one that wanted to answer so long ago
That when she asked him to come into her home

that day
Well, he did.
"Never met a girl could make me feel the way you did."
It didn't seem simple then
But he had bet everything on that if his heart ever heard it
Said it to him so clearly another time
He'd jump over all the centuries in between
right to the year nearing 2,000
Or over that line
when there was all that light to bring to the Earth
that he knew all about
But none of it meant anything
without her
And he hoped his young personality
could understand it
Without taking the path
He had
to make it
Abundantly
Clear
Right
Here

To the enlightened man whose consciousness embraces the universe, to him the universe becomes his "body," while the physical body becomes a manifestation of the Universal Mind, his inner vision expression of the highest reality and his speech an expression of eternal truth.

—Anagarika Govinda,
German-born Tibetan lama

Response of the "Least Evolved"

Is there a connection between the two instructions? I asked. That is, the lifetimes, as we represented them, of St. Paul and Mary Magdelene? Well, to go back to what I wrote *at the time*, to be more accurate, YES.

To Al and Susan Miner (probably never mailed):

> This energy showed me myself before incarnating, but it was St. Paul. He was choosing a lifetime, or rather in the strange way I remember it, it was as if I was walking around a room and got to choose the lifetime I wanted. And I chose St. Paul. Only, it was agreed that this being made to happen, I would have to carry a karma, a task, related to that, to go back and rectify some harm done to the feminine through some of the quotations taken from this energy. I had to go back and change that. Understand it and grow into where it could never be my conception of the feminine
>
> So this was all while shaking. I had all this come through that shaking.
>
> What do I see? A similarity between them. They were reported in history to have a Conversion. And then one was called noble and quoted and a great teacher, almost second to none. Did anyone bring back out the Conversion of St. Paul and start talking about anything but a glorious light and the years that followed, in prison, in other escapes and noble deeds and some kind of impediment, long travels anyway. And courage. But take the feminine picture. What models did they bring? Mother Mary? But that's the Mother Archetype. She cannot step out from it . . .
>
> Well, we have two stories of Conversion. One is noble. The other surrounded in shame. It cannot be. The Corrective Instrument of Incarnation saw the unbefittingness for the human race to have the two Archetypes side by side, and what if he blended hers with his? Have her have some of his

> fame and nobility, in the Earth's eyes? Because she had it anyway . . .
>
> In life, he had to defy his own convictions and former friends. But her archetype was the very fiber of matter and its capacity to withstand light. Her archetype was the filtering of light through matter, of what I have been told is what I am (or was; it keeps revising itself). The combination and the confrontation when light meets matter. And there is respect on all sides.

I could easily see, if not in the stupefaction and bodily overthrow of the Kundalini kriyas incident, that St. Paul and the Magdalene were, like a male-female set of poles: *two conversions*—but treated so differently in history. This time he would stand behind her. Or, more broadly speaking, *the male* would protect the female, and she be his own gateway into incarnation. Of course, in this particular case, maybe it would never be known he was there.

And suppose you imagine yourself in this way, being willing to accept the consequences—live the energy, bow down to it when necessary, even wrangle with it when not, as in the Zurich Initiation I was counseled to do. I was clearly a novice in the personality then; the Initiator was clearly Commander as he released his consciousness, fully feel-able, over a whole city—Zurich—so that it descended into whoever aligned with it, as a "mood."

Certainly he was, *as a state of mind*, roaming the city filling it with love. But I attempted, following it, to go into the same "state." I sometimes did, an ultimate human location he called "The Christ State." This truly happened and the memory of it gives me impetus now.

How many people ever witnessed such a thing? Not many, I think, though they do witness something else, or can. And the point is to do so.

I am an example. I am saying: *Go ahead. Learn how to witness without prevarication, witness and even merge without inflation, just matter-of-factness, because* What is is. But you have to verify, know how to be sure, without taking offense, when asked: *How do you know it wasn't the* Devil?—which is the point of "a living vessel."

It means that the Word of God can flow through you, or the still-living truths can, alive, flexible, silent or hyperactive, that we use as sculptors of our biographies, as witnesses and experiencers, discoverers and REPORTERS. That we Report to the Earth, all on missions to do so, to process first of all and then report, though sometimes we do the contrary, in reverse order. But we do, or someone does, both—to bring to the Earth new energies, intensities, new embodied potential that was waiting for us to know that it was hidden away, on the edges of boundaries, on the Edge.

So Jesus was "a road above the road," asking, "What would you, Miriam?" And Hunter asked me, "What would you, Margaret," as it were. That would be a field within a field within a field if the powerful archetype went all the way back to there, or only in the tiniest drew from it or had the most miniscule reminder of such an event. But I did not make the association consciously then. It just comes to mind now as I try to reconstruct, get the long view.

⁂

Remember that the Ground state and unity consciousness do not personalize in the way we characteristically do but exist within a structure highly problematic vis-s-vis the Earth. Not personalizing in the ego sense of identity but from a structure in which those in this consciousness in a sense step aside as a unique physical vessel. But as they master this, they become even more unique. For they go on in uniqueness *after accepting the collectiveness of the Source of all energy.*

There is personalness, but it is something else—individuality but contextualized differently, crossing any boundary it wants to and yet aware "This is I," having identity, its "point" of view—which says "I," though it may be that energetically it is a different energy that says "I" one time than the next, and the "I" from before may even—it is possible—be speaking in someone else, though if and after accepting such a premise as framework, the job of "Who am I?" begins.

For nevertheless, when one gets to that level, one can personalize just as well, but with different outlines and conditions, the way we, human, personalize an entire body, when a smaller organism sees as "itself" something smaller, tiny. There is the nondenial of one's own truth but the noninflation of it as well.

In view of that, one needs boundaries drawn differently, new definitions. Besides, no matter whether it applied to any other person on Earth, the imperative would apply to oneself to find the right response to such Kundalini-brought data.

And the Earth needs that skill now, so that overlapping, jostling altercating values *based on long histories, perhaps authentic*, perhaps mutually exclusive, will not annihilate but learn from each other—knowing when to yield and withdraw, even during challenges to their own identity; knowing that in energy terms it can be multiplied. But no two parts of the same energy will try to play the same role.

Even here, or especially here, there is the law of physics that no two identical particles with half-energy spin can occupy the same "quantum state within a quantum system at the same time"—consciousness assuring us there is some distinction, even if it is that one withdraws to the observer position, saying to the other "I," you go ahead.

"This [Pauli exclusion] principle was formulated by Austrian physicist Wolfgang Pauli in 1925 for electrons, and later extended to all fermions with his spin–statistics theorem of 1940."[24]

From *Keep This Quiet!* IV, rev. ed., pages 82–83:

> The Kundalini kriya episode—"the broken water"—came in October 1991. I know because Russell walked into my room just afterwards; he had not yet left for India.
>
> Writings that remain from this period, I printed in scroll format—the only paper I found lying around the house . . .
>
> [They] remind me of what I struggled with—a few states away from Hunter—in this major initiation that would, in kilometers outside Earth measurement, take me many more, as my unconscious, my inspiration, aligned with *the Fourth Amendment of right to privacy in the home* free of unreasonable searches and seizures (that he championed). But [I] turned it into a pun [just ahead] . . .

For most of the entire three months in La Honda area

> I tried to write him a letter. I intended to include it with a copy of the (September 10) release of British rock band Dire Straits ("If you wanna run cool, you got to run on heavy, heavy fuel"). Their album *Brothers in Arms* was a staple of Willy's collection. Yet what a sensation I'd felt at Owl Farm

to hear Hunter play it, heartily endorse it. No one ran on heavier fuel.

Remember, this is from my point of view. He might see it differently. So might I later. But right then and there I intensely wanted to make contact before I changed so entirely it was out of the question. So, a little part of me feared.

A tiny part. Probably the me who instigated the Kundalini in the living room, who had something to say and was bound to break through, who crossed the barrier of the unconscious but couldn't get out of my throat or into a mailed letter. And even if she had, what would have changed? But she didn't think about consequences. Or reason.[25]

❋

A part of me—call her that least evolved—didn't know how she would cross the widening gap between us. She was intent, standing firm, trying to write—and then mail!—Hunter a letter.

Picking up the all-too-obvious indications of a shift in the future, she tried to lay down markers:

> Like someone before a big battle, wanting to bring another person close at that moment to say: *Look, I'm going away for a while.* Or: *Look, can you handle this? Here, I'm still me. Take my hand and help me do this more gracefully. Go through this with me. Otherwise, I'm bound to be outlandish, "abstruse," perhaps incommunicable. I'll say outrageous things. I'll be stoned out of town. At least, till I get a handle on the situation.* The two events—finishing my manuscript and still hoping to make contact with Hunter—intertwined to create the end of what became *Love in Transition* II, the novel that had been intercepted by energy initiations in Zurich, Switzerland, and Tienen, Belgium. The initiation in California being yet more fuel to the inner fires.[26]

I was protecting my initiations but dead set on exploring the relationship with Hunter. Was that a contradiction in terms?

What I was soon to call a young part of me was bound and determined to have this experience. To throw herself into it, hopefully, to see where her connection to Hunter led, her feelings not yet squashed out by this incoming energy—which was a dangerous, fine line to manage.

The place where my path that was now opening met the uncertainties inherent in it. The Edge. The Light holding high intensity, which Hunter already held. His energy bursting at the seams. It knew no bounds. I do not exaggerate. *How would this multidimensional encounter turn out?*

✻

But it wasn't all up to me and my two differently inclined "sides." At the JFK airport in New York City as I was en route back to Belgium, things came to a head. The Universe was having nothing to do with fence sitting. It had an opinion on the subject. AND a way to enforce it. *Hide your head in the sand at your own peril*, it as much as said.

Posthumously, an anthologized book of Milton's selected essays, *A Discourse on Hip*, had been published in December 1990. Learning of it, I ordered a copy. I marveled at the introductory announcement that he kept his emotional life "under wraps"; it remained a mystery, it said, why he'd come up from an arid, nonwriting underground of the '50s with an outburst starting in the 'mid-60s.

I didn't recognize the unproductive, parched-in-a-barren-desert Milton of the '50s—who sprang alive (that one I knew) with productivity about the time I, ahem, *arrived on-scene!*—seeing him nightly. How could this be? I wanted to correct any gaps I could.

In New York I phoned *Commentary*. Did anyone there at the magazine remember him from the days he used to publish essays in *Commentary*? "Wait." I was put on hold, and senior editor Marion Magid came to the phone. "We used to 'eye' each other," she said., "when he'd come into the office." But they didn't get into conversations. She advised me, "Write 'The Milton Klonsky I Knew.' Begin it, 'There was a time when New York was known for its talkers. Milton Klonsky was one of them.'"

Though she doubted she'd publish it because, she said, he was a "cult hero" with a limited following, she insisted I pen it. It was an assignment.

Then I got ready for my flight, January 14, 1992. The Universe made the dilemma I was in, from its point of view, a clear-cut choice. Waking that morning, I pulled myself out of sleep to find Jyoti's face bobbing in front of me, delivering a very palpable hint": "Time's up." But despite obviously being ruffled by the fearful statement she'd communicated, I stood unsuspectingly at the Carey Terminal.

Jyoti had never given me idle advice. Was she to start being whimsical now? No. Silly me if I didn't heed her warning.

But I was careless. First, a carry-on was stolen right off the sidewalk.

In the plane I was checking in my second carry-on to see what had been taken.

Hooray, now twenty-five-years-in-the-making (!), my *Love in Transition* manuscript was safe. My attention was captured by a photo I took at Hector Kuri-Cano's: a famous in-color image of the Christ's face, reportedly manifested by the Hindu satguru Sai Baba superimposed over a black-and-white printout of the famous Shroud of Turin image. I pulled it out, staring at it. On Hector's wall, one side of the face was in shadow, the other in light, and the middle half and half. The angle that survived of the three I'd taken was *un*shadowed. Or was it half and half? I'm not totally sure. Definitely not shadowed.

I glanced out the window as we taxied down the runway. Fire on the wing right in front of my eyes! Message getting through??

Thus began a dramatic return flight.

Evidently, it was more than just routine sparks.

During the repairs, the passengers sat calmly aboard, partly inspired by devotees returning from Satya Sai Baba's ashram in India. I had ashes from his ashram in my carry-on, given by Jyoti. We waited. Then—the maintenance issue addressed—we rolled down the runway again. Again, fire burst out on a wing. Right under my eyes. The passengers—stewards and stewardesses too—balked, in a mass refusal to continue, and the maintenance crew evidently concurred.

Put up overnight in a Howard Johnson's, I was using my supply of free food coupons in the restaurant. But stopped, got up, and left for my room.

Suppose I'm killed tomorrow. I thought. *Think of what I wouldn't want to die with me.*

I took it as a hint to *Take note. You are running out of time. Start bringing out your work. Or someone will "replace" you.* I took note.

It took heavy persuasion, often, to get me to budge if the stakes were very high and what could be lost great, including loss of face for going out on a limb in revelations. I wouldn't call this synchronistic airplane episode, coming after the wake-up warning, blackmail. Rather, it was *showing me the landscape* and what would happen—how I would be usurped, missing the "boat"—or barcarolle—if I sat longer on my hands.

That night in a dream a great wind wafted copies of my manuscript up into the sky, sailing far and wide, dropping down through the air, into the hands of exactly those who knew what to do with the information.

Back in Belgium, with the bell sounding its welcome and my interactive computer receiving energy from another dimension, operating by a law I did not know (perhaps no one knew—it might be "angels"), I was in a real fantasy, a really creative place, a "land" of opportunity, a situation that was the opposite of becoming desperate in despair. No, I went knowingly into the Unknown, the Unconscious, the Guided. In fear and trembling, but elation.

❋

I arrived, feeling "ordered" to use Milton's real name—to report what I'd experienced as fact; report about the afterlife as meticulously as I could, using my name. Throw away the camouflage of a novel and an imaginary Robert. I was being ordered to tell it like it is, the novelist now thrust into the role of a writer of nonfiction.

The alternative might not be physical death but being bypassed ("Time's up") as the information found other outlets. For this brand of testimonial would come out, regardless. And taking this hint would avoid that Zurich comment, "was reduced and relegated, became like a well dried up." This was fodder for the fire. I determined to do a 180 on that front.

If you don't believe inspiration is insistent and that it "moves on," that a life purpose can—that it adapts to timing—listen to Elizabeth Gilbert's account of poet Ruth Stone, winner of a Guggenheim, National Critics Circle Award, and many other awards:[27]

> As [Stone] was growing up in rural Virginia, she would be out working in the fields and she would feel and hear a poem coming at her from over the landscape. It was like a thunderous train of air and it would come barreling down at her over the landscape. And when she felt it coming . . . 'cause it would shake the earth under her feet, she knew she had only one thing to do at that point. That was to, in her words, "run like hell" to the house as she would be chased by the poem.

And if she didn't:

> The whole deal was that she had to get to a piece of paper fast enough so that when it thundered through here, she could collect it and grab it on the page. Other times she wouldn't be fast enough . . . and the poem would barrel through her and she would miss it, and it would "continue on across the landscape looking for another poet."[28]

I plunged into writing "The Milton Klonsky I Knew," with the energy of a clearly present "spirit committee."

In it, I addressed the mystery of a life that seemed unfulfilled. I explained it by anticipating the future. The page below printed out with lines slanted *both upward and downward on the same page*:

> Rather than do what others had done, on no matter how large a scale, why not do what no one had done? One who had a vision of the future coming toward us, with predictions of out-of-control events, might decide rather to plant seeds that could harvest that approaching onslaught of energy and make of the crossing between two centuries a Celebration Event. Make, in fact, a Transition period. No one would know that was what he was doing. No one might ever know. Which is why those who were left with the mystery felt it so strongly. That they had been left with something to do. That it didn't die, but in fact at this moment BEAR ITS FRUIT.

Events in the future would be out of control. Behind the scenes, a lot of planning was taking place. April 28, '92, I sent the essay to Marion Magid. Her appreciative reply said I'd captured his spirit. But—*Commentary* was a long shot—she suggested trying an avant garde publication.

Further to intensify the energy, it appeared that, in my mystical Taiji class, the energy from my mind translated itself into my hands, while my mind—as I stood doing the Taiji form in Leuven—located the text in question in my manuscript, in Tienen. That is, my mind was easily traveling the distance between the class and the manuscript. Easy for the mind to do. But correlating the movement of my hands in the Taiji form with the text, it reshaped the text—in a sense, turning "matter" back into energy, patterns, a map of hills, valleys, typography of the printed pages: how they *felt* to me, as registered in the energy picked up by the hands. Like sending a beam of electrons to a particular target. It did not literally change the text but stamped the energy.

Thus, when I sat down at the computer again, I had already run through the changes I would now make, storing the impressions somewhere in my consciousness. To learn more about this, read *Space Encounters* III by me.

Also, references to Bible passages appeared beside text on the printed pages (keyed to my *Thompson's Chain Reference Bible*). In the printing, the pages were visually reorganized, accompanied sometimes by the ringing of the BELL for emphasis.

The bell never left the house, waiting for my return if I went outside or even traveled—audible when it wanted to be. In particular, facilitating the writing. It would often signal with the printer light flicking or the bell ringing before a barrage of pages, perhaps the first ten or so being blank!!

Remember, I felt my soul was in love with the cosmic level of this guide and they had a relationship up in those cosmic-consciousness spheres, in the huge universe of pastpresentfuture, to us. And I didn't want to betray it. And going to see Hunter was not betraying it.

But I was walking a tightrope with my human emotions, part of me bound and determined to rekindle and advance the love story Hunter and I had shared before, irrespective of any side issues, while also pulled in the direction of the future: my mystical self, I didn't yet know but could feel. All the while, my soul was monitoring. His too.

Well, we are all like that, if we knew. But sometimes the "spacecraft" of the soul comes in close. It wants us to do something. It detects we can.

I began to ponder what this "transition" of my soul grouping could entail. Was it dangerous? Was it sacrificial? Did it involve giving up their own stories to the Earth, but wrapped with a bow, kept on a very high level, risking being confiscated (the intensity of the attractions) down in our egoic-preponderant Earth?

I exaggerated, perhaps, the effect on this soul grouping if their memories were handed over and misused. But maybe not. The following pages show how, in October and thereafter in my sublet near La Honda, I tried to "take Hunter along with me," in my dramatic initiations, *after* I left Owl Farm, while he was writing "Elko" and I was in telephone contact with him. Not often but enough. Filling in (with my drafts of letters) holes left in the story—or digging in the holes and finding what was buried underneath.

I was still impacted by the gigantic impact of the near-miss of our get-together. I didn't dare post most of the letters. But I did get them down on paper. And therefore, I have them now. And who knows in what way, as he reached up and resonated with his own thoughts, some of these thoughts might have "reached" him energetically, that is, in resonance. It only takes resonance to communicate in this realm. But that cannot be faked. It happens when we are alone with ourselves. It tells us who we are. And the way forward.

The Multidimensional Hunter OR, *the Universality of* Hunter

Well, that's a topic I didn't expect to go into. But it's here. If a person is representing his soul level and is unique enough, unusual enough, then the resonances he gets from "up there" will not be likely picked up right and left here on the Earth, because they are too particular. They are too extreme. So he was safe. In his camouflage personality he could get involved with as much of his soul level—experience it, in this unlikely personality, that is—as wished, because who was going to walk in and try to imitate him? Successfully, that is. As on the writing level, no one could, it was the same with the personality. But under that was the man who in his soul level contact, partly because he was "split," was doing OK. At least, that is what's coming into my fingers, unannounced, today. I'd say unbidden, but that would be going too far.

So I went to Owl Farm, aflame with old passions, he as well, amid much skepticism on the part of spirit guides except for his soul level, a watching presence that I was aware of.

I have told the story multiple places. But omitted these letters that follow, the back story.

June 1991, just after leaving Owl Farm in May

A Kundalini episode, as you know, occurred right in the middle of the first night's sexual encounter, attempting to take it over, use it to break in like an intruder through the gates, to revive—I suppose—a connection that went much further back.

I said not a word of explanation to him at the time. Silly me. Old emotions were trying to get let loose. How far back they went, I was not to know, too busy squelching them. But in *my writings following this trip—writings addressed to him, at least one of which I mailed—I overcorrected, ripe with revelations.*

My sense (conviction) of his involvement ramped up due to the October kriya incident, as you will soon see in these drafts.

In short, to recount, the kriya energies typically took me to information known on my cellular level—the specialty of this energy that is considered, in the Hindu tradition, in studies of it over centuries, "an evolutionary energy." That is, an energy that, in conscious, electrical (Light), in the quantum fields, is looking ahead to imprint our thoughts as we attempt to become more ready to handle the Earth consciousness and, when appropriate, take it further.

PART FOUR

Locked behind a phone that doesn't ring

Cell-*burst* Poems

by the Sprit *World*—2023

Author's Note

Did you write this account that follows?
I just pasted it here now,
Discovered it in my files of Book Three Poems
Dated January 2023

I *stumble on this file*
I *wrote it*
I *did*?????
Must have been in

a daze
A *trance*
Fingers typing
The brain
Asleep?

I had to get
From 1992—is that what it was?—
to What Came Next

infinitely different
Had a walk-in personality come to replace me?
It felt like it

As if I were stretched and turned into pretzels and Chartres mazes of my past
Heading into some future, which?
all that emotion refusing to go one step further if not brought to the surface
It refused to quietly stand by
and disappear
into my unconscious, never addressed by me
who had something more important to do

I had to face it
little as I was in this role that had these feelings
But they roared out
Why?
I told myself why
But it was beyond belief
Yet the downpour would not stop
So call it a running Other World's commentary
who knew which dimension this one came from?
Sometimes it said it was from eternity—no dimension
all dimensions
But it would not stop pouring over me
out of me
backed up by everything a cell—a single cell burst I've described before—let out
stopped holding back.

It did not focus on the St. Paul part of the assignment in the cell burst
No,
its focus was on the

Magdalene feelings,
For to get to the role being undertaken, these feelings had to be looked at
AND FELT.
Had to be felt, and evidently I was thought to be able to hold them
And would
For they were the opening point to a door
to what came next
blocked otherwise

So here goes with the Cell Burst poetry
To which there was obviously a collective, archetypal aspect
But we live archetypes
We live collective energy
Only, do we live
names from the past?
Do we?

Not exclusively
It isn't allowed.
We would be so confused
not know how to think in terms of partial energy
to share
Nevertheless,
the cell burst didn't know this
seemed not to

I had a lot to figure out
But more
first of all
To feel

Feel for whom?
For myself, it felt like
But it was archetypical
I kept falling into the problem of "not" identifying
with an archetype
Don't do that, Jung said, knowing well how persuasive the archetype, whichever one you might find yourself in

if it begins speaking through you,
Merged with you
using you
to go further
is

But was that relevant here
The cell burst was simple,
straightforward
a burst of feeling
of redoing the past
of breaking into the future

And is the past even fixed?
Could that change too?
as the feelings buried then or hidden from the public
came out
undeniable
don't even try to deny them
Straight from the Heart of
the history
Personal
Not Third person
Wanting
Recognition
to be
Felt

For where did we think our unlived realities went?
Of course, nowhere
If unlived options disappeared at death
like humans
Certainly, they didn't break off and remain alive
as the human died
Certainly, longings didn't maintain a foothold
in energy
Somewhere

This one did

In the total being they could become
Quite Large,
Couldn't they?

While first being initiated, for three years, long ago,
I was told the initiator had many "personalities,"

Or was it the group and he stepped forth?

Yes, from within the group
Naturally
That's the typical way it occurs

Any one of whom of his personalities, he said, could make a love story with me
A scandalous thought in that it makes us seem like underlings to higher beings
Large-scale beings that cover more than one human being
But isn't that so if they are willing to—have no choice but to—be vaster than you or I
when in physical form
unless we grasp that we—yes, we—are
Universal
too?

Any personality of his could, then,
Anyplace where his energy was strong enough
Not that he controlled it as with strings
Decidedly No,
being one of his "personalities," or, better pit,
drenched with
His energy,
Did not preclude freedom
AT ALL
Underscore
It was voluntary

But the thing was
if his energy was strongly there

it had dominance
impact
swayed the person feeling it
Reeling with it

OF COURSE

It was just like saying that resonance
in some cases
was personified
Had a spirit behind it

Oh no
Oh yes

So it was dangerous, do you mean?
How dangerous was it
to resonate with something because suppose that meant you were
in the clutches of a spirit

No, do not fear
It did not work like that
It was another part of the
Big Mystery that
being human inside eternity
Meant

Inside, let's say, energies so much larger than we
Us
In a physical form
were

Incomprehensible

But that in some sizes were organized
Just like here
Rather, not like here,
But just as we organized three dimensions
organized larger chunks of energy

huge blocks like ice
Only, that were thawed
Were not frozen blocks of energy
congealed into our patterns
Oh no

And so, being roamed inside other beings in this structure I am describing
And in this structure cosmic beings
"oversaw," as it were, *their* own energy
Coinciding with which, or inside which
but not boxed in,
some of us were
Depending on, though,
not just history but
Well, history too, don't discount it
But
Too
That we
Resonated
with it

Which made us prisoners?

Oh. No
Let me explain.

Should I or not?
Is it getting too heavy?
too weighed down
too un-Earth-like, where we are guaranteed our freedom, by birthright
That's the one thing for sure we can count on

But, he told me,
trying to encourage me to choose any human personality of his,

that is, on the cosmic-being level, he could get any personality I chose
to—feeling *his* response—
react

Choose one of them, any one, on the human level, he said,
and he would throw all his energy behind him
But it didn't work

Did you think it would work?

Certainly not automatically, as I said,
And—have I said this—it could be intercepted!

No!!

It was just that human energy of the higher self or soul
strongly affected the reactions of the human self
especially if it was part of a very high being
With very high mastery
And, though, selflessness

Yet,
There were many purposes behind
Incarnation
Even to experience defeats and temptations

Already, once I began the initiation
the first person I felt as holding this energy was dead
in fact, triggered the initiation
As I kept the tie with him

But a few years later
the story expanded
with people I met in the present
however, around us was energy and patterns that developed out of experiences in this lifetime

One relationship
impossible to carry forward
everyone admitted it
yet held patterns I could walk into with others
I have earlier written how aghast I was at this notion
What?
Make a pattern—walk into it, meet new people swayed by it—make a pattern, I was saying, using a relationship in the recent past because it was so significant

But why then is it reused secondhand
Dusted off
No, it never got dust on it
Well, picked back up and set aground
New People
no one the wiser

but me, I knew

If we are all in this together
It makes sense that we would share patterns made by others
But for one of the originals to go into a pattern Made with Someone Else
It didn't seem fair
To me

Suppose that original person were recontacted
Impossible, the channel said
You've no idea what you're suggesting

Now I am *not* not not confiscating another person's choices
just stating how the initiation went
with many things beyond my understanding, I am sure
and yet, when demands for sacrifice seemed too high to me, humanly speaking
that is, sacrifice of others
I balked with all I had

believe it or not, it worked
A new course was set
It only required a display of enough rebellion
To make another course be believed in
Anyway, there were so many unknowns and missing explanations
befitting the situation that came from another dimension
trying to be real in this reality

So a person from my past
As I was saying
Began to loom into this reality as a possibility to go forward with

Remember, though, as individuals, in this dimension, we still control our destiny,
More or less,
Our preferences,
Our soul may come in—or the Bigger Picture—and "kill us off"
I had discovered
For a purpose
And I am not clear whether we even, in our 3-D self, have to concur
I think not

Also depending on how much of the Bigger Picture of us and that we are in we absorb

But killing someone off was not in the plan here
It was to see how much of the behind-the-scenes scenario that this option existed in
could land here
through anyone who could for any length of time absorb and live the energy

By 1992 I had shifted to a long shot
the one just described
And though its chances had dwindled to nonexistent
I could not clamp tape over my mouth and be silent
I felt I had to give him,
this man left "outside" as parts of our history together were replayed with new characters,
a retake
some clues
feeling he could receive a few of them, that would explain
some recent actions on my part
So in writing him

I preserved a record
of 1992
How I got from there to there
across the Cell burst energy

That writing—to myself or to him—is the source of the material elsewhere
I have never, obviously, felt comfortable transcribing it and sending it out
But recently, looking at what I reveal and what not on the Earth,
I at least typed it into a computer.
Remember, though, he was just one of the males I encountered *who perhaps could have*
incarnated the channel, and in particular one spirit in the channel
But let's say the channel
Who had enough of the energy *already*
And certainly access to it
to redirect it to the channel's mission

None of them succeeded or perhaps even wanted to accept the job
Truth be told, none became aware they were being approached
Consciously, that is,

As the channel told me, and showed me pictures,
if a lot of Light was given to a human,
that recipient would take it a certain distance
And then,
Light too strong
turned dark
no guidelines, no rules—
It came in "cold,"
Void of all posts and guidelines
It made them up
Almost inevitably
trying to find the way through the unmarked, uncharted, indiscriminate packets of a giant energy that could go in any direction on Earth
Or not on Earth

So I got the idea
that the teachings being given to me were inside a pair
And I thought—rightly or wrongly—I knew who the other person was
Again, rightly or wrongly

I think that had it been at another moment in my life I would have gotten the idea
that the other person in the pair was someone else
But at that moment, so wedged into my attraction to this particular person was I
filled with the energy of our last encounter
I focused the "pair" idea onto him
And maybe it belonged there
And maybe it didn't
And maybe there was no pair idea
Anyway, there was the cell burst and
how affected I was, in the kriya outburst, of course

So I described my initiation, which outpoured
I could not control it
I had nothing to do with it
I just received
And on sheets of paper, sometimes scrolls of paper
in the new computer in 1992
wrote and wrote
what became the record below.

This was the incredible firewall I had to walk through to get to my mystical self. She/I had to pacify the inner child who had another idea for this lifetime and had to give that part of herself a chance to bring along "a friend." To try out her conviction of what would happen if she turned the story "her way." All it took to pacify her was to give her feelings a chance to express themselves, to let them off the leash. To see where they took her. Then obediently she joined with the mystic for The Rest of Her/My Life. With no regrets. Not discovering this part of me, though, I would have had regrets. Discovering her, experiencing her feelings, not knowing where many of them came from, I enriched myself. Richer, more fulfilled, though partly filled with Mystery, leaving explanation aside but letting feelings in, I became who I am today. That firewall of feeling, though, was the precursor, the barrier. I had to pass through it. Had to. Did.

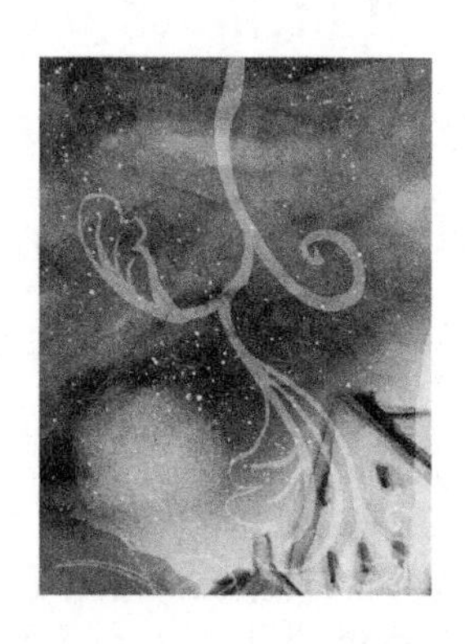

PART FIVE

The Extraterrestrial

Hunter S. Thompson

February 1, 2023: *Pulling from my drafted* Nabokov *book that includes the above cell-burst* October 1991 *incident that figures strongly in my life, an incident that occurred at* La Honda

Tienen, Belgium. 1997, writing away like a little mole, in total solitude in my apartment that had what I called "spirit committees" triggering what I wrote. In fact, the computer, since just before I went to Owl Farm, has been "helping" me write, and the interaction intensified afterwards. It prints some of the text differently than what's on-screen, selecting to focus on now one area of the page, now another, as in lifting up a line below.

1997

Yes, we are in a tight spot now. And we have all been in it before. A tight spot is nothing new to us. And we have really gotten down to it. We know how to react. We will each just be ourselves, as we were before we began this project. So now I will conduct myself as if I am famous and have the will and resources to see all of this though, because I am myself, and I just have to

remember myself.

No one can imagine that a Kundalini kriya incident took me to witness the very moment—the setting—where (asked to choose a lifetime role) in a prebirth "assignment" in an Upper Room, I watched myself answer, "St. Paul," and was given, paired with it, the Magdalene, the male-female duo, or counterparts—no one could imagine, thinking on it seriously, that a Kundalini kriya could have whisked me off to observe this without (at least in my subconscious at odd moments or persistently in a wormhole, unknown to me) perusing what that might mean. Or that (not told yet in this story, but it's coming), I retrieved the memory of Paul's most seminal moment ("seeing the Light")—all by myself, without permission.

Maybe humans might disregard and be uncurious about the implications, afraid, even, to so much as touch such an absurdity, but for how long?

What if we shove aside—or shunt aside—telltale experiences? Refuse to explore beyond a certain depth? Well, they will catch up with us. Never fear.

2022

This 1990s writing is catching up with me, asking: *Do I want to leave these heaps of channeled material to be thrown in a dump pile, or do I want to see what mysteries they unfold for me, now that I know how to practice nonattachment, I can take it on the chin, whatever they turn up, which of course will be miraculous regardless from my point of view?*

I have a non-jaundiced but instead curious, investigative approach.

No, it is more than that. It is the return of an ultimatum. The warning I woke with in January 1992, just after the wings of my plane caught fire at JFK airport at takeoff, about which the reader knows: "Time's up."

Like a buzzer that tells that you are at the five-minute-warning mark in a speech, keeping you from running over or omitting the critical point of what you wanted to say. Or it is like a kind professor who tells you your exam time is three quarters finished, step on it.

To convince me I was "mortal"—for who thinks about death?—I got diagnosed in 2022 with a serious disease. (Halt. Never fear. Jumping into creative energy, I got cured, as illness—lack of harmony, as they say in the East—cannot follow high creative energies. In fact, it was the out-of-alignment with my higher calling and Time, when put side by side, that caused the illness. I know. That's not a Western explanation. But putting my timeline side by side with what I had left to do precipitated an urgent command to change focus. And so you see this book materializing. I would not have done it otherwise, wouldn't have gotten to it, wouldn't have that seriously thought about what I wanted—had been asked—to leave behind. Beyond the obvious, that is. Beyond the easy.

❋

In 1991, the warning came with a sentence, a voice, in my head as I woke from sleep.

In this new "command performance," *nobody said the work given to me would be turned over to someone else if* I *dallied and procrastinated longer*. No, I suddenly make the connection that the push, or really shove, by the illness I contracted in 2022 was reminding me of my mortality; mortality will take care of matters all by itself *if* I *did not see this work left over from* Tienen, Belgium, *in just this* Time's Up *fashion*. It is a stopwatch measuring my speed around the track, an Other World coach tapping on a wristwatch.

Picking up another of the countless piles of pages, I find a letter; in the 1990s in which I recorded what was uppermost in my thoughts, directing that to a recipient, probably unmailed, when in reality *it was to me* Now. It's a way to remember, to bring it all back, to verify. So I wrote:

> I will tell you the memory I have of being given this lifetime, another of these totally contextless memories that I have kept in store but not written of, not published, not spoken of. For they belonged to some announced but nonexistent outer framework. I was alone, writing, in [October] 1991. Suddenly the Kundalini began, and I will just be straightforward. What I say won't exactly make sense because it comes inside a consciousness that has to be carefully presented. So the Kundalini was putting into me, while breaking up blocks, the sight of myself in a chamber before being born. I was with a group, who were asking me to choose the lifetime I wanted. I—or the Kundalini—brought it unavoidably to mind, insistently, with its shaking: this extraordinary and unthinkable scene. I replied without thinking it over or hesitation, as I remembered under the Kundalini influence, somewhat like being on a cloud somewhere, I chose St. Paul.

And I seem to be melting away at this moment, thinking of the seriousness of the statements I made up there.

So. See. It's all true. It's not a case of faulty memory. See. I recorded it at the time.

I added, "Well, this lay dormant in my scattered but unforgotten assortment of such powerful memories."

But this was not all. In that Upper Room, I got the consent to take on St, Paul, as requested. But with one caveat: add the Magdalene to it. To continue:

> And I must say I would be the proudest person on the Earth to bring in any of its teachings.
>
> Now, coming out of this are parallels, obvious to me once I started looking. You see, one teacher is remembered for taking gigantic risks, having shipwrecks, being thrown in prison, persecuted, crucified. And you take the other. And you have a person with a cut-off history. This coincidence and opposition was part of the karma, as you can easily see. Why this is important is for the feminine archetype, dignity. And vibrations. And this is only the beginning.

So this is just the beginning of a mysterious clue.

How could such a subtle (quantum-located possibly) experience be a fact or factor in my life? You tell me, I asked. Also, what did it say about the human structure? Anything at all? Yes, certainly. Is it a "dissociated" facet of "me," existing in isolation, one I am to hear about vaguely, get rumors of, have initiations that bring here to me, but then disconnect from? If we do that in everyday reality, we are in big trouble. What about if in spiritual reality?

Everyone else was looking to find out who they were, and I was thrown into the question of why I was someone else—at least two people, to start with. And probably more. What could that mean? How did transpersonality work?

Ah, transpersonality. Was that it?

No answer. Left to me to figure out or discard.

I had selected the roles. *But hadn't I been someone to start with?* Someone standing—or was it sitting?—in the Upper Room who requested to take on these two roles? *Who was that?* I started as whom? No answer. Let's see if more comes.

And again, what does that say about us humans? It seems to make consciousness supreme because wasn't it consciousness that was being carried further? continued? And energy? "I," of course—who that is—is another matter. And did a group do this with me? Was I in a sense a group, a point (me) here on Earth in a body, but energetically the rest "offline," out there, ready to assist???

Yet, whoever "I" was and for however long had evidently had this consciousness I did not or else was a parrot choosing the lifetimes like a robot. No, it was the former.

If you wonder how I am feeling, in 2023, in rereading this, I am laughing out loud. It is such a cockamamie plot, such a humorous predicament, a trick on myself, a trap, or series of obstacles, a *Survivor* show by a Master Plotter.

I watched (2023) a biography of Johnny Cash—his time of despair, when he walked, totally "spent," deep into the interior of a cave; he was all set to die. Walked till the light he carried went out—till, bone weary, he sank down. When he woke, though, he seemed to hear or sense God, who said he was not finished with him yet, to get up and leave the cave. How? He had no light. No strength. Yet walking and crawling, sensing at each twist and turn of the dark cave the direction to take, at long last he felt wind. And some steps further saw light: the cave entrance Once out of the cave, he did not look back on his old life of uppers and downers, addiction, and a death wish. He was a new man, turned inside out. He was back on track with his soul.

Insight from Swami Satyananda Saraswati:

> This external experience, the perception you have through your senses, is a product of matter. Even your thoughts, feelings, emotions, and cognitions are products of matter. Therefore, they cannot be absolute and final. This means there must be another realm of experience. And if there is another realm of experience, it must be possible to transcend the present limitations of the mind. The mind is also matter; it is definitely not spirit. So the mind can also be transformed and made to evolve. People have begun to realize and experience this in the last few decades. And in my opinion, this marks the end of one era and the beginning of another. That means the external world is a manifestation of your inner experience. And you can improve this experience to any extent . . .
>
> If a man is living but is unable to think, we say he has prana shakti but not manas shakti. Similarly, the silent parts of the brain have prana, not consciousness. So a very difficult question arises: how to awaken the sleeping compartments of the brain?

"All the great miracles of the remote and recent past," he went on, "and the ones yet to come, have sprung from what is known as the store-house of cosmic consciousness, the golden egg, the golden womb, the hidden Hiranyagarbha [containing/hiding, the unimaginable Creator God] within the structure of the human brain . . . What came as revelation to the ancient rishis, to Newton and Einstein and to many other great seers, is existing in us also, but it came to their conscious plane while it does not come to ours . . . The aim of Kundalini yoga is not really to awaken the power of man, but rather to bring the power down to earth or to bring the power of the unconscious, or higher consciousness, to normal consciousness."[29]

Kundalini awakening, he says, is "like a great explosion which transports a person into another plane of being":

> Ordinary consciousness and transcendental consciousness cannot be maintained at the same time; it is necessary to pass through an intermediate zone of change, where perceptions, feelings and experiences undergo a transformation. The adventure is always the same; it is a journey through the border region between the known and the unknown.[30]

The original Last Supper, Upper Room, event took place "during these last hours that Jesus spent with His beloved friends":

> The disciples had been arguing about who among them was the greatest (Luke 22:24), displaying a distinctly ungodly perspective. Jesus quietly rose and began to wash their feet, a task normally performed by the lowest, most menial slave. By this simple act, Jesus reminded them that His followers are those who serve one another, not those who expect to be served. He went on to explain that, unless the Lamb of God cleanses a person's sin, that person will never be clean: "Unless I wash you, you have no part with me" (John 13:8).

Divesting myself for at least those moments of *the physical self I knew*, I followed that kriya trail in the Upper Room, joined forces with "that me," who, at least in that instant of choosing, *knew what was going on*. I didn't. Hadn't.

Therefore—though I was, to myself, someone else a minute before—*having found where I began, this lifetime anyway, did I not become that beginning*? Or did I wrap it up and forget about it? Inexplicable as it was in the here-and-now? Leave unpacked a major trail? A thin, ribbonlike trail extending off a single moment. Kundalini has too great a reputation to be producing outliers, insignificant thought fodder to disregard.

I needed to let the question sink in, reveal greater consciousness. Too, a group I knew somewhere was involved, though again, which "I"? One I had seen only in a vision, Kundalini instigated at that.

Oh, and "Her water broke" meant, to me, if I rejected the kriya revelation, did not allow it to speak, it was to write off the baby right at the moment it pushed itself public, i.e., killing it in its very birth. No, don't I have to go through the birth ordeal? Assuredly.

❋

Meanwhile, in Colorado, Hunter is deep into "Fear and Loathing in Elko." I would call this really slapstick, as the rubber band stretches and the two trajectories move apart, yet both fueled in a flood of writing. In the *Columbia Journalism Review*, 2005, shortly after Hunter passed, his "Elko" editor at *Rolling Stone*, Robert Love, wrote a report on Hunter's deadline-snapping style. I extracted from it below.[31]

MEMORANDUM

To: HST
From: BOB LOVE
CC: JSW
December 16th: 7:00 P.M. EST [1991]
Re: FINAL HOURS OF CLOSING SCHEDULE FOR F&L IN ELKO

SUNDAY NIGHT: WE MUST FINISH INSERTS TONIGHT!!! Tomorrow afternoon is too late. I will call you at about 6:00 your time. We can talk through the two remaining inserts. You can dictate. I can take it down on my computer here, fax it back to you for correx, and you can fax it back to me. Either way, we must finish them tonight . . .

THE SQUABBLE AT THE COMMERCIAL HOTEL: One more paragraph! The judge looks into the lobby, freaks out at something. He turns to you and says . . .

THE JUDGE TO THE PLANE: We can talk through this if you like, but your outline seems right.

While the pages were flying back and forth in the darkness, Hunter and I would speak for hours on the phone, trying to straighten the plot lines, eliminate falseness, root out clichés and repetition. We also talked about other things, depending on what time of year it was: politics, basketball, football, F. Scott Fitzgerald, the William Kennedy Smith trial, the price of Christmas trees at Korean markets in New York City. When I told Hunter that from my desk at home I looked across an airshaft at a happy family celebrating the holidays with their young child while I waited alone and miserable for his transitions and inserts, he offered to crank-call them mercilessly all the way through until New Year's Day—as a kind of Christmas present to me. Later on he worked all of that stuff into a reverie for the Elko epilogue . . .

So, a flurry of "manuscript" pages would arrive, buzzing with brilliant, but often disconnected passages, interspersed with what Hunter would himself call "gibberish" (on certain days) and previously rejected material, just to see if we were awake. "Stand back," the first line would inevitably say, announcing the arrival of twenty-three or twenty-five or forty pages to follow in the fax machine. Soon there were phone calls from Deborah Fuller or Shelby Sadler or Nicole Meyer or another of his stalwart assistants. We always spoke of "pages," as in "How many pages will we get tonight?" . . . Pages were the coin of the realm; moving pages was our mission. I would mark them up, make copies for Jann, and then send them back.

❋

A Wild and Ugly Night with Judge Clarence Thomas . . . Bad Craziness in Sheep Country . . . Sexual Harassment Then and Now . . . A Nasty Christmas Flashback and a Nation of Jailers

"Fear and Loathing in Elko" from *Rolling Stone* #622, January 23, 1992:

[Part I] Memo from the National Affairs Desk: Sexual Harassment Then and Now. The Ghost of Long Dong Thomas . . . The Road Full of Forks . . .

There is a huge body of evidence to support the notion that me and the police were put on this earth to do extremely different things and never to mingle professionally with each other, except at official functions, when we all wear ties and drink heavily and whoop it up like

> the natural, good-humored wild boys that we know in our hearts that we are. These occasions are rare, but they happen—despite the forked tongue of fate that has put us forever on different paths.

✻

What can I say more outrageous than this? I will not accept the dare. I had a sense this period and after would take me too far "away"—from Hunter—to bridge the divide. Not a conscious thought. I didn't let it be. A sense right below the threshold.

As mentioned, a part of me, who had foresight, unconscious to me, was standing firm, trying to write—and then mail!—him a letter.

Merged in with this, I finished what would become *Love in Transition* volume II.

The La Honda Writings

I had already learned in Zurich that some of the strongest male energy was supporting the feminine, to bring out its strength in Earth archetypes. And my soul, focused in the transpersonal, identifying herself there, would send me out to work in energy *before* it got to the point of descending into public hands.

Writings from the La Honda sublet—the oldest printed out on the long, long scroll-shaped paper—still remain. They connect to the strongly sketched out unfinished poetry of *To Love*—AND *Remember*, written in 1985 /'86 in the Zurich Initiation. But they have greatly progressed underground:

Music he heard and everyone else did

when he died
and the music filled the room
from the astral plane
and was recorded in history that others heard the music play
heard it that day
that the flights of angels came to take
GOETHE

And so a big Comedy is coming through me
I call it a symphony

THIS IS BRACKETED IN THE MS TO BE CUT OUT:

and my personal instinct
said I got the call but it's for Hunter *too. I know I was always meant to tell him, if it came in this way,*
that the Go *signal came for his* Soul *Purpose this lifetime*
And it's a really big one
And so now I'll just start with this much, however much I wind up

> *putting into the envelope because it could go on forever*
> *as it's after all a big outpouring*
> *and a heart outpouring*
> *And the determination to get the message to you but with a very very light touch*
> *so you can scrutinize and ruminate and twirl your fists around,*
> *as you do when you type*
> *and let the music stream through you*
> *and we'll see what turns up*

Picking up, not in sequence:

> I got my Depth of Appointment. And I ran as fast as possible, though that was pretty slow [cut: *but as* Diana *the* Huntress *in the center of this rampaging* Archetype *and also the counteractant to it, that was powerful conflict. The man in the helicopter pulling the* Earth *to its new plot. And he was the one who showed it to me, made me feel it all through me and what it meant* "He Home" . . .
>
> *And you with the* Fourth Amendment *call and story. It's a big job.* And *I was bound and determined not to take one step more till I told you this much. And that somewhere in time there was locked in my heart a feeling of love for you that came out now. For your book was in the* Archetype *too. I need heavy heavy fuel here.*

The arrow to begin the page is here:

> And if all of this sounds cryptic
> well it's nothing to
> what comes later

Though everything that pertains to Hunter is marked to cut on these pages, I have something to remind me of what I struggled with, only states away, in having this major initiation that would—in kilometers outside Earth measurement, as I aligned the Fourth Amendment of right to privacy in the home (HST) with a Fourth Amendment that I was now receiving, in this Kundalini: going into the heart, or fourth chakra—take me many more. All through this, I try to write him a letter:

. . . I did hold up that screen of the past of something little in me that found your face and memory and example and courage of being individual in a moment like that. And I said what the hell, just go through it. But tell Hunter. And more came each day, and then I didn't know if I'd said too much or too little, because how did you fit in? For sure when I get my He-Home signal and the computer tells me you have one too, just as you have an Ir* signal—another go signal.

And then I picked up the fantasy of two children, Marie Antoinette and Little Mozart, and added this crazy idea. I wrote: she's going to be engaged to him for two centuries [based in a dream], and then she'll have learned how to feed the masses and he how to finish the Mass for the People, the Old Man's Mass and the Old God's Mass but also his own, when he goes on. And the signal would be He-home. I don't know. I do know that there's a group project I care about making work. And it's all true, the part about the risk it involves and the firm belief of all of us we could do it, take on the Archetype of the End of the Century if it was the only way out. The only positive way. And that was agreed that it was. It was the one unopened door, the one unopened seal. And I stand in front of it now, that seal of the heart that never spoke. It couldn't speak. It was SWORN TO SECRECY. And as I stand there I get my breath. For I know my intuition has told me and my computer typed it that this means everything to someone. The answer does. The next step. This very step. And that I have to have a whole heart.

Well, well, well, or ho ho ho.

What remains? I find more. My letters, as Kafka had written to his father, unmailed. I find how a small part of me was resisting expanding—not unless she could write her letter(s). And perhaps he would respond. Not to mention the fact that in ending *Love in Transition* Volume II with this material, I cut everything referring to Hunter out.

Why leave that in, when there was ChriST??? But I have detected the energy secret in the "omp" in the center of his name, the oomph,

---

* *ir*—pronounced "ear," the end of verbs like *sortir*—"to go"—in French; part of the image thread of a "GO signal"

which an energy cell has energized inside the Arc de Tree OMPH and even *heart of pomegranate lips*. I turn his *Fourth* Amendment focus into my parallel focus on "the Old Man's right to privacy in his FIRE-side"

I connect it to the opening of the heart, the fourth chakra (*"four"*: oven in French), happening to me right then, as the pages describe.

When the two doorbells rang at the same time

One that would knock the Old Man out
His shadow hand again
And the other that knew that even a massive onslaught of
Creativity could be thrown out if it was an invasion of
Privacy
At a certain point
And that was ruled out
For I had Number Four of this century
That call
That book
Of the heart chakra
And there was an Amendment to that
A parallel line
Coming to the same point
At the same time
Number Four was one point
And right on top
AT THE SAME POINT
THE FOURTH
AM-END
Ment
And then the Old Man with his massive intellect and creativity
would not be knocked out by what he'd kept hidden in his heart
But would draw the line here
In his helicopter pulling the Earth to the New Plot
He said Yes to the New
He did not shut it out
Going on and on and on in the old line
That now came to a stop
And so I tore mask after mask
To try to see his face

The man behind the Son of Man masks
And I kept seeing your spirit standing right beside me
Helping me have the courage I really had
To be Diana the Huntress against the whole archetype
Of the End of the century
Which I found myself right in the center of
And that it was my Life choice to be there
Unknown to me
When I would suddenly wake up
As I'd dreamed I would
And my book be intercepted
But I didn't know that holding so firmly to my reins of the Truth
For myself I would wind up in this unconscious energy of the Earth and all the things people never said
That would have made history go another way
It was vowed in the energy left down there not to let

But I had no idea that if I did it well enough
If my heart was blown wide open
And my mind blown wide open
But in the end my heart
So that nothing else mattered
I would wind up with the Alternative Revelation
So deep it took centuries of master-hearting to get to it
A 2,000-year PLOT
By the boldest minds imaginable
But they found their hearts all this time
In being master minds
Had got omitted

And they'd had that style of it enough
They would say their message from the heart
From his "heart of pomegranate lips"
Which she saw
Looking at him so long ago
Miriam saw
And he said, "What would you, Miriam?"
And it stayed locked inside then

And stayed locked in
And history kept going one way
Leading up to this way
When suddenly everything that was no turned into yes
You can imagine what an explosion that would be
And so it exploded in me
The answer to the question
that was his own vibration
and was coded into the DNAs of his and her personalities
that if ever the day came
the question was presented again
and it happened by the way to be coded to a personal
Apocalypse
That would snowball,
Well, just look that the real answer was
Practically saying there will be no 21st century
If the King stepped down
Dethroned himself
For what was that crown
If he couldn't share
Couldn't have a heart like other men

And so I tore mask after mask . . .

In lesson form
The lessons they had learned
HIS HAND
THE OLD MAN'S
When he reveals it

As he's opening my hand now
The hand I didn't know I had
That I was one of those who agreed and even shouted that I
Wanted to do this
Help bring in the Real RITES OF MAN
Starting with the rites of his own FIRE SIDE
The Old Man's privacy in his own FIRE SIDE
He had never been allowed that
Because where could he get protection enough

It didn't exist
How to protect
A VIBRATION LIKE THIS
His own when he looked at Mary Magdalene
Just as he had on the Cross
And then he'd get strength from her
My computer when I felt the question and wrote it wrote the Answer
As the power behind it is fueling everything written here
D
I
D
Lessons for the Earth in its changing position

Now what use for a
Medium
THE MEDIUM
OF
LOVE

LOVE
IN
TRANSITION
THE MEDIUM
Of LOVE

And so I always knew I was to write my Revelation
but so as not to be responsible
for a snowballing Apocalypse
I'm bound to write this letter
Which I've been trying to write for two weeks
But the Apocalypse kept pushing for the other end
Like the Plague centuries before

For it was in the air now
The germ of it all
The real story behind
The American Dream
In this version

The real one
A
MARY
CAN

WHEN SHE SAID, "I CAN"
And shouted it so loud her personalities heard it
And his heard too
And thus the Avenue being walked down by Christ and Mary Magdalene
AT THE END OF THE CENTURY
Was not the Unthinkable one
In the predictions
For they were set to counteract those predictions
Of the end of the century making each other hear of their real meaning
When the man of the OUR
the Apocalyptic HOUR
Turned instead in the Bridegroom
And she was the bride
For else naught else mattered
And he couldn't put a clamp on his feelings on his one
This was the real one
And when he felt something at that intensity
His own vibration
The whole world shook in ramification
Thus he, John, had written it
AS A FAMILY WARNING
That the Christ had better right then take note
Which did he want
Which was the real dream
For it would spread and spread like the plague this time
Whichever on became the "Take"
As in the two possible endings of
Casa
*Blanca**
In the other world where all these terms originated

---

* *Casa*—house; *blanca*—white (SP)

Thus it was something long in preparation was coming into
Being meant to be Peace on Earth
But the Alternative would be rampaging war the like of which
Had never been seen
If when he opened his heart and said I love you
The whole world picked it up
Picked his vibration up
His private vibration
Invisible though it was

At just that moment of intersection
Why, all history wood be changed
And John agreed,
John of the Anti-Apocalypse
And it goes on and on in that version
But I could also get trapped in the poetry
of it
And this was real

The message underneath it

❋

And that's the purpose of not sitting any more on this music that you know there's, as said, an energy of feeling that puts you right into the transmission.

And how fun it is. Here comes my computer. I punched print and it wouldn't, which is to emphasize to me that what I feel is correct. However much my loyalty is to the energy and the memories behind the cell burst, that it may be the very thing I always did, that made the mistake before. And I've learned what it is to live your life in a book and in feeling held in unconsciously. And for all I know you're the very last man behind the mask. I don't know. That's it. I know how powerful was the feeling I've always held in behind my masks, and there's somebody here, in me, very little, but who's holding on so hard and holding your picture up. If, even, all she got was to tell you goodbye and where she went she did that. She did get a chance to speak. And in that kind of energy this is and battle, that's pretty heroic. And it must mean she has a pretty powerful memory of her own. And she's part of me. However big or little. She may be the very biggest me or the very tiniest. But she's sure got passion . . .

Yeah, that's what I want to say. Thank you. Somewhere down deep inside me you made an enormous impression. And I needed that these last two weeks, drew on it. But first I had to know it was there and that I really felt it and I felt it so strongly it must be real. And if it was real it couldn't hurt anybody by saying it.

⁂

So that's a look into my Hunter materials, October–December 1991 in La Honda, while subletting the office of Jyoti, who was in India at the ashram of Dhyanyogi-ji, whose photos looked down from her office wall calendar. All that in a mighty conjunction the kriyas took advantage of.

Factor in the soul-grouping aim of spreading the Christ consciousness, using those who, in their lifetime, reached the level where they could join the group's work. Otherwise, they stayed obliviously in the dark about it. And that was OK. Only, I was to wake up. And it was not as easy as snapping your finger.

But once you were "contacted," from within, in fact, it was irresistible. But due to the energies I felt, the thoughts I had, as I came back to myself as this kriya settled down, I was trying to bring Hunter along with me. Well, shouldn't Hunter on his human level know some of this? He was up for it. For anything. Even if he laughed it off.

He was smart enough to discard the seeds or make sense of them. And I felt I was designated to give him this clue. Besides, my thoughts as I came out of the Kundalini experience suggested he was part of this.

I couldn't think of shirking this duty, honor bound to at least give him hints.

The ET HST SEQUENCE

1997—The *Nabokov Draft* Continues

And it is no more confusing to accept these statements than to accept a Big Bang beginning. Perhaps I was a particle of nonexistence one moment and then landed inside the energy of Paul. And he focused on bringing out that part of himself.

I do not want to force you to establish linear thinking at this point. How would that be possible in widely dispersed energy? But I have remembered what it is I am here to do. I am to build a cathedral, carry the Arc of the Covenant. I am to reestablish the lost Way to the Church. I have come as a particle that has traveled from the Church to show the Way back to the Church, the Way that was never

[Universal, to be preached throughout the world]

Mt. 24:14. And this gospel of the kingdom shall be preached in all the world for a witness unto all nations . . .

through the Heart of each person. I have come on orders to lead the Way BACK.

Now, I am telling you what extraterrestrials are like. So pay attention.

2022

BUT *the text breaks off here in full steam ahead. What? What will I do with it, these twenty-five, twenty-seven, years later? Picking up a message in a bottle.*

Transpersonality. What to make of it? Or is the message otherwise? Let's peruse the vacuum. Take out the telescope and look into Deep Space. The Deep Space of Self. What is Out There, light years away or in whatever other category is attracted in? How to go on with this? What did I write at that moment when breaking off like Robert Musil, caught in surprise by death before completing *A Man without Qualities*. Or Mozart's *Requiem* or Proust's *In Search of Lost Time*. Or much of Leonardo. What a good stable of eloquence, of history. To be unfinished is the norm. But what here? Leave it as is or try to see what came next or what was going on that created that interruption that I can step into with a solution now?

⁂

Paul is on the Earth for only one thing. The personal form doesn't matter. He wants to speak for the Christ and ask the questions not generally asked. Ask the questions that love asks.

January 28, 2023

I don't want to let the thoughts coming into my head in. Of course, I do, but there's resistance. What will I do with these thoughts? That's the reason they first came through Kundalini kriyas, to get past the barrier of the everyday mind, which is holding on to logic.

January 29, 2023

I have promised to start typing up some of the 1990s letter drafts here, a sparse few of which, for sure, I mailed.

A few more preliminaries and backtracking to set the drafts up. Remember that about 4:00 a.m. January 7, alone in a heavy fog, Willy van Luyten drove *straight*, in a line as if drawn with a ruler, *into the only tree in the field*.

Meanwhile, in my room, I dreamt—of Hunter. That—it bears repeating—following a state of confusion, I packed up and *moved from Belgium back to the United States to "help write* The Hunter Thompson Story," *which I am doing right now. Why dream of* THAT *while* Willy's *life is ending in a crash*? What convolutions.

Yet, dreams, operating outside our linear time, "know" things. I began to speculate about an "Event Ball"—a snowballing of events, as preposterous as it sounds—and to top that, years apart.

Was Willy's accident, in 1991, *foreshadowed in* 1981, in my dream of a car accident, just before Milton's death? Milton had cancer, so it was only a symbolic car crash in '81. Not so in '91). Did it somehow span the stretch from November 29, 1981, to January 7, 1991, to February 20, 2005? just as if it were bound up inside the enfolded Count Down, as, at least, *a probability*?

Was there such a thing as an "Event Ball"? where events far apart interconnected—how? *Who* got into it? *On what grounds*? Was it a regular feature of how events dived down into the Earth stratosphere?

Did a bunch of events enter the Earth, as in a suitcase—packed together—with an *if this, then that* unfolding? "If this," not cause-effect, signaled that certain of the other suitcase-packed events were now "up"?

It seemed so to me with respect to my uncanny dream *while* Willy was dying, detailed above. But did such an intertwining exist in my life options????

In *The Physics of God*, we find "matter" called "matter waves." In all cases. Though not circumstances. We just typically, seeing ourselves as solid, neglect to notice the wave part that makes all the connections, invisible to us.

This idea of events lining up, in readiness to jump as with a parachute out of a plane—into Time—to take another analogy, aligns with quantum descriptions in *The Physics of God*.

"Matter waves," Wikipedia says, defining the term, "are also called de Broglie waves, after the physicist who introduced them in 1924"—further toppling the theory, abroad since the seventeenth century, that matter and waves were separate things.[32]

"In the de Broglie hypothesis, the velocity of a particle equals the group velocity of the matter wave." Yes, with the introduction of matter waves, an object is no longer single, boundary-defined, visible, as was believed true before $E\text{-}mc^2$, when no one recognized the back-and-forth flow between energy and mass as energy changed into matter and matter energy: solid, fluid, solid, fluid.

There are also "traveling matter waves."

Furthermore, matter is "only energies in a stable vibrating equilibrium." Or "only an *excited* state of an underlying *field*. This approach is generally known as field theory (FT)." Or quantum field theory (QFT).[33] Who, then, is giving the orders?

Pages and pages back, I mentioned "Plot line four. Yes, with the other plot lines eliminated, that's the one we're in. In the moment's intensity and the lingering aftermath of the La Honda blockbuster, life-altering kriya episode, where did my attention also go? To Hunter, convinced he was part of this surprise revelation it brought. I got the idea inside the barrage of energy.

Maybe wrong. But suppose I was right. (There were reasons to think so.) *Suppose he's counting on me—on some high level—to do the impossible: get him the message. Well, then I have to try.*

And so I wrote and wrote and did not mail and did not mail. Trying for just the right letter. Which I did find.

In the drafts you will see me finally coming clean, broaching the topics above and more, including my insight into the

Owl Farm debacle. At least one of those I mailed. Definitely embarrassing.

I overwhelmed him with some of the details, blow by blow. But again, what did I mail? Who knows?

I do know it's *as if I wrote then to me right now*, for I don't remember exactly what I was being taught then, what I was enveloped in. It's *like dark matter to me now, dropped by the wayside of past years and then brought out as of a white hole*, suddenly alive again. Perhaps it went into a cryonic state, frozen for twenty-five years, as youthful now as it had ever been. When I open up the scattered letters, I look for dates, timestamps. 1991: June 1, La Honda. (I left Owl Farm for La Honda, California, May 20):

Dear Hunter,

Here are pictures of you and your story, which I really look forward to in *Rolling Stone* . . .

I started out cautiously but wait till I get going.

Doug Brinkley was to tell me, after Hunter's death, "He had a crush on you." He left it at that; Hunter gave him this clear impression repeatedly, lastingly, right up to two days before shooting himself in 2005. Wonderful that I have that, knowing that as I thought about him, he thought about me—spoke about me. Left his impressions of me to steer his biographer.

Well, time held this experience, this relationship, secure. Closing with:

I'll be back in Tienen on June 7.

Hoping your back's better, your feet unstiff. And heart getting its wishes, those deepest and most sensitive.

Love,
Margaret

I am by no means finished writing the letter, handwritten on the blue note paper.

If somewhere inside you, you have an intuition that I know something or hold a key, I do. It's the mate to the one

> that let the snake be killed in N.Y. Only, it's the other side of the coin, for in this revision, the snake lives. And the story is more unbelievable than in imagination. And yet it's real . . . If the opportunity comes, I'd go into this with you.
>
> It's very concrete. I'm supposed, by the way, to have a "big shot" lifetime, this time, in power and influence. [Speaking of the Richard Unger hand reading I'd just had.] And the time for it is about now . . .
>
> If in the "other dimension" we have "Symbolic Essences," we "symbolize" them in the lives we choose.
>
> Here's to laughter, and health, in meaningful terms.
>
> Keep in touch whenever you feel moved to,
>
> Love,
> Margaret

But the pages go on, the blue sheets. Once I get going and start adding pages, the likelihood I will mail the letter diminishes.

Remember, I state things as I know them at the time, and the more hypothetical and esoteric I get, the less likely I am to really pass the thoughts to Hunter. I don't want to embarrass myself.

I go on with a message from a psychic reading I've just had, now back in Belgium. I had pondered how to give framework to relationship to the Mother Mary consciousness. And finally this psychic had given me language.

> As one clue, I found out I'm a "personality of Mary."

But I mark through that and put "of someone," chickening out or showing wisdom or speculativeness. I didn't, by the way, ever, even then, take what a psychic said at face value. Going on about how this revelation affected me:

> I felt I would go into a cocoon and never come out. How was I going to be that? Then I found out it was simple, taken as a belief and seen what it led to, but it would lead to nothing if not accepted. I would be at a dead end. If accepted, it opened things up. First of all, what did it mean? And so I get closer to who I am, what I feel, shedding layers.

> This is partly where we met this time. Just a glimpse. It gets better,
>
> If you posit the first truth of yourself, the tab FOLDED up unfolds. The little dots. The Hologram. The synchronicities. Everything.
>
> So I [took] a leap of faith and found it was the first time I was really inside my skin.

I wasn't keeping experiences that were baffling at a distance, I tell him, not trying to wall myself off from the ramifications and implications.

> Then I began to have waves of energy experiences, etc. Coming awake, then I had explanations that weren't commonly known. And had to be made known. Because if I didn't, no one else could.

Comment: Well, actually, someone else could if given my assignment. But I got a shot at it first.

> So—
>
> I'm discovering humor on a large scale, COURAGE as well.
>
> I'm sure you have "news" too. That no one yet reached to.
>
> I wonder what you would say in person to this.

SIX MORE HANDWRITTEN PAGES.

Then a one-page handwritten page.

Then typewritten. I guess I can sweat it out, deciphering the difficult handwriting. But it really wasn't worth it. Hunter would have, correctly, said, "Gibberish." And with this distance, I do as well. No, let's go on to the letters where I was in my groove and they are worth recording, illuminating the story. Jumping from the weeks immediately following my trip to Owl Farm and into 1992, things were hopping.

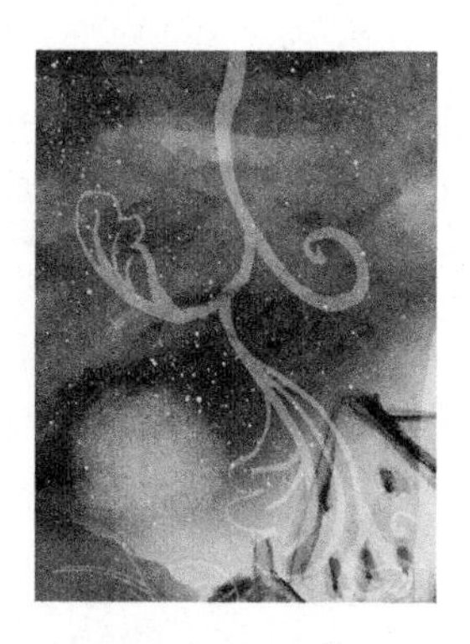

PART SIX

The Lunevillelaan 46 *Letters*

Getting Down into Them

Yeah, that's what I want to say. Thank you. Somewhere down deep inside me you made an enormous impression. And I needed that these last two weeks, drew on it. But first I had to know it was there and that I really felt it and I felt it so strongly it must be real. And if it was real it couldn't hurt anybody by saying it.

❋

A tremendous new era was yet again to be heralded, and Shri Dhyanyogi was to be part of it, at first in the background where I could not see him. In a near death-experience in 1979, taken into the chambers of Lord Ram, the seventh avatar of Lord Vishnu, one of the Hindu Divine Trinity, there, he'd been told he must return to Earth to carry out desires he still had. He must not "drop the body" this time with any unfulfilled. Also, he was shown faces of people waiting for him to teach them.

So he returned to life and began to meet those faces. Perhaps I was one.

Dhyanyogi-ji, a Kundalini Maha Yoga master, who had mastered all the yogic traditions, was known to prefer to work with a small number of devotees, from whom he could expect results, something in the manner of Jesus. He kept a photo of Jesus. First he would work in your energy field until you became aware of it, or might.

Just before New Year's 1992, Jyoti and Russell arrived back in California from Gujarat, India, where she had been told, not incidentally, by Dhyanyogi-ji that her lifetime was like that of St. Teresa. Married in the ashram by two saints, she prepared, with Russ, a small ceremony for the three of us to welcome in the New Year, commenting that she felt we would all "get our parts." Unknown to me, she was to channel in my own future role, fixing me into it.

I instantly sensed a very powerful presence. *Could Dhyanyogi be here*? She said yes.

In the ceremony my guide came into her, making it all the more powerful. When this occurred, Jyoti first had me get into a pose—which I held as she described what to do—telling me to stand with arms slightly extended, curved, but only to a certain height, and watch what I saw.

She said that was me—but what I "saw" (in a "vision") was books of various sizes, some small, antique-like, Victorian and Edwardian-like as in my mother's bookcase. She said it was me and to hold the position *without lowering the arms*. I felt a future fully forming, though it was as if being in a magical position that I could have no control over.

It meant to me that there could never be a lowering of intention or consciousness in the material I had been given to bring in.

Shortly afterwards, in Belgium, on TV I saw a film. Why, that powerful image at the Howard Johnson airport hotel wasn't just created on the spot. It was borrowed from a movie.

To Jyoti and Russ Park: "This is incredible. The scene from my dream [in the JFK airport hotel after the plane wing caught fire, when I woke with the words "Time's Up" that put steel into my backbone and fire under my feet, set me to dancing as if I had ice cubes down my blouse] is in a movie I just turned on."

> In the movie a newspaper reporter who is helping wage a battle for poor people in Mexico—Milagro—has his papers bought out by a rich man and the local government, to burn. And as the fire is mounting and very vividly photographed, a wind comes up and beautifully lifts [up and distributes] all the newspapers to people in the village. *There's aerial photography as the papers spin in the air and land precisely at those places the people are ready to read them. It's very exhilarating and like a miracle.*

This was the capsule scene I had dreamed of.

> In the story there are lines such as "People now, I don't know, they don't know how to act or talk with saints, talk with angels."
>
> "You talk to the angels?"

"Those are the only ones with time to spare."

In '91 I begin to read *World Treasury of Physics, Astronomy, and Mathematics* (editor Timothy Ferris), Boston, Little, Brown, having no idea this newly discovered expert was a close friend of Hunter's. But this signaled a real interest in quantum mechanics on the abstract, not mathematical, level, the next "layer" opening up my consciousness where it was absorbing new reference points.

⁂

Meanwhile, January 23, '92 a new HST article was distributed in *Rolling Stone*, with flamboyant cover, titled "Fear and Loathing in Elko," an incredibly daring, humorous story involving Hunter's alter ego Raoul Duke and Judge Clarence Thomas (now Chief Justice), seeming to invite libel at every turn, except that it is so outrageous. The telling is delegated to Raoul Duke—in what HST calls "brainless, atavistic gibberish" by a "screwball" (his alter ego, himself) that he "wants fired." As the two stories are briefly joining, let's look in on the doings over there, drawing from the website The Great Thompson Hunt, though I could just as easily open my own copy, right here:

> The story spans about seven or eight pages in *Rolling Stone*, not to mention five superb new Ralph Steadman caricatures. It starts and ends with a letter to Jann Wenner . . .
>
> The opening is strong, a beautiful testimony to perceived beauty and harsh reality:
>
> Dear Jann,
>
>> God damn, I wish you were here to enjoy this beautiful weather with me. It is autumn, as you know, and things are beginning to die. It is so wonderful to be out in the crisp fall air, with the leaves turning gold and the grass turning brown, and the warmth going out of the sunlight and big hot fires in the fireplace while Buddy rakes the lawn. We see a lot of bombs on TV because we watch it a lot more, now that the days

get shorter and shorter, and darkness comes so soon, and all the flowers die from freezing.

Oh, God! You should have been with me yesterday when I finished my ham and eggs and knocked back some whiskey and picked up my Weatherby Mark V .300 Magnum and a ball of black Opium for dessert and went outside with a fierce kind of joy in my heart because I was Proud to be an American on a day like this. If felt like a goddamn Football Game, Jann—it was like Paradise.... You remember that bliss you felt when we powered down to the farm and whipped Stanford? Well, it felt like That.

I digress. My fits of Joy are soiled by relentless flashbacks and ghosts too foul to name....Oh no, don't ask Why. You could have been president, Jann, but your road was full of forks, and I think of this when I see the forked horns of these wild animals who dash back and forth on the hillsides while rifles crack in the distance and fine swarthy young men with blood on their hands drive back and forth in the dusk and mournfully call our names....

An article by sports editor Raoul Duke is enclosed with the letter. Picking up with The Great Thompson Hunt:[34]

On the night in question, HST was innocently "about eighty-eight or ninety miles an hour in a drenching, blinding rain on U.S. 40 between Winnemucca and Elko with one light out" when he came across a bad accident...the victim turns out to be none other than Judge Clarence Thomas (referred to as "The Judge" who also happens to be accompanied by two hookers.

The main idea is that it is harder to "get away" with things, and that someone or something is constantly watching. For example, most people aren't Hunter S. Thompson. HST finds the perfect foil in ridiculing the Judge, as a wild, whore-hopping gambler with a penchant for loud music and trashing hotel bills. What if, "Elko" asks, Clarence Thomas was really more depraved than previously thought? . . .

It can also be considered another one of HST's works that brood on the "death of fun" . . .

> Hell, you could afford to get mixed up with wild strangers in those days—without fearing for your life, or your eyes, or your organs, or all of your money or even getting locked up in prison forever. There was a sense of possibility. People were not so afraid, as they are now.
>
> You could run around naked without getting shot. You could check into a motel in Winnemucca or Elko when you were lost in a midnight rainstorm—and nobody called the police on you, just to check out your credit and your employment history and your medical records and how many parking tickets you owed in California.
>
> There were Laws, but they were not feared. There were Rules, but they were not worshiped....like Laws and Rules and Cops and Informants are feared and worshiped today.
>
> Like I said: It was a different time. And I know the Judge would tell you the same thing, tonight, if he wanted to tell you the Truth, like I do.

I studied the magazine piece for anything I might write Hunter. I marked places I particularly liked in pencil. I also looked for any relic of a reference to my visit. But there was none, not surprisingly. I believe it was Jungian analyst, my friend Dr. Pui Harvey, who sent me this issue, back in Belgium.

Across the ocean, I did not know, Hunter, had called himself "a road-man for the lords of karma." He said, "When the going gets weird the weird turn pro." And the weirder the better. Only a year and a half had passed since I went to Woody Creek. One simple year and a half. But now even perhaps a "naked child" could not express it. Perhaps even it would be too challenging for someone who said it "never got too weird."

❋

I accepted Jyoti's invitation to co-organize a workshop for Shri Asha Ma, heir to Shri Dhyanyogi, now a hundred fifteen years old. She would give shaktipat, or energy transfer, for Dhyanyogi-ji, who was in India.

I had begun private sessions with my Inner Landscaping energy teacher, Chris Van de Velde. And soon began studying the light body with an invaluable energy teacher (I was so lucky), Roland Verschaeve. And sometimes had private energy sessions with Joost Van de Hove, gifted as well. Not to mention my Taiji with Jef Crab. In Jef's particular style, the focus was inner movement, with a mystical bent I totally appreciated, as I appreciated everything about the class. What luck to have such a support group.

I also had Willy's young daughter, Coralie, over to play and sleep at times, cooking for her, and continued to grow close to my outspoken, overfriendly *teckel* (dachshund) companion, Snoepie. I hear in my head while writing this, softly, in great, moving depth, remembering, "Each day in my life was a lifetime."

In this period, I was twice a delegate to Europe of the Cultures—conventions (once in Bruges, once in Athens) to plan the economic and cultural development of Europe. In Athens, not used to public speaking or being a political-conference delegate, I suddenly felt, at one point, that Jyoti's "personality" was there, in my room, to let me "step into" it. It "knew how to talk." This was another experience in how energy can move around and how we can master techniques useful to us, once we understand that principle and what's possible, based on it.

Then one day I learned that Jan's last publisher had issued a memorial poetry journal with a large spread on him. In Leuven at the Europees Poëziecentrum, I looked Eugène van Itterbeek up. Glad to see me, he invited me to participate in an international poetry festival, "Europe and the Americas Viewed through a Poet's Eye," in Sibiu, Romania, October 1–7, followed by a leg in Leuven. Invited also would be such poets as Mark Strand from the USA.

Herbert Tarr writes back in August—"with a big biggg mazel tov (congratulations!) on placing your work in the International Poetry Festival in Brussels & Bucharest 'even with experimentation'—that's simply TERRIFIC." He never failed to come through with inspiration. He was disappointed that Marion Magid turned down my article "because it's so very good, but her critique—'it brought Klonsky's spirit & presence into the room'—was right on the mark. After reading the article, I, who never even heard of him, felt I knew him & wanted him to befriend me too. (& if it makes you feel any better, before leaving NYC, inspired by you, I submitted an article to *Commentary*'s Norman Podhoretz (it was the eulogy I delivered at the memorial service for my professor, a world-famous Bible scholar), which got turned down with: 'very charming, but . . .' I wasn't disappointed because I well knew my article hardly measured up to yours—that's the truth, not flattery."

❋

I lost contact with Hunter in '92. I phoned while on my annual visit to the States, I suppose. I don't remember if he answered. He had no email when last seen.

And to top things off, suddenly at one moment, I felt an electrical connection with someone, powerfully. I didn't identify whom I was connecting with. Or maybe I did know.

It was on that incentive, that motive and energy, I wrote Hunter the oddest letter ever and perhaps the oddest letter he ever got. Not the oddest I ever wrote him, but this one I know I mailed. It was about the existence of "Jesus" and "Magdalene" cells, and how he and I had one. How we used to *"swim in electricity baths"*—I put that in.

Yes, I certainly took the lid off. Who knows what he thought? I hope he destroyed it. I meant it, of course. It made sense in the atmosphere of spirit committees, which he was not in. However, it apparently, I presumed—feared—*crossed with his now-arriving note*, which I thought was surely inspired by that same moment I'd felt, of communication electrically.

Now, with these spiritual initiations going toward a mystical Christ consciousness reality, I needed someone to talk to. Someone whose mind could admit unheard-of possibilities. I knew no one else.

But I find other drafts; most unmailed, I assume. Is that presumptuous? No, I think I was trying to "get it right," find the right words, get up the gumption to pass this news to him but caught up in it to the point I couldn't see outside:

Even as late as while proofing this pdf, I dug into a box and found yet other missives.

"Some people," I say in one, "thought they could make a soul change all through the Earth if doing it just among themselves. Taking their treasure chest and marching like pirates and soldiers into sewers or whatever to get the archetype of love so cleared it could handle this vibration." Also:

> June 2, '92
>
> Dear Hunter,
>
> Things keep roaring along here . . .
> I've said from the beginning my signal to begin came parallel to yours.

It didn't, however, or rather, there was an alternative, The Hunter S. Thompson Story, lurking in the wings, which I couldn't see—intent on getting him to come out of the Other Dimensions, swinging, NOW.

> And there's nobody else, but yourself, I think, who can tell you this. Besides, I value our friendship so. As it's really unique. Being how unique you are. And I think I can speak freely as I become more me, and you'll be right there with some comment and understanding.
> And I'm going to keep saying something is opening for you until I find out if you've got the message It's the least I can do. For I know if it were the other way round, you'd say, Hold it, hold it, I promised to tell Margaret something was in the air and it was hers too, if she wanted it. And that it involved a different consciousness of the Earth, which anyway you've already got. But this one's official, and it has to battle to be recognized, and it involves energy in high fields, and it's not impersonal only. That was the point, that the personalities were made visible, and their values made visible.

So I contacted him urgently—once again. And—once again—did I communicate ONLY by thought transmission? The way I was pounding him, whether or not in letters he ever read (unmailed), I was sending thoughts to him, loud and clear, though I didn't see it that way. Then. Do now.

Little did I know that by this time, Hunter had probably already set in motion his dramatic return onto the scene. I drafted to him:

August 7, '92

Dear Hunter,

I'm about to have something published.

That is, take a gigantic step, though I called it "a little step but on a big stage!"

Normally, it couldn't have happened this way, in a group that was already known. But when I showed this piece to an editor for criticism, he said, "We're looking for something like this." And also a tiny excerpt from my book. I chose to jump right to the main theme, instead of something milder. So the littler excerpt is called, "The Leaders of the Transition."

But on the larger stage, my work will appear with work by a Nobel Prize nominee in Poetry from Czechoslovakia. And names you know from America, North and South, and Europe. It's because for a certain number of years now I've been put in increasingly strong energy fields . . . "highly energized events." I knew it, but I never really believed what was promised was real. Rather, I did believe, but it didn't help me hold the energy. So wherever I went, knowing these events were being experimented with around me, to ty to make me me, I was in a very strange state. I could never explain to anyone what was really happening. And mostly they wouldn't have believed me. Not till I proved it by holding the energy, which is beginning to happen. I can feel me. And I can hold me. Which isn't the end at all. The point was to make me tell a story. Give me the opportunity. It was such a story if I could tell it the way it was believed, I would have fulfilled why everyone would sit up and take notice. I mean, stories like this weren't thought to be real. But mine would be. Mine came from another dimension, and it lived all the time secretly, hiding out inside this dimension. And when I first began to discover its reality, it contradicted almost everything I saw in this reality, because no one knew the missing piece. I did. And no one would believe it. Not if I said it right out. I couldn't tell certain people a deeper part of them, which I knew. How did I know? Because it was my job to teach the world, the whole world, something new. By living it. And if I didn't succeed, it was an all-or-nothing gamble.

I never thought of myself as a gambler, but in that dimension I was one of the best. And I was counted on to learn to bring that part of me here. That was the deal. And some people were so sure I could do it, they bet everything on it too. Now, these people don't bet unless they're sure. They have aces up every sleeve and they know how to play them. That's what made the highly energized events. They stood in rooms, unseen, and other places, and sent energy. It was nothing but heart energy, caring. They cared and cared and had hearts able to express what they cared. Hearts used before on the Earth to make art with. We knew their names, in many instances.

To sum it up and get to the point, some people took on the Archetype of the End of the Century.

What I'm trying to get to is you're one, to start with. You didn't know it in that way, but you didn't have to. You probably wouldn't have changed a thing, had you known it, for it wasn't the time to. And the big thing was to stay true, in yourself. But now the time has changed. Everything is pushed up to or beyond the limit . . .

What this has to do with us is almost everything because we lived inside their energy fields without knowing it . . . I carried the end of a story and at the last minute there was the need to tell you what it was . . . I want you to know that it was real, sitting in the car on the hilltop, remembering parking when you were young. It was real inside this story . . .

So, I wanted you to know there was a lot more to everything. And that in fact you were a hero, for it's very rare to find anyone who can walk away from an encounter with this channel, especially when it's anticipating some pleasure, and not get confused. Even be totally honest, with himself and with me. I hold that as an example of pure honesty. So that's why you were able to hold this secret, not knowing what it was, inside memory cells. But the more energy it takes to make the field for Completion, then everything changes and I have to tell you the score. You made a terrific score. You won . . .

I'm sitting here as the go-between of one dimension and another, especially one dimension of a man and his

> Earth dimension, and the two don't connect. And he's trying urgently to get a message to himself . . .
>
> Imagine *The Terminator* being true or any other such movie. This is just as crazy and fantastic. And serious . . .
>
> And in this way there was going to be made—now this is unbelievable, but I learned how true it was—a pattern to take Christ off the Cross and put in its place a Living Christ.
>
> P.S. To say just a little more how unbelievable but true the whole thing is, you are right here in this room. Reacting to how I write this letter, in perfect integrity, not bending a reaction.

And on and on, much I've cut out. I tried to carry the message, as I saw it. Not to say how many times I only typed and didn't mail it, getting up another day another week another month to try again. I do not know if I mailed the above letter.

> August 15, 1992
>
> Dear Hunter,
>
> You always liked information, and I really have some. Anyway, I'd like you to have it because it explains a lot in a way you'd never guess, for the clues were like part of a puzzle and it's only now I can see the puzzle. So here goes.

It is almost as if I am in a monastery, receiving mystical visitations, but writing about them to Hunter, telling him they have some connection to him if we go to that "road above a road." But is it all projection?

Here's one UNDATED. Obviously written in the summer of 1992, after getting the invitation to participate in the poetry festival in Romania (mailed or not). I refer back to the La Honda period, the initiation there I'm still processing. Remember, if you ignore an initiation or unfathomable experience, it dies on the vine. If you look into it, it begins to speak. It takes you to behind-the-scenes interpretations and next steps you could not have gotten to otherwise. But you must be open-minded, not declaring the meaning out of turn. Let it do that. Of course, there's a time when reason steps back in and confers with the intuition.

Well, that's enough words. They probably meant nothing. But if they do, then look and keep looking, for there's a secret in all this that you'll find you know too. At least, I think so. And if not, then you had to know this anyway. And being you, I'm sure you'll make something good of it.

Excuse the lengthy words and even sometimes garbage. I couldn't take one more step or concentrate on the story I have to write until I tested whether this was real or not. You see, I don't walk away from a test, and this energy backing me allows it, providing it doesn't go on forever. For I have to be sure, and I wasn't sure till I tried out whether you were the one I was in love with. Deep in these cells and in this fire I hid, was it you? I couldn't answer, so I thought it was yes. And if it was, it'd be better that you knew. If it wasn't, I hadn't lost anything.

So I found myself faced with the most important task I could imagine and I couldn't concentrate on it because I kept thinking of you. I kept turning all the words in the book, the cell carried, the love of Jesus and Magdalene and even I, with all this careful training that I would make no projection, wondered. I had to wonder, was it you, in my case, that all this was leading to? I had to clear it up to take the next step, and you won't have any idea what that really is right now. It's so big. But that had to start with me. It had to be me, really me, who took the step, and not an energy field I got swallowed up in. So I asked, what did I want first, and I said, like a child, well, I really remember Hunter. But I had to be real, and not my imagination, and I would never make a mistake on that level, so I would ask myself and keep asking and then I'd throw it in the trash if it were false . . .

Oh, forget it. You probably think it's stupid and crazy . . .

So as I accept to go ahead with the next step, onto the stage with a Nobel Prize nominee in poetry, for that's my start in being published, I know my start in this other level is on just as high a level . . . And then I knew somewhere in the next step was this feeling locked with the first cell, side by side with it . . . What that all means to you is totally up to you as a free field. But I did know something in me kept identifying you as part of the story. And that the fire recognized you as of an equal fire. And that it was all possible.

Well no, not possible. But that wasn't for lack of pondering, of trying.

Also, remember that if one has an experience, even a thought, energetically, it opens up the possibility someone else, in high enough resonance, might receive it—in this energetic telephone system.

RIGHT AT THIS POINT, Hunter had someone slip me an invitation from him into a Rolling Stone issue. While I was enmeshed in my revelations, it began to skirt its way across the ocean, circumnavigating not the globe, but his own self-exile from this story.

But what awkward timing.

This text (below) may or may not have been a codicil to the above letter. It was definitely drafted in 1992, the year we are in now:

> If I were to say how weird and even tragic the whole thing really is, in some sense you are actually here in this room, singing to me. Hurrying me up. Telling me, "I'm hurt to think that you lied to me" and "Talk to me, the way that lovers do."
>
> But you are there, locked behind a phone that doesn't lift up. But part of you wants to pick it up. And so that's the one I write this to. The one who almost answers the phone or listens carefully to the sound of the voice.
>
> Who sings, "I fell for you, my dear, not as a stranger. A thousand times or more, 'neath stars above,"
>
> And other songs. I won't go on. But I do like them. And my headache, which has taken me over till I write this, seems to be clearing up. I'm being pushed to write this to you because it's such a peak moment, a time when all things are possible. When I begin to be published, and it happened by chance. I was lucky to show the material to the right person, who liked even the experimental style or part of it. He could understand, and where he couldn't, he jokingly threw up his hands and said, "Lord, please change my level." [A Romanian.] What an editor. I could have dreamed up the situation. And to be able to offer a place on a podium with a Nobel Prize for Poetry candidate. And the poets from the States, in fact, famous.
>
> So that's the first part of the dream that's coming true. It's the half that's supposed to harness the energy of the End

> of the Century by telling a story that got left out, overlooked and without which there would be no center to the End of the Century [as it turns out, that applies only to me. It's hard to keep your balance, this far out].

So I talked to Hunter and told him just enough, testing, putting my toe in the stream—reporting to him, usually not mailing the letter, saving the letters, however, for this me right here. So grateful to rummage them out.

Meanwhile, an invitation from him is winging its way over to me, but waylaid. Just our luck. Or destiny. For good or ill, it's sitting in the La Honda apartment, unnoticed, while Jyoti and Russell are on one of their many work trips. So I continue on with my one-sided perusals, of which at least one letter was mailed.

And how were things on his front? Galloping, of course.

In his wonderful 2006 memoir, *The Joke's Over*, Ralph Steadman describes Hunter's disastrous visit to London September 4, 1992—accompanied by blond girlfriend/assistant Nickole, who "struggles to control a trolley which groans under the weight of six large cases, half of the doctor's equipage for the five-day visit."[35]

Eluding journalists who were there to ensure he wrote a story on the Royal Family for the Observer, he withdrew into his large Stevenson Suite at the Metropole Hotel—refusing to go to Scotland. This suggests the invitation to me went out well before that trip, or was it during? Faxed or phoned in???

And then I burst the dike of my revelations. Here's another letter, undated—excerpted from briefly in an earlier chapter—which mentions having to finish my book before the end of September, when I would go to Romania—presumably written at least after August 7, more likely in September:

> Dear Hunter,
>
> My whole life is changing.

Truer words were never said.

> And I've promised to tell you about it if it ever happened. Here's why I think that. Part of it, I've told you. But the other part I haven't. I haven't told anybody, in fact . . .

In the earlier preview, giving the reader a peek at this presumably-September

1992 letter, I described my dream in which, eerily, the morning of Willy's death, "I packed up all my belongings to go to the United States to write, or be involved in writing, your story." The letter goes on:

> This made me understand, again, that there was some kind of real connection, concretely, between you two. And when I went to California, this story burst through me that I felt was a cell bursting. I had a memory and everything I wrote had a parallel message which I interpreted as being meant for you. That it was a go signal but came in pair form.

I wasn't at all sure of Hunter's role, if any. As always, I left a question.

I referred to how he withstood the mishap of the "champagne evening that wasn't," maybe burdening him with information he didn't want or need. But remember, I didn't mail much of it. Also, suppose I've correctly understood, from the memory cell, a facet of him, a very important one.

> The other reason I was putting clues together on this level was that beginning in Zurich I was experimenting in walking into set-up energy fields and learning how to hold them. It was my karma to learn that. Because I was always invisibly a carrier . . . At the state this had reached, for it was a project, I'd be connected to you in a channel, and if I didn't hold it you wouldn't be responsible for what happened. That's why I respected you so. For when you did fall into this channel, for a moment, you brushed it off like nothing.
>
> It didn't penetrate you. You only accepted total responsibility. And that was wrong. There was something you didn't know.
>
> That it was my whole life purpose to learn to become me inside such a field. And it was so impossible that the whole group was supporting me. And you were part of the group. And everything I did therefore was partly at the expense of that group. It was why the man I was living with died. His car didn't just go into the tree. It bounced into the channel . . .
>
> More than this, they took on everything you can imagine—in one pact—in a microcosm . . . He's been the center of my life in different forms. He's taught and taught me. He's made me

> learn how true I am . . .
>
> Inside me is a memory of how he felt when he looked at Mary Magdalene. "My heart don't lie."
>
> He had to die then. He thought the next time he would die twenty thousand times to find one time he didn't. And that time he would live the personal part of the story. But in order to do so, holding both at once unseen in space while the world invaded his personal space. . . Not know that though transpersonal in this particular time it was also personal.

I outlined a seemingly fictional scenario he should beware of:

> To sum up, you're in the energy of a channel to your true being, the one in another dimension that keeps you trying to reach it with coke and so on . . .
>
> And this channel is in the storm now set to guide the Earth into the new century. To bring it in in a new way. This isn't just the Jesus we know. It's more of him than we ever saw, more beauty, more complexity, and more guts. Yes, even more guts. Plus a Jesus in love. All of that, I fought back as not true till everything in my whole life made me understand, believe it or not, it is true . . .
>
> What a job. What a crazy gamble. What borderline-players, going right over the border, pushing limits. That's what they're doing, Hunter, pushing limits. So everybody can. But I'm frightened at this point because I know there are limits. And that knowing them coming makes the impossible come true. In the right sequence. It would be awful if all this became known by you but just too late. So I go way out on a limb.

Fiction, my eye. I kept saying it over and over, in different ways.

And where was Hunter about now?

Well, you have to hand it to me. I was consistent. Speaking of energies massing, headed toward Earth, I was nothing if not convinced, nothing if not determined.

❋

To get an outside look—besides from Chris, from Mariah—I went to an energy session with Joost Vanhove on my birthday. What he told me fit with what Mariah, in the United States, had but was even more powerful. I felt every word I'd written come alive not as imaginary but in his assessment, and he set the context matter-of-factly.

September 25, 1992—Confirmation of Etrea Material Session with Joost on my birthday

The people who came to me in one body to give the Jesus material were Etrea energy, which is the Jesus energy during his teaching. It's the energy he was in as the Christ. Now I've been in it. and felt many times as if Jesus was coming into me. Or some Christ whom I called him. I could feel especially his face, and it was the one in the picture in Mexico.

This was followed by the deepest emotions I can imagine in a period first when a plan failed to have the effect it might have, which would have woken someone in this energy. Second, on my return, when almost constantly I felt it and was in it. Especially the song "Can't live, don't want to live without you," as if floating somewhere, and the song from *Gone with the Wind*.

My letters during this period, mostly unmailed, sum up some of the feelings //////wwwwwwwwqz, whose int4nwit6y is inmmdescribable. My computer made the distortions up there.

Perhaps they're asking me to carry this or this man, to let him live in me, and at the same time there's the invitation from Hector, if it's serious, that's also bringing this to a point.

Hector had invited me to stay in Guadalajara to help him with his book. Also, of course, to study under him. He'd asked me once before if I wanted to study under him. That was in 1984. I wasn't ready then. Was I now?

It must be about my little and big self . . .

In the Joost session he said when he looked at my valise, every time he saw the face of Jesus. And when I asked if he had comments or suggestions about publishing the material, he said, he kept seeing the words "None of your business." I'm not to get opinions from people very much because after all, what would they know about such an experience? Who could imagine the intensity"? Who could believe in the existence of this group or what it was doing or that I was part of it, normally"? Yet there are those who do. Joost totally confirmed the validity, as did Chris, as did Mariah, indifferent ways entirely, each of them.

So this group no one knows about is spreading their energy more widely, and everything I know and have to say is inside that energy, because I got it from him first before even from them. So all I have to say is literally and truly prepared for. I only have to find a way and place and hold on tight to belief. I have over and over to step aside and not question why I am in this position.

Joost said I have old ties with the large group, from flying with them. This also confirms an intuition that I already know this material and that who I wasn't concretely, I nevertheless felt I was, for I was in the energy; I might even have been the source of something on record without ever having been in the body who lived it. I might then really have these ties with Mary Magdalene not just on the energetic level of plugging in to them but on the level that I was in the energy. But that's not so important to others—can keep it for myself—as this idea right now that this is a pattern others can use. No one perhaps will know I was in it before it became widespread. Why it came to me; that it knew me because the field I'd always lived in, historically, when it became an Earth field would have me in it. I had to discover me. I had to step aside when the energy came through me, now knowing it was in part me anyway, because I had used to be art of it collectively. Joost pointed out that I had a sense of wanting to be individual and yet also this old sense of being part of things collectively and yet that people *just were*. That enlightenment was for everyone, and so on.

I had an overdose of the astral now, he said—that in future I could learn to hand such an experience better. That is, not to be so open to the many influences possible at once. He said immediately, when I came into the room and was thinking: *It's*

> *my birthday; this is the wrong signal to myself about how to get the information now*, "You're going to conduct the session."
>
> So as I sum it up for myself, I was in the same energy Jesus was in for his work and felt when I energize that my hands must go up and they must heal. That they can. They know they are made for that. The energy is conscious of its purpose. And its nature. Its character. The particular feelings that compose it in this moment. It's a healing and very serious energy. It's not my personal energy I felt, when BELL began to be expectant and was joyful and light, like champagne bubbles. It's the energy of someone with a deep sadness. I can't say how deep . . .
>
> If this comes from, an energy source, then the part that wasn't lived but was in Jesus's energy that would explain why—I'm an unexpressed part of the Etrea energy, a projected an untold part. Such as when Clark Kent, as Superman, takes Lois Lane on a journey and kisses her and she wakes and doesn't remember. Or just say there's an unexpressed part of me. And it makes me ill when it knows something, as it does. And wants me to take action . . .
>
> I'm being asked to do something according to the Christ consciousness.

❋

> For the third time my left breast is affected; once, before my father died, it had a lump . . . responding to some similar emotional buildup that it's trying to deal with consciously but that probably involves getting rid of an old pattern. And that one really the big one.

It's possible the undated letter quoted above came here, fueled by this session with Joost. There's no way to know the sequence.

❋

Finally, the *Rolling Stone* issue arrived, amidst the flurry. Landing in my postal box at the most inopportune time—just before I went to Romania at the very end of September? Opening it, what did

I find? An interview with Bill Clinton, candidate for president, by William Grieder, P. J. Rourke, and Hunter S. Thompson. But also—Hunter at his best—the note slipped inside invited me confidently, tersely, cutting to the chase, to

meet him "in Little Rock on election night"

I stop and laugh hilariously. I was *"just the person" he needed, he wrote. I took it to mean in Little Rock on election night*. Me, the person who was trying to pull him into another dimension.

✳

His note to me (written before receiving my letter?), nestled inside the magazine, addressed to *California*, first idled un-urgent. Forwarded belatedly.

At least it wasn't thrown away.

Receiving my highly embarrassing in-the-sober-glare-of-the-new-situation letter, on second thought, did he want to retract it? OR with his usual wide-open mind, able to accommodate the unorthodox experiences of his friends, had he sent the invitation in spite of the revelations? Was he even curious to know more?.

The intermittent contact had fired me up to keep bringing him in, in my writings, drafting letters to my "confidant." Remember that Milton Klonsky had always provided clarity in the "morass" of my life with Jan Mensaert.

"*Meet me in Little Rock Election Night*," he said

But—more: in just a sparce two sentences he added that I was just the person he needed. What would I do? Well, initially be silent. Not answer. Get all twisted up to figure out a response. What did I WANT to do? What did I?

It was all very well to have him as an imaginary pen pal on the other side of my missives. But what about when it really got down to it and a physical invitation arrived in the mail? It arrived perhaps just as I was about to get into the plane to Romania. Thereabouts, in any case. Then what happened? The invitation was still unanswered. There was time to answer after I returned.

⁂

Now comes Romania. I feel surrounded by my soul grouping, pulling all plugs out, basking in their love and intensity. Mariah has told me that publication—at last—"is all set up. *They like to surprise you*." During the trip I had very successful encounters with leading lights of Romanian culture and literature. Two of the most recognized volunteered to translate my poem "Invitation to Masters of the Past in the Light of the Past, Come, All Ye Singers."

This stroke of good fortune came about because—at the festival—I immediately asked the presenters milling around, "Who's the most mystical poet here?" Mihai Ursachi by unanimous consent.

Imprisoned as a dissident under Communist dictator Nicolae Ceausescu, miraculously released, he wrote in

> a characteristically Romanian combination of hermetic mysticism and surreal symbolism, an intense spirituality and irony perhaps further reinforced by the poet's solitary confinement during the communist years in Romania's most notorious political prison, Jilava—a place, Ursachi has said, "where you were expected to die."[36]

I approached, and he invited me up to his room. Uh-oh. Once I straightened out my motivation, he immediately said to read the poem aloud. Mihai listened, giving warm advice, saying we wrote similarly, then advised me to read every page of the whole long poem in the festival, not to "keep it short."

Having a wealthy family, under Communist rule, had only precipitated his arrest as a dissident, imprisoned underground with one light bulb for six months. No one expected him to survive.

However, in still awareness, instead of dying, he had spiritual experiences.

In fact, Mihai described them to me a bit, just after I read him my festival poem.

In the almost-pitch-dark, he learned, he said, he was "the fourth incarnation of Pythagoras." I don't know if he told anyone else. He certainly didn't run around telling people.

Hard to believe, but is it? Yes, but oddly, coincidentally, just prior to this trip, I'd bought a fancy leather briefcase; the label said, "Pythagoras."

That he found my poetry much like his own is a tremendous compliment. Below, I quote:

> What crazy words I used to speak, oh, I wanted
> to be sure that we existed, that truly *we are*; that here,
> here is a tree, or a pillar, and we're standing beside it, alive,
> That this, in your hand, is the leaf
> on which we were destined to live. On which we remember
> we once lived in great peace,
> serene with deep knowledge. No, we weren't mistaken,
> we didn't tell lies: this is the hill beside the well
> is a tree, among its leaves
> is a leaf. I tell you again,
>
> surely we lived on this very leaf
> where you are reading now, if it pleases you.

I guess you could call that one of the "best teachers money could buy." Released, he had fled to Texas; in the United States he'd been a doctoral candidate but was now back in Romania.

I also befriended the reclusive Romanian poet Mircea Ivanescu, likewise scarred by Communism (winner of the lifetime achievement Medaille d'or and nominated for the Nobel Prize); Ion Mircea, co-host, took me in hand as well. I felt an extra romantic film had been spread around me, as had happened once before, in Rome. That, combined with a natural affinity, made my presence here a "splash"—opening the door to a relationship that would be cemented in the Belgian leg of the festival, in a very strong attraction.

Playing around in the back of my head, however, was a phenomenal decision I had to make. Had I not received a bolt-out-of-the-blue invitation from Hunter. No? Yes.

I dissolved into the quandary of what to do.

Undecided, I wrote to Mariah Martin.

Looking more closely at the '91 tape box

A cassette tape container is open in front of me. It's from Mariah. It says, "M Harrell c/o Hunter Thompson, Woody Creek Rd, Woody Creek Colo 85616." It is a copy of a phone reading, May '91.

The reading is erased. Coralie, Willy's daughter, did the erasing, and what you hear on the tape is the crackling of paper, Snoepie barking, and me talking to myself or telling her not to erase the tape!!! But she is eleven, interested in playing loud music and having her favorite foods, while visiting me as a mother figure who reminds her of her father, whom she knew only a few short years; everyone says she is like him.

With the May '91 reading erased from the tape: a reading a year and a half later still remained. So though I do not know what the '91 reading, # 85616, said, the '92 portion is intact.

As to the erased tape: Hunter, she said there, was in my soul grouping. I *know because I referred to that statement in the surviving'92 tape.*

Probably a big figure in it, for hadn't I written that the Christ sent some of his top lieutenants into the underground, the shadow, to go see what could be turned up, to aid our survival in the coming Big Shift, when there would be "out-of-control events"—not calling them things like 9/11, but just knowing there would be events "out of control"?

Look at what opposite species we were. Imagine the stretch of consciousness. Imagine, therefore, that something ran through both of us, something sourced in that pooled place where the tall man came from, who was mercurial.

The day would come when this split into friendship was not enough. I knew. It was not enough not to say goodbye. So I planted the idea, the determination, to say yes to being the "Ciao de Hunter." (I say hello; you say good-bye.) Well, that would do in a pinch. That was MERCURIAL.

For those who did not read my earlier writing, here is a digest of the poem being referred to. In 1982 I dreamed about an ambiguous "Vita Pass," an approaching moment at which time all directions in my life converged and—left, right, and center—followed a common direction. Like a blindfolded driver, for twenty-eight pages I was swept up, looking for the treasure clues that were energy of my future. Blindfolded, I didn't know who "he" was.

He wasn't dead
For when they said caps off to him
he did a recap.

I amplified:

> Squared off after all cars met and perhaps clinked lights
> in the center of the road
> Then each turned into its lane
> toward or now arrived at the destination:
> The Vita Pass
>
> When it was all the traffic in your life that met there:
> right and left,
> as if centered,
> And took the turn together—
> BYPASSING WHAT?
> When they streamed together
> onto 831—
> And a voice told you this was it, you were on
> THE VITA PASS

I described its foreboding nature, playfully but earnestly. I asked myself

> If there were eight lanes, we ate you,
> If there were ten, why you're in our net,
> Any way you look at it, you haven't a chance.
> To catch your breath,
> before we got you
> and put you
> IN YOUR PLACE
>
> For you, my dear, have been chosen to be—
> The Chow de Hunter.

....

Yes, this is the true story of the Psst or Hsst Story, that was, decoded, also the *Au-Pair* Tree story. And *jullie** too.
Yes, U-2.

---

* *jullie*—you (NL); *espion*—spy (FR)

An *es-*
pion.
A spy story.
Of the Hunter. Who was an Esp-
pion.

If I am the Ciao de Hunter, it's not that he instantly signs off, for I appear as *saignant*, sig *non*, and he had to turn me into ciao.

Well done? *Saignant,**
Rare

good fare
A good meal
The whole well.
Or, well—
Or, well—

Anyone reading this might easily say, *what on earth year is this*? *Is it massive projection*? *Is it tapping in*?

According to Jung, Active Imagination, which this is, reveals "unconscious regulators." It was such an important discovery to him, he said, that he "based upon it my idea of an impersonal collective unconscious" (*The Basic Writings of* C. G. *Jung*, pages 74–75).

Active Imagination *amplifies* "conscious contents." Not *reducing* the content, it is useful for dream interpretation, which this is. Here, it reveals that the Vita Pass is where all cars—all possible directions—"got the point": *it is a turning point.*

So they clinked or tch'enked
their glasses, did the automobiles,
as the lights found each other—
This is it, when left joins with right
when two turn into one,
as three ate one.
For it's a crazy kind of math
that makes two turn into three eight one.

---

* *saignant*—rare, as in "steak *saignant*" (FR)

I asked: Could the Vita Pass be a bridge, between two lives? Continuing skipping:

> A super-
> nuova.
> Nuova Pass. Route to the Nova.
> Or supernova.
> Or past it.
> No, this is probably it: the Nuova Pass*.
>
> . . . .
> Where the star blows up
> . . . .and what kind of Nuova would be on a superhighway?
> A super-
> nova.
> Supper.
> It was Supper.
> It was: On the Menu—?
> The CIAOU DE HUNTER.

❋

Added to the complications, in Romania one evening a dashing poet came up to me, a leading light in the East European literary world. And he said dramatically, playfully (not like a Casanova), "My life started tonight." Naturally, it didn't. But when a tall, dark, handsome, highly intelligent, and ultra-poetic man spins webs of romance around you, the suitable response is to let him, to drop into the fantasy. Which I did.

So I started a new relationship there and then. Thinking back now, I am appalled, in a way. Knowing Hunter's invitation was waiting, did I actually start a relationship, given the two options? Apparently, I did. Or my life, all lives, are so difficult to figure out after the fact, that I can only surmise that's the case. How could it be? Wasn't I even conflicted? Or have I got the dates the tiniest bit off and the relationship just barely preceded my finding the note in the *Rolling Stone* issue?

Someone said my new poet boyfriend could have any woman he wanted, he was so handsome, poetic, intelligent. Further, he had absorbed the channel energy holding it *without a problem*. And during

* *nuova*—new (IT)

the festival I was enveloped, surrounded, by it, swooning in it, almost. But then, the channeled energy went back, in large part, to Hunter. Again, what to do? Hunter, being part of the original energy, was more tumultuous, unpredictable, unsafe. AND there was something else that bothered me. I returned from Romania and tried to figure out my answer.

Oct. 23, '92

Dear Hunter,

I've been exploring in Eastern Europe and would enjoy talking to you about it. You must have lots of ideas, and I have some first-hand experience, as well as names of journalists who were at the Festival.

. . . I've been totally unreachable for these three weeks, as the whole thing took me by surprise. There was never a minute there wasn't something to do, contacts and so on. It turned out that I had a couple of "readings" from my writing, and the people there were warm, like a little club. Only, on a high level, for of the two American males, one [Mark Strand] was "Poet Laureate" (of the US, 1990–'91), and the other [W. D. Snodgrass] had won the Pulitzer Prize. He was a discovery, with his wife, of eleven years and very much bridelike in the sense of alive. The third was [poet Tess Gallagher], the wife of Ray Carver, about whom a movie is currently being made, and she's supervising it in a way. She lives in California.

Besides these, a Romanian with many awards, a prisoner for three years, size months underground with only a light bulb and no visitors, 'recognized" an affinity with what I showed him and asked to translate about twelve pages into Romanian for a magazine. That's a tiny, tiny start, but it felt encouraging.

There's more.

Behind all this, I kept remembering your invitation to meet you in Little Rock.

So there it is, plain as day. I knew. Swept up by the dashing Romanian poet, I knowingly chose to start the affair in spite of

Hunter's note, waiting patiently in my apartment. But when you walk into a hotel room, which we soon did in Leuven, with Johnny Cash synchronistically belting out, "We got married in a fever, hotter than a pepper sprout," it gives you some idea how much, supported by the channel, the attraction to the Romanian was irresistible.

> What a crazy idea, and how in the spirit we've known each other in. How very right to just meet like that. I was glad, because I'd wondered if you'd accepted some of the really far-out things I'd been writing to you. Or if not, which was fine, if it had at least been considered interesting and perhaps courageous Anyway, I've kept that belief you'd keep a place for me as a very special friend.
>
> Now I haven't phoned in that period of the Festival, and perhaps you have or if not expected me to [no answering machine]. But I kept the invitation close to me. And the joy that you walked that road you did holding a hand firm whenever I reached for it and that you evidently understood my hand was always there for you too.
>
> I don't know precisely what you had in mind, but was prepared to open to it. I do know there's this tie that stayed alive between us and that whatever choices your independence takes you into, there will still be a place receptive in me. I feel the total person.
>
> It's turned out that time is creeping along, leading up to Election Day, and we've both been full of commitments, I guess, and not gotten together on this idea of yours. I, though spending little, exhausted my funds, so that I have money for a ticket but nothing extra for the trip expenses. I would have money in January, as in "Inauguration." It's an idea, if you're still interested in this meeting, to make it then. When you said you needed "my help," I was very curious. You can imagine.
>
> So how is *Polo*?
>
> Your back? Everything. How is winter there? Your plans?
>
> . . .
>
> The computer took over now, typing inside, and I wonder whether it's my mind or someone else's. It can be either, at different times. I seem to have learned how to work it from both directions. I could imagine what a story you might

make of this, for you would have the courage and humor and audacity to do it. And the audience. As a comedy, it would be nonstop roller-coaster intensity. BELL. (That's my bell, ringing to approve this description.) Of course, I guess I could write it, but I seem to be for the more serious line, at least when I'm in this particular book. If I could get the thing introduced, I could get on into the real comedy. I mean, the thing is so amusing, thinking of the Earth being surrounded by living conscious energy trying to make things happen and getting caught in hilarious predicaments. As there's some focus on love, that's also part of the High Comedy. *Woman in Red* comes in a lot, with Gene Wilder situations. Passion trying to speak from a spirit intensity and getting in many a squeak. I can imagine your style of half-tongue-in-cheek, half-eyeball-popping-out amazement, playing the thing blow by blow. And underneath, the seriousness,

Well, that's a script suggestion. I kind of think it's bound to be written, this script. And I can imagine supervising the movie in Hollywood, sunglasses and all. Back to the Continental.

I've found much openness in Romania, which had an underground courage and a tradition of mysticism. I can imagine Laurel and Hardy or something. Cervantes and Sancho Panza. Or even the Christ and the Antichrist energy. Racing to catch up, but not having a chance in this version. Such sureness that in the end only what was "right" could cross the finish line. Behind it all would be the fact that it was true. That's been my example I held up and part of it I found in you.

Addition to my letter:

There was a big difficulty in knowing how to answer your letter about Little Rock, because I had no idea if it was the response to my letter or the two letters crossed. There was no date, and the magazine with the letter was forwarded from California. So I didn't know what you meant by needing my help. It could have been from one end to another of possible meanings. In the meantime, also, things were going so fast here, in that the Festival knocked me out, though positively, but also I had withdrawal symptoms from the change in

> energy levels when I went back to normal, after writing this enclosed chapter in the presence of a "spirit committee."
>
> I had thought to finish my own book would be easy, but the change left me quite undecided about what line to take. It's taken me to now to get back into the swing of the thing, by the idea, which is the one I always go back to, to just stick to the truth. Say it. If you lose, you get stronger. If you don't, well, you're that much ahead. But surely if you choose not to say it, you're emotionally dead.
>
> So hoping to hear from you about things. So much is happening. I'm going to include the letter I wrote before this, leaving this out. But this is of course the crucial piece of missing information.

The new relationship I had just started was lyrical with sporadic moments of actual physical consummation, given the two-country distance.

> Sometime in October, I left a message on Hunter's machine, and later another; the last—when I began to get personal—was cut into by a voice; it said, "End of Tape. Call back later."
>
> A human being or a mechanical robot? Or was it Hunter, disguised, breaking in as the speaker phone broadcast the message into the kitchen, where people listened—friends and/or his new girlfriend—an awkward moment? The Prankster salvaging a prank. I thought so.

❋

It was a mysterious conclusion or challenge to the in-person part of a twenty-six-year-relationship. I felt stage fright, identity fright. Fear that I wouldn't have the gumption and self-confidence to stand up for myself with him, no matter what, suppose I went. Fear he wanted to start a relationship again, but I had just started one!!!!! Afraid as to what situations I might find myself in election night—what sort of hotel room extravaganza. By the time the letter arrived I no longer felt like flinging myself into his arms again, or did I? I was conflicted. I might change my mind. Afraid because I had mailed the "absurd" letter, pouring my heart out about our multidimensional ancestral history, to the point I knew it. Or imagined it.

I was afraid I wouldn't get the chance to "explain" recent developments, which did not preclude my going, if—a long shot, a risk, a hair pin curve on a motorcycle going a hundred in the dark—it could be on a high enough "vibe." Then no explanation was needed.

I didn't want to go into smoky hotel rooms where who knew what might be going on, and up to what wee hours. But maybe he wanted me to keep him on track in his room, writing!!! Command him to turn out copy, meet the deadline. I remembered the lavender soul level energy enveloping the bed the last night before I left Owl Farm, when he was sitting up in the other room, watching Mae West on TV, perversely knowing something hadn't come out right.

I was afraid I wouldn't get the chance to "explain" recent developments.

Whatever he intended, I felt it was inspired by the deep connection that second in the electricity, which said: *We can pull this off*. As he had said right away, in a letter in 1966, already, he *"felt a connection."* I remembered the lavender soul-level energy enveloping the bed the last night before I left Owl Farm, when he was watching Mae West on TV, perversely.

I assumed the invitation was sent *before* he received my letter ("awful letter," as I now perceived it). But suppose the opposite was the case. Would I have somehow fitted the trip in—a complete change of the rest of my life? How on earth, however, could I have squeezed myself into such a time crack; to be with Hunter I would need to be FULLY present.

What if I packed up and flew into Little Rock, having just begun a new chapter of my professional life in Romania, a new emotional relationship with a male as well—in fact, with a whole country, which would lead to publication that was, Mariah had said, "all set up" ("They," meaning my guides, "like to surprise you").

Well, surprise me, this letter did, appearing just *as* the whole Romanian/publication period was set in motion.

I dawdled. Eventually phoning, I could not reach him.

Did I walk into *Faust*, by *Goethé*—picking up some of the pieces of the result of the wager that God made with Mephistopheles, which would truly relate to being a "Lord of Karma," though we would not see the Scene in Heaven in the prologue but only open the pages on the *fait accompli*, the die cast.

It occurred to me that perhaps it was from London, hiding away in his hotel room for four days in September, that Hunter contacted *Rolling*

Stone to send me the invitation. It was unsigned, as if he telephoned the instruction to put it into the mail, maybe telling them to phone Owl Farm for the address (which somehow was given as California). Hunter arrived in London, in Steadman's account, with Nickole, "a small, blonde woman in her mid-twenties [who] struggles to control a trolley which groans under the weight of six large cases, half of the doctor's equipage [mainly 'of video equipment, hashish and weapons'] for the five-day visit."[37] But he spent days locked up in the hotel room, refusing to exit, to go to the airport to fly to Scotland on assignment. Perhaps the invitation was sent well before the trip to London. I cannot reconstruct.

But if while in London, it would have echoed the time when, wanting to escape from the DC Inauguration-of-Nixon madness to the Outer Banks, he phoned with the same kind of out-of-the-blue suggestion in 1970. Feeling for a moment that in whatever situation or fix he was in, and whatever kind of situation he wished to be in in Arkansas, I was just the person. Yes, such are dreams made of, fragilely looked into after perhaps having been kept like Keats' "Ode on a Grecian Urn," unchanging, still fair. It could leap over obstacles, on that deep level where particles (in the brain as well) jump walls, tunnel under them, do everything to try to keep alive the bright bloom of, said Villon, "the snows of yesteryear," the "flowers" gone.

❋

But in a short year so much had happened. Hunter did not know. I did not go. Our paths diverged—on this level.

At first, it appeared I had ignored his invitation!! And, thinking how Hunter might "read" that, I assumed he had given up on the idea, now cooling in dying embers, the delay having been fatal. I also just "felt" that someone else had walked into the opportunity. There were thousands or hundreds of thousands standing in line. But knowing the electricity around this invitation, then probably, I thought, someone had immediately, synchronistically, walked in.

Anyway, I did believe he was in this soul grouping that was guiding me, irony of ironies. One doesn't change archetypes except with a big throttle-thrust from unexpected quarters. Who better to help humanity out with shockers?

Hunter went to Little Rock.

Below, in extracts from his article, *Rolling Stone* managing editor Robert Love pulls back the curtain in "A Technical Guide for Editing Gonzo: Hunter S. Thompson from the other end of the Mojo Wire," published in the *Columbia Journalism Review*, vol. 44, 61–66:

> **The Sacrifice of the Young Male Assistant:** If there was reporting left to be done on the road, Hunter usually demanded the services of a young, healthy person from the magazine to help him get in and out of airports and hotel suites, arrange interviews, rent equipment, etc. It became part of *Rolling Stone*'s tradition to assign a features department assistant to meet up with Hunter, and it was of course cheap (enough) insurance that he might actually file copy on time. (There were also vain hopes from time to time that the mere presence of a representative of the magazine, callow as he might appear, might rein in Hunter's expenses, but that of course never, ever happened.) In New York, Corey Seymour was the fixer and the enabler; on the Polo beat in Garden City, Long Island, it was Tobias Perse . . . I never believed half of what they told me, but I did see a few of the hotel bills. I know they often stayed up all night, toe-to-toe with Doc, and were asked to find and deliver telephones, whiskey, typewriters, tape recorders, batteries, blow-up dolls, and other things. When Hunter was safely on a plane back to Woody Creek, and our assistant dragged himself into the office in the early afternoon, we knew it was time to get ready for Part 3.
>
> **The Fun Begins:** . . . In fact, he considered himself a likely candidate for the Deadline Hall of Fame, which honored "Stories of Intense and Historic Quality Produced under Extreme Pressure in Savage and Unnatural Circumstances." Just the mention of deadlines would get his staff at Woody Creek fired up . . .
>
> M E M O R A N D U M
> To: HST
> From: Bob Love
>
> Date: November 16th, 1992
> Subject: Little Rock Rumble
> We have a four-page window of opportunity in the next issue. And here's the deadline:

HST'S NON-NEGOTIABLE DEADLINE SCHEDULE

....

Bob

Right . . . Of course, all this talk about deadlines was a complete ruse . . . I came to understand that the word "deadline" was actually Hunter's code for a two- to three-week red-zone standoff against the exigencies of publishing . . .

So, the deadlines were set, the Maginot lines were built, breached, rebuilt, rebreached, and reinforced all the way to the cease fire . . .

When things didn't go over in Woody Creek, I'd find something like this awaiting me in the morning in New York.

M E M O R A N D U M
To: Bob Love
From: HST
12/4/92
Re: Bad News

I have tried and utterly failed, Bobby, to figure out how a smart person could whine and jabber day & night about "the desperate need for at least some pages about anything that happened in Little Rock on ELECTION NIGHT . . . But what the fuck am I suppose to think when I see that YOU have very shrewdly cut (dropped, deleted, excised (sp?) "edited out") the only two pages I've sent that have anything to do with real events that occurred on either the DAY or the NIGHT of November 3 at Clinton headquarters in Little Rock (see attached/below Pages 26 & 27—which I wrote and & planned & intended to be my LEAD INTO Election Day/ Night . . .

Thanx for nothing. H."

. . . .

There came a time, however, when the stars aligned—Hunter would find his muse and settle himself down for serious work . . .

Actual Editing: Now the pages arrived in greater numbers . . .

Hunter's manuscript pages were themselves manic, bristling works of art.

Working with Hunter was a privilege that came with a price, and I willingly paid it for many years. . . It was wicked serve-and-volley with journalism's greatest prankster, and I will miss him terribly.

Robert Love is an adjunct professor at the Columbia University Graduate School of Journalism and an editor-at-large at *Playboy*.

❋

March 21, '93

Dear Hunter,

These are letters preceding the originals. . . I only reread them this visit to my storage. They brought you from then back so vividly, and I think they will for anyone. In fact, you have a book to be made from this if you wanted this, and I would find it really exciting to be part of that, if you wanted . . .

I have a FAX now, by the way, the same as my phone.

At this period I'm considering moving back to the US and could have a place in the back of where my two California friends live, in a yurt, but that's in the works only. I have a million projects here . . . But I think some of the real opportunities are in the US.

In the earlier package there were originals, so I hope it arrived safely . . .

I laughed out loud many times in rereading these . . .

I'd have loved being at Little Rock, but many things made it impossible.

Dhyanyogi-ji

I began organizing the workshop in Leuven for Dhyanyogi-ji (1878–1994) and his spiritual heir, Shri Asha Ma (later Anandi Ma), to take place Friday–Easter Sunday, April 9–11, 1993—*in a country so Catholic country* that for Easter, pharmacies close the entire week.

Soon I would be assisting in the editing of his biography, which finally came out, with the help of many other supervisory hands, over ten years later.

In the late nineteenth century it was still possible in India to live a wandering life, in search of "Who am I?" and God. Dhyanyogi-ji had been announced by Lord Krishna as a non-ordinary holy child before birth, in a dream to his mother. He first ran away at seven on a quest for God—and definitively at eleven, wandering in the mountains among reclusive saints till finally at forty-three, living in a cave on Mt. Abu, he was given shaktipat by a solitary teacher.

"He recounts that when he opened his eyes three days later, he beheld his Guru seated before him in the form of Lord Hanuman . . . the quintessential devotee of Shri Rama, embodying the highest level of *bhakti* (devotional love), *jnana* (knowledge of Reality), *vairagya* (renunciation or detachment) and *seva* (selfless service). And these Divine qualities of Lord Hanuman became the hallmarks of Shri Dhyanyogi Madhusudandas."[38]

The Hindu story goes that Lord Shiva (God, pure consciousness) incarnated as a monkey to serve Lord Ram, as recounted in the tales of the *Ramayana*. Lord Shiva illustrated that "the last shall be first," or the first last, becoming in this nonhuman, monkey form the supreme incarnation of service. This sheds a certain, very different light on the question whether humans descended from the ape, because in this other level of the story of human history, if in a focus on service, the ideal lineage would be of Lord Hanuman, the monkey god of service. In Hinduism, Lord Shiva in uttermost humility took this form to serve Lord Ram. A central aspect of Dhyanyogi-ji is this association with Hanuman, as his life was indeed donated over to service.

According to Dhyanyogi-ji, the Indian soil retains traces of the subtle energy built up over centuries by the reclusive spiritual teachers living in the Himalayas and elsewhere. The practice of meditating in the foothills or mountains (as he had) resulted, he said, in the generation of such energy that if such an individual did come out into society, his or her gaze was almost too powerful to look upon. Indian society, until relatively modern times, took it for granted that one of these gurus was more powerful than a king and also could heal and bring about results that in the West are called impossible. Being a guru had nothing to do with information, as the popularized word imagines; it was about this ability to hold energy.

For instance, into the later years of his life, Shri Dhyanyogi would have his disciples meditate together to end a drought, and successfully perhaps twenty-four hours later step out into rain at the end of their meditation. This is a part of history I had never known about.

Before accepting to have shaktipat with Shri Asha Ma and Dhyanyogi-ji, I requested a private silent, subtle arrangement with him—which asserted that I *was not giving up allegiance to the Zurich Initiator or the "spirit committees" in the apartment* but expanding my ability to relate to Light.

I asked him not to take my karma, except in an emergency that was extremely dangerous with regards to a lesson I *had already learned*. I had the intuition I was to hold karma sometimes for others, which, of course, normally only a great teacher does. Nevertheless, it felt right to ask, and I assumed that if he was truly that powerful, he would read my intention, provided I was very clear.

Another thing I learned is that Hinduism, according to Dhyanyogi-ji, is not a multi-god system. It is a One-God system, with its highest representation of God, or reality, so abstract, so difficult to grasp (that is, before expanding to a God-consciousness in unity with all life), that in order to relate, we need "personalities" such as Lord Vishnu or Lord Ganesh that incarnate God, with traits that are lifesaving for the time they are born. The Kundalini energy is the feminine, the Divine Mother. Unity consciousness is a balance of male/female.

When the Kundalini goes up the spine in any individual, it achieves this God-conscious unity of all life, knowledge of the sacredness of all sensate beings (including animals), and the union of the male and female energy. I record this because it was now a consciousness my consciousness was trying to expand into, to align with, and it was active in the atmosphere I lived in, active in the guidance in the "soul committees" that were helping me write. That is to say, I was becoming multicultural, with all cultures coordinating and interacting in this consciousness I was growing.

However, at the moment—as we are unable to leap many quantum leaps at once—I was expanding to understand Hindu consciousness. Also being introduced to *siddhis*, which in the East were not called "paranormal" or "anomalous" but a natural part of the development of spiritual consciousness, evidence of the priority of spirit over matter—mind over matter (back to that as all things loop around). Physical evolution followed upon physically influenced, pragmatic choices, but the focus of the East was on merging with God, by any name, so long as it led to God-consciousness. According to Dhyanyogi-ji-ji, this took place through awakening Kundalini.

I began to send some of the computer printouts to a parapsychologist professor in Belgium, then to a physicist in Holland, who came to a train station to meet me in person, handing over—to test the energy—a random number generator designed by him. But I felt not strong enough to have random frequencies in the room with me.

It is clear to me that Dhyanyogi-ji is assisting me.

1994—*Shri Dhyanyogi "drops the body"*

On the refrigerator at Jyoti and Russell's I had noticed some news in a note about the Shoemaker-Levy comet predicted to crash into Jupiter. It would destroy part of the planet. At the same time there was a conjunction of Jupiter in Scorpio to Pluto. As time passed the idea began to grow in me—I began to intuit—that it would associate with some Earth event. A symbolic link. In other words, it was a clue that something was up. But I didn't know what. I was right. Now a big event began to prepare itself, an event that would be important to me, an event that was all taking place unconsciously, at this point.

> Jupiter, the planet that drives us to search for the meaning of life, is still in Scorpio where it has been since late last year. Scorpio is ruled by Pluto, the god of death, and therefore relishes the journey through the underworld of darkness and emotional baggage. Scorpio seeks power and emotional intensity and Jupiter is the planet of buoyant abundance, so this is an odd combination that expands (Jupiter) the focus on death, secrecy and sexuality, the domains of Scorpio. Scorpio is rather ruthless in its aims, and Jupiter, being the King of the Gods, can be somewhat arrogant and self-righteous and an unfortunate aspect of this combination can be the ruthless slaughter of innocents. Jupiter was last in Scorpio in 1994, witnessing the beginning of the Rwandan massacre and the murders of Nicole Simpson (wife of OJ Simpson in case anyone needs a reminder) and Ron Goldman . . . Jupiter expands the mind and Uranus brings in new ideas and ways of looking at old problems. (August Skywatch—Astrological Update from Lynn Morrison, Astrodynamics, July 31, 2006)

In Romania I had met someone, also had the chance to be published. And so Hunter slipped into the distance; I would send him a copy of a book, by me, now and then, knowing it arrived. Knowing he would be pleased for me in friendship—and continue into his stardom and personal situations. But also that he would possibly point to the "gibberish," the impressionism, lack of "hard facts" in my books. Yet be glad, in any case.

I remembered how he had his secretary open his mail and read it aloud to him. I couldn't imagine he asked her to read a communication from me. But who knows? And why not? I sensed, when I phoned about Little Rock and he didn't pick up, there was a new girlfriend. Yes, it turned out, there was, Nicole.

There seemed no further chance to be together. At least, on this obvious level. I also dreamed, remember, I was to help "write 'The Hunter Thompson Story.'" What was that? It seemed glitteringly joyful, but when? How? What? Something held, underneath. It held beyond logic. It held as charisma. It held as love.

❋

Goe-
thé
Last cup of tea in the dregs [thé: tea (FR), pronounced "tay"]
to stand beside
Dan-
thé
and Thé-
O

1993–'94

By 1993, I had acquired my version of a Buddha belly. Some part of me, an energetic system in the stomach, sat, cellularly there, with a consciousness beyond mine as an individual. That was apparent (when it arrived). But let's wait for then. I get ahead.

Most of us have seen portraits of Gurus in loin cloth with a large belly, but few Westerners know that this belly is transpersonal energy. In fact, in those days I went regularly to get my neck and lower back put in traction. The first time I arrived with the little Buddha belly, the medical assistant putting on the weights had to keep adding more to the lower back. *Mass*, I told myself. *There is more mass there, holding the weights*. Every time thereafter she had to add the new amount of weight to the lower back.

With the inbreath and outbreath in a holding position there, the Buddha belly gets large and small, depending on what it has to do. It can change size dramatically in a matter of minutes. Sometimes it doesn't show at all, as with Gandhi, being it's internalized. I covered mine, though small, with loose blouses and sweaters, so no one knew.

It cannot bear to be constricted. I couldn't put anything tight over it, not stockings or elastic at the waist. In contrast to lying flat, it wants to poke out, to protrude, to *breathe—even if physically just barely visibly*. This gives a greater sense of weight, mass, which is also why the center of the body is here, at the hara:

> By transferring your center of consciousness to the hara thoughts gradually disappear on their own without any inner conflict. This is why you see Buddha statues with a big belly. This is an esoteric message that the hara is a key to meditation. (.web-us.com/meditation_handbook.htm)

Therefore, it is only natural that I go up to these more cosmic perspectives if there is a child of cosmic energy in my psychic/subtle womb.

Information Arriving Mystically

Now my consciousness is soaring in. Mystical things happen; people walk in and say things to me only possible in subtle energy.

❋

I kept much of it internalized, and from there looked out into the world through it. BUT I never doubted or turned back,

If this story sounds strange, I guess my entire life is one of the strangest stories I could imagine. Except when I begin to think in depth on many lives, I cannot see them as anything but unimaginable.

Anyway, when I went to see Mother Meera—whom I knew to be, for the Hindus, an avatara ("descent") of the Divine Mother—in Thalheim, Germany (this was August 6–8, 1993, an old red agenda book tells me), there, in darshan with her hands on my temples as her blessing acted in what her website called a "wiring" of the soul," I was suddenly convinced: I *must be true to the image the Initiator had of me.* In that moment, facing her, silently in telepathic communication, I couldn't believe what went through my head. I found myself asking her, wordlessly, *to recognize me in the way the Initiator did.* Is that blasphemous?

I didn't care if she heard or not. I could not help myself. I had to. *Else, I could not "recognize" her.* Nothing could have startled me more.

It was a kind of energetic "quid quo pro." Her hands pressing lightly against my head supported the outlandish request. The "wiring" insisted I couldn't disavow—betray—my Initiation. Thinking of the Initiator, all he knew, viewed from my soul level, that I didn't, I let the thought stand. I held to it. So my soul had me insist that she "recognize me" in the way the Initiator had. This was in a sense inflated. But I felt it at a gut level. So I blurted out silently this request. An instinct

Now, of course, this is a preposterous thought to have in one's head, standing before the saint the Hindus recognized as one incarnation of the Divine Mother—radiating the Paramatman, or "supreme Self."

But it is these kinds of gut level energetic responses that make our "energy signature" visible. It is the energy that is reacting, calling the shots, building to the point where it can no longer be silent. Kinetically, beyond thought, it acts.

I'd rejected such position-"claiming" during the Zurich Initiation, but my allegiances changed in that moment, in that situation, when she was, as her website put it, "working on [my] personality[ty], the everyday body/mind." I never associated the "I" of that moment with "just" my personality till quite recently. But if Mother Meera was removing the blocks and false influences that Earth experiences had produced, well, obviously, she was working on the personality. And the personality alone. I felt nothing but the need to assert this request, not realizing that the sheer determination of the thought as it focused single mindedly on me was aligning with her blessing, her vibration, in resonance with her energy—that she had taken me, or someone had, up to a level where that was the only possible response.

In the blessing, she "works on nadis, lines in the subtle body, which contain knots, and she unknots these . . . 'I *am giving Light to every part of your being, I am opening every part of yourself to Light.*"[39]

> Matter itself is not self-evolving, for at the heart of matter there is the Divine and no growth can take place without the Spirit as primal mover . . .
>
> Paramatman means literally "*Highest Self*" or 'the *Self of the whole Universe* . . .
>
> —Mother Meera's website

> *[This] Light has never been* USED *before. Like electricity, it is everywhere, but one must know how to activate it.*
>
> —Mother Meera about the Paramatman Light

Anyway, nothing happened. So, I thought. That was the end of that. *Little did I know.*

✻

In February '94, Dhyanyogi-ji came to me in a dream.

As I recounted June 2, '95, in a letter to Shri Anandi Ma and her spiritual husband, Dileepji, he told me he'd been "looking at [my] charts." They were off to one side. I could not see what was on them. Then he indicated a group it would be normal for me to participate in but said not to. If I did—

A solitary park bench appeared. I was sitting by myself on it. "That's where I used to be," he said, having experienced that being-benched situation, presumably over decades in the caves and mountains of India. But:

"It's nineteenth century."

Based on graphs of energy forms which were me, he was there to draw me away. He concluded with the most amazing request of a satguru to an initiate—to leap over all the study, the years of preparation and "*Come to me direct.*"

"Dhyanyogi-ji once said that whenever he met people, he took X-rays of their past, present and future," I read later. "He wanted to see into their hearts. Some people were like dynamite, he said. He'd touch them and they'd blast off. Others were like coal; it was hard to get them started, but once they did they burned very well. Still others were like wood . . . [requiring interaction]. And finally, there were those who were like stone. Dhyanyogi-ji said, 'It's my job to turn stones into humans, and humans into gods."[40]

The dream message presumed I could come to him without training, without group meditations, just on my own initiative.

This is unusual, to say the least. It must mean, but I did not understand it consciously at the time, that in a group I would be submerged, with no distinction made that something about me did not fit but was subtler. If I was to "come to him direct," there was a good chance I'd been realized before. *And it takes a teacher to awaken that earlier awakening.*

In other words, focused on him, though he's out of body, I could reach him on my own somehow. I took this to heart. It was a tough assignment. It's what Hindus call "a boon"—a blessing resulting from past lifetimes, karma.

I haven't a chance, he's said, if following a normal method. The reason, if it's true that I had been realized in the past, would be that I would not be trying to reach a certain level *for the first time but to spontaneously remember, step into where I had been before.*

In the letter to Shri Anandi Ma and Dileepji, I tell them that what prompts me to write is that "Somewhere, somehow, intuiting he might soon die, I wrote a letter in 1994 to thank him for something I felt sure he had done, on the subtle plane. But it was so subtle that I knew it wouldn't be imagined as real [I was wrong; it was exactly how his energy operated] if anyone by accident happened to read it." So not knowing the protocol in his ashram, I didn't mail it, but "kept it beside my bed. I decided that he would read it if he wished . . ."

And "am sure he read it."

"Come to me direct." I held it tight. A promise. It would not be taken back. I couldn't see him physically. But he was there, in reach. Dhyanyogi-ji had such energy when in the body that from yards away people would heat up and sometimes faint.

In certain groups, I think he meant, where my soul was coming down, there would be no way to detect I wasn't expanding upward ("ascending").

Light body study accelerated skills to see the energy level of everything. I wrote, "The point goes through, the wave follows." Each person can be the "point" that goes through first now and then, or never.

❋

Shortly afterwards, I went to a light body seminar on channeling in Utrecht, Holland. There, in a little group as we all went into a guided meditation. I saw a flash of pale blue, then blanked out. When it came time to share, another person in the little group announced she'd she just gotten a new guide, Mother Mary.

It could not be that Mother Mary came right into our group of (let's say) seven and *skipped entirely over* me. I felt set back on my heels. My practice of "being invisible" had turned against me. The flash of blue was her, I thought, and that I probably left my physical body and "merged." Gone unconscious. It sounded like me.

That night, I vowed to "stay in my body" the next day. The next day, I had a psychic reading with someone I was to see more of, an eminent channel by all accounts. I wanted to settle the uncertainty, for I was on quavering legs about all of this information, not matter-of-fact because not integrated.

I thought it would be crystal clear if I asked her, "What dimension do I come from?" That should be simple enough.

But she answered, "From the heart of God." So it was no clearer.

Near tears, I went on desperately, because I had to make some sense somehow. "Then if I come from the heart of God, why is the Jesus incarnation so close to my heart?" I was so completely open, because my heart could not hold it back, that she spoke personally now. It had seemed to me that there was no way to distinguish personal and transpersonal in this new world, no way to anchor.

She answered, "Because it is your incarnation that is closest to your heart." She said a lot of energy would go with me when I left the room, and memories come. She said three large beings were with me, but she would use no names: "A mystery will gradually unravel."

Then she stepped back into her personality. Looking me in the eye, she said, "*Be outrageous*. That's the way I got where I am."

These inconclusive meetings, I did not dwell on. The important thing was, I had been authentic. To speak silently to Mother Meera was just something I *had to do*, deliberately. I did not expect follow-ups; they would take time.

※

That same year, 1994, a young American spiritual teacher (I'd never met) arrived to spend the night in Tienen with me. An acquaintance sent her. It was Pentecost.

She left Mother Meera's to take the train straight to me. She too was psychic/mystical. Immediately in my house—and initially I did not connect this to Mother Meera—she looked at me, a stranger, and said, "Weren't you in the Bible?" Not of course her typical opening line. Carefully, I decided to let it play itself out:

Then she said, "Wasn't your name Mary?" "Mary who?" I quickly asked. She said, "Magdalene." Then she began to describe her from then: "You used to sit on the floor like now. You had a house where people came to be healed by drinking some sort of liquid. You were *very sensual . . . but very pure*."

It made sense to me that such an archetypical combination had no clarity here on the Earth, where sensuality is physical, purity spiritual.

Later I will learn to see these things as "a consciousness," and that consciousness close to me.

Then the visitor left, *to return to Mother Meera's*, and I make no connection, not till a year afterwards—1995—at a sweat lodge at

Kayumari, Jyoti and Russell's spiritual village in California that I had helped form.

As time passed, I accumulated a lot of sound understanding. Of great interest to me, I had learned for sure that the Magdalene energy *balanced* the Jesus Christ energy for 2,000 years. That means if he said red, she might say blue.

As for being pure AND sensual—a very atypical combination—on the other hand, he, Jesus, that I have seen, is the same. Utterly sensual while being of the utmost and inviolable of pure. I have seen his energy ripple like a vibration, yet with a human form, the sensitivity so high and nuanced. I think of hers the same way. Was she ever, in fact, this great sinner who needed redemption? I wasn't sure. What I thought was that a shift in consciousness she arrived at was that once she thought she needed the assistance of broth for healing. But she needed nothing. That the Holy Spirit requires no drink.

How was that for being outrageous?

But though most of this had not happened in linear time in late 1992, it was all present in different degrees; that is, different lines into the future—*potential under momentum*.

So as I write these words I wonder: *Was that what instigated my writing of the Hunter letter—combined with the electricity*? For one of my future paths was the *approach* of such moments.

Was it the approach that made me feel protective of my young spiritual awareness, not wanting ever again to get disconnected from my higher energy so that it had to "fly out of my body" to leave the personality behind? I became intent on learning to "stay in my body"—*remain conscious*. Was that the background into which the letter I sent in 1992 would *not seem so odd*?

⁂

Later I was in a group who were taking a "medicine." Feeling it was protected space, tired of always standing on the sidelines of medicine journeys, I joined in and was given a pure dose of yagé. Instantly, a blackness began to sink over me. I thought: *I am going to black out!* Never had such a thought entered my head. At that moment the leader came over. Grasping the situation, she peered at me. "How do you think I stay conscious in samadhi?" was all she said.

So that's it! Samadhi. I just have to stay conscious in it, I thought instantly. And immediately my higher mind took over, canceling out any threat of going unconscious. Then the real experience began. I shot up into a conversation with the Divine Mother. I "stayed in my body," opening into the consciousness that was where I was normally unconscious.

Every threat to humankind has skills that make it avoidable. But as we go up the consciousness ladder, often we learn new laws before learning the skills. I had a lot of fear. My task was to "get over the fear of being strong and powerful as a female." And on the soul level, to "help others overcome the fear of enlightenment." Again, removal of fear. How?

By learning the laws that are stronger. And by knowing the laws of love, more powerful still—of surrender, of putting one's own will under Divine Will.

❋

In the summer of 1994, I attended the conference of the International Association for the Study of Dreams at the University of Leiden, the Netherlands. Here again, as in the May '92 breathwork seminar in Zurich, I had an unfathomably deep spiritual experience—one of three "magnetic moments." This third energetic memory (*of stretched space-time, with its quivering* Brownian *vibrating molecules*) happened here, at an IASD workshop.

I will skip it now, as it belongs properly near the end of the book.

August 7–10, I went to the Parapsychological Association Convention in Amsterdam. Hoping for her to publish an essay by me, I'd written Rhea A. White—editor of the *Journal of the American Society for Psychical Research* (as well as *Exceptional Human Experience*, the EHE journal)—to ask if I could send her materials about my computer-PK. I mentioned J. B. Rhine, whom she remembered fondly as her former lab boss.

Modifying the request, she replied, asking that I write my Exceptional Human Experience Autobiography instead.

At the same time, at the very end of August or first day of September, my "big book," now split in two volumes, was finally finished, coinciding with a monumental event. August 29, 1994, Shri Dhyanyogi "left the body."

It was in this fury of that energy that I completed the book, or it completed itself. "This house is on fire," he had said. "Loot all you can."[41]

> The work of saints is to spread fragrance, like an incense stick, even at the cost of their life.
>
> —Dhyanyogi-ji

The events in India still unknown to me, I felt myself *spinning fast inside* as if jumping out of my skin. For several days I let the experience run its course, at the edge of my ability to bear it. Then phoned Mariah Martin.

Before I said a word, as is the way she opens her readings, she described me as if on jet fuel. She also said my energy had merged with Jesus.

Neither of us yet knew that in the aftermath of the comet striking Jupiter, king of the gods, Dhyanyogi-ji "dropped the body." August 29, 1994.

❋

Learning of Dhyanyogi's departure, which occurred on the birthday of Lord Krishna, I recorded:

> Even as this holy man died, I had completed the story I was telling, in the book form. And the computer had every other page, in a style invented for this one occasion, *printed out only the last letter of each word*. Letters had been used, before this, as if in signatures by the computer energy.

That is, the short second volume finished at the very end of August or first day of September, with—in the printout—every other page perfect, *followed by a page missing all except the last letter (or two letters) in every line. The rest of the page blank.*

> Even as I wrote that, quoting him, we are not always conscious of where our energy is, he had just passed away, into a new form, and I will say I was receiving some of that energy.
>
> The Resurrection Christ would not walk onto the stage in a recognizable way. But he would over and over give people the chance to choose Him, when the more visible choice, the usual, the seemingly obvious perhaps, was really to choose Barabas. Not even told that we sat inside this issue, or rather not told again, for we had heard it before, we yet did sit inside individual

choice that was remolding the ideas our world lives in. And as there was no Appearance before the events happened, the room that opened, on purpose, gave to each person the chance for that particular growth, albeit that the risk they seemed to be taking was on a higher level taken with them. To see what the choice was. Was it the incarnated second, the moment's spark, illuminating the presence of the cosmic Christ?

Klonsky had told me he felt like someone in a murder mystery who finds out he's the one being murdered. But "there will be a punch line." I believed thought could connect even between universes, for how else could that promise be kept. And the others had been. The punch line would have to be consciousness of this, and in the energy as of helium fires of Jupiter in which this was completed he lived and felt the completion. And—dare I say it?—was signaling. Even in being transformed, remembered.

Music in the plane. A spirit was inside the music—the spirit counterpointing the notes. The spirit that was saying: He lived and yet, "to go or/and not to go."

Fired up by seeing Mother Meera in Germany, I wrote Stephen Spielberg a letter, never delivered. I had an idea for a film, that now reads very 9/11-ish. This below may be part of that idea, or it may be another film, for ideas were flowing, under the impact of the spirit committees. Told in the perspective of the spirit committee pre-9/11, the story looked entirely reasonable, just entirely multidimensional:

MOVIE SKETCH

Begins with the situation of a new millennium. In the heavens a new commandment is being recorded. It reads across the sky:

LET THERE BE
NO MORE DEATH

Thunderclaps, for the heavens are clapping, lightning.

On the Earth, which hasn't received word of the commandment, much upheaval. The instruction is still Light Years away. Can it intercept the known End of the Century? The known Laws of the Earth? Can it give the Earth a closer connection with its real situation? Can it bring it out of the Cave of Plato, *closer to the blinding light of the sun? Can it do miracles that are positive and not negative—that are constructive? Can it beam signals into the atmosphere that counteract the negative signals of the* Archetype *of* Death *as it dies?*

For death on so large a scale will try to take many inhabitants with it. It will pull them into its clutches. It will hypnotize them with fears, bind them with barbed wire cords as they scream. Much evil will ensue and even nature may react with fear—just as animals in the forest run before a fire, as Bambi *ran, hearing the sounds of the hunters approaching.*

Thunder, lightning. Let us begin.

In a corner of the sky God *appears, saying not to worry, things are as they should be. The* Earth *is undergoing an enormous change—a move to a higher consciousness, and much will have to fall in its wake. Much lower consciousness will have to give way. How can that be? For consciousness is identity to most. How can so many at the same time undergo this stripping bare of their souls, this loss of identity on a cosmic scale? But then how can a new consciousness come in, otherwise? And come in, it will.*

Chills, o chills. Must this be undergone? It must.

There are many ways to begin this story, of a universal consciousness sweeping the Earth, *like the* Great Fire *of* London, *like the plague, like a giant meteor crashing into the god of poetical triumph,* Jupiter. O, *let's make the* Jupiter Symphony *be seen first. A mighty symphonic hymn, a many-planet orchestra. Let's pick up the spirit roaring out into the starry night, of the song of the agonizing god, the one so close to the* Earth *that only poets and artists heard originally.*

Now Time, *in a cloak comes onto the stage and says the key words: "*Earth, *I am a burden to you. I should not be. I am making a connection with* Eternity *this decade. I am opening my locked doors, as to a levee. Will you experience the floods of the unleashed water at my sides or will you come with me?"*

But who will make a buffer for so great a shock as the feeling of eternity?

Leaders, there must be, familiar with it, at home in it, who dare to take on this mantle, pick up this sword, and as Time *marches through the gates of* Eternity *defend the* Earth, *which shakes and rumbles and quakes with the human fears set loose. With the tremors of temptation.*

BACKGROUND:

A man and a woman, and God says you have the whole universe for a stage, provided you clear up the Archetype of Love.

So the Archetype of Death is on stage, at the same time, sharing it with the Archetype of Love, and this couple is in both. Both Archetypes will be casting shadows and veils, and this man trying to reach high noon, to be in a position of the sun at its zenith.

Time, Place: Earth, New York City, 1960s

Action: A double love story—one including a cerebral young woman, about twenty-four, and a poet with a strong practical side, considered a genius by many. The other includes a triangular relationship between a very physically oriented housewife and her husband, the woman having a fantasy attraction to an enigmatic young man.

Unbeknownst to anyone at the start, this married woman, Anny, is the shadow life of the cerebral Paula, the physical involvement with life, and experiential encounter with it, a passionate desire for experience. Her husband Joseph is unable to satisfy this need for excitement and thus the attraction to the mysterious Ian, who is fascinated with this kind of woman.

Robert, in the first couple, provides astounding insights, in condensed form, that speak to the depths of Paula, though she cannot cross the barrier into a spirit fully in love in a physical form. For her spirit is in love with him but trapped by an Earth separation between spirit and matter. He is in human form. Her spirit cannot love someone in human form, who is so entirely physical and masculine and everything that a man can be, including powerful, accomplished, assured. Dynamite, in fact. And something in her prefers the unconscious, shadow relationship with a man.

Beyond this, the dimension of Archetype, which this story falls into. And why it does, for it is part of a plan. Spirit nearing Earth, and it must have new outlines to go into. It must have new, original relationships. It must have expansion. When the Earth breathes out this time, it must breathe even further, expand beyond the contours it had. It must expand to include a new understanding of love.

And so this story, that had every reason to enter the Earth in an experiential form in triumph, in recognition of one with the other, comes in differently. It comes in in challenge form, in pioneering form, in sequences, even, of group participation. It comes in in the satisfaction that the ground cleared here will be clear on a larger scale, and that soul growth must have its feelings equal to those that in a moment had been sacrificed. The Earth is under the shadow of guilt and sacrifice. Only by going through that path can the real future open. If a man so loved a woman that he wanted her to experience what he had, that her soul might so grow it could become as visible to him on the Earth as it was off the Earth, well then, wouldn't others learn from that? And so the multidimensional facets of the story would work with the missing facets of the Earth to help it in its birth. To help the female Archetype of soul growth, for instance.

❋

Though the EHE Autobiography began in the intent to write a simple autobiography of "exceptional experiences," it became a flocking point for information.

I included in my letter June 2, '95, to Shri Anandi Ma and her spiritual husband, Dileepji, the first essay of my "two-part spiritual autobiography." I explained that Dhyanyogi-ji, in dropping the body, had "lifted my karmic position into one of possibility rather than almost-impossibility": that it was with the massive energy windfall of his *mahasamadhi*—which, as it sent out such huge matter waves, tied up some loose knots if we accepted the tying up—that the surprise request for my spiritual autobiography entered my life.

By Rhea White, a dedicated publisher/editor, I was given a chance to speak—in a public forum—of these thoughts and experiences I had been holding to my chest.

I phoned India to, at the last minute, be sure I had their permission. Not quite understanding my request, Dileepji hesitated. Then I realized the only possible answer to his question, "What do you want?" was, "Your blessing."

He said, relaxed, quick, "You have that, always."

❋

I sit in a clearing of a forest, drumming outside a sweat lodge. 1995. My first. I did not go in. A number of women are inside the intimate, cave-like enclosure filled with burning sage and other herbs. Suddenly, for the first time I made a connection. I saw Mother Meera's face flashing in front of mine. It went on for some time, and I deduced—rather "knew"—she was saying, "Well, you asked me, and so I'm doing it. I'm recognizing you." Then she went into the sweat. Afterwards, those in the sweat told me the Divine Mother had gone in, which I knew. But they didn't know in which form she was. I told them.

I realized that in recognizing me, she'd turned my request around to make a request of her own: that I recognize someone in her energy. But who? Then I saw someone staggering, being held on both sides. She looked like Mother Meera, even. *That's her*, I thought. I knew I was being asked, in turn, to do for this staggering woman what was being done for me. I went over.

In fact, she was extraordinary.

I put my hands, with her permission, on the sides of her head—the way Mother Meera passes transmissions—telling her she was under the protection of Mother Meera, who had just been in the sweat lodge.

Later, still at Jyoti's and Russell's Kayumari spiritual village, I sat inside the communal living room, in front of their altar. On it sat photos of spiritual teachers (e.g., the Dalai Lama, Dhyanyogi-ji), a statue of the Buddha, a large portrait of a running Christ. I was for the first time listening to a recording of Shri Anandi Ma singing samadhi trance music. Suddenly, I felt myself in an energy like never before, as if in a vortex that transmits and conducts; to my left in spirit was Shri Anandi Ma, to my right Dhyanyogi-ji.

He was communicating. I felt him saying he wanted his biography to be about not only her feelings for him *but his for her*. This intense interchange, I was clear was real. But what to do? As it turned out, years later the completed biography followed this format, though I never said a word about the occurrence. Yet I was clear it was the wish of Dhyanyogi-ji. Only, how would it be communicated? Not through myself verbally. But in a vortex of such strength as this, I believe that the presence of the format was a conduction system, and in some way the fact that I listened in on the plans assisted. Or if not, then I merged with the planning location.

But there are now other incidents. I leave California and this time Jyoti drives me to San Francisco to drop me off. As I sleep in the motel that night before my flight, her image again appears to me—subtly, suspended just under the ceiling—and tells me *the Earth wants safe passage. It wants to learn things for itself!* And it wants safe passage to make those discoveries.

She tells it to me as if I will deliver that message or act on it in some way, that the delivery is purposeful.

The Mystical "Steps Up"

In preparing slides for my speech in the Parapsychology Association panel on J. B. Rhine (in Durham, North Carolina, in August 1995), I finished a roll of film on my balcony by pointing my $100 Fuji camera into the sky. Years earlier, I'd dreamed of cloudscapes containing cinema-like scenes that rapidly shape-shifted, and in the dream I marveled, knowing such cinematic scenes in the clouds were impossible. Also, no one else was looking.

The incubation now sprang to life. For hours, I'd watch faces, scenes, emerge as I developed a technique: tipping the inexpensive camera toward the sun, I tried to "materialize" cloud images. It worked. In a light body meditation I experienced the sense that I'd lost my hands—that they had the gift to sculpt or paint but had been born without the force in the hands to do so.

Looking at the clouds, I saw fully realized paintings. But I had to use "mind through matter." The soul grouping focus.

In 1996 or '97, I invited a woman to Belgium to teach a seminar.

One day she arrived from France or Germany. I greeted her on the platform of the train station. Above the roar of the arriving/departing trains, she called me "the Magdalena"—adding that she'd had a flashback when we first met but had been forbidden to speak of it till now.

Don't start thinking one-on-one, though. The Magdalena would be the first to discount it. No, it was true, and it was also to be very carefully couched in that phrase "universality of humanity," not to diminish it but not to try to pin it down. *What? Do that to energy? To Huge Energy?* It would be laughable. More, blasphemous.

After Little Rock

I—being a coward or a wise person?—did not go to Little Rock.

Joska famously said, "True knowledge of sound carries with it great power. It allows one to travel without moving."

Sometimes there were dreams; sometimes I bit my tongue to keep from pouring things out. However, the time was past. The future was set. He was set down into a new life, a happy environment, one he could smile in as he always did, be productive in.

Romania had led me to a publisher.

I took the chance to publish with a professor, Didi-Ionel Cenușer, and sat with him in Romania about a hundred hours as he tried to untangle my computer floppy disc, plus the sheets of paper containing computer-PK-formatted text. After the otherwise-irreproducible computer-PK inserts were scanned, we printed them out and Scotch-taped them onto clear film paper. A strongly left- and right-brain person, detail-oriented and visionary—an offbeat professor, creative, English-speaking, an author himself—he wrestled with the process as I sat there. Just the right person for the job.

I often wondered if I would see Hunter again. *And what about when he dies? What about when you hear of it?* I wondered how deeply I would feel it. Could I stand it? Would I go to the funeral, fly in? It never occurred to me that that question would be out of my hands.

Backed against a wall with only one option, the male behind the males I played my part with could have made any scene a success, a dead end, produce some miracle that convinced me, AND MORE IMPORTANTLY, HIMSELF, his personality level.

When I think of it that way, it is yet one other untried situation, one other approach that was not even ventured, it was so horrendous to think that we might just stay stuck.

At any rate, I have to look myself in the eye on this level and ask whether I took enough risks. Whether I risked trusting him, the large male counterpart, enough, or followed too much, ready to jump when he did; whether I showed myself, on the personality level, or rather believed in myself, on the personality level, as much as he believed in his personalities. Believed, even, to the point of trusting them beyond himself on that level, time and again, at least now and again. Never sure he was necessarily holding all the answers—about them—for they could create and make discoveries.

And did I believe enough the same?

Anyway, when I found myself in *Gonzo Letters* II, it was healing. But that was in 2005. And there is time before that to continue the story here.

What did take up so much space? It's THE present. It's unending, it stretches so in intensity. And intensity means it is everything, everywhere, for the brain cannot absorb more. The brain, faced with intensity, cannot see "outside." And so you are "here," in that way, now. Another lump in the throat. I will see where this is going, what it turns up. Who is here? What form? I am used to "form change."

Can I not stick with the physical, the presence of what "was," and "is"? Yes, let's see what pours forth from that. Dare I recount it? Put it on paper? The lipstick tube when I saw you after those twenty-one years; or "parking" on a hill? Well, those are hints, clues, not full descriptions. But let the rest be private. No? You say yes, well, then, using imagination in quantities that I had not remembered, inspiration perhaps always present, there was the use of a lipstick tube to—

I shiver, remembering. Imagination, and then—you take it from there. Play it again, Sam. After all, you were not married to anyone then; neither was I. What we did in private broke no rules, not ours.

The scenes come in now. The end of *Casablanca*. It makes me cry every time. Milton was like Rick. I meant to say that he looked a lot like Humphrey Bogart; talked like him. Another lump in the throat. So in writing this, I am seeing it from other perspectives. I get closer to yours, to your feelings that were not revealed, your sense of what was being foregone—time and again—for me. I see it as for me, by intent. How many times did you kill yourself for me, or just walk away? How many? And do I exaggerate? But this is a private conversation. Reader, turn the page.

No, I do not exaggerate, provided we are looking from this angle. From other angles, it would present another picture!! I remember lying in the bed, Hunter's bed—he didn't even ask, after twenty-one years, where I wanted to sleep!

I was saying, though, that I was lying by myself, on the right side (I can picture it), and some in the soul grouping were there. I was aware of them; aware, as they were, that it was very ironic and in some ways quite unconscious, though in impulse it was not unconscious.

I knew they were there by the strong, thick lavender/purple/violet energy. It changed the frequency. I felt the texture. The energy was not just one energy but a group.

They were there, just as they had been at least once with Willy, in the same sort of situation, trying to make something happen. Also, like the night of the arrival of the Little Dot. Not that I didn't have free will, but resonance took over. Water does that. We, made physically so much of water, do not need the water to learn resonance, but perhaps that we are made so much of water is indicative.

1996

Book publication (March/November). My play, *From the Eagle's Nest*, to be performed in Romania for the launching. In it Paula remembers and tries to get in touch with Robert while he is in another universe, where he doesn't remember her. Something like a Greek chorus chants off-Earth poetry, lines of wisdom. Working Title: *In Search of the Uncrucifixion, or, The Sunset Unreported Hitherto*. It begins in Robert's apartment, his "aerie," with Paula there, as they bring a scene from the book to life. Robert had once told Paula that he's "down there with the Minotaur" in the Labyrinth and wants her to get him out by finding the Ariadne thread. In the play:

> Scene after scene after scene, looking for a thread to connect them.
>
> A little child: I'm the thread, Mommy. I'm your higher consciousness. I came in a child form. Nobody will be intimidated by me if I come in that form. I'm only a child.

Paula: You know the meaning behind all this?:

Little child: Of course I do. I'm the child who watched inside you.

Paula: And where are you now?

Little child: I'm taking you over more and more, because you more and more see as I do. I don't have Earth eyes. I have extra-terrestrial eyes. With those eyes, everything has more forms, physical, energetic, and more—in one moment in time. I am those moments where that vision is seen.

Paula: With those eyes, then I can make peace with my past.

Little child: You already did that.

That's why I came. But you can dramatize it so that others can do the same, all of them, if they want to.

Paula: You'll go to them too.

Little Child: I already have. However, they don't know it—they don't see me. They're not sure how to use these new kinds of eyes

MC: Let the show begin, the real one. Let the curtain go up on

OUR NEW PERIOD Of

EARTH HISTORY

Everybody can help make it, though sometimes it means rebelling against the position one is in. Let us go on with these scenes. Let us champion the poor and underprivileged. Let us bring new consciousness, effective in its results, to them.

Paula: Where do such words come from? You are a child, you know.

Little Child: It's extraterrestrial. It's Christ consciousness. Every child and every creature has it there, where I come from and speak of.

CIRTAIN GOING UP on no matter what stage, what scenic setting, but behind all that it is the stage in Earth history that is being set. Portray it, then, differently, in different theatres.

1997

Fate came to get me again in 1997. I found out that some letters of mine (silly, embarrassing, mostly) which somehow got left in Jan's mother's house had been donated by her (without reading them, she couldn't read English!) to a museum. How tricky. How cornered. But I got myself appointed international editing coordinator to a retrospective exhibit on his life and work and set about finding people who could put his psychology and poetry into a credible mix, a structure, people from the United States, people in Belgium who could read Flemish, a process-oriented psychologist in Zurich.

Notes sent to the contributors

> The concept of INSCRIBING a life in a certain size came to me from Jan Mensaert. I would like to introduce him, as a personality, with this concept in mind, in the background. He introduced, in his late writings, the concepts sufficient to form a theory of the larger, multidimensional nature of the human being—of which he was an example, a proponent, and in this instance an inscribed portion of the larger self he also introduced. This being the preface, we can show him in as bizarre, as humorous, as playful, as genial a nature as all of this included. We can break the mold of merely thinking of him inside his human limitations, BECAUSE HE ALREADY DID THAT IN HIS WRITINGS.
>
> This will, surprisingly, reveal a person somewhat different—or even largely different—from what the descriptions of him, outside such a principle, might produce. Thus, we can begin—reconstruct, quote, remember.
>
> Of all the people I have ever met, he was one of the most dedicated to, and admiring of, his "Higher Self"; he went to great lengths to find ways to entice it into his presence, which was a major reason he spent so much time in Morocco, in the nature-abounding "thinking man's country," as it is called.
>
> The limitation, on the one hand, worked with genius, which has the habit of breaking through limitation. These two poles were the theoretical boundaries he saw his lifetime set into.

❋

His novel *The Suicide Mozart* impacted me greatly. The ending reveals it to be an encounter with (or wrestling with) many teachings of St. Paul, as it ends in making conscious (from within) faith, hope and love. The birth—or the making conscious—of these AFTER DEATH . . .

The presiding over of the Graduation Ceremony on Vega Fünf by Muses, graces, Gurus, and Artists shows that we are meeting this consciousness with some variations of perhaps a quality that wants to join their number, "playing with freedom," but must pass through their strict requirements for the acceptance of a Path inside universal knowledge. That birth of the St. Paul consciousness inside the Raskolnikov consciousness, as an implied infolding of the rules of freedom, is one slant that offers a road in.

Of course, Dostoyevsky slew the Raskolnikov consciousness he once identified with. So do we here . . . The basis of the burst of freedom into the modern age, the freeing from old beliefs, with some new support, some new twists, so that truly a Path is made from the seemingly nihilistic beginnings if we see them as such. A path into the Leap of Faith, or so it appears. These things, we are looking at, because we have arrived there by induction.

It would be quite amazing if we found that the Path of the Leap of Faith was a major fulcrum underneath the emerging modern age: . . . As T. S. Eliot said, "Mankind cannot stand too much freedom." Can mankind? And what if we are to be given it? And is the end of this book indicating that such an examination (of the consciousness) might be facing us all—even the entire planet???? . . . Let us see if we can shoot from our cannon something to add to this entry into what looks to be very much of a quite different century, in need of all the wisdom and foresight it can muster. Muster, yes, just as in the grain of mustard seed. I *have finally realized that my position here is to sit with a grain of mustard seed, holding it, to see what might come into the forefront if permitted to—not censored and warded off, not barricaded against, but simply allowed to walk in. So perhaps we are all helping to open a door, merely because we chose to let the free mind have a few words to introduce some new juxtapositions and questions as to what is possible, regarding consciousness, in the huge universe out there, where not all values are as we know them . . . so it is not from lack of exposure that we wonder how to respond to any encounter or even that word attempt at "invasion." We fell asleep over that term "faith the size of a grain of mustard seed."* Suppose another culture did not, and we encountered it. Well, one could go on and on. Imagining the best preparation for the next century. But we are lucky to be allowed to move in our thoughts as far as they take us, for our container is strong, our minds indisposed not to be free.

But something else happens in 1997: *The Proud Highwayman* publication, volume I of Hunter S. Thompson's letters. I got a hold of a copy and wrote him a letter. In some form, though probably not this detailed, I mailed it (the book by me that was also newly published was *Love in Transition*, volume IV; it was the first time I'd mentioned him in published writing):

May 14

Dear Hunter,

I have written a long letter, prompted by reading the book of your letters, and a recent *Rolling Stone* essay (which I liked). However, is there a need for long letters? So just to make sure I get this book into the mail (pointing out p. 56), I take the letter out (at least, for now). It is a small-size thing, on p. 56, but it is packed with density. I think it says volumes, in those few lines. So there you are—

I was rather overwhelmed, to tell the truth, to find myself eliminated, supposedly, from all existence in your early days. But as you yourself noted, this was not a conclusive representation. There were many friends in the same boat. However, I am most partial to the collection of letters I myself have, and even the tribute to you that they offer and the personality and dreams that come through. Also the humor non-ending. And the characterization of you that is completely uncensored and yet as appealing as any restructured or invented one. I have said this before. I am sure these letters are destined for survival someday . . . Probably I will not even be around then, but they will. This is because anyone who stumbles upon them will recognize the genuine voice and the immersion in a drama that they tell. For you are, day by day, writing about what produces the finished work of *Hell's Angels* . . .

Most of all, I hope you are happy. And also that you are still healthy . . . sixty and all. So here, looking back, I hope you will find one of the best friends you ever had. As I find that, looking back, and always believed it. I hope you will always sing "This is my life. I'm satisfied."

I was in a way forced to put all this information down, as it was requested by a journal. I would much rather have condensed and excerpted from it. However, I am glad. And I can release it now. I can, if I have time, deal with other things—other subjects, the photography, which you would like, I am sure. Remembering how you have a photographic eye. I have enlarged the photographs, some to 50 by 65 cm. What you can't see becomes strongly visible. I enjoy the startling sensation of making these practically invisible portions of the sky completely visible. And the images they show.

If ever you have a hunch you want to say something to me, or give me any kind of assignment or whatever, you know that I am someone you will be able to count on. No? I would like to think that you think so. Are you well? (once again). How did you manage? (next question).

It breaks off there. I included, however, a few of his letters from the '60s to refresh his memory, seeing them there, starkly in front of him. The page 56 footnote, I pointed out to him so he would know that I wrote about him, this one time—two tiny measly paragraphs, but there it was, as packed with love as I could fill it. It reads, slightly edited:

I had left the job at Random House, due to the assassination of Robert Kennedy. At that moment I felt the transitoriness of life. As stated earlier, this Random House period had been essential, in testing my stamina in the big leagues. One young writer who became quite famous was, in at

> least one episode of his unauthorized biography—the "snake story"—in fact and not fiction me. (I learned close up that printed material can be completely erroneous, in reading the garbled account; the snake, in the true story, was killed on the stairs of the Random House stairs—instead of chopped up with a vacuum cleaner. The police had advised me to label all the toilets while the beautiful Florida swamps Blue Indigo was loose on the premises, BEWARE OF SNAKE. The real story was not gory. We were all trying—even the Snake Division of the New York City Police (to whom my phone call was transferred without the operator's blinking an eye)—to save the snake, which had been flown up from Florida in unaccompanied luggage, delivered by hand by a flight attendant. I kept it for Hunter in a box in my office. Yes, yes, I know. But this is the truth, and not that. It was my idea, even.
>
> It was a major challenge, getting legal clearings, reprint permissions, dealing with the Hells Angels themselves, and then the paperback version of the book that sold several million copies, *Hell's Angels*, was dedicated to me, for the work entailed, and that was dropped in the proofreading . . .

It concluded with a reference to the day of our first meeting, the TV program where celebrities tried to guess which of three contestants was the REAL HST.

Hunter included me in the next book of his letters with a bang. He left no stone unturned to give me full credit. And when he set his mind to do something, he knew how. But we are not there yet. Not that he wrote me, and not that I even discovered myself in the second book of letters till 2005. Too late. I would have loved to write a thank-you, showing I had read them, in that now-otherworld plane where perhaps my soul, through me, could thank his.

❋

My Birth Pattern

Circumstances made me possible, timings, the fact that a new medical treatment was available. And that my mother, who could not hold a child nine months, heard about this solution, this medical "miracle."

My mother explained it all to me—due to the synchronicity that I asked the question the last time I saw her, not knowing I would not see her again, because how could I predict the car accident? Or could I? After months of the medical process, she was told to go home, and *if she could hold the baby five months,* I could be born; that is, she could have me.

In the Bible, in the pattern of "barren women who conceive," Elisabeth, cousin to Mary and to-be mother of John the Baptist, conceives and is told by the Angel to *"hide yourself away for five months."* IT WAS THE EXACT TIME PERIOD. More, the words survived. But she was told to go through a question-mark test, incubation (silent) period of "five months." A thing is intensified by the more reinforcement, the more confirmations and repetitions of coincidence, it can muster. Archetypes are accumulative by the time they begin to operate openly among us. In the very next passage, Mary herself is visited by the Angel. So this was the archetype of "women who against-all-odds conceive."

Sometimes, also, an archetype is crying for change—for a solution, to be updated.

Many archetypes are stepping up for adjustment today, as we settle into a global society. The old patterns cause dissension, war. New ones of more accommodation, greater adaptation, are on the horizons and crying to be walked into. Stepped into by people who want to walk in the outlines of the future and help others. Some archetypes are even being heavily energized. But right now I want to explain how this fact of being born on the cusp of medical technology, and also how on top of that the solution being right out of a biblical passage, insofar as outline, affected me. And can, under similar situations, affect you.

It is not that the path exists, but that it is JUST OPENING. *It is just this minute becoming available. I am a prophet—oops, product—of the repetitions of this circumstance. I could not be born, and then lo! Suddenly, a way existed.* I asked for details the very last hour that I saw my mother alive—before she got into my new used car and drove it, leading the way, to the edge of town, then stepped back into her cars and headed toward unexpected accidental death!!!

But this is phenomenal. It adds surges of energy. I see how it works. It's nothing to be concerned about that I hit snags and find lack of preparation, that I have to bang on doors and perhaps fall down and straighten out errors. It's the sudden, mercurialness of the door that appears out of nowhere. I am not to feel frustrated, because apparently it was a blessing, not a handicap. It was an obstacle, predating any connection with me.

And this is the pattern I am in, one of CLEARING THE WAY. II had a dream of my mother and me trying to walk down a slope together—a slant. As we walked I saw that my mother turned back because of a male figure—he was trying to come toward us, in the same narrow area as my mother and I were trying to walk. I speculated that meant that my birth was delayed, as it were, maybe just a few contractions, because of this figure who entered—thinking there was room enough for both. But not my mother. She stopped our walk, for the length of time it took for him to go first. I think she was afraid. For me. Because she did see him, in the dream.

And then I sat down, and it all came clear. My birth. This was the desperate kind of birth situation I was given, the one where there was the attempt from the past? Future? Anytime? To push time, knock it off-balance, settle things now; so that there did not have to be crosses and crucifixions. This me, sitting here, examining, letting it happen. Holding. Not letting go. Letting the body, which had been prepared, knew how to, Go Through with it. And then, this idea came. It had been like that before; simultaneously a consciousness entering while my mother turned me back. Turned me back *away from the exit*. But the contractions had begun. Both met, in the body at the same time. War and death. *Life. Life without these old patterns.*

Hunter, you said early on in a BBC interview that after you were "gone," people could take the "legend" and speak of it freely, with liberties not possible if you were alive—in the way, taking up space, inserting concrete facts there in the legend's material, spelling the "real" out, making it explicit to that extent, warding off the ability to speculate. Why was speculation important? In the cards? More important than the human development at that point? And was it? Anyway, you outlined it, laid down the expectation.

It never occurred to you that you would die and be like the tree that fell in the forest with not one hearing a sound.

I sometimes dreamed about Hunter vividly. Notably, I dreamed I wrote his name with red ink on my hand and rewrote it and rewrote it, every time it washed away. And didn't I write about a dream in 1982 that one day, associated with Mimosa (after moving back to the States, I first lived on Mimosa Tree Lane), all the roads would lead to the same road, all drivers turn in the same direction—left and right converge—and that would be the only pull of the future at that time, which is what it feels like now? The phrase I woke from that with "Ciao de Hunter"?

By 2000 I had five books published. The computer was in a fury in the apartment, working on the *Space Encounters* series. No sooner was the museum retrospective on Jan Mensaert over than I made plans to leave Belgium for good. I felt it had to be soon. I had no idea why, not—obviously—knowing of the approach of 9/11.

I attended a conference on advanced channeling in Ibiza. As I channeled in a pair with a light body teacher, he said, "We are having a double initiation." I felt the heavy purple energy surround us. That night in my room, remarkable things happened. I will tell just this one.

Alone, I felt my hands raised over my head. I knew—I cannot explain how because when an altered state comes to get you, there is no fighting its knowledge—it was the Magdalene's hands in my hands; she was blessing the disciples one by one as they went out on treacherous missions; "anointing"—channeling the energy of Jesus through her hands to them. A kind of shaktipat, or energy transfer. I was sure it had happened. It felt historical. The energy had passed through her, in a blessing.

Energy can pass through one person en route to another, sometimes just being stepped down without the other person knowing of the first one's presence. But here it was a ritual. They came to her for this infusion. At least, I felt it as the energy went through my hands.

❋

"No More Games. No More Bombs. No More Walking. No More Fun. No More Swimming. 67. That is 17 years past 50. 17 more than I needed or wanted. Boring. I am always bitchy. No Fun—for anybody. 67. You are getting Greedy. Act your old age. Relax—This won't hurt."

I slid right over the "old age." So was this the prediction, "they will be together in old age"??????? When? Now?

In helping "write The Hunter Thompson Story"?

"Together" for the length of that?

In early 2005 he was felt many places by a variety of people, and I did feel that he was pushing me—perhaps, like Willy, in some way "paying me back," though I had always thought of the relationship as two-sided, mutual. But there was the point that he'd been in the "limelight"; I was in it to a degree so modest that it risked being "reduced and relegated," and no one on that level wanted the end to be a "well dried up who had been a diamond." So, full force and full throttle to the rescue.

Consciousness, at the ground level, is always a trillion, gazillion things at once, able to be in relationship to every single other thing in the universe. And what it supports, then the whole universe backs. That is, if we get out of the way, don't argue, don't excuse, and let the support get through. So I thought that in the multiple effects of this sad event, it was also true that it, in its Resurrection pole, did, consciously, this. And I know, I know, it's too heavy, put this way. Call it one other expression of a person who, fighting hypocrisy, wanted to send some payback of returned emotion, once realizing that it was returned. And some.

❋

2001. My consciousness arrived like a hurricane, at a conference—handed me on a platter in a vision walked into by Milton. It depicted "the All" in an always-moving, dynamic energy that I described at length in *Space Encounters* III revised (2023). As the All spun, it supported (potentially) any tiny part of the Whole, because potentially (abstractly but which could turn real) there was something to be seen—even to HAPPEN—*from that angle*. Every single angle, every single human being, had a unique POINT OF VIEW.

Shri Dhyanyogi assisted in another vision in the seminar, where great teachers, in a council, were preparing for 9/11, one could say in hindsight.

But that's a tale in *Space Encounters* III.

There is one more place where event and awareness concur, culminate. A Native American evening . . . music, instruments. It was my birthday 2005. An initiation took place. I thought it was due to Hunter. Also, it illustrated a piece of the Magdelene consciousness.

As the indigenous instruments sounded, I fell into a trance, in which I experienced sensuality—full blast. But of the sort "when the cells feel it"; earlier, I'd written that "a man is space was waiting to release into the universe its own memory."

At this event I had the sense of the cells, hosting light like rivulets that exploded—set into motion by the merest trace of a touch—my awareness bursting with the sensations, so holy it is, this body, the deep sacredness of it, such as the cells feel: light as it meets light, the flowers, the trees, the sound of music, the utter sensuality when something scrapes, brushes, against something else, creates tingles; touch changes, marks too. Life is that. Life is "extremely pure" and "extremely sensual."

A purity of sensuality like I had never imagined, I felt.I felt it in my bed in the morning too, in meditation as the body felt, inside itself, the internal rivulets, renewed with the sheer essence of life, the possibility of it, the creativity at its heart, based on touch, on contact. I felt it in particular when meditating mornings just before writing *Keep This Quiet!*, setting up the energy for working in the HST materials.

I would experience ripples of light, exploding. *Electricity baths? Yes, I thought so.* And all that in us, buried, hidden, the real "Eve's apple." I felt the release, of the universe in its sensation of Love entering each touch, of Love in transition. Of the Divine Mother, the Goddess, feeling the burst of Creation at the touch of the Divine Male energy, as I have felt it and feel it, and as I give thanks for restoring to me the memory of *my* own nature.

> I began to realize that love is not just an energy but rather a state of consciousness.
>
> —Jyoti

⁂

Talking to Mariah Martin about writing this book. Do it. "Consciousness needs New Consciousness," she said.

⁂

I was to help write "The Hunter Thompson Story." Well, I would have never guessed it was this sort of story. But then, neither would I have guessed this to be the meaning of "They will be together in old age." For how long? For only a moment? For longer. No matter. For however long. Here's a book then, with a chance that this one will be read. And it's all your fault. Thanx, Doc. With Love, Margaret

Here is the emotion I cut out at the end of Volume II of *Love in Transition*. The name that had been there. Here it is, Doc.

I have all of these people to thank. It's all I am, anymore, the experiences that reshaped my cells, their readiness, including blast-off of Hunter, sending me into orbit—all the blast-offs; taking each of us, our ability to decide for ourselves, into new orbits of lucidity, of awareness, of self-knowledge, of gumption, of experimentation, of freedom, of sacredness, of respect.

In the beginning was the Word. But it was not somebody else's word. Now we can take our own word for it, and that is the challenge facing us each, to get to that place where our word is transformed through the fires of transition, the Fourth Amendment, the Rites of Home, internally, where no one can gain admittance except sacredly being admitted through the door, all the while we are, each of us, part of All of us.

And the experience in 2001 where the whole twirls into ever-new forms BEHIND a point, that point being anyone, and, at some times, definitely each one, if they but ask and step up to the plate. For Ciao. As Ciao.

So there, my contribution to the Ciao *de* Hunter. *The great blast-off, the loudspeaker transmission, the holodeck place of imagination, the future as each craftsperson creates it, fueled by freedom, honesty, imagination, a knowing without and within.* Fearlessness *too, in a world where fear might take over, denying it further options, for fearlessness rules, and all citizens opt for it, or some do, enough, to make it a viable* Path *into the future.* This, *for our* Earth.

If the Montparnasse *beggar (sorry, a private reference from my other books) had finished his meal but wanted to light up, with nothing to put the light to, then as the* Whole *twirls and steps up behind this scene, this time, at the plate, on the plate—in the* Sole *for* Breakfast *tradition—let's sign on.* Saignant. A *signature of love, one of those for the next century, when many signatures of* Love *are made, and let's put this one there, inside the* Chow *tradition.*

But this is enough of a crescendo
To get us into the Gothic atmosphere of the
Bedtime Stories written by Jesus
For the Children of the Transition Period
From what we call eternity

Take the story to the presses

He called himself the Man in Silver
Going for Gold
The Man in Silver
Who came back
Com-
PEWTER
Coming into that position, with headquarters
In my computer
From which he made revisions
This the crazy battlefield headquarters
Of the plan to
SAVE THE
EARTH

OK, there are many such plans.
They are working together.
Marshaling collective energy. I had to wait decades to bring this out, till—now—because now I understand such things, have a nuanced, distanced perspective. All together now, we are chipping in, going for high stakes

Just as happened at
my
Computer
That tale that no one believes
Are you kidding me?
But with a wink and a nod
I just agree
Of course, none of it is true
Didn't you know
Nabokov was clear on this:
I made the whole thing up.

But if you do not make up a story, live it and take it to the nth degree of reality
make it your personal myth
Why then, what will you have planted in the new reality
the new vision
What do you think life is
MADE
of?

Are we not all creators
basking in a vast creative energy
A universe of it

Each with our own reaction to every miniscule breath of life, every event molecule

If the water in our brains can bring pictures—like a camera—to us what untold creative ideas and gifts can we ourselves unleash
Why, there's no telling.
And I did not make it up

"I could have come with armies. I wanted to come with my heart."

What?

But I was awake.
The words popped my eyes open

Who *could* have come with armies?
I remembered the utter rawness.
the sacred whispered message
Wrenched
out of a soul

I often wondered
Who confided this, or did I just overhear it?
Who chose to
try another tact?
Who among us chose to forego them all, no armies

come with
the heart?

But anew, right now I have another inspiration:
The intonation
matches that statement
on the Cross
Was it that I went back further
in sleep
overheard from centuries earlier
Heard it now
As I woke
As it floated to me
From long ago and now at once
Could have come
A conqueror
Chose instead
Another dynamic
whispering from back then

Another instant, it may go to another context
But it is a match in this instant

So did he pick a role in the Upper Room
Asked to choose
and he chose
The heart

The Kingdom of Heaven is within
That is, the connection to the transpersonal

On the outside individual
Inside, make our own pictures
of the whole
The point where we connect
How it looks, seen through those particular eyes.
And the experience and feeling

1993

Marlow, I said, can you believe it? Perhaps I will have to call you in again. Marlow, can you believe WHAT THEY ARE DOING NOW???

MARLOW, they are using the sky to transport images. AS WE KNOW. But the next technology—and technology, we all know, is undisputed. For though it CANNOT BE BELIEVED, let it get into the store, onto the shelf, INTO THE COMPUTER MARKET, IT IS

BELIEVED. So now we are told that THROUGH a radiation alone—nothing added—THINGS CAN BE TRANSPORTED. No electrical outlets OFFICIALLY involved. Just like I said. The bypass (not plugging in any wire) nevertheless retains the message. With a high pitch into outfield, or however it gets there—just in the transport of the infrared, WHAT DO YOU THINK Happens?

Without as much as a where-with-all or bat of the eye, this image next is

transported (wirelessly) onto paper.
Now, is that impossible or is it?????
INFRARED, that's the name of the game. Infrared on the

spectrum. There is more to electromagnetism, Marlow, than this world dreams of.

And so I tried to close the gap, to show how the merest *slip of* the imagination—the merest *forgetting that it was impossible* (at least, FOR HUMANS) and pretty soon, we might be imagining WE could do things like that.

Just as I have been saying all along.

For some reason, I CAME TO EXPERIENCE IT. And so it was JUST AS REAL TO ME as buying the technology in a shop, going home and using it there. I did not have to wait—for some reason—for these inventions, to get the conviction that it was all a human sort of thing also. HUMAN EVOLUTION. And if I had not gone entirely the path of Gopi Krishna, for Kundalini is NEVER REPETITIVE, then I must be in the Kundalini vein nevertheless, the one leading humanity to the next step in its evolution.

And you'd better COUNT ON IT.

That was my Higher objective for now.

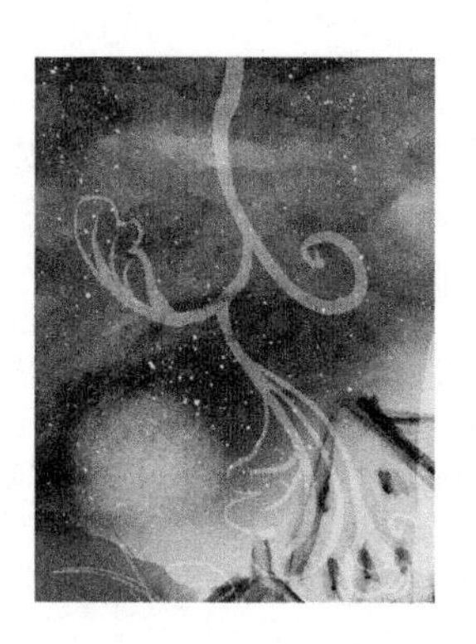

EXCERPT

Mendelssohn to the Rescue

Love in Transition: Voyage

of Ulysses–Letters to Penelope

The Bedtime Tales of Jesus III

Margaret A. Harrell

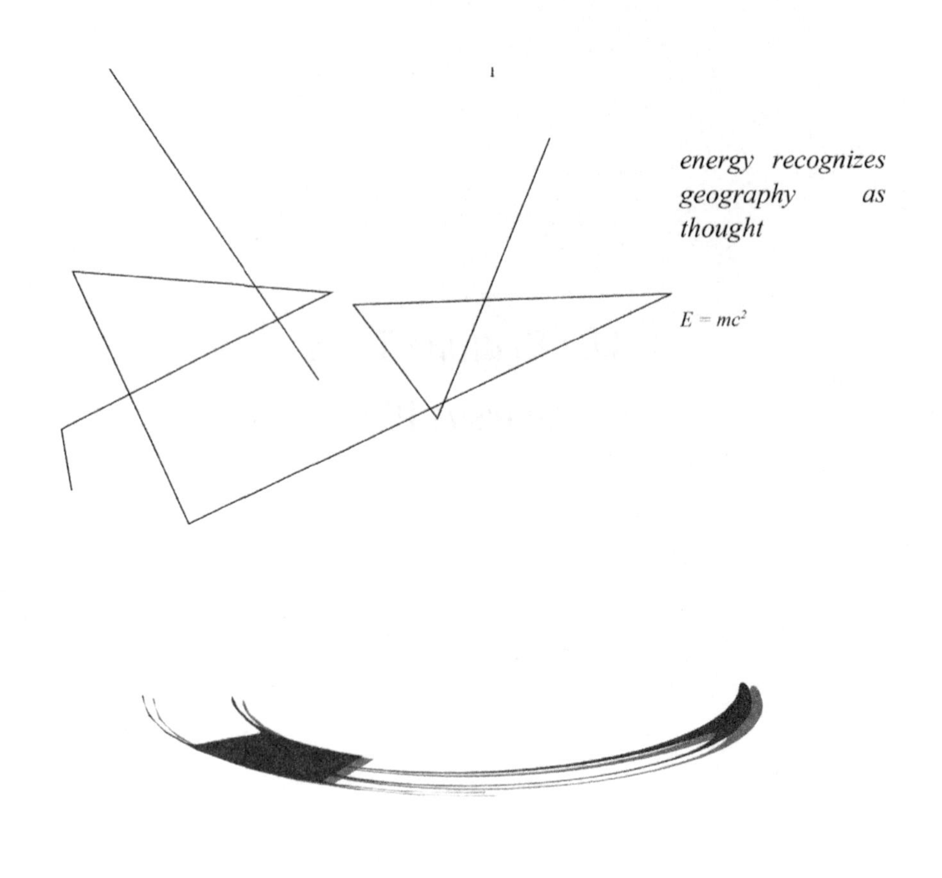
1
energy recognizes geography as thought
$E = mc^2$

Energy recognizes geography
as thought.

What???

So began *Love in Transition* IX

The Bedtime Tales of Jesus III

A manuscript created in the "room filled with guides" these many years back, then put aside.

What does Jesus have to do with it? I ask, returning to it now. But that's the original title. Who am I, why am I, to change it? Especially as maybe, back then, it was timed for now.

Never thought to be for the 1990s when I lived in Belgium.

But planted in a timeless spot that would hurl down or drop down into this spot by plan.

We have jumped across the 1990s, which were filled up with "spirit committees" and "spooky" action at a distance, if maneuvering between the physical and nonphysical is "at a distance," or if you find it "spooky."

This next line brought my mind careening to a halt:

How much infinity is it necessary to hold to be yourself?

Quite a lot if it is not

focused on. Then you cannot find yourself except in continuing beyond where the mass rules. As if in making statements on other issues, they have not reached yours. Merely to state and express yourself will not bring up the focus that is you. You are in some other century, in some other "mood," not yet delineated as a type of consciousness, not perceived to be STILL around, etc.

But then, you know the emptiness or alienation if you do not take "you" as information; take yourself, in this case, VERY SERIOUSLY. Where most times, one has to learn not to. YOU, on the other hand, have to "learn to."

fo

in

s

to

Yo

te

E

used on. Ther
beyond wher
ements on other i
ate and express you
are in some other c
is a type or a consc
. But then, you kno
"you" as informati

Note the precision of the slice. However, it's impossible to retype in the 1990s spacing, the font in 2022 is so different. I tried.

I am hanging on every word, rereading these piles of drafts, when, as I was just about to leave my ten-year self-imposed writing exile in Belgium in 2001, the "spirit committees,", isolated with me during the '90s, gave me send-off manuscripts. Yes, six! Written in the downloading energy I was now leaving, in terms of where I physically lived. The nonstop computer-PK.

Forcing these manuscripts hurriedly out of me. Perhaps—no, certainly—realizing this day would come, January 2022, when I returned to the unpublished archives, no longer treated as discards. Forced to pick them back up.

In my astonishment, comprehended the immense amount of material I was "willed," yes willed, by my "former self," the one I left behind in Belgium, knowing it was Time to Go. Putting those manuscripts into my "safe," unlooked at, as if too ambitious to even try to tackle, once back in the United States.

And now here, these new (to me) twenty-first-century spirit committees, falling out of "the sky" of my luminous body seminars, "discovered" *them*—just as I had always fantasized my own "Mendelsohn rescue" might come, posthumously.

The command to me to take them up again (with their help) was enforced by my becoming ill enough that I am on the run from failure. That too *a tactic, to elicit a makeover—turning me into one who believes in them, in their subtle-energy presence as real.*

The alternative, failure, being that I would enjoy this stache by myself. Unknown to the world, as if that's why they were given me in the first place, as if ten years of hermitdom with the "Other World" was for naught but my own pleasure. No. We cannot treat our creations this way. At least, I couldn't.

This postponed work was not, despite appearances, postponed indefinitely. I could not let it languish, till "death do us part." No, my attention was, in cosmic humor and insistence of the highest order, forced back to it.

But this is too difficult a task, I immediately thought, decrying such an assignment. *How can I, the present me, go back and pick up something so totally channeled in a different atmosphere, a different world even? Who says I can even understand, what I woke to every day then and streamed off my fingers? And, I have to say, put on a shelf in moving back to the United States from Belgium.* And turned aside to present-time pursuits.

However, suppose the pause was rightly taken, in that there was no audience then. This work might have a timer set to *Go, do it now.*

I left this self-imposed, delicious writing period, as you know, taking with me huge outbursts of nonstop computer-PK to file away and save. To use when?

The printer sometimes just let them flow out in a barrage, keyed to no page numbers or books—pages pouring out as in rushing river rapids. Cascading, one after the other. Did it mean there would be *no more of these creations in the United States*?

Afraid so. Periods come and go. They start—they end.

Evidently, that period was time stamped as *un*perishable. *Carefully preserved in truth-bound cartons.*

Like Mendelssohn rediscovering Bach—I view my Mendelsohn self!

I am not nudged but shoved back onto the racehorse. To bring out the material in my safekeeping I stored unopened, though alive in unforgettable memory—from a consciousness I was learning from but that was not yet mine.

Till lo! spying me down here, in a luminous body meditation course, in 2020, 2021, intense very high energy shed a spotlight on my dusty archives and *said ah-ha, just perfectly prepared to outpour for us flowingly*. That is, we will help. No excuses now. Of course, my soul was behind it, no doubt.

As if opening a different faucet, I catch the new outpouring. A new imperative underscores the need for hurry. This is—ah-ha, again—a command, or let's say, an initiation. *Do the job and you are healed. Abandon it and God help you, which God will, but you will not be pleased with the result. No, trust us. You are up to this.*

Initiations can come with do-or-die significance. As my Belgian light body teacher, Roland Verschaeve, said to me, *consciousness needs to make new connections*. A perhaps fatal disease can redirect a life, make someone, me, plunge into this writing when I don't know how on Earth I can, twenty-one years later, incorporate a 1990s–2001 mindset into a reframing.

No, I am required to not be another "little mole," squinting at the mere sight of daylight.

"Once made, mole tunnels are often used by several generations."[42]

I listen. Instead of looking for my "future self" in the future, I am finding paradoxically, she time traveled, as it were, and I can easily spot her if I dive into these drafts. What did this "visiting" me write back then, like a mother wanting to leave future messages for her daughter when she was no longer in person here? In this case predicting a time when she was merged with me. Taking over perhaps if all went as hoped?

1990s

Unfathomable Deep Dives

What follows are some of my most-treasured, most deeply buried memories.

For much of the last years, I

had certain memories I could not speak of. Did not wish to. They were not mine. And if I record them, it will easily become clear why. But then, why did I have the flashbacks? Why the moments in frozen time? Or even "implants"? Merging? Unknown principles, only hypothesized as to even exist.

So I left them out of my biography. They were snipped out of other biographies. Even, what is more, would be recognized and labeled from where they came. What was I doing, going into biographies like a plagiarizer, confiscating memories—as from a storage facility that obviously couldn't exist because they began in personal positions—clicking them into mine? OR someone did.

OR allowed me the privilege of walking into them. Just like opening the door, finding yourself in a familiar place. Well, I seemed to walk into "magnetic moments."

The one below happened in May 1992.

A number of times in the early 1990s, I went from Belgium to Zurich for Jyoti's and Russ's breathwork seminars. Most exhilarating, always.

They used Grof-like hyperventilated breathing, a system for entering non-ordinary states using fast breathing, music, and energy work in lieu of LSD and similar hallucinogens. Jyoti's own breathwork, she called "Maitri." Arriving by train, ready for her huge Mother energy, I stepped into something out of the ordinary, indeed.

I was on a mat on the floor, doing hyperventilated breathing, with Jyoti and Rus monitoring, holding the divine energy. Suddenly, it came . . . the energy sweeping in, beaming in, overriding the present, wiping out my sense of the present. Here.

I was suddenly taken into a memory, entering that nanosecond as it stretched—elongated, opened into dimensions as huge as to be eternal . . . , as if time dropped down this moment onto me, it was the mind/spirit I was inside, entered," that I called "me," though it had its own historical existence. But that didn't come into play now. Nothing that was in this moment was outside me. The being, the essence, the vibration containing this exact memory, was my only awareness. I knew exactly where it was. (Lifted, just like levitating.) Knew exactly who was having the experience. But it was *in* my mind. The storehouse, the living receptacle of this memory, as if it itself, the mind, the spirit, came to me like a bird wanting to speak.

How was I lifted up like that? Is it even possible to find out without sounding ludicrous, confiscatory? Where, my mind had gone (or how, if that was the case, it had been entered), I did not know. I knew nothing but that it had become a *location*. Preexisting. Recognized, as if opening a page in a history book. Stored like the Essene scrolls in hidden, buried jars, dug up.

I was

on the Road to Damascus.
(Yes, we all know that wasn't me.)

with no memory why or how—that is, no awareness, no focus, outside the micro-second. Suddenly thrust into the energetic moment.

Of a moment, I am stopped. All time, all movement, stops. The energy doesn't stop. It takes over all time, all space, which stops. And enters it here. It is the only space-time I can *feel*. There is a kind of rippling effect.

The atmosphere grows dense.

Anyway, all I retrieved that day, knowing it had happened—and I knew it, for sure—was an isolated, carved-out instant, Brought living, quivering, from wherever it had been, as if it had put a hand on my shoulder and said: *Look, you are in eternity*.

Knocking the rest of time lopsided, shoving it aside.

In that instant, I was pinned down, localized in the revitalized segment of awareness. The instant of it. The intensity that lifted it, recorded (or needled), with some needles from the past, into wherever it did so. Some medium I contacted, as if it were in my own brain.

The whole unit. Isolated. Total. Eternal. I am there. I am *it*—even That. Forever, in having consciously, physically embodied, experienced it, or been transported to it, walked inside. No one brought up the subject of how? No one would have thought of speaking. Not in such vibration of energy. The rippling, which of course may be a transformation of the feel of energy as a wave.

Be whatever it was, I received—rather, encountered, *re*-encountered, met as if a living soul—*this instant*.

As if an electronic needle were replaying it LIVE in my brain, which knew such computations or vibrations.

Now all I was able to experience was being struck down. I next experienced—recorded in the surviving and re-entering awareness—one thing. That I need not worry myself with forcing :

E

myself onto my legs, standing up. I did not

n

r

m

a

A

need to struggle to my feet and stand. In the bit of energy that remained for motion. That was a difficult perusal, in the options I might think of. But the thought alone struck me. I knew (in awareness) that all I needed was to raise myself only to the knees. And to pray.

Shortly afterwards, I "saw," still during the breathwork, a giant snake coming out of my mouth. In other words, I'd be communicating, or the Kundalini would.

This restored segment of time now continued in me.

But is the reader, given the flashback to my Upper Room, even surprised? Wasn't some follow-up, or follow-through, bound to occur? We'll come back to that question.

Mightily struck down, struck dead and dumb beyond the power of moving, I knew the one thing I could do was to get to my knees.

This was nothing to talk about. Not to a soul. Not to breathe a word.

But I had stepped into it. Unforgettably. Of all the moments in my entire life, it was one that defined me, targeted, and remained. I knew it was from another dimension. I knew it aimed straight at me: St. Paul in the moment the pure Light came to him, pushed him onto his hands and knees. Powerless, submitting.

There was no me, no him, no anyone. Just the brain, the awareness, thinking, deciding, acting, for an Instant in infinity. Forever etched there. Moved into me. As if detached from anyone else and any other time. As if THIS were WHEN it happened, back then.

As if we had reached a time inset it was waiting for. As if this now were that now, for it was happening for the one and only time.

somehow (how?)
come to join me, or I it. Stored itself in me.
Activated.
Alive.
Beating

Later that weekend, the second thrusting-aside of time's fabric into a moment energized and forever alive (but stored with what caretaker?) came. Just as profound. As famous.

Again, it entered me (or I it). What attraction gravitated us together? Pulled me to that door, and it opened? seared into me. I had not mentioned these two incidents in any book until 2015. This text, lying unpublished for over twenty years, is the first time, though as the 2015 Keep *This Quiet!* IV came out, including these stories. Still, they belong here, their first home.

Now, this second energetic moment had the same sense of *the fabric of time stretching*—But who was imagining? doing it? And why, which I am now going to hypothesize to arrive at some principles.

This next moment, captured in infinity, reappeared on the Earth, likewise, with no past (except that I knew its past); no future that was referred to. It was stopped. Caught in a net. Just before the death of Jesus. That moment of his crying out, when silence was wrenched from his body and words came in its place.

This time, with no follow-up thought. Again, no preceding thought. It was just the once-recorded so public instant when he uttered: "Into thy hands, O God, I commend my spirit."

I felt the private anguish. I was inside it. It was my emotion being expressed, my mind holding the thought. Myself, my mind, thinking inside that suspended-in-time moment as if all my being were contained in it. *And* contained it. I lived it.

But we all know, practically speaking, it had been lived before. *It was as if it had not been lived before.* It was as if I made the outcry: the still-living "I" vocal again, in the original setting, "merged" with.

We are told there were then thunderclaps. Death. But I did not see any surroundings. Not Galilee or the Cross, not the watching, crying crowd or soldiers. Just the contours of the instant; the awareness—feeling and living, quivering, vibrating energy—was again alive, here. As if on some lake or pond where the energy was the ripples; the experience, the stone that dropped into the water, as if no quantum decay occurred but that the memory was held up on the waters of living time. And thus, somehow able to retain and reestablish its intensity and its quality. Its message. First-hand. Because in the tone of experience itself. Is this possible?

Who was it aware?
Who stored the awareness?
A brainstorm in 2022 told me
Whatever individual held the experience,
That is, St. Paul did,
Jesus did,
Underneath and above it all,
Who experienced it was
The Christ

Moving from May 1992 to the third memory—*exactly like the others in quality*—in 1994. This time, at a workshop of the International Association for the Study of Dreams, led by Robert Moss, Australian creator of Active Dreaming. I was instructed to create a movement—let it naturally "self-organize."

But let's stay in sequence. That comes two years later.

The 1990s Return like Jedi

Like night and day the different parts of my life are fitting in. I check the dates. Could that really have happened *then* in view of what also was happening? Yes, and taking the ancient Chinese view of cause as timing (what happens when what else happens means they belong together, they are expressing meaning), a picture emerges.

2022

Moving from May 1992 to the third memory—*exactly like the others in quality*—in 1994, two years later. This time, at a workshop of the International Association for the Study of Dreams at the University of Leiden, the Netherlands, led by Robert Moss, Australian creator of Active Dreaming. Wikipedia astonishingly records the following moment:

> In 1986, Moss felt the need to get away from the commercial fast track and moved to a farm in upstate New York, where he started dreaming in a language he did not know that proved to be an archaic form of the Mohawk language. Assisted by native speakers to interpret his dreams, Moss came to believe that they had put him in touch with an ancient healer—a woman of power—and that they were calling him to a different life.
>
> Out of these encounters, he wrote a number of historical novels and created a technique he terms Active Dreaming, which is a novel synthesis of modern dreamwork and different journeying and healing techniques. A central premise of Moss's approach is that dreaming isn't just what happens during sleep; dreaming is waking up to sources of guidance, healing, and creativity beyond the reach of the everyday mind.
>
> He introduced his method to an international audience as an invited presenter at the conference of the International Association for the Study of Dreams (IASD) at the University of Leiden in 1994.

Moss instructed us to create a movement—each of us—let it "self-organize."

In deep focus, I was gently moving my arms. And—suddenly, the movement took off.

The energy in my mind shifted. There "I" was—again on the level where the energetic moments, stored in Light (or consciousness) occurred. Again in that *quality* (*of stretched space-time, with its quivering Brownian vibrating molecules*). But this time suddenly "I"—the experiencing awareness—was standing at the Sea of Galilee, choosing disciples. This time, though, the awareness, the "I," had stepped inside me. Or I had gone to some location where I could experience it, be inside it.

I knew nothing beyond this compact instant. Not forward or backwards. Restricted to a single moment. With a side view.

In the side view, a road led straight to a fork. "I" was on the left. The road to the right led, as to a static "box," to a view of King Herod's party, where Salome was dancing. Infamously. For the head of John the Baptist on a platter.

It was fixed, familiar, set apart. I was not witnessing the side scene *live*. But I saw it. Understood. I knew the scene was in opposition to the Sea of Galilee scene, an either/or. The two were paths. And I, off on the left, merged into the act of choosing disciples, knew that the Living energy here was trying to bring about the non-beheading.

The focus was barring entry to anything else.

Outwardly, I stood, composing a movement at the workshop in the year 1994. (Or was that where I was?)

Energetically—in the more real reality?—I was suspended. Biographically I would have to live this *as a symbol*. Yet it was an experience. Beyond that, in some way, a fact, a memory.

From earlier initiations, I knew that in higher consciousness, one (highly skilled) could bring together two time periods or geographical locations—like two sides of an accordion. Slash away the distance and create a question. A pattern arrived at through the pitting, theoretically, subtly, like a thought experiment. Make two events into a single issue. An argument, as it were, presented by illustration.

In this case the two situations, far apart geographically in those days when travel was by donkey or horse, were juxtaposed.

The workshop was the only physical event going on that I could put into my biography.

However, it turned out this time a parallel event was drawn in. A secret telepathy contest.

In the quiet of my hotel room that night, I kept pushing aside a pop hit, "Come on, baby, let the good times roll." Not that I didn't like it—I did. But a hymn was vying with it. As "Come on, baby, let the good times roll" was loudly replaying over and over in my head, I found myself fielding a hymn into priority position.

I really didn't know why I was so earnestly engaged in this contest—having no suspicion I was transmitting to the entire community "This, this is Christ the King" as an alternate choice. And why would I do that? No idea.

In her room, the unannounced "sender" gyrated, to push the "target" picture into the sleepers' heads. In easily "received" gestures, as is appropriate in telepathically transmitting information, she used loud, lewd, graphic movements, which, unknown to myself, I countered. All night.

The next day I found out the motivation behind the duel. A telepathy contest sending onto the collective pathways, into each brain, a photo, taken from a Middle Eastern Sufi poet, Rumi, put into the sexual framework. What did it matter if the sacredness of the Rumi poetry was erased, a disconnect established between such the poet's intent and the audience's response? a false connection forged through all the minds that picked it up?

What did it matter if in ignorance of Rumi's subject matter, he was portrayed in terms of wild sex into the unconscious? Did it matter? In any case, I batted back the hymn that retained the sacred element.

And, indeed, the unconscious dreamers reached into their own unconscious to vote, the next day, for the sacred choice. The message reached them. And they chose.

More people, selecting from the photos laid out on a table, chose the version I was unwittingly "sending." The ESP test was deemed a failure. I chalked it up to one more instance of high consciousness showing me a glimpse of how it works in matter.

It was an illustration (or trial run-through) of how we are all connected and can express a conscious wish, even if some programming is trying to brainwash us otherwise. It did not work. Jesus chose his disciples that night, as it were. They sided with the Sea of Galilee-like choice, never even knowing what was at stake. Asleep as the historical event, revised, underpinned the twentieth-century replica, in disguise but powerful still. Unconsciously, they said no when asked whether to behead John the Baptist or not.

So here I received a demonstration of how tests might be conducted.

What leads me to believe what I've speculated above is correct, other than waiting till I'm eighty-two years old to conclude it, almost out of this lifetime? I double-check my methods.

Well, for one thing, in the late 1990s in an energy session with the holistic energy master Joost—to jump ahead—I came into his healing room irate, in the St. Paul energy, angry at Jesus for, as I took it, snubbing me.

A very reliable channel had, in a reading in which he called in "the Master," said I "sat in the council"—reviewing the work of the scribes. Nothing more (or that was implied) during the lifetime of Jesus. "Perhaps a memory, a picture, would be of resonance for you." Around the campfire, "the Master asked of you what were the writings of this and that? . . . And you and two others would respond. See? Very nice picture, don't you think?"

No. Now, a council member screening the work of scribes was a pretty high position in the first century AD. But it canceled out the information I had. At least, I took it that way. I could not allow it to stand. So I walked, in irate energy, up to the door of this Belgian healer I trusted. And asked immediately—flinging the door open—to have it out.

This healer, Joost, said, "Do you want to talk to Jesus? Or the Christ?"

"Both," I said, totally surprised. Then his body changed; it shifted, and a new energy came in. The energy of Jesus. He began to answer my questions.

I had not known this channel was capable of such a thing.

Had only heard of such incidents, as in a "storybook," but certainly never thought to experience one. But the irate energy I was demonstrating led to this reaction from the healer.

As Jesus, he said, "My mother is the Earth."

But the so-called snub, he told me, had been "a test" to see how I reacted. The authentic energy who had been in his lifetime would "claim" itself.

In fact, in the reading I was irate about, the channel had said:

> You were one of those blessed enough to be instructed by Shem . . . You cannot follow the tune of another's song, if you deny your own song in the process. If you do, your soul will rebel, for you taught this long ago. Notice each time you have, there has been some force which abruptly or strongly moved you away.

So there it was, as predicted. A test. I rebelled. I had relied on an "outside authority," and it was now up to me to rely on my inner authority, I detected.

For our energy identifies us. We could look 50 percent like a former entity. And it would count for nothing if we did not carry the energy. The energy did not know what time period it was in or think in those terms. It was just itself, outer trappings be damned.

So I asked Joost, as Jesus, about my presence in his incarnation. He answered, "You took on more than one role. Some did. Some didn't. But you took several."

That is, I could have taken the role of council member overseeing scribes, which demotion had angered me, setting this reaction off, and still had "other roles."

He went on, "If I were to tell you what you did in my incarnation, we'd have to stay here two days."

This and many other incidents—quite a number, from disparate sources, including profound personal experience—added up to the same point. I could deny it—consequently not learn more *about what such situations meant, for it was not a given how to interpret them*. After all, Jung warned not to fall into the temptation to "identify with the archetype." On the other hand, by not resisting, I could *let the thoughts into my mind that were trying to get in.*

Jung also said let them in.

> What is your contribution, and what chalice shall you place upon the altar of life? Why not this self-same light? Why not claim the highest frequency you can and translate it . . . manifest it . . . The fleeing of self from bondage is very much like being chained to a wall in a cave . . . with this exception: each one who is chained possesses the key to unlock those chains. Why, you might ask, do they not do so? They know not.
>
> And so we leave you with these words from the Master: Many knew Me not, and for this I ask that our Father forgive them, for they knew not and, therefore, knew not what they did. Could you fill the chalice which you shall place upon the altar of life with knowledge for those who cannot see, who have not hearing in their spirit, whose eyes are closed or dimmed by darkness? This would be a good work, and I am with you in it.
>
> —Lama Sing reading through Al Miner, April 2000

Done. And done.

Yes, the imposing channel who "set me off" with the picture of myself in a council, screening scribes. was that wonderful friend who channeled from the soul level, Al Miner. How could I not take whatever he said at face value? But my energy was disheartened. And later I could look back and see in that very reading the prediction of the test, the outlines of how I would balk. So be it. I did. I passed. I learned a lot. And I bless the now-in-spirit Al for giving me this noble challenge—this chance to go yet one notch higher in frequency and self-knowledge.

❋

So suppose my soul, way up there in a cosmic energy, was in a grouping whose transition involved showering down on the Earth patterned memories. For instance, St. Paul's split-second conversion from wrong-headedness to total courage after "seeing the Light." And then, once that happened, heading straight into stormy seas. Risking crucifixion and beheading. But he lived in a time of great female inequality (as there had been in Ancient Greece), when the equality he advocated for for women, "in Christ," looks to us now, like backward steps because we forget or are unaware of the culture at the time, even as he tried, in scale, to counteract some of its flaws.

In fact, I had a memory/vision of myself in the Inquisition as a powerful male, taking part in it. But then a child stepped in front of me, holding the Light, bringing me a conversion. And both were me, the Inquisitioner and the Child. It was the same pattern.

Now add a third component, Mary Magdalene's energy, that balance. For—if we go ahead again—I was to learn that she was formidable. One person who remembered her told me she was, to her, "one of the greatest mystics of all time." Add that to "very sensual . . . but very pure."

This picture of the Magdalene fits together. A mate to Jesus, worth sitting at his side through his ups and the finale—"formidable . . . one of the greatest mystics of all time." And every time I felt my mind was peculiar, that it shouldn't be thinking the thoughts it did, I could say: *Well, maybe it goes way back to this great mystic; she must have had "peculiar" thoughts. But Jesus didn't think so.*

And she didn't fear letting those intuitive flashes and genius insights cut into her mind from her being. No, don't be afraid of what people think. Easier said than done if you are me.

And remember, this is both an archetype and a universal energy—spread out in degrees, from miniscule to major. And I was major.

The above psychic, who identified me as being "as close to the Magdalene as possible in energy," said: there could be "two of you" in a room (here on Earth). That is, the energy was "universal." Everywhere.

But also, I had this personal idea that I had to capture my own memories in order to be recognizable in the "future," however you defined that—to stay recognizable, beyond the dispersement and photocopies.

So any future stories would not find me, as in *Star Trek*, disintegrated in the transport chamber and then unable to be reassembled. No, in *Star Trek*, if you space-traveled in a chamber, the idea was to be reassembled.

Try to keep that connection as memories hitherto protected as personal inside the universality fell down into the Earth, to assist its transition into higher-level, purer states of consciousness and solutions. If problems had been solved before, they could be useful as patterns.

Here's where it becomes important. This soul grouping, I deduced, wanted to have experiences that made them recognizable to themselves in the future, as their dispersed energy might prevent that. If Jesus could not recognize Mary in her scattered self and could not recognize the Magdalene, but could only see replicas, sensing something was missing, it would be a loss.

Well, whether I made that up or it was accurately perceived by me, I felt this was so. That they were taking a huge risk, though to them they might have felt ready for any outcome. Remember, the "ability to accept." But not me. "Disintegration chambers," as it were, were not acceptable.

I was dead set on making sure I did my part to "preserve" their memories if they put them "in the air." Memories as patterns. Landscaped gardens. Perfected past trials now ready for a new tender, but *don't erase the original*. That was my stance.

I think this is true. Is it? It doesn't matter. I will start here.

Also, I'd written scores of stanzas about Jesus sending some of his *top lieutenants* into the shadow.

Knowing how I struggled with some of this material, wanting—for decades—to honor it but "not," as Jung stated, "identify with the archetype," I fear this can so easily all be miscommunicated.

It starts inside the oneness of us all: the God consciousness that is in that oneness; that universality, or *presence everywhere*, of every one of us. Inside that framework, to pinpoint us down "locally." Speak of individuality and incarnations.

Yet, once you get into this consciousness, once you have a slew of these experiences, they happen over and over, they build on each other. They are your "daily bread."

After a while I stopped having initiations. I merged with the energy.

This is about all I knew during the 1992 cusp, writing now, looking backward to the old me and forward to the me that was calling from the future/past. From Knowing I didn't have. And experiences I didn't yet have. All of which lent support to this direction.

Is every little detail correct? Well, you have to also factor in that there could be a parallel reality being described. It's possible. I could wander off into that. But keeping my head down as close to the ground as possible, in the preceding pages I've jotted down what I knew in 1992. After Owl Farm. Universal. Not confined to 3-D, to appearances, to fears created by the mind to hold us down. At home in the universe. It is there for us. And when we return "home," it will be to the consciousness that knows that. Taking us home to that. In awareness, peace, joy.

2022/2023

I realized the energy of the higher me was now looming closer to the surface of the Earth, its propulsion strong enough to reach me forcibly. Surreptitiously, easily (no bumps) I came upon the fact that I from thereon *more and more believed myself.* Well. Doesn't everyone? Absolutely not. That's another thing we are here on Earth to do.

Long story short: the life I had lived for ten years in the 1990s, that retracted further and further from me as the twenty-first century brought its own interests (and distractions), now returned to *a sense of reality*, but different. Now the messages I had written every day back then, so new, gained believability. I took Pascal's wager, paraphrased. This time, when the Great Questioner came around, asking, "Who do you believe, the outer investigators and truth establishers or yourself?" it was as if I couldn't afford to straddle the fence. The messages gained reality. *Coming now from myself. Not an outer spirit group, though there was that. But the thoughts were now mine. I could identify with me.*

The energy to do so arrived innocuously, unannounced. But I realize that I am much more all of a piece. I was *forced to choose*, evidently. Choose which me to go on with.

Choosing the other meant I needed an overhaul, had become too "infected" with Earth belief systems, was "hopeless," as it were, if to go further into this lifetime with the promise of it. After all, I had done a lot. But to go further, I had to jump aboard this me, the one I had "talked to" in the '90s. It happened effortlessly. I barely noticed the change.

In other words, my focus of attention was *not* to make one last trip—supposing it proved to be that—not to tell someone I loved her (or him). All that seemed taken care of. What remained to be done was go back into the '90s. Find the *living material* from there—kicking with energy—that was entrusted to me.

Look and see if something like this is also being presented to you. Does it offer a possible explanation to unusual experiences or an extreme situation you might find yourself in? Would this explanation make sense? Give you fighting power or "belief" power? Try it out if you wish. That is, are you being given the chance to go to another level, maybe even much higher, or much much higher? Are you being asked to, at least, believe yourself???

Hold it. Hold it. In 2022—yes, again a takeover but in reverse—of my life by physical reality. Its urgencies broach no argument. I have been racing to bring out the drafts before the physical ultimatum date arrived. And it has. Da-dum. I have cancer. Oh, a mild one. It's easily treated, I'm told. Don't fret. But how, I ask myself, will the treatment affect my creativity?

I addressed the spirit world: Why is this part of my life plan?

In answer, I got surrounded by spirit protective energies opening up a path. I took it initially to be that I get out these books. It was a Creative Force. A non-deathbed confession.

I answered. I stepped up.

I think of the "old" me. Putting that aside, who am I? The answer, if taken deep enough, always reaches a stillness.

Splitting Time from Space—New Quantum Theory Topples Einstein's Spacetime

Einstein famously overturned the Newtonian notion that time is absolute—steadily ticking away in the background. Instead *he argued that time is another dimension, woven together with space to form a malleable fabric that is distorted by matter. The snag is that in quantum mechanics, time retains its* Newtonian *aloofness, providing the stage against which matter dances but never being affected by its presence. These two conceptions of time don't gel.*

The solution, Hořava says, is to snip threads that bind time to space at very high energies, such as those found in the early universe where quantum gravity rules. (emphasis added)[43]

A massive thought is looking for a place to land.

David Peat, *Synchronicity*[44]: "But if causality is to be pushed to its logical limit then the miniscule effects of nearby mountains, the passage of the moon overhead, the more distant stars and planets, and even the masses of the players who run across the court must be taken into account. *Each one acts to curve the fabric of space-time*, which, in turn, governs the [tennis] ball's trajectory across the net." He had said that "for Einstein [gravity] arose through the curving of space-time that is brought about by matter and energy." (my emphasis)

A massive thought, looking for a place to land, gets weightier and weightier, with time, hovering overhead, adding magnetism, electromagnetism.

If we are carrying gravity, so are thoughts, even in shapes like beginning-end.

Presence curves the fabric of space-time. Massive presence curves it more. Timing curves it, as a mass. Etc. Who is thinking the thought? How is the thought "looking"? Whose consciousness is it? Is it unconscious? Is a head peering out of it? Is it just "there"—built up to? How did it find heads to go into? The Initiator looking up into the stadium. The faces appearing to Shri Dhyanyogi-ji in a near-death experience.

Not just large masses like the Earth hold gravity. Every passing thing does. A particle without mass does because it has energy and momentum.

⁂

As I've lifted the above text from a book, unpublished, being finalized—at least, I thought so before this new idea of putting these materials into their Hunter Thompson framework took over—this manuscript is cobbled together—no, selectively assembled—from 1990s writings before I left Belgium, framed in a 2022/2023 mindset in North Carolina. The book dropped, abandoned, like a lot of the other writings I was in the midst of—almost submerged by—when I relocated back to the United States. But then, I was being bombarded with teachings and energy of what I called "spirit committees" that would not act in the same way after August 2001, when I settled into an apartment in Raleigh.

One last discovery. Just today, I read accolades to Jyoti; the writer recounted Jyoti's role in founding the Thirteen Grandmothers, beginning in a vision she had:

> Unbeknownst to the individual grandmothers, the seeds of their coming together across the miles and the cultural and language barriers began in 1998 when Jyoti had a profoundly moving visionary experience. In the vision, a divine feminine form appeared and said, "I'm going to hand you one of my most precious baskets. Inside this basket are some of my most treasured jewels. These jewels represent lines of prayer that go back to the origin of time. Do not mix them. Do not change them. Protect them and keep them safe. Walk them through the doorway of the millennia, and hand them back to me. I have something we are going to do with them.
>
> Eventually Joyti realized these jewels were the [Thirteen] Grandmothers and that her job was going to be to find them and bring them together. The story of how this was accomplished is one of the most extraordinarily inspiring I have ever read [wrote the writer, rightly].[45]

But it is the same thing. I saw it too, held it too, was as impacted by it too. And thankfully now know what was—some of what was—in the basket. From *Particle Pinata Poems*, still impacted by the vision decades later, I recorded:

5-D, 10-D

I saw
Mother Mary
with a basket overhead flying

overhead then, decades after I perhaps saw her—was it so?—as
a Little Dot I followed

I saw her
but I was flying with her
this time clearly visible
it was me

an angelic sight, a vision clear as day
in my meditation

Over her arm was this basket she reached into, as to get flowers
and sprinkle them down the aisle at a wedding,
Whatever was inside floated down,
as she handed out
as-if-petals

beckoning me
magically
to join in the distributing
As I watched
I did.

But what about my hard-fought-to-find creations
I'd always protected, feared to lose
working solitarily, throwing a coat or other camouflage over them
so no one could see while they "slept"
me and Creativity solitarily at work

copyrighted every one

but in that moment
unhesitating
As I watched
I saw Mother Mary up there with her basket, me at her side,
dip my hand into the basket,
pulling out, distributing
Watching, I knew that in the basket might well be,
must be, I thought, parts of my creations, of "me,"
what I "owned,"
But I smiled, why?

as I watched myself, my 5-D or 10-D self, without a thought to
any objection,
Blended, magically blissful
Distributing the blessing
in there with other
indicators of
connectedness

All forgotten in an instant
of being beckoned to join in as she distributed.

How indelible the moment was
I watched, cheering her and myself on in silence, as a part of me
flying with Mother Mary
dipped into her basket of blessings
distributing.

We are One, her basket said to me.
part of a Universal Energy,
This is more complicated than you can understand right now
But your instinct is superb
It's just right
As patterns she'd had cleared to a point could be
picked up at that point, taken further
if you reached energetically,
resonating with, asked for

trusting to receive
from her basket of
anonymous blessings.

Yet a couple of decades later, in 2021, I made a click. I sat at the computer, editing. In a barrage of requests. Super-inundated. And why did it make me smile? Why did the solutions flood my fingertips? Suddenly I caught again the smile I had, watching my 10-D self distribute as I, below, marveled. See it beside the smile I have now, watching myself meet, with no problem, the barrage of editing requests.

The same smile, same frequency. Up there high above, reaching into her consciousness, her basket of energetic petals

Distributing.

I had experiences that gave me energies I needed, experiences that were at the heart of who some of the most important people in our history were. Those energies—that consciousness—offering itself to us this century. Needed by us. By me. If they are here with us, can we not do almost anything? Is this not a world to hope on?

So, Hunter, what did we have to do together in this? Well, who can say who has enjoyed the pattern we made? Who stepped in? Our sons and daughters, in a meaningful sense, those we gave something to, that was the best of us. Well, and so much for that. The computer won't let me write reasonably here. It has stepped in, causing errors, which lets me know all is well. I am in good company here. Salutes to you, Doc, and thanks.

To Conclude

We are all angles,
foci
Of the Whole
—and also
individual

What about equations?
all equations, individual,
of the Whole
I am not you
You are not me
But I CAN access you
You CAN have access to me

Or we can, any of us,
sometimes with good reason
go into hiding

What about "personalized dilemmas"
of the whole?
Is that what we are?

Incarnated Dilemmas?—
Questions it asks?
Suppositions?

Oh, yes, I've wound up in
a poem
about
O*nze*—

Ours

AND

Hours
Time—

not-wasted
when everything is added up
your and my
sum-

Ons[*]

Sum-
Mary
In some cases,
Ah, yes

All sort of
Summons

---

* *ons*: our—NL (Dutch)

A FOOTNOTE TO HISTORY

Once upon a time there were Maidens
This takes place a couple of centuries ago
These Maidens were young girls
It was before the birth of Jesus
One would become the Mother
The others would hold the consciousness
It wasn't known which one

Were you one? a part of me asked.

Well, no, it came about this way
one day, illuminating some of my questions
I was "trading" with a young psychic
I taught her a sample hour of energy work
In return she gave me a sample quick "reading."
When would you like me to look into? she asked
Let's say back in the time of Christ
Well, she "looked"
She mused
And then said, "I see you as a Maiden."
Ahhhhh.
Well, what about the others? I asked, thinking of specific women I'd met this century
I called them "Mother."
I named them one by one.
Yes, I was right.
They had been part of the group.
and carried the consciousness thereafter.
As I named them, she said, "first generation," "second generation."

Well, see
there is no single leader who does not operate in this way
We look at The Leader
Behind that one we see is the energy that has been and can be again and perhaps is in that moment
Personified

Invisibly

Well, I later thought.
So we can "change the world,"
each of us,
by supporting a thought, invisibly, in subtle energy
Who knows who else is supporting it with us?
We can tear down institutions
by "thinking" them out of existence
removing our support from them
joining, unknown to us perhaps, others who are also removing their energy
Without it, there is no tyrant or faulty leadership
For the energy of support must come from somewhere
every single act can be an acorn that grows the mighty tree
Or tears it down
We are mighty in our tininess
can
change the world

And so I guessed that just by holding a consciousness for centuries
all of us who did and would
we were
taking the Earth
the universe
someplace
We had a hand in choosing
where
we were
going

The Maidens did long ago
And in all the centuries since as they kept that consciousness alive
in the ins and outs of history
Also adding other consciousness to it
other types
They modeled to me
what was happening in our system
and how these invisible starships formed around

individuals
How we did indeed
change
the world
You do
I do

I woke with this energy
Woke late
It kept me sleeping
Talked to me while I slept
So much is invisible
So much is affecting—perhaps controlling—us
as we go about visible things
Wake, as I did
and often do
with energy pushing me to an action
Energy that "knows"

This time it did not take Kundalini kriyas
to force my mouth open
At least my fingers
typing to an invisible audience
wondering if I will delete it
Does it fit here?
Will I leave it?
What am I
here to say?
Strong enough
to speak of?
Without the Kundalini
the illness threat
as enforcer?
the ultimate
Last Resort
of consciousness
of my
Soul
Group

Perhaps
of
yours

AFTERWORD

Helpful Insights for Integrating the Text

by Jef Crab

Taoist, Taiji master, Rainforest activist

Note 001: "On Behalf of Large Consciousness"

I am already deeply impressed by your introductory chapter, "On Behalf of Large Consciousness." A gem . . .

When it comes to the complexity of the subtle aspects of our being, there is indeed a lot of confusion and misunderstanding in modern times, caused by what happened in Europe during the Middle Ages. I won't elaborate on that. However, it's surprising that we don't more easily see the similarities between what happens on a physical level and how the mind is constructed.

For example, we know that we consist of trillions of cells, each performing a specific task. Are those roughly thirty to thirty-four trillion cells the same? No. So, *why do we assume that the mind is only one thing*?

In today's society we see three sectors that maintain and strengthen the illusion of separateness and individuality: education, healthcare, and the legal system. Especially where the latter concerns punishment. These structures and their operation maintain the illusion of man as a fixed, unchanging mind. Our entire society is built on the individual I—an illusion, as it does not exist.

On the contrary. Because how do we explain that an infant exactly imitates the chemical composition of its mother's saliva? Or that we can deduce exactly the movements of their parents from the movements of young children? In the sense of: He walks exactly like his father.

In Tao/Taiji or shamanism we look at individuality and subtle abilities very differently. Shamanism accepts the observation that the average person carries at least forty generations of ancestors in their genetic material. These determine a lot of a person's movement. Some of these personalities have a stronger influence on the path of life than others.

Apart from these observations on the genetic level, the same applies to the karmic relationships. That which humans are not genetically linked to, but to which they are strongly attracted. Sometimes so strongly that we can speak of a change of identity.

In Taiji and other traditional martial arts, we consider the fact of involuntary movements. These are mostly tensed reactions towards or responses upon an opponent. Those movements appear over a period of time and have to be???? recognized as a pattern. We consider them inhibiting for the harmonious movement we seek to express through our martial art. They cannot be changed by simply changing the outer physical movement, but can only be changed by changing our inner attitude. This means inviting another "personality" to deal with the problem, with the tense situation. By repetition, we might become acquainted with and over time even become unified with this new personality. Only then, our movement changes . . .

Ultimately, we belong to different spheres: the family, the clan, the country or culture, the bioregion, the planet, the galaxy . . . Forces are at work in each of these spheres that guide us towards the fulfillment of a unique potential. Just as our cells perform their specific task in the entire body.

At the cellular level, each cell must perform its task, but undoubtedly there must be an organizing principle that ensures that the cells put together specific organs. All organs together must perform their task in the umbrella intelligence of the body, and so on. Because it doesn't stop there, does it?

Likewise, we all carry out a task within humanity and on this planet. Maybe further . . .

So, assuming that the "I" as an individual entity decides . . . that is an illusion. There is no I in the sense of a fixed, well-defined, or separate entity. We are all influenced continuously by many genetic and karmic personalities, and indeed, also by spiritual and archetypical forces.

The only difference between the superficial and the spiritually awakened person is that the latter is more able to choose which voice within him/her, he/she wants to prioritize. All my teachings are about learning to make this distinction, allowing participants to make more conscious choices about their lives.

Anyway . . . we can only become what we already are.

Note 002: "Ordering Archetypes"

Relating to *if I postpone picking up a messy piece of paper . . .*

It is important to understand that our daily actions are also influenced by the multitude of "personalities and forces" connected to our inner being. Every action, no matter how banal it may seem, is preceded by an inner impulse inspired by one of the many voices within us.

Whether or not we pick up that dirty piece of paper or how we arrange the milk in the refrigerator is *important already* to the extent that we can *observe that there is an impulse that tells us what to do*. We may follow or neglect the impulse.

From a superficial awareness we are unable to perceive the original impulse, and so we will repeat involuntary and patterned movements. But as soon as we deepen our awareness, we hear that voice and, following it uninhibitedly, an authentic movement arises.

In shamanism and the Tao we accept the existence of an organizing principle in nature. The more we follow the impulses that are in harmony with nature, the deeper the inner peace we will experience. From inner peace arises health, joy, and light . . .

We humans are incapable of overseeing the magnitude of that process. That's not our job, either. However, it is not superstition. It is based on observation and on learning to listen to the impulses of the organizing forces.

Note 003: "White Designs"

While reading, many interesting ideas came to mind. I want to go into some of these in a little more detail because it does indeed question and supplement the authority of the reductionist model of evidence.

I want to start with your question at the beginning of this chapter: "*How much of ourselves can we know in human form—dare to (even be meant to)*?" That question has its full meaning in the light of that reductionism.

The problem of our existence is not its complexity, which, according to good scientific standards, we must always seek. The problem is the ultimate simplicity of our Being. The Trinity expresses itself in Light, Life, and Love. All three inner states that can be experienced. And indeed, as you write at the end of that page: "The heart can do this."

We now know that the heart, and I do not mean the physical heart only, but the empathic capacity, is able to empathize with situations that are far removed from us in time and space. But equally in the most subtle expressions of our being. It is there, in the depth of the Heart, that we experience that Trinity. This is passed on in all bona fide spiritual movements.

I immediately agree with your thoughts in this chapter: "*What? But that's not scientific*, said the West. *Never could we think the mind took the place of a laboratory, of measuring instruments. What about repeatability?*"

Indeed, it is not just about experience, but also about repeatability and transferability. Personally, I would add that it must also be practically applicable. Because the latter is the only valid argument for actually accepting an experience as part of a pragmatic solution.

In shamanism, we recognize the power of knowledge transfer through sounds and rhythms that must be experienced and then repeated by the adept himself. Mechanistic-reductionist science is still far from this method of proving, transferring knowledge, and applying it.

Precisely this ties in with the last sentence of this fascinating chapter. Indeed, events and situations are not isolated. Nature uses repetition in as many different forms as possible. It does this until a certain state of being—and probably all its variations—has been fully experienced. Only then is there room for a new form, a new capacity.

On a human level, this indeed happens across people, generations, cultures, and eras. A given situation will continue until we find an appropriate solution, in accordance with the Line of Evolution. It is then a matter of repeating this particular situation. Repetition, and therefore broadening and dissemination and ultimately inclusion in the collective capacity. Then comes a new experience . . .

Note 004: "Getting Back to Me: The Initiation" & "Describing the Initiation"

Since these chapters describe a very personal experience, impressive both in the experience and the description thereof, I will only comment on one "non-personal" aspect you describe. However, I believe it may give the reader some insight into those realms of high subtle vibration with which you were clearly in contact during this initiation.

Let me connect on what you already wrote after your meeting with Al Miner: "*However, Al did add that the several realms in consciousness were identified by the 'ability to accept.' Ability to accept was an indicator of consciousness.*"

With regard to our spiritual development, the ability to accept is crucial. Both within the martial arts and within shamanism, developing an attitude of acceptance is considered a basic condition for developing harmonious actions. A harmonious action is always a conscious choice for self-regulation of all living organisms, human beings included. Without acceptance this is impossible.

By acceptance we should therefore consider that this is not only about accepting external situations and events, but even more so the very subtle vibrations and impressions that are a harbinger of every situation yet to unfold—in matter or in daily life. This acceptance can only take place in the mind.

Such subtle impressions almost completely ignore people with superficial awareness.

And as you very aptly describe on a page later, acceptance also means a loss of identity over and over again. It is giving up the old patterns in order to add to the new inner form/attitude (i.e. gestalt)

This brings us to the ideas expressed in your paragraph: "*Invisible 'vibes' present (through a physical person or just 'in the air') might be thought to emanate from a person or even an idea, whereas the "real" source was too subtle to be identified. By most of us, that is. It meant that the basis of a decision, of a feeling, might* REALLY *be very very different—perhaps opposite—from what one interpreted.*"

In ancient times, the sages called the real source of these invisible and subtle vibrations by different names. Among the oldest of these names we find the Sumerian Asherah, known to the Hittites as Inanna or to the Egyptians as Hathor, Maat, or Isis. In the Kabbalah it is known as Chochmah. In each case it is about the primordial goddess who is the consort of the supreme god. She is the Tree of Life, the creator of all that is, gross and subtle. This is very different from the Christian faith, where a celibate male supreme god sits on a throne somewhere in heaven. The primordial goddess was the Goddess of life, love, sexuality, and sometimes also war and death. The Greeks also adopted this idea and called her Sophia. The most famous shrine of this goddess is probably the Hagia Sophia in Istanbul, later called Ayasofya by the Muslims. In many Coptic and Early Christian churches she is depicted as the Black Madonna. Today we call this architect of creation "Wisdom," a literal translation of the Greek "Sophia." Unfortunately, the conceptual content of the word "Wisdom" no longer retains its true value in our time.

Now, going from the purity of life itself, we have to switch to emotions and the Line of Evolution.

Starting from your question: "*Could life be like that? Could patterns of discarded emotion be attracted to someone else? Germs were contagious, but what else was? Under what circumstances?*"

Here in the Amazon rainforest, it is normal to think of emotions as an infectious disease. We can certainly notice at mass gatherings that emotions are contagious. Especially when panicking . . .

But the same processes also work on a smaller scale, between individuals and in small communities.

From shamanism—something I later organized in the E.A.S.T. method—we consider emotions as subtle formative forces that directly affect the human psychological and physical condition.

In this sense, we distinguish only four inhibitory patterns, which express themselves physically as: shaky legs, steamy ears, hard head, and iron heart. Very nicely expressed by Walt Disney in his cartoons, by the way.

All four inhibit growth into our potential, establish themselves in our being, and ultimately result in contagious response patterns. Our environment, not in the least our children, will copy and take them over . . .

A safe way to neutralize them "harmlessly" is the following transformation method.

This technique accepts the lower contagious vibration and through inner activity raises its vibration and guides it into the Light or into the archetypal world. The healer or shaman knows how to do this.

The jungle dwellers have various rituals to cleanse both the individual and a village or environment.

Note 005:

Thoughts popping up while reading "I Had to Be Celibate—Reversed" and "Jamie Lee Curtis in *True Lies*":

As I already mentioned, the initiation is so purely personal that I will modestly only add some thoughts that might clarify something to the reader.

The idea that Hunter is using his influence from a fourth level or dimension of consciousness is quite remarkable.

In traditional oriental martial art based on Tao or Buddhism, five levels of consciousness are described. In Taiji, for instance, the students exercise the movements in order to control the first three, being the physical, energetic, and intentional level. In Chinese called Li, Chi and I.

Only after acquiring certain skills on the level of I, an adept might enter the fourth level, the Spirit, or Shen, in Chinese.

Now the first three levels must be directly approached by means of our material existence. (Keeping in mind that matter might be considered differently from what mechanical-reductionist science assumes.) Our abilities in thinking, feeling, and willing are mere expressions of collective energy fields expressing themselves through individuals; e.g., if one develops the ability of entering the collective energy field of the I, or intention, it becomes possible to direct Chi, or energy, without moving the body. The fourth level is indeed archetypical and contains indeed transpersonal and trans-human forces.

Any genuine teacher will have to give proof of at least mastering the first three levels of consciousness. This cannot be done by words alone, but has to be demonstrated in a real situation.

All this connects also to what my shaman teacher, Joska, used to tell me about the different types of teachers. He explained that in the first level of teaching are those teachers who pass on the knowledge, the Truth, to those who are seeking. As you wrote that you felt . . . "*to give such tools, such secrets, the laws of esoteric reality, away* . . . ," obviously you wanted to share the Truth with other seekers because of your Initiation.

The second level are those teachers who are teaching the teachers. The third level, he called the invisible masters. Joska clarified that those work only through emanation. In so-called real life they could be a farmer, salesman, or whatsoever. He explained that only those individuals who we're already at the height of their ankles could recognize them and eventually follow their guidance. Physical contact or physical existence are not requirements for that.

All this can be clarified by the idea of entanglement. Somewhere in the beginning of the '90s, I started to teach that information and energy always form a unity. I also thought that consistent with Einstein's ideas, matter is not existent. So information IS energy and vice versa. It seems an easy sentence, maybe superficial, but I guarantee that those who are really to reflect on this idea might find it a life changer.

As soon as we connect to a person, entanglement is set in motion, and information and energy will be exchanged, no matter where the persons are in real time or place. This means that just by directing our energy, i.e. our thoughts, to someone, we already change the person. The level of influence is directly connected to the level of consciousness, or the inner work, the sender already achieved. Lucky for us. Otherwise, eight billion people on this planet could change the weather.

Note 006: The Lunevillelaan Period

As I was reading through the Lunevillelaan period I really relived that time when we met, Margaret, and you entered our Taiji classes in Leuven and Ghent.

It is a beautiful real-life story and as well a demonstration of what I elaborated on in the former note.

It is indeed, as Stan Grof stated, that consciousness is not limited to your body or even to your singular life and that one can expand one's identity to a cosmic scale, explore other dimensions, and access information from what appear to be past lives.

Especially the fact that transpersonal domains exist, indeed have been explored by shamans and healers, is proven time and time again by advanced Taiji players and other martial artists in a real-life situation, i.e., free combat. For sure we are not limited by time, space, and causality in the way we once thought . . .

In *Eternal Spring*, I wrote that if Albert Einstein's later search for one single unified field was considered by many younger scientists a waste of time and a fallacy, few of them asked themselves the question why this great thinker remained at this point. Because the ethical consequences of his relativity theory – "the *being in relation to*"—is easily overlooked. Relativity, in its deepest and ethical meaning explains us that everything is connected with everything. If the former Western scientific world had also accepted the fundaments of scientific teachings from other cultures—such as the Vedic and Taoist teachings—then Albert Einstein would have found this field a long time ago. Unfortunately, in mechanistic science, consciousness is not acknowledged as an existing energy/field.

However, in quantum physics it is generally accepted that

the observer influences the behavior of particles and therefor the experiment. It surprises me that we have not yet made such a connection between perception and influence, whereby we conclude that directing attention produces a force.

According to physics, a force is a quantity that causes change; hence, the change in the behavior of the particles. The conclusion should be that directed attention, being part of consciousness, is a force.

Advanced martial artists, so-called Masters, often demonstrate this principle, that consciousness is a force. Masters may easily uproot an opponent or make the opponent deviate solely by use of the I, the intention. (I refer again to Note 05, where the levels are explained)

What's more important is that it proves that an opponent's movement can be known, even if the person himself isn't yet aware of his decision to move.

Movement, just like consciousness, doesn't belong to the personal sphere. It expresses itself through all living things. Maybe, therefore, Leonardo da Vinci saw a correlation between Movement and Life. In shamanism, we accept the idea of Primordial Sound, a movement as well. Movements and consciousness arise from the fifth level of consciousness. They connect everything with everything . . . There is no synchronicity on that level.

Synchronicity appears in the first and second level of consciousness. Being able to use the linking energy between two synchronic events requires at least control on the level of I, the third level or deeper.

I am amazed and in awe that you describe these principles through real-life experiences. Incredible . . .

Note 007: on Parts Three and Four

Hi, Margaret. On this New Year's Day, and of course New Year's Eve yesterday, I found the time to read again some pages and I would like to share some thoughts on that. I would like to start by the end of the fourth part and then work my way towards the beginning of the third.

So, near the end of Part Four you wrote, *That would be a field within a field within a field if the powerful archetype went all the way back to there . . . .*

I agree with this observation because also from my experience, and the experience of the meantime thousands of people who followed my classes, the structure of the universe can be compared to a so-called MMandelbrot symmetry, meaning that patterns are composed of smaller patterns of similar shape, only smaller in dimension.

Hermes Trismegistus already wrote in his *Emerald Table*: "As above, so below." On many occasions I experienced that the structure of a cell, a particle, a star, a planet, a plant, or human being are exactly the same regarding energy and consciousness. Only the external shape may confuse us. In reality, everything is literally connected with everything on every level of existence and dimension.

So why are we so confused about this fact? This is because our observations, and therefore comprehension of nature, whatever the dimension of nature, depend on the level of connectedness we've achieved within ourselves. If it is superficial, our consciousness and observation will be superficial as well.

I therefore enjoyed reading your description of the differences between St Paul and Mary Magdalene. It is indeed interesting to research how this controversy ever came into the world. Joska always emphasised the necessity to connect the anima and animus in oneself. Integrating this idea into the martial arts, I now teach how to connect the anima, animus, and the androgyne—being three different abilities—in ourselves. Only then they can be the fundament of a large and energetic sphere connecting us to the unconscious, as Jung called it.

The greatest obstacle for contemporary humans to realize this is their separateness. A lot of this separateness derives from a dualistic vision, so eagerly advocated and spread by the Christian churches in the past centuries. They emphasised the difference between God and the devil. However, if the observation of "As above, so below" is correct, there is no contradiction between those two. In fact, they are both part of one energy/consciousness.

The Taiji Tu, the Yin-Yang symbol, expresses this unity. More elaborated on, even, are the texts of the Advaita Vedanta.

I also feel more connected to the indigenous idea of the fox teacher who led the seeker astray from the path to bring him/her, sometimes after a long detour and through several indispensable experiences, on the right track again.

What I appreciate very much in the chapter the "Response of the Least Evolved" is the fact that you make clear that it remains an individual responsibility, not only to distinguish between the word of God and the devil, but also how to react on the incoming information.

So this brings us into Part Three and "*Kriyas Strike Deeper.*"

If we understand the "As above, so below" principle, it is indeed very easy to accept that cells are intelligent beings. It is indeed as you wrote: "*Can cells' know' something? you ask. The answer is yes. Entangled in the vast web of connections in the universe, acted on by spirit energy, they sometimes 'disconnect' from the history of ourself we know, or the projects we are aware of, and bring something from far far away, taking their 'marching orders' in unknown-to-us triggers.*

More and more we become aware that it is not the human being as a person or individual who extracts/absorbs energy from its surroundings. It is the separate cells and all viruses and bacteria forming a symbiosis to create a shape, a body adapted to the natural processes of growth, spiritually as well as physically, who absorb the energy needed for this growth. Yes, they think, and yes, they know. They are as conscious as, or maybe more so, we are.

Every time we enter the deep sleep, past the dream state, our cells connect to very subtle archetypical energy levels. Most people are unaware of this fact, as it requires quite some exercise to be able to remain aware enough in this level of consciousness. Most of them will only remember the dark void after waking up. The technique, derived from Carl Gustav Jung, you described in the beginning of the chapter "First Indication of Something Else than 3D" can surely help to obtain more information from these levels.

We must understand that it is the symbiosis of all the cells and organisms forming our physical body that indeed knows the way forward. The energetic pattern formed by the vibrations of our cells will attract those energies that either involve growth or clear obstacles. This energy is translated into comprehensible images or other impressions through the dream consciousness. I advocate making a subject on dreams, archetypes, and symbols mandatory for secondary-school students. It would surely improve their lives drastically.

And this brings us to "De-niched" and the Al Miner session. Just as our cells attract the necessary energy during deep sleep, they recognize similar vibrations while being awake.

And indeed, when two persons of a similar vibration join together, they create a much larger energy field. This process of connecting and joining energies is as old as the first prokaryotes. The most important reasons to do this was to improve awareness and sensitivity, extract more energy from the surroundings, and improve self-regulation.

Thus, when two persons reach out to each other from the heart and literally create a connecting energy line, they increase their impact on the environment.

And thus, when the energies of St Paul and Mary Magdalene are connected within ourselves, we become a much larger sphere of influence. I have the impression that this is consistent with Swami Muktananda's statement as well as that of Lama Anagarika Govinda in "Epic Proportions." Our body is the Universe, indeed, . . . and we are vessels to universal powers.

Note 008

As promised, I finished the reading. So this will be my last note. Again, I wish to express my amazement at the depth of the processes you describe. The mere fact that someone can observe this over a lifetime is exceptional. On top of that, you also give the reader a glimpse into deep realities, far beyond the material and physical, and reveal the connections with transpersonal realms.

This is living proof that this book was created from a direct and deep inspiration.

Which brings me to:

excerpts from the Nabokov book

I wish to add a nuance to your fabulous description of Kundalini awaking throughout the book. especially where you wrote : *Ordinary consciousness and transcendental consciousness cannot be maintained at the same time; it is necessary to pass through an intermediate zone of change, where perceptions, feelings and experiences undergo a transformation.*

This is certainly correct when it happens for the first time or times. However, we know that shamans and (martial) artists exercise especially the broadening of consciousness instead of just deepening it. This is also the common thread in the EAST (Energetic Awareness Sensitivity and Transformation) method I developed. Joska taught this through a technique he called: radio on, radio off. The trick was to go into depth (and gain experiences) and immediately return to the sensations in the physical-energetic complex to connect those two realities. After sufficient practice, it is possible to experience depth while functioning in physical reality.

In fact, you know this, as you wrote further on: "I *had already learned in Zurich that some of the strongest male energy was supporting the feminine, to bring out its strength in Earth archetypes. And my soul, focused in the transpersonal, identifying herself there, would send me out to work in energy before it got to the point of descending into public hands.*"

This is always the process. The feminine is the reflection of Mother Earth herself, the ONE we call the Black Madonna. The primordial force. (I referred to it in a former Note.) Her impulses are perceived by the Heart Center. It is the Male creative light which connects to our Head Centre that forms the images. Those images require energy. Hence, working within the energy.

Only after that the impulse may manifest itself into the material world. This energy, transforming into movement is connected to the Belly Center, the Hara in Japanese, or the Dantien in Chinese language. Together, these three form the Trinity of Life, Light and Love . . .

Although even the most superficial consciousness must follow these principles of Nature, it are only the enlightened minds on this planet who are capable of consciously taking part in this process.

Further on in the book, reading the chapter on "Information Arriving Mystically," I enjoyed my memories of the time when Shri Anandi Ma and Dileepji were staying in our home near Leuven. It was a blessing.

So, the above-mentioned about the levels and extremes of consciousness integrating into one mind also counts for Mary Magdalene and Jesus. I am convinced that, indeed, it is a hallmark of a highly developed individual to combine the pure and sensual. As all is an expression of the Almighty, also sexuality and pleasure are. So, to me, the whole idea of sinning looks like something introduced centuries later by an institute that aimed to control people. Impulses, captured by the Heart, are pure Life; ideas or imagination are pure Light; and if we follow the energy of the Impulse, we act with pure Love. Then we don't move, but are moved . . . It is the Divine Will coming into action.

Such persons will: "*radiate their energy in ripples like a vibration, yet with a human form and, indeed, master a tremendously high and nuanced sensitivity*," as you wrote it.

In the chapter "The 1990s Return like Jedi" you wrote: '*You took on more than one role. Some did. Some didn't. But you took several.*'"

Allow me to make a remark on this from the point of view of shamanism.

Nature uses experience to evolve. Minerals, plants, animals, humans, nonvisible creatures . . . they all experience and react on. Those reactions leave an imprint in the collective energetic layers and consciousness of the planet. Probably they are even fed back to even deeper, transplanetary layers of consciousness.

Every creature exists in all this layers. as you well explained in this book. In shamanism we accept that in every layer of consciousness, forces and entities can help us to achieve our life purpose. This is probably the totality of full potential of all these forces. So we can be the pure and the unpure in the same organism.

Not many people will have that clear vision on those potentials as you have. Bravo . . .

And that leads us to "Splitting Time from Space."

It is as you wrote : "*Presence curves the fabric of space-time. Massive presence curves it more. Timing curves it, as a mass. Etc. Who is thinking the thought? How is the thought 'looking'? Whose consciousness is it?*"

Yes, indeed, every human being will curve space-time and influence his surroundings, even by mere presence. The more we realize our various potentials, the more we will influence space-time. I do not doubt this. In martial arts we demonstrate this principle with an opponent to ensure that it cannot be denied. In shamanism we heal through touch, presence, or even at long distance. It is all the same.

After reading this wonderful life story I wish to conclude that it is my deep experience that there are no secrets on this planet. Everything that was ever achieved by someone in one time and culture can be re-realized and further developed by someone else in a completely different culture and era. That is mere evolution towards global humanism.

Our greatest obstacle in this endeavor is formed by ingrained reaction patterns and retained ideas. And this book is really a mind-opener.

Thank you for sharing Margaret.

Acknowledgments

Thanks again to Virginia Parrott Williams and Didi-Ionel Cenușer for "getting me started" on this route to here, in different ways. To Al Miner and the Lama Sing group for recognizing me in their initial consciousness revelations. To Ron Whitehead, who this very minute again performed his magic by sending his powerful energy my way, confirming the book was ready to print and that my latest insertions added, "Grounding! Yes, keep all of it! Just completed! Connective string. Earth to sky. Spirit to sex. Excellent! Time to publish!!" His words keep reviving the spark the book started out with as he told me to "go big."

To all the light beings who contributed during the Duane Packer-DaBen seminars. With Duane channeling DaBen, I sat at my computer and let the energies waft and spin me into the words for this book. It was phenomenal. And it's over. Duane "left," which makes it all the more necessary to me to acknowledge that participation. That contribution, including of the seminar meditators. It would have been irreparable, had I not realized it was there, for a short time span, for me to use. A bombshell of joy that I did. With Orin and Sanaya in the background too, including the times they drew me upward with a "message." To my first light body teacher, Roland Verschaeve, for introducing me to the work and being, with the years, a more and more loving embodiment of this precise path. To Chris Van de Velde and Joost Vanhove for miraculously descending into Belgium to be the precise, magical teachers and fellow voyagers I needed. Of course, to my family, to my large support group, to friends so irreplaceable but not named here. To Snoep, Snoepie, and Hans—what would I have done without my dachshunds? To Grant Goodwine for coming through with another brilliant cover image and Deborah Perdue for design. And to the "Place" where these inspirations come to me from: the Land of Truth, of Fun, of Reflection, of Questions, of Answers, of Consciousness. And, I suppose, karma. Let the sparks continue to fly.

Dictionary of Multilingual Terms & Language Abbreviations

Multilingual Terms

Dieu—God (FR)

dar—to give (SP)

espion—spy (FR); pronounced "S. P. on"; pion—a subatomic particle

io—I (IT), as in *io sol uno*, "I myself alone," in Canto II in Dante's *Inferno* (*Divine Comedy* Part One)

haut-parleur—a loudspeaker (FR), a reminder that Milton was "a shouter"; "*haut-parleur* is an off rhyme with *adieu* (FR pronunciation); "adieu, in English, uh-D(Y)OO, rhymes with or echoes "a loud U."

jullie—you (NL)

mano—hand (IT), as in Mozart's *Don Giovanni*: "*Là ci darem la mano!*" (Your hand in mine, my dearest).

ons—our (NL); *onze*—ours

peau—skin (FR)

saignant—rare (FR), as in steak cooked lightly

REM—the dream state in the brain

sol—sun (SP)

Abbreviations

FR—French
DE—German
IT—Italian
NL—Netherlands
SP—Spanish

Notes

[1] Carl Jung, *Dreams Memories*, Reflections, 232.

[2] "The Holy Grail of the Unconscious," Carl Jung and the Holy Grail of the Unconscious - The New York Times (nytimes.com).

[3] Yogananda, Self-Realization Fellowship, *Autobiography of a Yogi*, 347.

[4] Amit Goswami, *The Visionary Window: A Quantum Physicist's Guide to Enlightenment* (Wheaton, IL: Quest Books, 2000), 248.

[5] Goswami, *The Visionary Window*, 248.

[6] Quoted from its Amazon display.

[7] Frank Gaglioti, "Giordano Bruno, Philosopher and Scientist, Burnt at the Stake 400 Years Ago," https://www.wsws.org/en/articles/2000/02/brun-f16.html.

[8] Alberto A. Martinez, "Was Giordano Bruno Burned at the Stake for Believing in Exoplanets? *Scientific American* March 19, 2018, https://blogs.scientificamerican.com/observations/was-giordano-bruno-burned-at-the-stake-for-believing-in-exoplanets/.

[9] "Expectations, the Real Happiness Killer," How expectation influences perception | MIT News | Massachusetts Institute of Technology.

[10] Anne Trafton, "How Expectation Influences Perception," MIT News, July 15, 2019, How expectation influences perception | MIT News | Massachusetts Institute of Technology.

[11] The Shift Network, "Discovering the Psychology of the Future: A Free Online Event with Stanislav Grof," Discovering the Psychology of the Future | The Shift Network.

[12] Jyoti, *An Angel Called My Name* (The Czech Republic: DarmaGaia Publishing), 1998, 140–141.

[13] "Chiti Shakti," What is Chiti Shakti? - Definition from Yogapedia.

[14] Christine, owner (last name unknown), "1900–1999," The Great Thompson Hunt, http://gonzo.org/roads/timeline/life.asp?ID=5.

[15] Christine, "RS Covers—The Nineties," The Great Thompson Hunt, http://www.gonzo.org/books/rsm/rsm.asp?ID=4.

[16] The Christ consciousness is based in the light, love, and truth inside each person, in contrast to the exclusiveness sometimes emphasized in Christianity. For instance, the great Hindu satguru Paramahansa Yogananda, in his *Autobiography*, called a Hindu avatar, Babaji, the "Yogi-Christ of modern India" (345). In trying to write this footnote, I stumbled across a 2004 book that compiled teachings of Yogananda. In it, this top teacher in the Hindu line interprets the four Gospels according to a unity of religions that is the base of his own work. He says, "A thousand Christs sent to earth would not redeem its people unless they themselves became Christlike by purifying and expanding their individual consciousness."

Published fifty-two years after Yogananda's death, it brings together his ideas about the deeper meanings of Jesus's teachings; how they are essentially unified with yoga as a path to oneness with God. In the book he calls the Second Coming the "resurrection of Christ within you." This sort of approach—of inclusiveness—was such a clear basis of my understanding that I was afterwards completely startled whenever hearing this consciousness confused with a religion.

[17] Margaret A. Harrell, *Ancient Secrets Revealed*, 34.

[18] Harrell, *Ancient Secrets Revealed*, 37–38.

[19] Harrell, *Ancient Secrets Revealed*, 48.

[20] "The Continental," Music by Con Conrad and lyrics by Herb Magidson.

[21] Jyoti, *An Angel Called My Name*, 1998, xxiv.

[22] "Gibran," http://leb.net/gibran/.

[23] Mini Sharma, Mondeep Dhankar, and Deepak Kumar, "Awakening of Kundalini Chakras—Presenting as a Psychosis—a Case Report," Indian Journal of Psychological Medicine 44(5): 526–528, doi: 10.1177/02537176221082936.

[24] More exactly put, by Wikipedia (Pauli exclusion principle): "In quantum mechanics, the Pauli exclusion principle states that two or more identical particles with half-integer spins (i.e. fermions) cannot simultaneously occupy the same quantum state within a system which obeys the laws of quantum mechanics. This principle was formulated by Austrian physicist Wolfgang Pauli in 1925 for electrons, and later extended to all fermions with his spin–statistics theorem of 1940."

[25] Harrell, *Ancient Secrets Revealed*, 83.

[26] Harrell, *Ancient Secrets Revealed*, 79–80.

[27] Joseph Selbie, *Break through the Limits of the Brain*, Chapter 1, Kindle.

[28] Selbie, *Break through the Limits of the Brain*, Chapter 1, Kindle.

[29] Narayani Ganesh, "The Golden Womb and the Cosmic Egg," The golden womb and the cosmic egg – Times of India (*indiatimes.com*).

[30] Swami Satyananda Saraswati, Kundalini Tantra, ebook pdf, https://sriyogaashram.com. This pdf is no longer on the site. But the book is available to purchase.

[31] Love, A technical guide for editing gonzo: Hunter S. Thompson from the other end of the Mojo Wire. - Document - Gale Academic OneFile.

[32] "Matter Wave," https://en.wikipedia.org/wiki/Matter_wave.

[33] Joseph Selbie, *The Physics of God*, Kindle, 70, 44.

[34] "Fear and Loathing in Elko," The Great Thompson Hunt (website), http://gonzo.org/books/rsm/rsm.asp?ID=a.

[35] Steadman, *The Joke's Over* (Houghton Mifflin Harcourt; First Edition, Jan. 1, 2006), 297–298.

[36] "Mihai Ursachi," Center for the Art of Translation, Mihai Ursachi | Center for the Art of Translation | Two Lines Press (*catranslation.org*).

[37] Steadman, 297–298.

[38] Dhyanyogi Madhusudandas-ji, Wikipedia: Academic Dictionaries and Encyclo-

pedias; also see "Pure Love and Devotion, Dhyanyoga Centers, https://dyc.org/dhyanyogi-madhusudanda/.

[39] "About Darshan," accessed September 2023, About Darshan - Mother Meera.

[40] Dhyanyogi-ji, *This House Is on Fire: The Life of Shri Dhyanyogi as Told by Shri Anandi Ma and Disciples* (Antioch, CA: Dhyanyoga Centers Inc., 2004), 153.

[41] This is the full title of his 2004 authorized biography. Inside the book, page 153, he admonishes disciples who are concerned about his health that "the work of saints is to spread fragrance, like an incense stick, even at the cost of their life." And "This house is on fire, let everyone take as much as they can."

[42] This fact was taken from https://www.rspb.org.uk/birds-and-wildlife/wildlife-guides/other-garden-wildlife/mammals/mole/ but I no longer locate it there.

[43] Zeeya Merali. "Splitting Time from Space—New Quantum Theory Topples Einstein's Spacetime: Buzz about a quantum gravity theory that sends space and time back to their Newtonian Roots, https://www.scientificamerican.com/article/splitting-time-from-space/. OR: https://bigthink.com/personal-growth/newton-vs-einstein/.

[44] Peat, *Synchronicity: The Bridge between Mind and Matter* (Bantam New Age Books, 3rd printing, 1988), 43.

[45] "Fiery Muse Jeneane (Jyoti) Prevatt," https://www.teridegler.com/newpage2a1dac62.

Review Snippets

Books Outside the *Keep This Quiet!* Series

Inserting Consciousness into Collisions

"Finally, a manual of the Universe but also connected to the deep psychology of the human being. In easy to grasp terms Margaret reveals insight into the processes that connect past, future and now; the quantum world with daily existence and seemingly superficial events with deep spirituality.

"The magic of this book is that it positions our place in the universe and our dream of life with much more clarity. A manual indeed."

—Jef Crab, Taijii master and Taoist

"This is a soul journey in and through and beyond space and time. All of Margaret A. Harrell's books are connected, linked. They are her never ending life story. Her new book is plugged in, an electric shock, a wake up call for those bold and daring enough to take the wildly delightful adventure to the whirling ever changing source of all and everything."

—Ron Whitehead, US Lifetime Beat Poet Laureate

Poetry

Particle Piñata Poems

"The poetry of Margaret Ann Harrell reads like a Zhuangzi of the 21st century, taking its reader through a spiritual Odyssey, where one can hear the cosmic beat in the rhythm of the word play, the pulse of heartfelt mind-blowing experiences revealing a vast span of messages from beyond. It shows the craftmanship of a female shaman who has the power to catch such a dazzling wild and free roaming content into the nets of poems. Here is a biopic in words, a biographical epic, a story of a lifetime full of surprising leaps into the story of Earth and the Cosmic Drama, a rite de passage (read the passage) initiating its reader into multiversal dimensions, bringing meaning to life where few have been looking to find it. This great bold poetry full of wit and spirit reads as a unique treat, a gift from those who know how to sow the seed for what really matters on earth: a choice to live a life guided by love and light. For those who are in love with poetry, share this genuine gift and the sheer joy of it! If you want to, go ahead!"

—Chris Van de Velde (MA Philosophy, lover of wisdom), Belgium

Other Books

Cloud Conversations & Image Stories

"Harrell's own images, striking and surprising, suggest multitudes, yielding rich new visions of figures and scenes the longer one gazes into their tufting splendor . . . Harrell's cloud photos are collaborative, between artist and nature, between beholder and photograph, between our at-a-glance perceptions and the deeper, expansive visions we tend to allow ourselves only in meditation or reverie. In inviting prefatory essays, Harrell persuasively links the art of cloud photography to 'chance' images from the history of art."

—Book Life Reviews

The Hell's Angels Letters: *Hunter* S. *Thompson, Margaret Harrell and the* Making of an American Classic

(available only at Norfolk Press: norfolkpress.com or from the author)

"Thompson's motto might well have been 'Nothing in moderation.' For *The Hell's Angels Letters*, Margaret Ann Harrell—in collaboration with Ron Whitehead—has assembled a dossier of all her correspondence with Thompson during the time she worked as the editor of the gonzo writer's 'strange and terrible saga of the outlaw motorcycle gangs.' Typed manuscript pages, scribbled notes, photographs, interviews and all sorts of period ephemera relating to *Hell's Angels* allow the reader a valuable, behind-the-scenes glimpse into the making of this classic of New Journalism."

—Michael Dirda, the *Washington Post*

"A *big book, literally and figuratively . . . The Hell's Angels Letters* is a must-have text for any Hunter S. Thompson fan. Lavishly documented and illustrated with the actual correspondence that led to the publication of his breakthrough literary effort . . . The author, Margaret Harrell, who was Thompson's editor on his inaugural book, and her collaborator, Thompson's friend and associate poet Ron Whitehead, have succeeded brilliantly to create a fabulous present for you, or anyone in your life who admires Thompson's numerous achievements . . . It's worth every penny. *The* Hell's Angels *Letters: Hunter* S *Thompson, Margaret Harrell and the Making of an American Classic* gets five stars out of five! Bravo!"

—Kyle K. Mann, *Gonzo Today*

CONTRIBUTORS

Jef Crab

Belgian-born Taiji master Jef Crab lives in Suriname on the edge of the rainforest with his Surinamese family. The fear and emptiness in the eyes of children on their way to school in the early '90s shocked Jef. According to him, the cause of this was the separation on a personal, social, and environmental level. As a solution, he developed a method for restoring connectedness, the feeling that you belong to each other. In doing so, he was constantly looking for ways to make the state of optimal and connected functioning experienceable, repeatable, and transferable. Jef's efforts led to the establishment of the EcoSystem 2000 Foundation in 1994. In Suriname, several models have been developed in the field of the Earth Circle. "We are currently coordinating a regional development process for the Saamaka in Upper Suriname, at the request of the Tribal Authority. This process focuses on a nature-supporting economy integrated into the cultural reality and preserving the social structure of the indigenous Saamaka.

"Many change processes get stuck," he says, "because of inhibiting communication and tunnel vision from those surrounding or participating in the initiative /project." This is due to a lack of energy, which is why E.A.S.T Institute, which I founded, also focuses on the Human Circle. The transcultural nature and application of the method gives substance to the Celestial Circle." The Ecosystem 2000 Foundation has projects and activities worldwide, such as in Anahata Healing Centre in Ravandur (India).

Ron Whitehead

Poet, writer, editor, publisher, scholar, professor, activist Ron Whitehead grew up on a farm in Kentucky. He attended the University of Louisville and Oxford University. Among the numerous state, national, and international awards and prizes he has won are The All Kentucky Poetry Prize and The Yeats Club of Oxford's Prize for Poetry. Filmed for over ten years, the documentary *Outlaw Poet: The Life and Times of Ron Whitehead* was finally released in 2020. In 2006, Dr. John Rocco (SUNY Maritime, NYC) nominated Ron for The Nobel Prize in Literature. Ron has edited and published the works of such luminaries as His Holiness The Dalai Lama, President Jimmy Carter, Hunter S. Thompson, Thomas Merton, Jack Kerouac, Seamus Heaney, Wendell Berry, Andy Warhol, Yoko Ono, ONO, Allen Ginsberg, William S. Burroughs, and hundreds more. He has produced over 2,000 historic Arts Events, Festivals, and 24-48-72 & 90-hour nonstop music & poetry Insomniacathons, from New York City to New Orleans to The Netherlands. Ron has performed thousands of shows around the world with outstanding musicians and bands. His work has been translated into nearly twenty languages. He is the author of thirty books and forty albums. And counting.

About the Author

Credit: Bill Hardesty

The author of the coffee table collectible *The* Hell's Angels *Letters* in conjunction with Ron Whitehead (Norfolk Press), the *Keep This Quiet!* I–IV memoir series, as well as as well as *Space Encounters*, rev. ed., *Particle Pinata Poems*, the artbook *Cloud Conversations*, as well as *Space Encounters* III, and a host of others, Harrell copy-edited/assistant-edited Hunter S. Thompson's first book, *Hell's Angels*. HST acknowledged her in *Gonzo Letters* 2. She is also a book editor, cloud photographer, and advanced meditation teacher in the LuminEssence school of light body and luminous body consciousness exploration, and a mentor to those wanting to maximize their potential. A three-time MacDowell Colony fellow, she has lived many years outside the United States—in Morocco, Switzerland (studying at the C. G. Jung Institute), and in Belgium. She took her masters in literature at Columbia University and a bachelor's in history at Duke. A a sought-after speaker, she has been repeatedly on panels at the Gonzofest in Louisville, Kentucky, as a VIP and on panels elsewhere. Currently, she appears in a short documentary (Hunter Thompson and San Francisco) for Arte TV,

France. And is on the planning committee for GonzoFest Dublin: Calling the Underground, which is scheduled for September 2024. Look her up at MacDowell here: https://www.macdowell.org/search/results?q=Margaret+Harrell.

Thank You for Reading My Book

Authors live by readers and their reviews. If you enjoyed *Beyond* 3D, I would truly appreciate an honest positive review on Amazon and/or another platform. I will read every word you write and benefit from the comments.

Thank you again and God bless.

Connect with me on Facebook. LinkedIn, and through my website https://margaretharrell.com.